JEHOVAH'S WITNESSES
AND KINDRED GROUPS

SECTS AND CULTS IN AMERICA:
BIBLIOGRAPHICAL GUIDES
(General editor: J. Gordon Melton)
Vol. 4

GARLAND REFERENCE LIBRARY
OF SOCIAL SCIENCE
Vol. 180

BIBLIOGRAPHIES ON SECTS AND CULTS IN AMERICA
(General Editor: J. Gordon Melton)

JEHOVAH'S WITNESSES AND KINDRED GROUPS
a *Historical Compendium and Bibliography*

Jerry Bergman

GARLAND PUBLISHING INC. • NEW YORK & LONDON
1984

Library of Congress Cataloging in Publication Data

Bergman, Jerry.
Jehovah's Witnesses and kindred groups.

(Sects and cults in America. Bibliographical guides ;
v. 4) (Garland reference library of social science ;
v. 180)
Includes index.
1. Jehovah's Witnesses—Bibliography. 2. Sects—
Bibliography. 3. Sects. I. Title. II. Series.
III. Series: Garland reference library of social
science ; v. 180.
Z7845.J45B47 1984 [BX8526] 016.2899'2 83-47603
ISBN 0-8240-9109-4

289.9016
B499j

Cover design by Laurence Walczak

Printed on acid-free, 250-year-life paper
Manufactured in the United States of America

CONTENTS

ACKNOWLEDGMENTS

A project such as this involved a large number of people whose suggestions and contributions were most important and appreciated. Foremost are Dr. Gordon Melton, Jim Parkinson, and my editors Julia Johnson and Dick Newman. I am also very grateful to William Chamberlin, Dr. Edmund Gruss, Dr. M. James Penton, Duane Magnani, Rodney Bias, Mick VanBuskirk, Carl Hackensack, Dr. Robert Morey, Dr. Alan Rogerson, Dr. Melvin Curry, Rud Persson, Carl Olof Jonsson, Dr. Joseph F. Zygmunt, Gaetano Boccaccio, and Richard Rawe for their hours of help, hundreds of references, and, most important, their persistent encouragement. And mention must be made of my typists, Nancy Tucker and Susan Schwarz, who struggled through the many drafts of this manuscript.

ABBREVIATIONS

1. *WtBTS* refers to the *Watchtower Bible & Tract Society,* the legal corporation of the Jehovah's Witnesses. Often used as a synonym for the Witness organization.

2. *JW* means a *Jehovah's Witness,* the most common name for the followers of the Watchtower Society; used to refer to a follower or believer of the Jehovah's Witnesses' doctrine.

3. *IBSA* is the International Bible Students Association, another one of the many legal corporations the Jehovah's Witnesses have used in the past and still use today. The legal corporation of the British branch is the International Bible Students Association.

INTRODUCTION

Almost every household in the United States has been visited
by a Jehovah's Witness offering for sale a book or a copy
of the *Watchtower*. Many school children have had the experience of a fellow pupil's refusing to salute the flag "for
religious reasons." Newspapers and magazines frequently
carry stories about Jehovah's Witnesses' refusing to accept
blood transfusions, celebrate the holidays, become members
of the armed forces, attend college, vote, run for public
office, or involve themselves in the political arena.

In short, among America's many religions the Witnesses
in many ways stand apart. They are separated from the cultural
mainstream and take pride both in their differences and in the
fact that others perceive them as "different." To emphasize
this difference, they call their meeting houses not churches
but rather "Kingdom Halls," and (except in the period from
1975 to 1981--see *The Watchtower*, 3-15-1981) all of their
baptized members are legally ordained ministers. For years
they insisted that their belief structure was not a religion
(they used to say that "religion is a snare and a racket").
During the 1930s and 40s they proclaimed that religion was
from Satan the devil, whereas their belief structure alone
was of God, and, therefore, simply "the truth." Few organizations can boast of as many "true believers" as the Watch Tower
Bible and Tract Society (the legal corporation of the Jehovah's
Witnesses). Their growth until the "great disappointment of
1975" (when the end of this world was confidently expected)
was phenomenal to say the least. From a handful in the 1880s
they now have almost 6 million adherents and sympathizers
(see the 1982 *Yearbook of Jehovah's Witnesses*, p. 31).

The Witnesses, even though a relatively small sect, have
been highly influential in shaping American society and law.
Their court cases in regard to proselytizing and first amendment rights have been extremely influential in molding constitutional law. Almost all contemporary freedom of speech and
press cases and even the recent court decisions regarding
pornography have relied heavily on the cases which Jehovah's

Witness attorneys fought and won before the Supreme Court.
Edward Waite in his article "The Debt of Constitutional Laws
to Jehovah's Witnesses" (*Minnesota Law Review*, Vol. 28, March
1944, No. 4) concludes that Jehovah's Witnesses have done more
to guarantee basic freedoms than any other religious group in
America.

J. Gordon Melton, in his *Encyclopedia of American Religions*,
classifies the various groups which broke off or were highly
influenced by the movement started by William Miller, such as
the Watchtower Society, in the "Adventist family." C.T.
Russell, the Society's founder, openly borrowed a great deal
from and was highly influenced by the Adventist movement as
a whole. He was originally a part of a group led by Jonas
Wendell, a minister of the Advent Christian Church. The
modern Adventist movement began with William Miller, a Baptist
layman (later a Baptist preacher), who settled in New York
after the War of 1812. For some time Miller was a Deist
(one who believes that God does not rule or run the universe
but has only created the laws which control it); but after
a three- or four-year study of the Bible he became a believer
and also became convinced the "end" was near.

In 1831, Miller spoke at a revival at Dresden, New York,
and from this date proved to be so popular that within a year
he was able to accept no more than half of his speaking invita-
tions. Miller attracted Methodists, Baptists, and persons of
other denominations to his teachings. In 1833, he published
his first book, *Evidences from Scripture and History of the
Second Coming of Christ About the Year 1843 Exhibited in a
Course of Lectures*. In 1839 Joshua Himes invited Miller to
preach in his Boston church. Himes, a man with much promo-
tional and organizational talent, was so impressed that he
soon brought the new movement into national prominence. The
movement's first periodical was entitled *Signs of the Times*.

Miller believed that he had deciphered the "hidden Biblical
chronology" which by the use of symbols enabled one to discern
the exact date of the "end of the age" or the end of this
world. He made many assumptions, such as that a prophetic
day is equal to a year or some other span of time, and that
the Biblical passages in Daniel and Revelation apply specifically to the 1800s. By this means, he set the date for the end
of the present world and the coming of Christ in 1843. As the
movement grew, it encountered increasing opposition from the
established churches although the established churches usually
supported him until about 1843. Many church laymen and
ministers who joined the movement were disfellowshipped after
1843, which resulted in more publicity. This caused Miller's
movement to crystallize after 1844 and separate itself from
the mainline churches.

Although at first Miller was vague about the exact month of the end, etc., he finally decided upon "between March 21, 1843 and March 21, 1844." Natural events such as the appearance of a large comet in February of 1843 gave impetus to the movement. When March 21, 1844, came and went, many of his approximately 50,000 followers became disappointed and left the movement but the rest had come to firmly believe that Christ's return was "soon" and so other dates were predicted, such as October 22, 1844 (this new date came from the realization that the key date on the Jewish calendar was seven months). From the original group of about 50,000 followers, a number of churches and sects developed, including the Advent Christian Church, the Seventh Day Adventist Church, the Primitive Advent Church, Church of God, Abrahamic Faith, among others.

One of the offshoots of the Adventist movement was the Bible student movement founded by "Pastor Russell," from which sprung approximately 200 splinter groups. Charles Taze Russell was born in 1852 in Pittsburgh, Pennsylvania, of Scottish-Irish Presbyterian parents. In 1876 he met an independent Adventist by the name of Barbour. Although Russell worked with him for only a short time as co-editor (according to Barbour, in name only) of *Herald of the Morning* and co-author (Russell claimed, but Barbour denies Russell's contribution) of *The Three Worlds or Plan of Redemption*, he was greatly influenced by Barbour. Russell was very concerned about the prophetic failures of the Adventist movement, especially the 1874 error. (Barbour later reasoned that the Greek work "parousia," usually translated "coming," actually meant "presence"—so Christ might have returned in 1874, only he was actually *invisible*! Thus, Russell felt, Jonas Wendell's 1874 prediction may not have been wrong after all!)

During this time, Russell worked with other Adventists and Bible students such as A.P. Adams, A.D. Jones, and John H. Paton. Partly because Barbour incorrectly predicted April 1878 as the month when the church would go to heaven, and because they had several doctrinal disagreements with him, Russell, Adams, and Paton withdrew their support from Barbour. They immediately began, primarily under Russell's leadership, their own journal, *Zion's Watchtower and Herald of Christ's Presence*. The first issue was published in July of 1879 and had a printing of 6,000 copies (this issue was reprinted later). Russell obtained Barbour's subscription list (without his permission, some claim) and sent a free copy to each *Herald* subscriber. Russell, in effect, began his movement as a mail-order religion, and the printed page has played an important part ever since. The Watchtower Society itself, which was, according to Russell, originally "nothing more than a publishing house," in time became "God's organization, the only ark of salvation" and the Witnesses now believe that to be saved, one must be firmly inside of that ark.

Paton and almost all of the early followers eventually left Russell's organization. The Watchtower movement, especially in its early history, has always had a constant flow of individuals in and out of "God's organization." Relatively few persons have stayed for a long period of time. Periodic schisms cause high-ranking members to leave for a variety of reasons (the most recent schism occurred in 1979).

By 1880 scores of congregations existed in most eastern states and several in the central states, all from the one small Bible study which Russell began in the late 1870s. In 1881 *Zion's Watch Tower Bible and Tract Society* was formed and incorporated in 1884 with C.T. Russell as its first President. There were fifty full-time workers in 1888 (a number that would grow to over 100,000 by 1980). In 1909 the headquarters moved from Allegheny, Pennsylvania, to Brooklyn, New York: Russell wanted to "start over" after such embarrassing episodes as his "messy" divorce in Allegheny.

Opposition from the Established Churches

Although Russell borrowed a great deal from the Adventists, he also borrowed from other movements as well. He was influenced by not only the conservative churches but also the Universalists, the Unitarians, and even the Plymouth Brethren and the Mennonites. Because Russell vehemently insisted on the correctness of his teachings and because his position on several major issues conflicted with the orthodox churches, many in the religious world disliked him. The *Brooklyn Daily Eagle*, an influential eastern newspaper, constantly criticized Russell, his religion, and his followers. Some sample headlines should illustrate the flavor of the attacks: "Girl Kissed Pastor and Sat on His Knee" (October 29, 1911); "Pastor Silent to His Wife for Months" (October 31, 1911); "Give Up Their Homes, Following Russellism" (December 26, 1911); "Russell's Latest Outburst" (May 1, 1912); "Sold House for $50.00 to Defy His Wife" (November 27, 1911).

Russell became famous, however, not so much for what he believed but for what he did *not* believe. Among the Christian doctrines which he denied were the immortality of the soul, hellfire, the Trinity, the bodily resurrection of Christ, the full deity of Christ (Christ was believed to be a lesser god, created by the father), the personality of the Holy Spirit, and the legitimacy of the Church and all its branches after the apostles died. An article in the *Advent Christian Times* of July 18, 1877, provides a good example of opposition to Russell:

One N.H. Barbour, called Dr. Barbour, with his con-
freres, J.H. Paton and C.T. Russell, is traveling around
the country, going everywhere that they can find Adventists, and preaching that Jesus has come secretly,
and will soon be revealed and mingling in their lectures
a lot of "Age-to-come" trash, all to subvert their
hearers. They are not endorsed by Adventists, "Age-
to-come" folks, or anybody else, yet having some money
and a few sympathizers they will probably run awhile.
They have been to Ohio and Indiana and are working westward. We are credibly informed that one of them boasted
in Union Mills, Ind., a few days since, that they would
break up every Advent church in the land. We guess not.
Their whole work is proselytizing. The Lord never sent
them on their mission. Give them no place, and go not
near them or countenance them.

At first the various groups were only loosely affiliated
with Russell, i.e., each "ecclesia" was largely independent.
Ecclesia were held together primarily by representatives
called "pilgrims." The structure gradually became more and
more autocratic, until today the Society owns all of the local
property, and individual "congregations," as they are now
called, exercise almost no independence. They follow strictly
all of the instructions from the Watchtower Society. Every
congregation studies the same Watchtower lesson on the same
Sunday and even sings the same songs, etc. The "meetings" as
their services are called are, with very slight variations,
the same the world over.

Russell's death on October 31, 1916, was a blow to the
movement which should have been anticipated. His health was
always somewhat poor, but he tended to feel his life was
shielded by God. Thus, he evidently did not take care of
himself and toward the end neglected necessary medical treatment. When he did die, the organization was thrown into a
turmoil which resulted in the formation of a number of large
splinter groups, for Russell was seen by his followers as the
faithful and discrete slave, God's spokesman on earth--His
only spokesman! The changes made in policy and doctrine after
he died were so drastic that many scholars now consider the
Jehovah's Witnesses to be an offshoot of the original movement
which Russell started. Today a number of movements claim to
be the "faithful" followers of Russell's teachings.

J.F. Rutherford

Joseph Rutherford, who became the second president, was probably the most controversial of the Society's four leaders. He was born on November 8, 1869, in Morgan County, Missouri, near the town of Boonville, the son of James Calvin Rutherford and Elona Striclyn, both Baptists and farmers. Rutherford showed an interest in law while still very young, but his parents allowed him to go to law school only if he contributed to the wages of a hired hand to replace him on the farm. He financed his education at a local "academy" by learning short-hand and working as a court stenographer. After two years of tutoring by a local judge, he was admitted to the state bar at age 22 and started practice with a small Boonville law firm. For several years he was a public prosecutor and also substi-tuted (for four days) for the regular judge as was required of all of the prosecutors in the city. He was never elected or appointed a judge and, thus, the title "Judge Rutherford," which both Rutherford and his followers relished, was purely honorary.

During this period Rutherford became involved with the Kansas City Court of Appeals (October term 1896). Here he ap-pealed a lower court conviction of "stealing" a cash register for his client (although it was actually more of a case of improper repossession). The court ruled that Rutherford was wrong in taking possession of the cash register in the way he did. In 1896 Rutherford campaigned for William Jennings Bryan and for the rest of his life adopted the collar-up style in imitation and honor of Bryan.

Rutherford was first introduced to the teaching of Russell when several women Witnesses visited his law office in 1894 and sold him some Watchtower books. He did not join the move-ment, though, until 1906, at which time he wrote his first religious book, *A Lawyer's View of God* (privately published). Russell utilized Rutherford, one of the few lawyers in the Society, to defend him in many of the court cases in which he was involved.

Watchtower Arrests

On April 6, 1917, the United States entered World War I. The Society's stand on conscientious objection was part of the reason for the arrest and subsequent conviction of J.F. Rutherford and his close associates, W.E. VanAmburgh, Alex-ander H. MacMillan, Robert J. Martin, Clayton J. Woodworth, G.H. Fisher, F.H. Robison, and Giovanni De Cecca (the warrant for the arrest of R.H. Hirsh was later issued on May 8, 1918).

There is some evidence that those who opposed his religious ideas on doctrine were instrumental in the arrests and convictions.

During the imprisonment of the eight Watchtower leaders in the Atlanta prison, C.H. Anderson acted as President and J.F. Stephenson was Secretary-Treasurer. They moved the Watchtower offices to Pittsburgh on September 25, 1918, for slightly more than a year. At the Society's annual meeting on January 4, 1919, in Pittsburgh, J.F. Rutherford was reelected as President and W.E. VanAmburgh as Secretary-Treasurer even though they were in prison at the time. The others elected to the Board of Directors--C.A. Wise (Vice-President), R.H. Barber, W.E. Spill, W.F. Hudgins, and C.H. Anderson--were free to carry out their responsibilities. When those imprisoned were released, R.H. Barber resigned, and A.H. MacMillan replaced him.

While in prison, Rutherford organized "Bible study classes" among the inmates and began writing weekly letters to his followers. He also launched another magazine, *The Golden Age* (renamed *Consolation* and, later, in 1946, *Awake!*). In March of 1919 the case was appealed, and the defendants were released on March 26, 1919. A new trial was ordered in May, but with the war over the government lost interest and *nolle prosequi* (dropped all charges) on May 5, 1920. Thus Rutherford came to be seen as a martyr, and partly for this reason at the first convention since his release (Cedar Point, Ohio, in 1919) the group took on new enthusiasm. Rutherford now stressed that each individual Witness should be an active minister. This was the first of many changes in Witness doctrine that he instigated. The prison experience had seriously affected Rutherford's health and caused him life-long suffering, which was partially alleviated by moving to a warm climate during the cold months (usually California).

Dignified and self-confident in his appearance, Rutherford, according to a contemporary newspaper account, "looked more like a senator than most senators." Although much in the news, he made far fewer public appearances than Russell and secluded himself for long periods of time at Beth-Sarim, a mansion in San Diego, California, which was donated to the Society in 1929 to house Abraham and the prophets upon their return to the earth (which was believed to be imminent). His wife, Mary, was crippled for most of her life and died in December of 1962. There is some debate as to whether or not she accepted the ideas of her husband; however, their son, Malcolm G. Rutherford, was for some time quite active in his father's movement, even working as Russell's secretary. Later Malcolm became disillusioned and eventually left the organization and has since lived in California. Rutherford himself

died of uremia January 8, 1942, at Beth-Sarim at the age of
72, a few weeks after an operation for cancer. He had requested burial on the property of Beth-Sarim, but this was
not permitted under local ordinances, and so five months
later he was interred in Staten Island, New York.

Rutherford As the Leader of the Jehovah's Witnesses

Rutherford's writings were seen as almost inspired.
Hayden C. Covington, probably one of the most knowledgeable
men in the movement (Vice-President of the Society for
several years and head of the Society's legal department),
stated in an interview with this writer on March 3, 1975,
that "God was writing through [Rutherford]" and he was
"definitely inspired to do what he did." Covington asserted
that Rutherford had absolute power over the organization and
the Board of Directors "only rubberstamped his [Rutherford's]
will and did nothing more and that's the way it should be."
During this interview, Covington also maintained that
Rutherford was an extremely dynamic person and once he made
up his mind no one could change it. The "Judge" also "en-
joyed a good physical fight." Covington's favorite example
of this characteristic took place at Madison Square Garden
where Rutherford allowed the fistfights with the "opposition"
at a small riot during his talk, whereas, according to Covington, "Knorr [the man who became the Society's third President]
ran like a gutless bastard." Covington's opinion of Knorr
was further clarified during the interview. After Rutherford
died Covington said he received 99% of the votes for President, but Knorr convinced him to become Vice-President.
Several years later, Covington stated, Knorr convinced him
to resign from the Vice-Presidency as well. In his own
words, Covington was "the dope that put that bastard [Knorr]
in office." Covington added, "I should have been smarter,
for I didn't realize I was lying in bed with a snake. Knorr
can't be trusted--he slithers around like a snake; he is a
cobra."
The "Judge" was a flamboyant, coarse, outspoken man who
spent much of his time attacking the churches of Christendom.
Except for some *Consolation* and *Golden Age* articles, Rutherford himself wrote virtually everything published during his
administration. He coined a number of phrases that Witnesses
used for years, such as "millions now living will never die"
and "religion is a snare and a racket." His forthright
personality often antagonized local government and religious
authorities, and he delighted in ridiculing and criticizing
his opponents in the pages of the *Golden Age* and the *Consolation* (both journals make fascinating reading today).

The Witnesses were given to strong language both in speeches and in their publications. This approach and their strict neutrality stand repeatedly caused difficulties with various authorities and resulted in a number of riots, arrests, beatings, and even murders (for many examples see the 1940s ACLU booklets). As a result of this, in America and many other countries the Witnesses hold the dubious honor of being one of the most persecuted religious minorities in modern times.

Probably the practice that gets them into the most trouble is their refusal to align themselves in any way with the national or political powers and institutions. A 1941 pamphlet published by the American Civil Liberties Union entitled *The Persecution of Jehovah's Witnesses* stated "Not since the persecutions of the Mormons years ago has any religious minority been so bitterly and generally attacked as the members of Jehovah's Witness's ... documents filed with the department of justice ... showed over 335 instances of mob violence [occurred] in 44 states involving 1,488 men, women and children."

Ironically, during World War II Witnesses were often accused of being German spies or pro-Nazis, yet in Nazi Germany, some of Hitler's most outspoken foes were the Witnesses. Timothy White, in his book *A People for His Name*, stated that thousands of Witnesses in Germany were imprisoned and "those in prison were treated extremely harshly, some losing their lives or being forcibly sterilized." The remaining Witnesses fearlessly went about their business and openly defied the Hitler government, even sending Hitler numerous telegrams informing him that "God was going to destroy" him if he "did not permit the Witnesses to continue their work." In 1936 at a convention in Holland, it was announced that thousands of tracts explaining the Witness position and denouncing Hitler were to be distributed. No one, including the officials in Nazi Germany, knew the distribution date. On the 12th of December at 5 p.m., 3,540 Witnesses began to go from door to door distributing these tracts. At 6:15 p.m. the SS began radio broadcasts telling people not to accept the tracts. The work was successfully completed by 7 p.m. the same day.

By the end of 1937, almost all of the adult male Witnesses in Germany and occupied countries (and many of the adult females)--well over 6,000 people--were in prisons or concentration camps.

Probably few countries in the world have not banned the work of the Witnesses at one time or another, including Canada and most European, Asian, and South American nations (and in many countries such as the Soviet bloc nations and several Asian and South American nations they are still banned).

A number of Nazi officials claimed that Hitler had a "love-
hate relationship with the Witnesses." Hitler admired them
for the strength of their convictions and their determination
to carry out what they believed was God's will--he often felt
that many of them would make excellent Nazis. However, the
Witnesses' obstinacy frustrated him more than that of any
other group except possibly the communists.

Doctrinal Changes

   At the very start of his control Rutherford's teachings
differed slightly from Russell's. From 1925 Rutherford began
to reinterpret many key Bible passages and introduce new and
different teachings and doctrines. In 1925, the war between
Michael and the dragon (Rev. 12) and the 1260 days was reinterpreted (the interpretation was now literal). In 1926
the "abomination that maketh desolate" was interpreted as the
League of Nations; and in 1929 the Society's followers were
told they were to obey the Society first: if a conflict between the Society's teaching and the Earthly governments
occurred, they were to obey the Watchtower. (They used
Rom. 13 as a text to support this.) This later led to the
refusal to salute the national flag of any country (a conflict which climaxed in the United States in the 1930s). In
1932 their ranks (including those that had died, both recently
and in Christ's day, excluding those they believed were of
the Earthly class) exceeded 144,000, so they created a new
class, the "Jonadab" class (also called "great crowd" or "other
sheep"). These were to participate in the destruction of
Babylon and had the hope of an "Earthly reward"--everlasting
life on Earth--not a heavenly reward like the 144,000. In
1935, the "Great Multitude" was reinterpreted to be an Earthly
class and was identified as also Jonadabs. In 1938, it was
proclaimed that only the Great Multitude would survive
Armageddon and that they (and the dead and resurrected
Jehovah's Witnesses) would procreate so as to fill the Earth
during the Millennium (1,000-year reign of Christ). It was
first taught in the 1930s that Christ gave himself as a ran-
som--not for all people as formerly believed--but for Jehovah's
Witnesses only or at least only they would benefit from it.
This last teaching was partially withdrawn by 1965 (the
Sodomites and other people who were destroyed by God, it was
now taught, could also benefit). To many, Rutherford and
his Society were going into "outer darkness" but the Society
claimed that the changes were an example of "the light shining
brighter and brighter unto the perfect day."

The matter of centralized government over all Bible classes was a heated issue for some time. In Russell's day, the various Bible study classes were autonomous: they voted on elders and deacons and on other class matters and voluntarily cooperated with the Society. Then, starting in 1919, Rutherford appointed a service director for each class participating in the *"Golden Age* work." In 1920 he required weekly reports from all class workers, and by 1932 he had stopped the appointment of elders by election and replaced the existing elders with a local "service committee" which was appointed by the Society. In 1938, he removed the last vestiges of autonomy, and all classes were now fully organized and controlled by the Society. Although Rutherford called his system "Theocratic Organization," his dissenters called it a ruthless takeover and the establishment of a dictatorship.

Numerous other areas of dissension occurred at this time and caused many members to leave. The Society stressed that the only way to serve God was to go out and "sell books." The concept of personal character development was abandoned and later declared a false doctrine. The Society claimed to be "God's exclusive channel of Truth," representing "God's visible organization on Earth," whose teachings were not to be questioned. Some felt that answers directly from the Bible were now banned in some local Watch Tower classes. Many readily accepted these changes but others dissented and left the Society even though personal reasons made departure difficult and unhappy. Still others believed that Rutherford was "smiting his fellow-servants" and that the Society was now part of Babylon (false religion); such persons usually joined one of the many splinter groups.

Some of those who left the Society were able to quietly withdraw but most were publicly "disfellowshipped." Many were anathematized and treated with indignation and animosity by their former brothers. Those who associated with various other Bible student groups were labeled by the Society as "evil servants" or "the evil servant class" until recently when the meaning of "evil slave" (Matt. 24:48) was modified to mean only those who are still part of the Society but who do not cooperate with it.

In spite of these problems, the Society grew. The 1918 Watch Tower office staff was about 10, but in 1929 there were about 180 persons at Bethel, a few more than in the last years of Pastor Russell's administration. Today the number is close to 1,500. Conventions held in New York in 1950 and 1953 filled Yankee Stadium, and in 1958 Yankee Stadium and the Polo Grounds together packed in one quarter of a million Witnesses. In 1963 they drew 140,000 to the Rose Bowl in Pasadena, California (the same week Billy Graham was drawing an equivalent number to the Coliseum).

In 1915 the Memorial (partaking of the Lord's Supper) was celebrated by over 15,000; from 1917 to 1920 it had around 20,000 participants, and in 1925, the date of the great prediction, the number was over 90,000. Attendance then declined for several years (in 1928 it was only 17,000). In 1942 the number was 141,000, in 1950 one half million, and 1957 over 1 million. In 1982 over 6 million attended the Memorial, but only about 9,000 partook and a large portion of these were overseas.

As has been noted, the Watchtower work in the 1930s was complicated by World War II. The work in Germany was stopped when Hitler came to power in 1933 and was slowed or stopped in most countries until the war ended. During this time, the Society expended a great deal of effort on winning a wide variety of legal cases, mostly related to freedom to practice their brand of religion.

The Years After World War II

Following World War II, the Witnesses experienced spectacular growth. This growth continued until shortly after 1975 when hundreds of thousands left the Watchtower Society when Armageddon did not arrive. A continual problem with the Witnesses is prophetic failure. They have announced Armageddon with varying degrees of certainty several times (1914, 1915, 1918, 1925, c. 1972, and 1975); each failed prophecy produced both disappointment and schisms (see Zygmunt in the May 1970 *American Journal of Sociology*).

Rutherford's first big "message," which began in 1918, was "The World *Has* Ended--Millions Now Living Will Never Die." During the time of the "Millions" slogan, the Society emphasized that the Church would probably be complete and the Ancient Worthies (David, Moses, etc.) raised in 1925. After 1925 had passed, the study of time prophecy was discouraged slightly although in the 1930s and 1940s speculation abounded. Even though 1975 marked a major failure, Armageddon still figures prominently in the Society's message.

The Witnesses and the Printed Page

The movement has always emphasized the importance of formal study, particularly the study of first Russell's writings, then Rutherford's, and today "the Governing body's." The movement was first called by some "Millennial Dawn Bible Students," and also "Bible Students" in addition to "Russellites" and "Dawnites," and other names. In 1931, members became

known as "Jehovah's Witnesses," a name selected by Rutherford
to separate them from the "Bible Students," most of whom still
held to most of Russell's teachings.

The Bible Student groups as a whole, including contemporary
Jehovah's Witnesses, have consistently stressed the importance
of religious knowledge and study and minimized the value of
ritual, edifices, music, and poetry in their worship. One
must study, they believe, to become approved by God. This
study requires publication, which partially explains the
prodigious output not only of the Jehovah's Witnesses but also
of the 200 or so different Bible Student groups formed since
Russell's day.

Ironically, the Society has been for almost a century
opposed to higher education, high school at first, then college. Of late it has not been as critical of junior college
or technical school education as it formerly was.

The Society's opposition to education is difficult to
understand. According to Covington, Knorr disapproved of
higher education because he did not have much formal education,
barely graduating from high school. Covington also stated
that Knorr fired Quackenbush (the editor of *Awake!*) because
"he had brains."

Russell became famous not only for his prodigious output
of literature but for his widely syndicated newspaper column
and speaking tours. By 1913, the newspaper syndications were
in four languages and in three thousand newspapers in the
United States, Canada, and Europe.

The Witnesses have not shied away from using new tech-
nology as it develops. The "1914 Photo-Drama of Creation,"
a multi-media presentation, first utilized colored lantern
slides (painted by hand) and phonograph records, synchronized
to present a photo-phono coordinated presentation. The
"Photo-Drama" also included music, a script to be read, and
a short motion picture of Russell at the beginning. It was
presented in four parts (two hours each) and viewed by some
eight million people.

Portable phonographs were also popular with the Society.
The Witnesses asked householders if they would like to listen
to a record, which was almost always a short talk by Judge
Rutherford. In the 1930s and 1940s the Society designed and
built hundreds of wind-up portable phonographs which the Witnesses carried door to door for years. Engineers at Bethel
(the Society's headquarters) in the 1940s designed and manufactured a portable phonograph which could be played while
the cover was closed.

Radio was used extensively in the 20s and 30s, and many
of the Society's booklets during this time were printed radio
broadcast messages. Rutherford was especially fond of phone

and radio hookups so that he could speak at one convention
and conventioneers in a dozen or so other assembly cities
could simultaneously hear his presentation. He made his
first radio broadcast in April 1922, and the first radio
chain began in 1927 (the Detroit Convention tied together
over one hundred stations). The Society built radio station
WBBR in 1922 and operated it from 1924 to 1957. The peak
radio work was during 1933 when 403 stations were broadcasting
the Society's message. In 1937, the radio work was virtually
abandoned (except for WBBR) in favor of the portable phonograph work described above. The Witnesses also utilized sound
cars (automobiles or trucks equipped with loudspeakers) which
drove around blaring the Watchtower message (often sound cars
operated in front of churches on Sunday in the hope that those
in attendance would listen to the Witness message rather than
their minister's sermon).

During the 1940s, Witnesses were trained to go individually
from door to door with oral presentations. The Society came
to feel that this method was more effective than playing
records, which had irritated many people. Many of Rutherford's
records were bombastic and highly critical of the Catholic
Church in particular, religion as a whole, and all earthly
governments.

In 1943, a special training school for the Society's
missionaries, The Watch Tower Bible School of Gilead, was
established. The school graduates two classes each year, and
for most of its history the graduating class was around 100
students, but has decreased markedly during the past few
years to as few as 25 students. Recently, special courses
have been established for training congregational elders,
branch personnel, and full-time ministers. These courses
are held in various cities in the United States, Canada, and
other countries.

We have already remarked on the movement's large production of literature. Thousands of books, booklets, tracts,
etc., have been published, many with printings in the multi-
millions and one book of almost 100 million. Few religious
organizations have been more preoccupied with the production
and dissemination of religious literature. Books printed by
the Watchtower Society have achieved greater circulation than
almost any other books. First printings of 2 or 3 million
are common, and 20 million or more copies of many Witness
books and booklets are produced before they go out of print.
The 192-page *Truth* made the *1983 Guinness Book of World Records*
(p. 175) with 103 million copies in 116 languages by April
1982. At the Society's peak in the mid-70s, their official
journal, *The Watchtower*, had average printings of almost 11
million copies per issue, bi-monthly; and at the start of the

1980s it was printed in over 100 languages, more than any
other journal.

The Society As a Publisher and Provider

The Society's first printing press, a small job press,
was set up in Brooklyn, New York, in 1909. All previous
literature had been printed by commercial firms. During
World War I, as a result of the imprisonment of the Watch
Tower's President and several of its officers, publication
slowed almost to a standstill although *The Watch Tower* magazine
(in 1939 changed to *Watchtower*) was published on schedule even
then. The Watch Tower's "Tabernacle" building was sold; the
Bethel headquarters closed; and the staff went to Pittsburgh,
Pennsylvania. By 1919, the Society's officers had been released from prison, reopened the Bethel Home in Brooklyn, and
began producing literature again. A rotary press was purchased in 1920 and installed in a building the Society rented
on Myrtle Avenue close to the Bethel Home. The first issue
of *The Watch Tower* printed on the Society's own press was
dated February 1, 1920. In the latter part of 1921, the
Witnesses began making their own metal printing plates and
doing their own electroplating. Four years later, the Society
expanded its printing operation and rented three floors of a
building (including the basement) at 18 Concord Street. The
Society soon purchased some property on Adams Street, and in
1927 an eight-story factory was built there (117 Adams Street).
Within ten years, a four-story addition was completed; in
1950 a nine-story addition was finished, and four years later
a thirteen-story building. In the 1970s the large Squibb
Building complex was purchased, a number of large apartments
were built to house the 2,000 New York workers, and apartments
and printing facilities were built at Wallkill, New York;
Canada; and elsewhere. In addition, large (and in some cases
multi-million-dollar) assembly halls were built in almost
every state in the United States, in Canada, and in Europe.
      The main Watchtower Farm at Wallkill, New York (1,700
acres), produces most of the food for the Bethel family in
both Brooklyn and the farm itself. At Wallkill there are 800
head of cattle and pigs, a slaughter house, a smokehouse,
and other facilities (all parts of the animals are used,
even the spleen and kidneys). In addition, a flock of 4,000
chickens and 3,300 white leghorns lays an average of 2,700
eggs a day. Ninety-two cows produce over 420 gallons of milk,
part of which goes into the ice cream, butter, and cheese
which is made at the farm. The farm also has a cannery and
a bakery where 700 or more loaves of bread and other foods

are baked each day. The Society also owns a fruit farm in
Washington, New Jersey, and a grain farm in South Lansing,
New York (see *Harpers Magazine*, March 1973: "A Case of Self-
Sufficiency" by Nadine Brozan).

International and National Conventions

      The Witnesses are well known for their large conventions
which serve to show each Witness that there are many others
like himself. These conventions serve as tremendous publicity-
generating events as well as important morale boosters for the
Witnesses attending. For many Witnesses, these conventions
are the high point of their summer. The first major convention was held in Chicago, Illinois, in 1893 and was attended
by 360 persons with 70 baptized. The largest convention to
date was held in New York City in 1958 at both Yankee Stadium
and the Polo Grounds. The Sunday peak attendance was 253,922
with 7,136 baptized. The year 1978 saw a set of international
conventions which included hundreds of assemblies located in
45 countries attended by hundreds of thousands of persons.
      After J.F. Rutherford and the other Watch Tower officers
were released from prison in 1918, their first convention was
at Cedar Point, Ohio, on September 1-7 (attendance exceeded
6,000 and about 200 were baptized). Rutherford went to
Europe the next year to revitalize the overseas work. The
1922 Cedar Point convention drew 18,000 to 20,000 with 144
baptized.

Witness Beliefs

      The Society teaches that all 66 books of the Bible are
the "inspired Word of God." They believe that while many
passages of the Bible are figurative, most of it is literal,
much of it can be used to predict future events, and the
whole Bible is historically accurate. They call the New
Testament the Christian Greek Scriptures (because they were
first written in Greek) and the Old Testament the Hebrew
Scriptures (because most of them were originally written in
Hebrew). Jehovah's Witnesses stress that the name "Jehovah"
is an improper translation, but nonetheless they use it
because it is the commonly accepted English word for the
tetragrammation. The Society teaches that a "proper name"
for God is important because of such Scriptures as Psalms
83:18, which says "that men may know that thou, whose name
alone is Jehovah are the most high over all the earth" (KJV).
They are not averse to using some other form, such as Yawa

or Yahweh but consider the term "God" a title; thus, some
specific name is to be preferred. They reason that the word
"Jesus" is also not a correct translation of the original
Hebrew ("Y'shua," "Joshua," or "Yehoshuah" is more accurate)
but because "Jesus" is understood in English, it is preferred
over the more correct "Yehoshuah." The *Watchtower* stresses
that Witnesses are to use the "language of the people," and
as "Jehovah" is commonly understood in English, it should
be used. Because they have used "Jehovah" for some time, it
would probably be difficult to change. The name "Jehovah's
Witness" comes from Isaiah 43:11, "ye are my witnesses saith
Jehovah, and my servant whom I have chosen."

1914 was an important year for the Witnesses. 1878 and
later 1914 were to have brought "the glorification of the
saints," the end of the harvest (Witness work), and the beginning of the Millennium (the 1,000-year earthly rule by
Christ). Since that did not occur at either date, the Bible
was reinterpreted to the effect that in 1914 the Gentile times
(rule of worldly rulers) "legally" ended and a "period of
trouble" began. Within one generation from 1914, everlasting
peace would come to Earth in the form of a New World run by
Christ.

Jehovah's Witnesses teach that God created Adam and Eve
with a specific purpose in mind, namely to live forever on a
paradise earth free from sin, suffering, and sorrow. Their
sin temporarily interrupted God's plan, but provision was
made through Christ to restore mankind to perfection. As a
part of this restoration, Jesus established a church which
started to become corrupt after the death of the last apostle
of Jesus Christ, John, and in time completely fell away. At
the time of the emperor Constantine, the church which Christ
established became totally corrupt and, although throughout
history various small groups maintained allegiance to what
they called "the truth," it was not fully restored until the
late 1800s by Charles T. Russell.

Russell was "specifically guided by God," according to
contemporary Witness doctrine, to restore the work and prepare
the world for Armageddon, a decisive battle in which most
non-Jehovah's Witnesses are to be destroyed. After Armageddon
the "thousand year millennial reign of Christ" begins. The
survivors will "clean up the earth" and restore it to paradisal
conditions. During this time both those who never heard the
message preached by the Jehovah's Witnesses and those who
died faithfully will be resurrected to earthly life. Most of
those resurrected during this time will remain faithful, but
a few will "fall away," creating pockets of rebellion (yes,
even during the reign of Christ).

The final cleansing of the earth will occur at the end of
the millennial reign of Christ when Satan will be let loose to

tempt those who can be tempted, and then those who fall away
will be destroyed. Those who survive this last test will
have "everlasting life" but not "immortality." The Witnesses
teach that "immortality" is a state or condition in which one
cannot die, but "everlasting life" is life which is conditional,
based only upon the continual obedience of the individual. In
other words, everlasting life could mean that one could live forever, but this is not guaranteed, whereas immortality means
that one cannot die.

The Watchtower also teaches that there are two classes of
believers, the heavenly class (which is limited to 144,000)
and the Earthly class (to which most Witnesses belong). The
heavenly class will live in heaven with Christ and rule over
the earth. This is, to some degree, "a higher calling,"
although most Witnesses claim that they would prefer to live
on the earth. Part of the heavenly class, they believe, lived
during Jesus' day, but most lived during Russell's day and
the remaining ones, less than 10,000, are still alive today.

During Russell's day the "gathering" was limited to those
in the heavenly class, but since the 1930s it has been taught
that most of the new converts were part of a new class called
"the great crowd" (the Earthly class). Outsiders feel that
this class came about because Witness growth exceeded 144,000
because of the delayed end of the world. The Witnesses consider it is imperative that they spread the "good news of the
kingdom" to as many as possible before Armageddon. In order
to survive Armageddon, one must accept the message preached
by the Witnesses and in order for someone to accept this
message, it must be preached. If one neglects to preach this
message to someone and that person dies in ignorance, losing
out on everlasting life, the one who neglected the preaching
could also lose his or her life.

The Witnesses are very strict regarding moral behavior.
They condemn fornication, adultery, masturbation, abortion,
pornographic pictures, dirty jokes, worldly songs (especially
religious hymns), traditional holidays, drinking (except in
extreme moderation), the non-medical use of drugs, etc.

The Congregation

Each local assembly of Jehovah's Witnesses is now called
a Congregation (previously termed a "Church," an "Ecclesia,"
and later a "Company"). The hierarchy within the Congregation
has changed somewhat over the years, but the duties of
officials remain fairly similar. The Congregation organizes
the proselytizing work, primarily the "door-to-door" activity,

which is almost a sacrament among the Witnesses in spite of
its ineffectiveness and the antagonism it arouses among the
visited. Congregations doggedly and continually pressure individual Witnesses to pursue this unrewarding mode of proselytizing. However, this activity does generate income, and
Witnesses have today almost totally neglected other methods
of outreach (although in the past, as noted above, the phonograph, radio, and film were utilized). For some reason they
have avoided television, even though this medium is extremely
effective. They have also strongly discouraged individual
Witnesses from taking the incentive in new ways and have insisted primarily upon formal "one to one contact" in the door-
to-door activity. Individual Witnesses are strongly discouraged from writing books, articles, producing films, television and radio shows, etc. Groups of Witnesses have recently
tried to set up schools and hospitals but have received no
cooperation or encouragement whatsoever from the Watch Tower
Society. The Society has solidified into a certain rigid
mold and will probably continue in it for some time.

Each congregation has a Presiding Minister (also called
the Presiding Elder or Overseer). One of his duties is to
insure that all those Witnesses living in the congregation's
territory are behaving in the proper manner. The Presiding
Elder has had many titles--at first he was called an Elder,
then the Company Head, then later the Company Servant, the
Congregation Servant, the Congregation Overseer, before currently being called the Presiding Overseer or Chairman of the
Body of Elders. He oversees most of the legal aspects of
the congregation, makes arrangements for speakers for "hour
talks," and assigns different congregational duties to
qualified persons. The vice president, or second in command,
at one time called the Assistant Congregation Servant, is
the Field Overseer. He is in charge of the congregation if
the Presiding Overseer is absent and is responsible for
filing the reports of the door-to-door work and keeping other
records. Once a month he sends a report to the Society's
branch office which eventually reaches the world headquarters
in Brooklyn, New York.

The Field Overseer now also fulfills the duties of the
Bible Study Servant, who used to supervise, encourage, and
sometimes work with individual publishers in conducting Bible
studies based upon systematic studies of the Society's publications although Scriptures are read primarily as "proof
texts," in order to support the Society's teachings. The
Literature Servant (formerly called the Stock Keeper and
later Literature Overseer) is the only person authorized to
order literature from the Watch Tower Society. This person

stocks, collects the money, and pays for the literature the
congregation uses. The Magazine Territory Servant or Overseer orders the *Watchtower* and *Awake!* magazines for door-to-
door work and is in charge of assigning territory to"publishers" (baptized Witnesses) who work from door to door.
The Secretary now serves as a "go-between" between the Society
and the local congregation. The Accounts Servant (formerly
called the Treasurer) counts the contributions and, under
the direction of the Presiding overseer, is responsible for
the bills and the congregation's bank account.

Each congregation's boundaries are divided up into territories, usually city blocks, apartments, etc., which can
be canvassed in ten hours or so by a carload of Witnesses.
Most congregations have one to two hundred territories, de-
pending upon the size of the congregation and the number of
persons living in the territory assigned to it. Members work
territories by alternately offering issues of *The Watchtower*
and *Awake!* (which sold for years for a nickle and, as of
1981, are now 10¢) or books (the Society's latest hardbound
book, or sometimes several Society books). A year's subscription to *The Watchtower* and *Awake!* was $1.00 each from 1879 to
until a few years ago and, as of 1981, subscriptions are
$2.50 each or both for $5.00.

The United States, Canada, and most of the rest of the
world are divided up into "territories." Wherever there is
"unassigned territory," the congregations nearby endeavor to
work this territory during the summer and holidays.

Local Meetings

Each congregation has had, since 1943, a theocratic ministry school (or after 1976 a "theocratic service school"). This
45-minute weekly meeting teaches Witnesses to give talks in
front of an audience, and indoctrinates them in history,
theology, etc. This school covers Biblical material much as
theological seminaries do, but in far less depth. Such subjects as Biblical Greek history and other subjects not
directly part of Witness doctrine and teaching are largely
ignored.

The school consists of four talks. The first talk, prepared by a spiritually mature Witness, is 15 minutes long,
and the second talk, prepared by a new Witness, is 8 minutes.
The last two talks or presentations are given by female Witnesses, usually at a table or the platform in front of the
Congregation, to a female Witness who acts as a Bible Study,
householder, or friend (female Witnesses are forbidden to
use the podium to address the Congregation, except when re-

lating experiences, because they are not allowed to teach the
Congregation directly).

Material for these talks is to be taken almost verbatim
from various Society publications. Counsel (constructive
criticism) by the Theocratic School Servant is given after
each talk in front of the Congregation.

The Service Meeting is usually on the same night as the
Theocratic Ministry School, and is also 45 minutes in length.
The Service Meeting is designed to help each Witness to
present his or her message effectively door to door. The
Return Visit Overseer (formerly called the Back Call Servant
and the Back Call Overseer) is in charge of helping congregation members make return visits, i.e., bringing follow-up
literature or "calling back" on persons who express an interest in the Witnesses and their message.

During the middle of the week (usually Tuesday) the
Society has "Book Studies" (at one time called **Berean Classes,**
a term from the **Bible, Acts 17:10-11), a study of some** *Watch-*
tower **publication,** usually a hardbound book. This study is led
by the Book Study Conductor.

On weekends Witnesses meet at the Kingdom Hall (where
congregational meetings are held) to arrange for door-to-door
activity and, during the week, at the Book Study houses (at
the home of a Witness). This meeting place was formerly
called the Contact Point, later the Service Center, still
later the Rendezvous for Field Service, and finally the
Meeting for Field Service. Those who engage in full-time
preaching work (their hours vary but usually range from 75
to 100 per month, according to the type of "pioneering"
missionary work) were first called Sharp Shooters, then Col-
porturs (during the Colportur stage, the primary goal was to
sell books) and now are called Pioneers. There are two types
of Pioneers, a Regular Pioneer and an Auxiliary (temporary)
Pioneer (at one time called Vacation Pioneers).

Directly above the congregational level in the adminis-
trative hierarchy is the Circuit Overseer or Servant (at one
time called a Zone Servant and earlier a Pilgrim) and the
District Overseer has charge of several circuits. The Branch
Overseer supervises several districts. Finally, the Governing
Body, made up of the President, the Vice-President, and a
number of other individuals (the number is currently 17), is
in charge of the branches. The Circuit Servant is actually
a representative of the Governing Body (or, at one time, a
representative of the President of the Watchtower Society).

Congregations are visited about three times a year by
the Circuit Overseer who supervises about twelve congregations.
This official has regained much of his former status after
almost having been reduced to the level of an elder in the

Figure 1
The Watchtower View of the World of Humans

Satan's Organization Hierarchy	God's Organization Hierarchy
Heaven Satan ↓ Fallen Angels	Jehovah (The Father) ↓ Jesus Christ (God's Son) ↓ 144,000 (The Anointed or Remnant) ↓ Millions of Angels

Earth Religious--Political Leaders ↓ World of Mankind ↓ Disassociated Witnesses ↓ Disfellowshipped Witnesses in General ↓ Witnesses Disfellowshipped for "forming a sect" or heresy (worst of all humans)	The President of the Society ↓ Governing Body (17 members) ↓ District Servant ↓ Circuit Servant ↓ Congregation Overseer ↓ (Body of Elders) ↓ Assistant Congregation Overseer ↓ Field Service Overseer ↓ Bible Study Servant ↓ Book Study Servant ↓ Regular Pioneer ↓ Temporary Pioneer ↓ Publisher ↓ Newly Interested Ones ↓ Bible Studies

congregation. Evidently, the Society has tried a number of
techniques to ensure an efficient organization and, especially
during the 70s, has had considerable problems. The Society is
very organizationally minded and is most concerned about both
cost efficiency and the development of an efficient large-
scale operation.

The only meeting to which the general public is invited
is usually on Sunday (commonly at ten o'clock in the morning)
and is called the Talk, the Hour Talk, or the Public Talk.
This meeting consists of an hour lecture given by an experienced baptized Witness. Since the advent of the elder
system in 1975, only elders and ministerial servants are
allowed to give hour talks to the local congregation and,
except in unusual circumstances, only elders are allowed to
give talks in other congregations. These talks are generally
little more than extemporaneous presentations of Society
materials. At one time a one-page outline with a number of
references to Society publications was followed, but currently
a much more detailed outline of four pages or so must be
followed almost word for word.

The Watchtower Study follows the Sunday public meeting
and is conducted by the Watchtower Study Conductor, who must
also be an Elder. It is conducted in a very formal but per-
functory manner: The Study Conductor asks the questions
printed at the bottom of *The Watchtower*, and after someone in
the audience answers correctly, the paragraph is read out
loud by the Reader. This is considered the most important
meeting of the week because *The Watchtower* is considered
semi-inspired. At one time there was a ten-minute break between the public talk and the Watchtower Study, but in an
effort to keep people from leaving (usually more people
attend the public talk because the Watchtower Study is rather
boring, and one can read the magazine at home), this inter-
mission was eliminated. Since the 1940s a song is sung between the Public Meeting and the Watchtower Study and after
the Watchtower Study as well as before the Ministry School
and the Service Meeting, which are now also conducted back
to back.

Nathan Homer Knorr

Nathan Knorr, the third President of the Society, was
born in Bethlehem, Pennsylvania, on April 23, 1905. He
graduated from Allentown, Pennsylvania, High School in June
of 1923. At age 16 he first associated with the Witnesses,
and at 18 he became a Pioneer and soon was called to Bethel
headquarters where he made rapid progress. In 1932, he

became general manager of the publishing office and plant, and
two years later, at 29, he was elected to the Board of
Directors, and, at 35 in 1940 he became the Vice-President of
the Society. He became President when Rutherford died in 1942
and remained in this position until June 7, 1977, when he died
at the age of 72 of a brain tumor.

Knorr has the reputation of having been an astute business-
man who worked extremely hard and expected others to do likewise. He is said to have run his workers "ragged" but generally
did it with a "never-failing good humor." Knorr's talents were
predominantly in organization and business, and he was not
noted as a theologian. During his administration, the chief
theologian was Fred Franz assisted by several others.

Knorr was far less colorful than either Rutherford or
Russell, and thus much less is known about him. He was moderate
in habits and kept a low profile, rarely making the bombastic
announcements that Rutherford or Russell were known for.
Virtually nothing is known about his personal life. He was
married to Audrey Mock and had a sister, Isabel Knorr. He was
raised in the Dutch Reformed Church. Aside from various rumors
about his personal life (he broke the Society's ban on marriage when he himself married), he avoided the scandals
of his predecessors. Like them, however, he spent a great
deal of time traveling, supervising the growth of the Witnesses' worldwide empire. He also was evidently at least
partly responsible for the toning down of the Witness message
and for the more conservative orientation which the Witnesses
developed during his administration.

Fred Franz

The fourth and current President, Fred W. Franz, was born
in Covington, Kentucky, in 1893. He is considered by Witnesses
to be a first-class scholar with a marvelous mind and a photo-
graphic memory. He is supposedly fluent in five languages
(Greek, German, Spanish, Latin, and English). He spent two
years at the University of Cincinnati studying theology but
because of the expectation of Armageddon in 1914, he left
school to enter full-time Witness work. It is claimed that
he was offered a Rhodes Scholarship but turned it down to
become a full-time minister for the Society. According to
Covington, he is "humble and easy until he learns which way
the wind is blowing."

Franz and Knorr evidently got along fairly well. Franz
is, and has been for a number of years, even during Knorr's
presidency, the main driving force behind the Society, more
powerful than any other individual person. He is in many ways

the Society. Unfortunately, extremely little is known about
Franz as a person. His life has been accompanied by none of
the scandals that were such an important part of the lives of
Rutherford and Russell. Franz and Knorr have been very care-
ful to conceal their life and any possible criticisms from
the public, and their close associates have respected this
wish. Recently, however, in 1982, Raymond Franz, Frederick
Franz's cousin and a longtime member of the governing body
of the Witnesses, left because of a number of disagreements.
He is now writing a book about his 35 years of experiences as
a Witness; the book should be extremely illuminating relative
to the organization, and especially its current President.
This is the first time since the 1917 split that a major ad-
ministrator has left the Society.

Franz never married, is quite retiring, and spends much
of his time in his room studying and writing. He is evidently
somewhat absent-minded and reads prodigiously. Franz is one
of the very few Watchtower leaders who are respected by both
friend and foe although some Bethelites have referred to him
as an egomaniac.

The Division of the Material in the Bibliography

Our rationale for dividing the literature in this bibliography into book, booklet, and tract sections is the
nature of the literature on the Witnesses. Most of the Witness and non-Witness tracts are brief and repetitive and of
minor value to researchers. It seems necessary to separate
books and booklets and tracts for other reasons: the books
are readily obtainable whereas the booklets and tracts are
almost impossible to obtain except from private collectors
or, at times, from libraries. In addition, almost all tracts
are purely of a proselytizing nature, as are many booklets.
Many of the books, on the other hand, are not theological
but sociological and psychological studies.

Sometimes a non-Witness tract or booklet contains a section on Jehovah's Witnesses, but as there are so few of these
publications, they are listed under non-official tracts and
booklets. The fact that only a section deals with the Witnesses is also noted.

Our definition of a book, booklet, or tract was based
primarily upon binding and size. Tracts are two, four, or
six pages of folded and unstapled printed matter. Booklets
are usually eight- to twenty-five pages, occasionally as many
as ninety pages, and always bound by saddle stapling. Books
are perfect bound (glued) or stitched (sewn) and are usually
from one hundred to three hundred or more pages. Both hardbound
and paperback books were included in the category of books.

During the Rutherford era, almost all publications were authored by "the Judge" himself (and the books and booklets gave this information). After Knorr became president in 1942, all Watchtower publications were published anonymously, although Fred. W. Franz probably wrote many or most of them. This policy continued under the presidency of Franz.

There is a very clear distinction between official literature and non-official literature. Although a few non-society publications have been accepted as official or semi-official, such as Marley Cole's *Jehovah's Witnesses* and *The New World Society* and A.H. Macmillan's *Faith on the March*, generally Witnesses are strongly discouraged from reading anything not published by the Society except possibly concordances and Bible dictionaries. Even the reading of publications by active Witnesses is strongly discouraged. Although Marley Cole's first book was approved by the Society and written in conjunction with the Society's editorial staff and Governing Body, his second book, *Triumphant Kingdom*, was not, and thus sold very poorly. Very few Witnesses knew of and read the book, and the rest would probably have refused to read it had they known it existed. When attorney Victor Blackwell (*O'er the Ramparts They Watched*, 1976) and Professor James Penton (*Jehovah's Witnesses in Canada*, 1976), both life-long Witnesses and both very active in defending the Witness movement, wrote books, they were severely chastised and in time forced out of the Movement. This attitude has existed since the early days of the Society. In the early 1900s A.B. Dabney of Virginia wrote a booklet entitled *Questions Answering Questions* that was totally in harmony with the Society's position at the time. He was forced to withdraw it from circulation. In a letter to Russell, published in the April 1, 1911, *Watchtower* (p. 110), he stated:

> Owing to much literature being circulated by the opposition within our ranks ... I concluded it wise to discontinue the distribution of the *Questions Answering Questions* booklet. Since then I have received many orders for these booklets from friends who are not advised of their discontinuance, and some do not understand why they are refused. I would thank you for the publication of this letter in the *Watch Tower*, notifying the friends of their discontinuance and my reason for this. Prayerful meditation on Mark 9:38-40 leads me to the conclusion that we can be workers in the Harvest, and yet not followers of the Lord. To be followers of the Lord, we must not only be workers in the Harvest, but must also be workers according to his will. The fact that the majority of the Lord's "little ones" now disapprove of the circulation [of] all literature other than that

published by the Society, and my belief that the expression of the majority in such matters is the expression of the will of the Lord, are other reasons for
its discontinuance. Feeling sure that all the Lord's
faithful ones ... may receive a greater blessing by the
discontinuance than by the circulation of the booklet,
I remain

A.B. Dabney

It is unlikely that this letter was Mr. Dabney's idea but
probably was written at the encouragement of C.T. Russell.
The message is clear: in any case only the Society is to publish literature.

An active Witness is never to publish anything about religion even if the work is totally in agreement with the current teachings of the Society. The Society wants exclusive
control of publishing although it will allow letter writing--
not too many difficulties have been encountered in publishing
letters in the newspaper in defense of the Witnesses. Commercial publishing almost invariably spells expulsion for
a Witness today as has been true during the whole history of
the Society. Witnesses view the literature that comes from
headquarters as semi-inspired, the latest installment of the
Bible. Even the "mistakes" are designed to carry out Jehovah's
purpose (such as a means to remove the weak or "faultfinders").
Some Witnesses also sometimes believe that Jehovah "misleads"
His people for His own purposes. For example, the explanation
for Rutherford's sometimes embarrassing behavior, especially
his strong language, drinking, and pugnacious behavior, both
in print and in person, is as follows: "God's organization
needed a leader like him during times of difficulties like
1930-1940." Few Witnesses realize that Rutherford's behavior
caused many of these "difficulties."

Witnesses are discouraged from reading "older" Watchtower
Society literature because usually anything over five or ten
years old is "old light." As each new president took over,
doctrines changed and old literature was phased out.
Rutherford's book soon replaced those by Russell and today
Franz's books have replaced Rutherford's. The last of
Russell's books were published by the Society in 1927 and
were last circulated in 1932 (see the *Bulletin*, December 1,
1932).

A NOTE ON THIS WORK

Although scores of indexes, bibliographies, persons,
libraries, etc., have been consulted, some items have un-
doubtedly not been included in this list. Readers aware of
additional references are strongly encouraged to contact the
author.

Existing indexes were of limited usefulness in compiling
this bibliography. For example, of the booklets listed in
Section Three, fewer than five percent are listed in any of
the standard indexes, and of the books, only one-half were
listed in *Books in Print*. Thus, the items in this bibliography were obtained not only from indexes, but also from correspondence and conversation with researchers in this area.

Another major weakness in this list is the result of
lack of access to indexes of smaller, local publications and
some publications which are not included in any of the standard
library indexes. While the indexes of a large number of
smaller journals were consulted, nonetheless, thousands of
small, local publications, especially religious publications,
have very limited circulations. Many booklets and limited-
circulation publications are produced locally and are not
commonly available.

The researcher's main source of much of this material is
through interlibrary loan. Few libraries, even large university libraries, contain, for example, more than four or five
of the books listed in the book section and, except in private
collections, almost none of the other material is publicly
available. The "official" material is available primarily
in private libraries and a very few large university libraries.
Probably the most complete collection belongs to the author
and to the Institute for the Study of American Religion (ISAR),
Box 1311, Evanston, Ill. 60201; Witness Incorporated (c/o
Dwayne Magnani, 5733 Verna Way, Clayton, Cal. 94517); and
CARIS (c/o Walt Davis, 471 Archibald Ct., Colton, Cal. 92324).
The Watchtower Society has a fairly large collection, although
they are missing many important items because their library
was confiscated in 1918 when the United States government

outlawed them as an organization. It is rumored this material
is stored in a government warehouse somewhere, but this is
unlikely; it was probably destroyed. Although, as I will
discuss, the Witnesses are usually not cooperative with outsiders (and often insiders as well), for those who wish to
write, the address of the Watchtower Society is: 25 Columbia
Heights, Brooklyn, N.Y. 11201.

When this writer was at Bethel (the Society's world headquarters) in the middle 60s, he made extensive notes of the
library holdings. Much of this information is incorporated
into this bibliography. Since then, while preparing this
bibliography for publication, he contacted Bethel several
times and was told the Watchtower Society was "not interested"
in helping with this work. Spokesmen for the Society stressed
that "it would not be profitable" to read either non-Witness
publications or older Witness works. What they wanted Witnesses to know was only what was now in print.

The Society has several large libraries and at least three
largely complete sets of their literature. One is available
to the writing staff, another to the school of Gilead, and the
third to the Bethel family members. In addition, at Bethel
there is another library with very old and rare material, many
non-Society publications, etc., which is available only to the
President and some of his close associates.

In addition to its publications, the Watchtower Society
has a large number of books in their libraries on religious,
medical, and scientific topics, many of which are quite dated
and most of which were willed to the Society. The Society
also has a bound set of all their Supreme Court cases (about
50), as well as most of the other court cases they have fought
(hundreds). A large collection of anti-Society tracts, booklets, and books is available, but only by special permission.
For example, William Schnell's books are listed in the library
catalogue, but the card entry says they can be seen only by
special permission--which is rarely granted.

Much of this literature is extremely rare, and thus fairly
valuable. For a discussion of its value see "Witnesses to a
New Area of Book Collecting" by this author, in *Book Collector's Market*, Vol. 4, No. 3, May-June 1979, pp. 1-9.

Readers who are able to provide any further information on
the entries or new entries are cordially requested to submit to
the writer in care of Garland Publishing, Inc., 136 Madison
Ave., New York, N.Y. 10016. In this way, future editions of
this work will be more complete. Also, since individual contact
is the main source of information in classifying much of the
material in some sections, mistakes may have been made. Most
important, there is probably much Bible Student literature that
is not listed. In either case, the reader is invited to offer
corrections and additions by writing the author.

SECTION ONE

OFFICIAL WATCHTOWER BIBLE &
TRACT SOCIETY LITERATURE

The Watchtower Society makes a clear distinction between
acceptable and unacceptable literature. Most active Witnesses
believe that the Society's literature is to some degree inspired, and all other printed matter is suspect. Witnesses
are therefore discouraged from reading all non-Witness literature. God's holy spirit directs the Watchtower Society, and
God uses the Society to direct His people (the Jehovah's Witnesses). Although the Society has not directly said so, nonetheless, it is clearly inferred and believed by most Witnesses
that their literature is inspired. Thus, it is important to
make a distinction between official literature, which has the
official seal of approval, the Watchtower Imprimatur, and
nonofficial literature.
This distinction was not quite as clear in the early
history of the Society as it is today. Several other Bible
students who wrote much of the early literature, such as
Paton and Barbour, later left Russell and began their own
ministry. Thus, it is more difficult to determine what would
be considered "official" literature, especially from the
1870s to the early 1900s. The imprint of the Watchtower
Bible & Tract Society (in America, in the early years, Allegheny, Pa., and later Brooklyn, N.Y.) or inclusion in the
official *Watchtower Bible & Tract Society Publications Index*
from 1930 to 1960 indicates "official" literature. Also included in this section are the publications sold by the
Society and published with their approval, such as those
edited by L.W. Jones, M.D., an early active Bible Student
who lived in Chicago.
Much of the very early literature was written by Russell,
and from 1917 or so until the early 1940s most of the literature was written by Rutherford. During the Knorr administration the writing was done by several different persons, especially F.W. Franz. On only a few of the works published
in Russell's day is the author indicated. On the other hand,

in the Rutherford era, at least for the booklets and books, the author is almost always listed (usually it was Rutherford himself). During both the Knorr (1942-1977) and Franz (1977 to date) administrations, works are only "published by the Watchtower Bible & Tract Society." The only books *not* included in this section which probably would be considered official Witness publications are *Jehovah's Witnesses: The New World Society* by Marley Cole, and *Faith on the March* by A.H. Macmillan, both of which were written with full approval of the Society and in cooperation with the Society by active Witnesses (the Society's staff actually did much of the writing and editing for both books) and were sold by the Society. The Society wished, in both cases, to produce a pro-Society book by a secular press. A number of other active Witnesses have written books favorable to the Society, but none of these has achieved the official approval of the Society although they are occasionally quoted in the Society's literature. These works are listed in the nonofficial books section.

A. BOOKS

Books Printed in the Russell Era
and the First Part of the Rutherford Era
(1877-1924)

Barbour, Nelson H., and C.T. Russell. *Three Worlds and the Harvest of This World*. Rochester, N.Y., 1877, 197 pp.

Bond, M.R., ed. *Thy Word Is Truth*. c. 1920, 114 pp. From Russell's writings.

Paton, John H. *The Day Dawn*; or *The Gospel in Type and Prophecy*. Pittsburgh, Pa.: A.D. Jones, 1st ed. 1880, 334 pp., hb., pb. (For later editions, not all of which were acceptable to Russell--for by then Paton had left Russell's group and made changes in the second edition--see below, p. 61.

Russell, Charles Taze. *Food for Thinking Christians: Why Evil Was Permitted and Kindred Topics*. Sept. 1881, 161 pp., supplement to *Zion's Watch Tower*, Pittsburgh, Pa.

——. *Tabernacle Shadows of the "Better Sacrifices."* Allegheny, Pa.: WtBTS, 1881; revised ed., 1899, 1908 (for reprints see below, p. 265, and the reprints of the *Divine Plan*, p. 272.

————. *The Tabernacle and Its Teachings.* Feb. 1882, 97 pp., supplement to *Zion's Watch Tower*, Pittsburgh, Pa. For reprints see below, p. 272.

————. *Studies in the Scriptures.* Titled *Millennial Dawn*, published by Zion's Watch Tower Co., Allegheny, Pa., or WtBTS, Allegheny, Pa., until 1903, thereafter *Studies in the Scriptures* (all published by the Watchtower Bible and Tract Society in Brooklyn, N.Y., although some list International Bible Student's Association as the publisher—another name the WtBTS uses). The *Millennial Dawn* editions were published in Allegheny, Pa., and *Studies in the Scriptures* were published in Brooklyn, N.Y. The *Studies in the Scriptures* are also available in a deluxe edition. The volumes are also called "Series" (Vol. I is called Series I, etc.). The six volumes are still in print, reprinted by several of the Bible Student groups; see below, pp. 257, 265, 272-273, 311, 312, 313.

Vol. I, *The Divine Plan of the Ages.* Pittsburgh, Pa.: Zion's Watch Tower, 1886, 356 pp. (originally called *The Plan of the Ages*).

Vol. II, *The Time Is at Hand.* Allegheny, Pa.: Tower Pub. Co., 1st ed. 1888, 366 pp.; 2nd ed. 1889, 387 pp. with index.

Vol. III, *Thy Kingdom Come.* Allegheny, Pa.: WtBTS, 1891, 399 pp.

Vol. IV, *The Day of Vengeance.* Allegheny, Pa.: WtBTS, 1897, 672 pp. (retitled *The Battle of Armageddon* in 1912).

Vol. V, *At-One-Ment Between God and Man.* Allegheny, Pa.: WtBTS, 1899, 500 pp. (later editions bound with *Tabernacle Shadows*).

Vol. VI, *The New Creation.* Allegheny, Pa.: WtBTS, 1904, 752 pp.

————. *What Say the Scriptures About Spiritism?* Brooklyn, N.Y.: WtBTS, 1897, 126 pp., pb.

————. *Russell-White Debate.* Cincinnati, Ohio: F.L. Rowe Publ., 1908, 196 pp.; 6th ed. 1928. Reprinted about 1974 by Campbell's Bookshelf, Magadore, Ohio.

————. *Outlines.* Pittsburgh, Pa.: Tower Pub. Co., 1909, 493 pp. (six booklets under one cover: *Chart Discourses*, *Our Lord's Return*, *Tabernacle Shadows*, *Spiritism*, *Hell*, and

Evolution), hb. with the same cover design as the *Studies in the Scriptures.*

―――――. *Poems of the Dawn.* Pittsburgh, Pa.: WtBTS, 1912, 286 pp. For reprints see below, p. 265.

―――――. *Scenario of the Photo-Drama of Creation.* Brooklyn, N.Y.: International Bible Students Association, 1914, Parts 1, 2, and 3, 99 pp. (reprinted by the Chicago Bible Students, p. 310), pb., hb. Bound separately in 3 volumes, also 3 parts bound in one volume.

―――――. *The Divine Plan of the Ages as Shown in the Great Pyramid.* Brooklyn, N.Y.: WtBTS, 1915, 438 pp. (A special edition of *Studies in the Scriptures*, Series I, *The Divine Plan of the Ages*, with chapter 3 of *Thy Kingdom Come* [Series III] included.)

―――――. *Pastor C.T. Russell's Articles for the Twelve Months: February 1911 to February 1912.* 1012, 60 pp. (reprinted from *Overland Monthly*, identical, only renumbered). (Probably each year was reprinted by the WtBTS.) See also Chicago Bible Student reprint, p. 310 below.

―――――. *God's Chosen People.* 1915, 288 pp. (a reprint of Russell's articles printed in *Overland Monthly*, 1910-1915).

―――――. *Pastor Russell's Sermons: A Choice Collection of His Most Important Discourses on All Phases of Christian Doctrine and Practice*, edited by L.W. Jones. Brooklyn, N.Y.: People's Pulpit Association, 1917, 804 pp. (reprinted by the Chicago Bible Students, see below, p. 310).

―――――. *What Pastor Russell Said; His Answer to Hundreds of Questions*, edited by L.W. Jones. Chicago, 1917, 776 pp., hb. (reprinted by the Chicago Bible Students, see below, p. 310).

―――――. *The Revelation of Jesus Christ According to the Sinaitic Text with Explanatory Notes and Comments.* Brooklyn, N.Y.: WtBTS, 1918, 200 pp., hb.

―――――. *What Pastor Russell Taught: On the Covenants, Mediator, Ransom, Sin Offering, Atonement*, ed. by L.W. Jones. Chicago, 1919, 398 pp. (reprinted by the Chicago Bible Students, see below, p. 310); original ed. 320 pp.

—————. *Tabernacle Shadows of the Better Sacrifices, A Helping Hand for the Royal Priesthood.* Pittsburgh, Pa.: WtBTS, 1919, 131 pp., pb. (Questions: 30 pp. bound with book: total = 161 pp.); Brooklyn, N.Y., 1920 ed. reset = total 182 pp., pb.

—————, ed. *The Watch Tower.* Brooklyn, N.Y.: WtBTS, 1919. (Reprints of all major and most minor articles.)

Vol. 1, 1879-1887, pp. 1-996
Vol. 2, 1888-1895, pp. 997-1908
Vol. 3, 1896-1900, pp. 1909-2748
Vol. 4, 1901-1905, pp. 2749-3692
Vol. 5, 1906-1910, pp. 3693-4732
Vol. 6, 1911-1915, pp. 4733-5820
Vol. 7, 1916-1919, pp. 5821-6622 (including index)

These reprints were in turn reprinted by the Chicago Bible Students; see below, p. 310.

Seibert, Gertrude W., and Hattie Woodward, comps. *Daily Heavenly Manna for the Household of Faith.* Allegheny, Pa.: WtBTS, 1905, 386 pp.; enlarged ed. 1907 (later published in Brooklyn, N.Y.); some eds. titled *Daily Heavenly Manna and Birthday Record.* Several bindings available. One printing was titled *My Friends--Their Birthdays and Autographs* (reprinted by the Dawn Bible Students, see below, p. 273, and by the Chicago Bible Students, see below, p. 309).

Smith, J.G. *Angels and Women.* New York: A.B. ABAC Co., 1924, 268 pp. (a revision of *Seola* by J.G. Smith), introduction and appendix by WtBTS.

Van Amburgh, William E. *The Way to Paradise.* Brooklyn, N.Y.: IBSA, 1924, 1925, 256 pp.

Woodworth, Clayton J. *Bible Students Manual.* Pittsburgh, Pa.: WtBTS, 1909, 654 pp. (all 5 parts bound in one volume). (Reprinted by the Chicago Bible Students, see below, p. 309).

Part 1: Zion's Watch Tower and Dawn-Studies--Comments, 481 pp.
Part 2: Instructor's Guide, 18 pp., compiled by Gertrude W. Seibert.
Part 3: Berean Topical Index, 28 pp., compiled by Gertrude W. Seibert.
Part 4: Difficult Texts Explained and Spurious Passages Noted, 14 pp.

Part 5: Index to Scripture Citations in the Watchtower
(from Jan. 1, 1908, to Jan. 1, 1916), 15 pp.
Appendix: 98 pp. (including index).
Total: 654 pp.

Woodworth, Clayton J., and George H. Fisher. *The Finished
Mystery*. Brooklyn, N.Y.: International Bible Students'
Association (IBSA), 1917, 608 pp. (also available in deluxe pocket edition). Woodworth wrote the section on the
book of Revelation and Fisher the section on the book of
Ezekiel. This work was banned by the American and Canadian
governments because of statements which were viewed as
critical of the American war effort. As a compromise the
Society agreed to ask its members to tear out pp. 247-258.
Thus, many copies of this book lack these pages. The book
was claimed to be the posthumous work of Pastor Russell but
was not accepted by many Bible students and was an important
factor in the split that took place in 1917-18.

————. *The Finished Mystery.* revised ed. Brooklyn, N.Y.:
WtBTS, 1927, 380 pp. (contains only Revelation discussion).

Books Written by J.F. (Joseph Franklin)
Rutherford, often called "Judge Rutherford,"
although he was never elected a judge
(The Rutherford Era)

Rutherford, J.F. *Man's Salvation from a Lawyer's Viewpoint.*
Pub. by Auth., 1906, 96 pp., hb.

————. *Millions Now Living Will Never Die.* Brooklyn, N.Y.:
WtBTS, 1920, 128 pp., pb.

————. *Tabernacle Shadows.* Brooklyn, N.Y.: WtBTS, 1920,
192 pp.

————. *Talking With the Dead.* Brooklyn, N.Y.: WtBTS, 1920,
156 pp., pb. (reissued as *Can the Living Talk With the
Dead?*).

————. *The Harp of God.* Brooklyn, N.Y.: WtBTS, 1921, 1928,
384 pp., hb.; also published in smaller pocket edition.

————. *Comfort for the Jews.* Brooklyn, N.Y.: WtBTS, 1925,
128 pp., pb., hb.

————. *Deliverance.* Brooklyn, N.Y.: WtBTS, 1926, 384 pp.,
hb. (two different covers, identical contents).

————. *Creation*. Brooklyn, N.Y.: WtBTS, 1927, 368 pp., hb. (two different covers, identical contents).

————. *Restoration*. Brooklyn, N.Y.: WtBTS, 1927, 127 pp., pb.

————. *Government*. Brooklyn, N.Y.: WtBTS, 1928, 368 pp., hb.

————. *Reconciliation*. Brooklyn, N.Y.: WtBTS, 1928, 368 pp., hb.

————. *Life*. Brooklyn, N.Y.: WtBTS, 1929, 360 pp., hb.

————. *Prophecy*. Brooklyn, N.Y.: WtBTS, 1929, 358 pp., hb.

————. *Light, Book One*. Brooklyn, N.Y.: WtBTS, 1930, 350 pp., hb.

————. *Light, Book Two*. Brooklyn, N.Y.: WtBTS, 1930, 352 pp., hb.

————. *Vindication, Book One*. Brooklyn, N.Y.: WtBTS, 1931, 350 pp., hb. Also called *Vindication*.

————. *Vindication, Book Two*. Brooklyn, N.Y.: WtBTS, 1932, 350 pp., hb.

————. *Vindication, Book Three*. Brooklyn, N.Y.: WtBTS, 1932, 384 pp., hb.

————. *Preservation*. Brooklyn, N.Y.: WtBTS, 1032, 352 pp., hb.

————. *Preparation*. Brooklyn, N.Y.: WtBTS, 1933, 384 pp., hb.

————. *Jehovah*. Brooklyn, N.Y.: WtBTS, 1934, 382 pp., hb.

————. *Riches*. Brooklyn, N.Y.: WtBTS, 1936, 386 pp., hb.

————. *Enemies*. Brooklyn, N.Y.: WtBTS, 1937, 384 pp., hb.

————. *Salvation*. Brooklyn, N.Y.: WtBTS, 1939, 384 pp., hb.

————. *Religion*. Brooklyn, N.Y.: WtBTS, 1940, 384 pp., hb.

————. *Children*. Brooklyn, N.Y.: WtBTS, 1941, 382 pp., hb.

Books Printed in the Franz-Knorr Era

The New World. Brooklyn, N.Y.: WtBTS, 1942, 384 pp., hb.

"The Truth Shall Make You Free." Brooklyn, N.Y.: WtBTS, 1943, 380 pp., hb.

"The Kingdom Is at Hand." Brooklyn, N.Y.: WtBTS, 1944, 380 pp., hb.

Theocratic Aid to Kingdom Publishers. Brooklyn, N.Y.: WtBTS, 1945, 382 pp., hb.

"Equipped for Every Good Work." Brooklyn, N.Y.: WtBTS, 1946, 382 pp., hb.

"Let God Be True." Brooklyn, N.Y.: WtBTS, 1946, 320 pp., hb. (The basic Witnesses doctrine book, used until the revised New York edition replaced it in 1952; green cover.)

"This Means Everlasting Life." Brooklyn, N.Y.: WtBTS, 1950, 318 pp., hb.

What Has Religion Done for Mankind? Brooklyn, N.Y.: WtBTS, 1951, 352 pp., hb.

"Let God Be True." Revised ed. Brooklyn, N.Y.: WtBTS, 1952, 320 pp., hb. (The basic Witness doctrine book, used for over 10 years.)

"Make Sure of All Things." Brooklyn, N.Y.: WtBTS, 1953, 416 pp., hb.; revised ed. 1957.

"New Heavens and a New Earth." Brooklyn, N.Y.: WtBTS, 1953, 380 pp., hb.

Qualified to Be Ministers. Brooklyn, N.Y.: WtBTS, 1955, 384 pp., hb.; revised ed., 1967.

You May Survive Armageddon into God's New World. Brooklyn, N.Y.: WtBTS, 1955, 380 pp., hb.

Branch Office Procedure of the Watchtower, Bible and Tract Society of Pennsylvania. Brooklyn, N.Y.: WtBTS, 1958, 158 pp., hb. (A procedural guide only for branch offices, not available to the public.)

From Paradise Lost to Paradise Regained. Brooklyn, N.Y.: WtBTS, 1958, 256 pp., hb. (for children; covers the basic Witness doctrines).

"Your Will Be Done on Earth." Brooklyn, N.Y.: WtBTS, 1958, 384 pp., hb.

Jehovah's Witnesses in the Divine Purpose. Brooklyn, N.Y.: WtBTS, 1959, 315 pp., hb. (official history of the Watchtower Society).

Kingdom Ministry School Course. Brooklyn, N.Y.: WtBTS, 1960, hb.

"Let Your Name Be Sanctified." Brooklyn, N.Y.: WtBTS, 1961, 384 pp., hb.

"All Scripture Is Inspired of God and Beneficial." Brooklyn, N.Y.: WtBTS, 1963, 352 pp., hb.

"Babylon the Great Has Fallen!" God's Kingdom Rules! Brooklyn, N.Y.: WtBTS, 1963, 704 pp., hb.

"Make Sure of All Things: Hold Fast to What Is Fine." Brooklyn, N.Y.: WtBTS, 1865, 512 pp., hb.

"Things in Which It Is Impossible for God to Lie." Brooklyn, N.Y.: WtBTS, 1965, 416 pp., hb. (also deluxe ed., smaller with thinner paper).

Life Everlasting in Freedom of the Sons of God. Brooklyn, N.Y.: WtBTS, 1966, 416 pp., hb. (also deluxe ed., smaller with thinner paper).

Did Man Get Here by Evolution or Creation? Brooklyn, N.Y.: WtBTS, 1967, 192 pp., hb.

"Your Word Is a Lamp to My Foot." Brooklyn, N.Y.: WtBTS, 1967, 224 pp., hb.

The Truth That Leads to Eternal Life. Brooklyn, N.Y.: WtBTS, 1968, 192 pp., hb.

Aid to Bible Understanding. Brooklyn, N.Y.: WtBTS, 1969, 544 pp. (A to E only; a Bible encyclopedia covering Bible topics from the Watchtower viewpoint.)

Is the Bible Really the Word of God? Brooklyn, N.Y.: WtBTS,
1969, 192 pp., hb.

"Then Is Finished the Mystery of God." Brooklyn, N.Y.: WtBTS,
1969, 384 pp., hb.

Theocratic Ministry School Guidebook. Brooklyn, N.Y.: WtBTS,
1971, 192 pp., hb.

"The Nations Shall Know That I Am Jehovah"--How?" New York:
WtBTS, 1971, 412 pp., hb.

Listening to the Great Teacher. New York: WtBTS, 1971, 192
pp., hb.

Aid to Bible Understanding. New York: WtBTS, 1971, 1,696 pp.
(A Bible encyclopedia covering topics from the Watchtower
viewpoint, very similar to a standard Bible dictionary.)

Paradise Restored to Mankind--by Theocracy. New York: WtBTS,
1972, 416 pp., hb.

Organization for Kingdom Preaching and Disciple Making. New
York: WtBTS, 1972, 192 pp., hb.

God's Kingdom of a Thousand Years Has Approached. New York:
WtBTS, 1973, 416 pp., hb.

True Peace and Security--From What Source? New York: WtBTS,
1973, 192 pp., hb.

*Comprehensive Concordance of the New World Translation of the
Holy Scriptures.* New York: WtBTS, 1973, 1,275 pp.

God's "Eternal Purpose" Now Triumphing for Man's Good. New
York: WtBTS, 1974, 192 pp., hb.

Is This Life All There Is? New York: WtBTS, 1974, 192 pp.,
hb.

Man's Salvation Out of World Distress at Hand! New York:
WtBTS, 1975, 382 pp., hb.

Good News to Make You Happy. New York: WtBTS, 1976, 192 pp.,
hb.

Holy Spirit--The Force Behind the Coming New Order! New York:
WtBTS, 1976, 192 pp., hb.

Your Youth--Getting the Most Out of It. New York: WtBTS,
   1976, 192 pp., hb.

Shining as Illuminators in the World. New York: WtBTS, 1977,
   253 pp., hb. (Pioneer Service school textbook.)

Our Incoming World Government--God's Kingdom. New York:
   WtBTS, 1977, 192 pp., hb.

Life Does Have a Purpose. New York: WtBTS, 1977, 192 pp.,
   hb.

Books Printed in the Franz Era

Making Your Family Life Happy. New York: WtBTS, 1978, 192 pp.,
   hb.

My Book of Bible Stories. New York: WtBTS, 1978, 250 pp., hb.
   (for children to replace the *Paradise Lost* book).

Choosing the Best Way of Life. New York: WtBTS, 1979, 192 pp.,
   hb.

Commentary on the Letter of James. New York: WtBTS, 1979,
   222 pp., hb.

Happiness: How to Find It. New York: WtBTS, 1980, 192 pp.,
   hb.

Let Your Kingdom Come. New York: WtBTS, 1981, 192 pp.

You Can Live Forever in Paradise on Earth. New York: WtBTS,
   1982, 256 pp. (Many pictures, most in color; for neophytes.)

B. SONG, HYMN, AND POEM BOOKS

(Note: most of the early song books in this
section contain the same songs.)

Songs of the Morning. 1877, c. 67 pp.

Songs of the Bride. Allegheny, Pa.: Tower Pub. Co., 1879.

Poems and Hymns of Dawn (without music). Allegheny, Pa.:
   Tower Pub. Co., 1890, 1902, 495 pp.

Zion's Glad Songs for All Christian Gatherings, by M.L. Mc-
Phail. Allegheny, Pa.: Zion's Watchtower and Tract Society,
1900, 79 pp.

Hymns of Millennial Dawn (with music). Brooklyn, N.Y.: WtBTS,
1905, 332 pp. (also 1909, 1915, 1916, 1924 eds.).

Zion's Glad Songs, No. 2, by M.L. McPhail. 1907, 65 pp.

Zion's Glad Songs for All Christian Gatherings, by M.L. McPhail,
1908, 248 pp.

Poems of Dawn. Brooklyn, N.Y.: WtBTS, 1912, 286 pp. (also
available in deluxe ed.).

Angelophone Hymns. New York: Angelico, 1916, 100 pp.

Hymns of the Millennial Dawn (without music). Brooklyn, N.Y.:
WtBTS, 1924, 120 pp. (also 1905, 1915, 1916 eds.).

Kingdom Hymns. Brooklyn, N.Y.: WtBTS, 1925, 63 pp.

Songs of Praise to Jehovah (with music). Brooklyn, N.Y.:
WtBTS, 1928, 300 pp.

Songs of Praise to Jehovah (without music). Brooklyn, N.Y.:
WtBTS, 1928, 143 pp.

Kingdom Service Song Book. Brooklyn, N.Y.: WtBTS, 1944, 62 pp.
(also 1948 ed., hb.).

Songs to Jehovah's Praise. Brooklyn, N.Y.: WtBTS, 1950, 96
pp. (also 1962 ed., pb.).

Singing and Accompanying Yourselves with Music in Your Hearts.
Brooklyn, N.Y.: WtBTS, 1966, 128 pp. (both paper and vinyl
cover).

C. YEARBOOKS

     The first yearbook, *Yearbook of the International Bible
Students Association with Daily Text and Comments*, 1926, contained data for the year 1925 and the daily text for the year
1926. With the new name Jehovah's Witness in 1931, the title
of the yearbook likewise changed. Thus, from 1934 forward it

was called *Yearbook of Jehovah's Witnesses*. The most recent
yearbook is the *1983 Yearbook of Jehovah's Witnesses*.
   All the yearbooks contain roughly 260 pages of discussion
of the worldwide Witness work; approximately 80 pages of what
is known as the "year text," a quoted scriptural text; and
finally, comments on this text from the previous year's *Watchtower*. The comments do not always closely relate to the
scripture, but the commentator tries to create a relationship.
These comments are read each morning in all good Witness homes.
   Until 1971, the first half of the yearbook included a report of the Witness work in each country, as well as the
general discussion of the work worldwide. As of 1972 a history of the Watchtower work in a few selected countries, "Acts
of Jehovah's Witnesses in Modern Times," is given instead.
For example, in the 1972 yearbook the history of the work in
Argentina, Czechoslovakia, Dominican Republic, Nicaragua,
Pakistan, Afghanistan, Taiwan, and Zambia is discussed. Such
histories provide a more complete story of the work of the
Witnesses in these countries than any other reference. Each
year a different group of countries in covered.

D. BOOKLETS (GENERAL)

Barbour, N.H. *Evidences for the Coming of the Lord in 1873
or The Midnight Cry*. New York: D.T. Cooper, 1871.

Dabney, A.B. *Questions Answering Questions*. June 1908, 60
pp., hb., pb. This booklet was written by an active follower of Russell but was later withdrawn although its author
evidently continued to follow Russell (see the April 1,
1911, *Watchtower*, p. 110).

Fisher, George, and Clayton J. Woodworth. *The Parable of the
Penny*. Scranton, Pa., 1904, 6 pp. Printed abstract from
an address given at the Boston Convention, Aug. 4, 1917.

Herr, A.S. *A Letter to Major Whittle from the Berean Bible
Class of Tiffin, Ohio*. 1898, 12 pp.

Manda, Sister. *How Hiram and Manda Found the Truth*. Washington, Pa.: Press of Observer Job Rooms, c. 1919, 26 pp.
An interesting booklet published by Hiram and Manda about
how they became followers of Russell. The language and
grammar are Southern Black: "When Hiram and me was married

we didn't care much about religion: we didn't seem to care
for nobody but ourselves" (p. 1).

Russell, Charles Taze. *The Object and Manner of the Lord's
Return.* Privately printed, 1872 (no known copy exists).
Most likely the first edition was in 1877.

————. *Three World Tract.* 1876, 1877, 32 pp. Evidently a
series of booklets bound together as the book *The Three
Worlds* (see Books).

————. *The Object and Manner of Our Lord's Return.* Pittsburgh, Pa.: 1877, 64 pp.

————. *Tabernacle Teachings.* 1881.

————. *Dr. Talmadge's View of the Dawn of the Millennium.*
1890, 32 pp.

————. *Thy Word Is Truth--An Answer to Robert Ingersoll's
Charges Against Christianity.* 1892, 32 pp. (reprinted in
the July 15, 1906, *Watchtower*).

————. *The Wonderful Story.* 1892, 60 pp.

————. *Harvest Siftings.* 1894, 31 pp.

————. *A Conspiracy Exposed.* 1894, 90 pp.

————. *A Conspiracy Exposed* and *Harvest Siftings.* 88 + 32
pp. Bound together as a special number of *Zion's Watchtower*, Vol. 15, No. 8, April 25, 1894 (Tower Pub. Co.,
Allegheny, Pa.).

————. *Outlines of the Divine Plan of the Ages.* 1896,
47 pp.

————. *What Say the Scriptures About Hell?* 1896; new ed.
1911, 82 pp. (See below, p. 312, for reprint.)

————. *The Bible Versus Evolution.* 1898, 48 pp.

————. *Gathering the Lord's Jewels.* 1899, 16 pp.

————. *Which Is the True Gospel?* 1900, 16 pp.

————. *Death Is the Wages of Sin and Not Eternal Torment.*
1901, 32 pp.

————. *Epistle to the Hebrews.* 1902, 48 pp. (some English and mostly Yiddish).

————. *The Scriptures Teaching on Calamities and Why God Permits Them.* 1902, 16 pp.

————. *Christ's Death Secured: One Probation or Trial for Life Everlasting to Every Man.* 1903, 32 pp.

————. *Criticisms of Millennial Hopes and Prospects Examined.* 1904, 32 pp. (Also found in Vol. 1, *Studies in the Scriptures,* 1914 ed.)

————. *The Sin-Offering and the Covenants.* Privately pub. at St. Louis, Mo., 1907, 28 pp.; reprint ed. 1954, 32 pp.; reprinted by the Chicago Bible Students. The booklet was taken from a stenographic report of a question meeting directed by Charles T. Russell in St. Louis, Mo., Aug. 11, 1907. It consists of audience's questions and Russell's answers.

————. *Instructor's Guide and Berean Index.* 1907, 68 pp.

————. *What Do the Scriptures Say About Survival After Death?* N.d. (about 1909), 64 pp.

————. *Comforted of God.* 1910, 48 pp.

————. *Die Stemme.* 1910, 64 pp.

————. *"Jewish Hopes"--Jerusalem--Restoration Prospects for God's Chosen People.* 20 new pages and reprint of Chapter 8 from *Studies in the Scriptures*: "Thy Kingdom Come," pp. 243-300 (57 pp.). Total, 77 pp., 1910.

————. *Charter of the Watch Tower, Bible and Tract Society.* 1917, 12 pp.

————. *A Letter to International Bible Students.* March 1, 1918.

————. *An Open Letter to the People of the Lord Throughout the World.* N.d., 1 p.

Rutherford, J.F. (All published in Brooklyn, N.Y.) *A Great Battle in the Ecclesiastical Heavens.* Privately printed, 1915, 64 pp.

————. *Harvest Siftings*. Aug. 1, 1917, 24 pp.; Pt. 2, Oct. 1, 1917, 7 pp.

————. *The Bible on Hell*. Brooklyn, N.Y.: WtBTS, 1922, 96 pp.

————. *World Distress--Why? The Remedy*. Brooklyn, N.Y.: WtBTS, 1923, 64 pp.

————. *A Desirable Government*. Brooklyn, N.Y.: WtBTS, 1924, 64 pp.

————. *Hell: What Is It? Who Are There? Can They Get Out?* Brooklyn, N.Y.: WtBTS, 1924, 64 pp. (printed with two different covers; the contents are identical).

————. *Comfort for the People*. Brooklyn, N.Y.: WtBTS, 1925, 64 pp.

————. *Our Lord's Return: His Parousia, His Apokalupsis, and His Epiphania*. Brooklyn, N.Y.: WtBTS, 1925, 64 pp. (printed with two different covers; the contents are identical). (See below, p. 312, for reprint.)

————. *The Standard for the People*. Brooklyn, N.Y.: WtBTS, 1926, 64 pp.

————. *Freedom for the Peoples*. Brooklyn, N.Y.: WtBTS, 1927, 64 pp.

————. *Where Are the Dead?* Brooklyn, N.Y.: WtBTS, 1927, 64 pp.

————. *Prosperity Sure*. 1928, 64 pp.

————. *The Last Days*. 1928, 64 pp.

————. *The People's Friend*. 1928, 64 pp.

————. *Judgment of the Judges*. 1929, 64 pp.

————. *Oppression: When Will It End?* 1929, 64 pp.

————. *Crimes and Calamities: The Cause: The Remedy*. 1930, 64 pp.

————. *Prohibition and the League of Nations--Born of God or of the Devil, Which?* 1930, 64 pp.

————. *War or Peace--Which?* 1930, 64 pp.

————. *Heaven or Purgatory.* 1931, 64 pp.

————. *The Kingdom: The Hope of the World.* 1931, 64 pp.

————. *Cause of Death.* 1932, 64 pp.

————. *Good News.* 1932, 64 pp.

————. *Home and Happiness.* 1932, 64 pp.

————. *Jehovah's Organization.* 1932.

————. *What You Need.* 1932, 64 pp.

————. *Liberty.* 1932, 64 pp.

————. *Health and Life.* 1932, 64 pp.

————. *Hypocrisy.* 1932, 32 pp.

————. *Prophets Foretell Redemption.* 1932.

————. *Keys of Heaven.* 1932, 64 pp.

————. *Who Is God?* 1932, 64 pp.

————. *The Final War.* 1932, 64 pp.

————. *The Kingdom: The Hope of the World.* 1932, 64 pp. (reset reprint of 1931 ed.).

————. *What Is Truth?* 1932, 64 pp.

————. *Where Are the Dead?* 1932, 64 pp. (reset reprint of 1927 ed.).

————. *Hereafter.* 1932, 64 pp.

————. *Can the American Government Endure?* 1933.

————. *Dividing the People.* 1933, 64 pp.

————. *Escape to the Kingdom.* 1933, 64 pp.

————. *Intolerance.* 1933, 64 pp.

————. *Bethel Home Rules.* c. early 1930s.

————. *Bethel Home Rules and Regulations.* c. early 1930s,
24 pp.

————. *Jehovah's Witnesses--Why Persecuted?* 1933.

————. *The Crisis.* 1933, 64 pp.

————. *America's End.* 1934.

————. *Angels.* 1934, 64 pp.

————. *Beyond the Grave.* 1934, 64 pp.

————. *Favored People.* 1934, 64 pp.

————. *His Vengeance.* 1934, 64 pp.

————. *His Works.* 1934, 64 pp.

————. *Jews.* 1934.

————. *Justifying War.* 1934.

————. *Religions.* 1934.

————. *Righteous Ruler.* 1934, 64 pp.

————. *Supremacy.* 1934, 64 pp.

————. *Truth: Shall It Be Suppressed? Or Will Congress
Protect the People's Rights.* 1934, 64 pp.

————. *Why Pray for Prosperity? Why Famine Threatened?
The True Answer.* 1934, 31 pp.

————. *World Recovery?* 1934, 64 pp.

————. *Government--Hiding the Truth--Why?* 1935, 64 pp.

————. *Universal War Near.* 1935, 64 pp.

————. *Who Shall Rule the World?* 1935, 64 pp.

————. *Choosing Riches or Ruin: Which Is Your Choice?*
1936, 62 pp.

———. *Marriage.* 1936.

———. *Protection from Those Who Seek to Hurt or Destroy Me--How Can I Find It?* 1936, 64 pp.

———. *Why Serve Jehovah?* 1936.

———. *Armageddon: The Greatest Battle of All Time--Who Will Survive?* 1937, 64 pp.

———. *Safety, Comfort.* 1937, 64 pp.

———. *Uncovered: Things Which Have Deceived Millions to Their Hurt Now Exposed for Your Protection.* 1937, 64 pp.

———. *Cure.* 1938, 32 pp.

———. *Face the Facts and Learn the Only One Way of Escape.* 1938, 64 pp.

———. *Warning.* 1938, 64 pp.

———. *Fascism or Freedom.* 1939, 64 pp.

———. *Government and Peace* (bound with *Victory*, pp. 34-64). 1939, 64 pp.

———. *Government and Peace.* 1939, 32 pp. (same as above except bound without *Victory*).

———. *Conspiracy Against Democracy.* 1940, 64 pp.

———. *Judge Rutherford Uncovers Fifth Column.* 1940, 32 pp.

———. *Refugees.* 1940, 64 pp.

———. *Satisfied.* 1940, 32 pp.

———. *End of Nazism.* 1940, 32 pp.

———. *End of Axis Powers--Comfort All That Mourn.* 1941, 32 pp.

———. *God and the State.* 1941, 32 pp.

———. *Theocracy.* 1941, 64 pp.

———. *Hope for the Dead, for the Survivors in a Righteous World.* 1942, 64 pp.

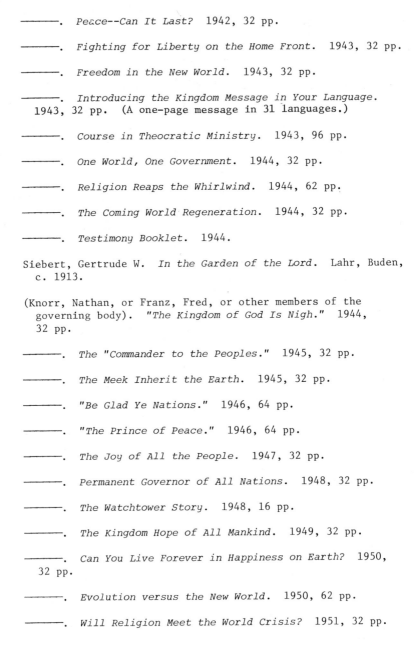

———. *Peace--Can It Last?* 1942, 32 pp.

———. *Fighting for Liberty on the Home Front.* 1943, 32 pp.

———. *Freedom in the New World.* 1943, 32 pp.

———. *Introducing the Kingdom Message in Your Language.* 1943, 32 pp. (A one-page message in 31 languages.)

———. *Course in Theocratic Ministry.* 1943, 96 pp.

———. *One World, One Government.* 1944, 32 pp.

———. *Religion Reaps the Whirlwind.* 1944, 62 pp.

———. *The Coming World Regeneration.* 1944, 32 pp.

———. *Testimony Booklet.* 1944.

Siebert, Gertrude W. *In the Garden of the Lord.* Lahr, Buden, c. 1913.

(Knorr, Nathan, or Franz, Fred, or other members of the governing body). *"The Kingdom of God Is Nigh."* 1944, 32 pp.

———. *The "Commander to the Peoples."* 1945, 32 pp.

———. *The Meek Inherit the Earth.* 1945, 32 pp.

———. *"Be Glad Ye Nations."* 1946, 64 pp.

———. *"The Prince of Peace."* 1946, 64 pp.

———. *The Joy of All the People.* 1947, 32 pp.

———. *Permanent Governor of All Nations.* 1948, 32 pp.

———. *The Watchtower Story.* 1948, 16 pp.

———. *The Kingdom Hope of All Mankind.* 1949, 32 pp.

———. *Can You Live Forever in Happiness on Earth?* 1950, 32 pp.

———. *Evolution versus the New World.* 1950, 62 pp.

———. *Will Religion Meet the World Crisis?* 1951, 32 pp.

———. *God's Way Is Love.* 1952, 32 pp.

———. *Dwelling Together in Unity.* 1952, 32 pp. (Rules for living at Watchtower headquarters.)

———. *After Armageddon--God's New World.* 1953, 32 pp.

———. *Basis for Belief in a New World.* 1953, 64 pp.

———. *"Preach the Word."* 1953, 32 pp. (A one-page message in 31 languages.)

———. *"This Good News of the Kingdom."* 1954, 32 pp.

———. *Counsel to Watchtower Missionaries.* 1954.

———. *Christendom or Christianity--Which One Is "the Light of the World?"* 1955, 32 pp.

———. *What Do the Scriptures Say About "Survival After Death"?* 1955, 94 pp.

———. *World Conquest Soon by God's Kingdom.* 1955, 32 pp.

———. *Healing of the Nations Has Drawn Near.* 1957, 32 pp.

———. *Aprenda a leer y escribir* (Learn to Read and Write Spanish). 1958, 64 pp.

———. *God's Kingdom Rules--Is the World's End Near?* 1958. 32 pp.

———. *"Look! I Am Making All Things New."* 1959, 32 pp.

———. *When God Speaks Peace to All Nations.* 1959, 32 pp.

———. *Security During the "War of the Great Day of God the Almighty."* 1960, 32 pp.

———. *When All Nations Unite Under God's Kingdom.* 1961, 32 pp.

———. *Sermon Outlines.* 1961, 32 pp.

———. *Blood, Medicine and the Law of God.* 1961, 62 pp.

———. *Take Courage--God's Kingdom Is at Hand!* 1962, 32 pp.

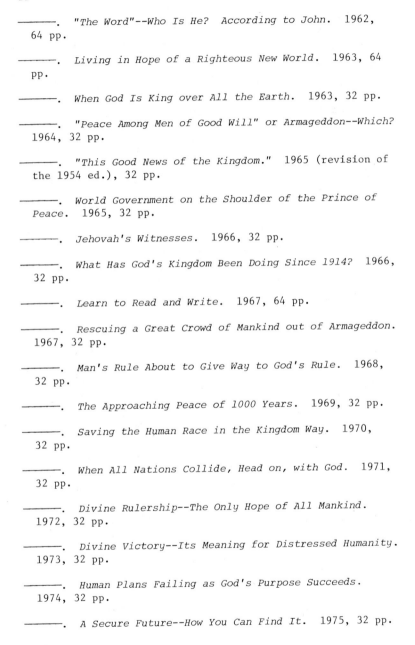

————. *"The Word"--Who Is He? According to John.* 1962, 64 pp.

————. *Living in Hope of a Righteous New World.* 1963, 64 pp.

————. *When God Is King over All the Earth.* 1963, 32 pp.

————. *"Peace Among Men of Good Will" or Armageddon--Which?* 1964, 32 pp.

————. *"This Good News of the Kingdom."* 1965 (revision of the 1954 ed.), 32 pp.

————. *World Government on the Shoulder of the Prince of Peace.* 1965, 32 pp.

————. *Jehovah's Witnesses.* 1966, 32 pp.

————. *What Has God's Kingdom Been Doing Since 1914?* 1966, 32 pp.

————. *Learn to Read and Write.* 1967, 64 pp.

————. *Rescuing a Great Crowd of Mankind out of Armageddon.* 1967, 32 pp.

————. *Man's Rule About to Give Way to God's Rule.* 1968, 32 pp.

————. *The Approaching Peace of 1000 Years.* 1969, 32 pp.

————. *Saving the Human Race in the Kingdom Way.* 1970, 32 pp.

————. *When All Nations Collide, Head on, with God.* 1971, 32 pp.

————. *Divine Rulership--The Only Hope of All Mankind.* 1972, 32 pp.

————. *Divine Victory--Its Meaning for Distressed Humanity.* 1973, 32 pp.

————. *Human Plans Failing as God's Purpose Succeeds.* 1974, 32 pp.

————. *A Secure Future--How You Can Find It.* 1975, 32 pp.

————. *Is There a God Who Cares?* 1975, 32 pp.

————. *One World, One Government, Under God's Sovereignty.* 1975, 32 pp.

————. *There Is Much More to Life.* 1975, 32 pp.

————. *Du ar ju ett Jehovas vittne farjag fraga dej Jarfalla.* Sweden, 1976, 16 pp.

————. *Pay Attention to Yourselves and to All the Flock.* 1977, 96 pp. (The Kingdom Ministry School textbook for elders only.)

————. *Bible Topics for Discussion.* 1977, 32 pp. (Replaced Sermon Outlines, with some revisions.)

————. *Jehovah's Witnesses and the Question of Blood.* 1977, 64 pp.

————. *Unseen Spirits: Do They Help Us? or Do They Harm Us?* 1978, 64 pp.

————. *Jehovah's Witnesses in the Twentieth Century.* 1978; revised ed. 1979, 32 pp.

————. *Enjoy Life on Earth Forever.* 1982, 32 pp. (A full-color booklet for new or interested persons.)

E. QUESTION BOOKLETS

(all published at Brooklyn, N.Y., except as noted). These booklets were to be used in a group study of one of the Society's books.

Berean Studies on the Divine Plan (Vol. 1). 1912 and 1915, 44 pp. (1911 ed. called *Berean Questions in "Studies in the Scriptures" on The Divine Plan of the Ages,* 48 pp.). (Another ed. was titled *Study Questions in "The Divine Plan,"* n.d.)

Berean Studies on The Time Is at Hand (Vol. 2). 1912, 1913, 1915, 48 pp.

Berean Studies on Thy Kingdom Come (Vol. 3). 1912, 43 pp.

Berean Studies on The Day of Vengeance (Vol. 4). 1912, 40 pp. (also entitled *Berean Studies on the Battle of Armageddon*).

Berean Studies on The At-One-Ment Between God and Man (Vol. 5). 1910, 86 pp. (1915 ed., 60 pp.).

Berean Questions on Tabernacle Shadows of the Better Sacrifices. 1917, 40 pp. (also bound with lined paper). (Also called *Berean Studies on The Tabernacle*, Pittsburgh, Pa., 1910, 44 pp.; 1919, 32 pp.)

Berean Studies on The New Creation (Vol. 6). 1914, 71 pp.

Berean Studies on "The Finished Mystery" (Vol. 7). 1919, 88 pp.

Questions on Deliverance. 1927, 59 pp.

Model Study No. 1. 1937, 64 pp. (one ed. entitled only *Model Study*).

Model Study No. 2. 1939, 64 pp.

Model Study No. 3. 1941, 32 pp.

"Children" Study Questions. 1942, 64 pp.

"The New World" Study Questions. 1942, 64 pp.

"The Truth Shall Make You Free" Study Questions. 1943, 64 pp.

"The Kingdom Is at Hand" Study Questions. 1944, 64 pp.

Questions on the Book: "Babylon the Great Has Fallen! God's Kingdom Rules!" 1964, 96 pp.

Questions on the Book: "Then Is Finished the Mystery of God." 1969, 64 pp.

Study Questions for the Book: Is the Bible Really the Word of God? 1978, 16 pp.

Study Questions for the Book: Is This Life All There Is? 1979, 16 pp.

F. *LEGAL TRACTS AND BOOKLETS*
(all published at Brooklyn, N.Y.)

Booklets

Loyalty--Questions and Answers on Whose Servant?; Saluting a Flag; Last Days. 1935, 32 pp.

Liberty to Preach, by Olin R. Moyle. 1937, 26 pp. (revised ed. by J.F. Rutherford, 16 pp.).

Advice for Kingdom Publishers. 1939, 16 pp.

Neutrality (from Nov. 1, 1939, *Watchtower*). 1939, 32 pp.

Jehovah's Servants Defended. 1941, 32 pp.

Organization Instructions. 1942, 29 pp.; 1945 ed. called *Organization Instructions for the Kingdom Publisher*, 47 pp.

Freedom of Worship. 1943, 64 pp.

Briefing and Arguing Appeals, by Hayden C. Covington. 1944, 36 pp.

Counsel on Theocratic Organization for Jehovah's Witnesses. 1949, 64 pp.

Defending and Legally Establishing the Good News, by Hayden C. Covington. 1950, 96 pp.

Procedure of Jehovah's Witnesses under Selective Service, by Hayden C. Covington. 1953, 30 pp.

Preaching Together in Unity. 1955, 64 pp.

Preaching and Teaching in Peace and Unity. 1960, 62 pp.

Memorandum on Procedure of Jehovah's Witnesses under Selective Service, by Victor V. Blackwell. 1964, 94 pp.

Tracts

Order of Trial. 1933, 2 pp. (Confidential instructions for Jehovah's Witnesses who are arrested and face a court appearance. Updated periodically. Instructions for 1939 are four pages.)

To the Police Department of the City of ____. 1939, 1 p. (An open letter to local police departments informing them of canvassing work in the area for the purpose of avoiding conflict with opposers.)

Law Abiding. 1940, 2 pp. (Mentioned in *Informant*, Nov. 1940. See *Jehovah's Witnesses in the Divine Purpose*, p. 251.)

G. NEWSLETTERS

Bulletin (*Watchtower Bulletin* from 1913 to July 1, 1931; thereafter *Bulletin for Jehovah's Witnesses* until Aug. 1935). 1917 to 1935, usually 2 pp. From 1913 to 1919 this bulletin was a typed 2- to 4-page letter.

Morning Messenger. 1918 (Canadian).

Special Colporteur Bulletin: Winter Edition. 1928, 16 pp.

This Kingdom Gospel Must Be Preached. 1929, 16 pp.

Bulletin: Special Colporteur Edition. C. 1930, 16 pp.

Director. Sept. 1935 to June 1936, usually 2 to 4 pp. Monthly.

Informant. July 1936–Aug. 1956, usually 2 to 4 pp. (special issues Aug.-Sept. 1936, March-July 1938, and March 1939). Monthly.

Kingdom Ministry. Sept. 1956–Dec. 1975, usually 4 to 8 pp. Monthly.

Our Kingdom Service. Jan. 1976 to date, usually 4 to 8 pp. Monthly.

H. MAGAZINES

The *Watchtower* with its slight title changes is the official doctrine magazine; the *Golden Age* and *Awake!* are more secular journals.

Zion's Watchtower and Herald of Christ's Presence. July 1879–Dec. 15, 1908. Renamed *The Watchtower and Herald of Christ's Presence* in 1909.

Bible Student Monthly. Vol. 1, No. 1 (Jan. 1909) to Vol. 9, No. 12 (Dec. 1917). (In 1911, Vols. 13 and 14 were printed. In 1914 two different editions of Vol. 6, No. 1, were printed: in the first the lead article was "End of World in 1914"; the second had "Battering Down the Walls of Hell.")

The Watch Tower and Herald of Christ's Presence. Jan. 1, 1909–Dec. 15, 1938. Renamed *The Watchtower and Herald of Christ's Kingdom* in 1939.

People's Pulpit. Vol. 1, No. 1 (Feb. 1909) to Vol. 5, No. 1 (Jan. 1913). (Most of the material in this magazine was reprinted from the *Bible Student Monthly.*)

Everybody's Paper. Vol. 1, No. 1, to Vol. 4, No. 12. (Very similar to *Bible Student Monthly* in format and content; often the same articles were printed.)

The Golden Age. Oct 1, 1919–Sept. 22, 1937. Edited by Clayton J. Woodworth and published by Woodworth, Hudgings, and Martin, 1265 Broadway, New York. Vol. 1, No. 1, to Vol. 1, No. 14; then at 35 Myrtle Ave., Brooklyn, until March 1, 1922; and 18 Concord St., New York, until Feb. 9, 1927 and thereafter at 117 Adams St., Brooklyn, N.Y. Renamed *Consolation* in 1937 and *Awake!*, Aug. 22, 1946.

The Watchtower and Herald of Christ's Kingdom. Jan. 1, 1939–Feb. 15, 1939. Renamed *The Watchtower Announcing Jehovah's Kingdom* in 1939.

The Watchtower Announcing Jehovah's Kingdom. March 1, 1939–to date.

Awake! Aug. 22, 1946 to date.

I. TRACTS

1. *Religious Intolerance--Pastor Russell's Followers Persecuted Because They Tell the People the Truth.* March 15, 1918.

2. *The Finished Mystery and Why Suppressed--Clergymen Take a Hand.* April 15, 1918.

3. *Two Great Battles Raging--Fall of Autocracy Certain--Satanic Strategy Failing.* May 1, 1918.

4. *Attempt to Wreck Garden Assembly--The Facts--An Open Letter to Mayor La Guardia.* July 1939.

5. *Can Religion Save the World Disaster?* Oct. 1939.

6. *Time of Darkness-Isaiah 60:2.* July 1940.

7. *Do You Condemn or Wink at Unspeakable Crimes?* Oct. 1940.

8. *If the Bill Becomes Law.* April 1941, 2 pp.

9. *Victories in Your Defense.* Aug. 1941, 2 pp.

10. *Life in the New Earth under New Heavens.* Feb. 1942, 2 pp.

11. *The People Have a Right to the Good News Now.* Sept. 1942, 2 pp.

12. *The Last War Wins the Peace Eternal.* April 1943, 2 pp.

13. *Education for Life in the New World.* March 1944, 2 pp.

14. *Overcoming Fear of What Is Coming on the Earth.* Nov. 1944, 2 pp.

15. *World Conspiracy Against the Truth.* Feb. 1946.

16. *Is Time Running Out for Mankind?* Sept. 1973, 4 pp.

17. *Has Religion Betrayed God and Man?* Dec. 1973, 4 pp.

18. *Government by God, Are You for It--Or Against It?* May 1974, 4 pp.

19. *Is This All There Is to Life?* Nov. 1974, 4 pp.

20. *Would You Welcome Some Good News?* May 1975, 4 pp.

21. *Your Future: Shaky? or Secure?* Nov. 1975, 4 pp.

22. *How Crime and Violence Will Be Stopped.* 1975, 4 pp.

23. *Why So Much Suffering--If God Cares?* 1976, 4 pp.

24. *The Family--Can It Survive?* 1976, 4 pp.

25. *Why Are We Here?* 1977, 4 pp.

26. *Relief from Pressure--Is It Possible?* 1978, 4 pp.

27. *What Has Happened to Love?* 1979, 4 pp.

> *Promotion of Christian Knowledge Tracts*
> (actually booklets), all published around
> the turn of the century in Pittsburgh,
> Pa. They were used to introduce out-
> siders to the Society's beliefs.

1. *Where Are the Dead?* 4 pp.

2. *What Is the Soul?* 16 pp.

3. *Calamities--Why Permitted.* 16 pp.

4. *Spiritism Is Demonism.* 16 pp.

5. *Christian Science.* 16 pp.

6. *Is There a God?* 16 pp.

7. *Hope of Immortality.* 16 pp.

8. *The Rich Man in Hell.* 16 pp.

9. *Weeping All Night.* 16 pp.

10. *Do You Believe in the Resurrection?* 16 pp.

11. *The Liberty of the Gospel.* 16 pp.

12. *The Dawn of a New Era.* 16 pp.

13. *Demons Infest Earth's Atmosphere.* 16 pp.

14. *Comforting Words of Life.* 16 pp.

15. *Golden Age at the Door.* 16 pp.

16. *Why God Permits Evil.* 16 pp.

17. *Joyful Message for the Sin-Sick.* 16 pp.

18. *Gathering the Lord's Jewels.* 16 pp.

19. *Earth to Be Filled with Glory.* 16 pp.

20. *Our Responsibility as Christians.* 16 pp.

21. *Thieves in Paradise.* 16 pp.

22. *The Bruising of Satan.* 16 pp.

23. *Predestination and Election.* 16 pp.

24. *Do You Know?* 16 pp.

25. *Is the Soul Immortal?* 16 pp.

Old Theology Quarterly,
Allegheny, Pa.: WtBTS
(some tracts, some booklets)

1. *Do the Scriptures Teach That Eternal Torment Is the Wages
    of Sin?* April 1889, 32 pp. (same as No. 53).

2. *Calamities--Why God Permits Them.* Oct. 1889, 16 pp.
    (same as Nos. 57, 73).

3. *Protestants Awake! How Priestcraft Now Operates.* 1889,
    32 pp. (same as No. 61).

4. *Dr. Talmage's View of the Dawn of the Millennium.* Jan.
    1890, 32 pp.

5. *Bible Study and Students' Helps.* 1890.

6. *The Hope of the Groaning Creation.* 1890.

7. *The Wonderful Story of Wisdom, Love and Grace Divine*
    (Poem, 156 verses). Oct. 1890, 32 pp.

8. *The Wonderful Story.* Illustrated. Dec. 1890, 60 pp.

9. Swedish translation of No. 1.

10. *A Basis for True Christian Union.* Also called *The Faith
    Once Delivered to the Saints* and *a Broad Basis for
    Christian Union.* Aug. 1891.

11. *Tabernacle Shadows of Better Sacrifices.* Illustrated.
    Oct. 1891, 104 pp.

12. *Why Evil Was Permitted.* Jan. 1892, 16 pp. (same as Nos.
    62, 74).

13. Norwegian translation of No. 1.

14. *Bible Study and Needful Helps Thereto.* July 1892, 4 pp.
    (same as Nos. 27, 54).

15. *Thy Word Is Truth; An Answer to Robert Ingersoll's Charges
    Against Christianity.* Oct. 1892, 32 pp. (same as Nos.
    16, 71).

16. *Thy Word Is Truth.* Jan. 1893, 44 pp. (same as Nos. 15,
    71).

17. *Purgatory.* July 1902, 16 pp. (same as No. 58).

18. *Representative or Substitute?*

19. Dano-Norwegian translation of No. 14.

20. Swedish translation of No. 14.

21. *Do You Know?* April 1894, 8 pp. (same as No. 66).

22. *The Scripture Teaching Concerning the World's Hope.*
    1894, 32 pp. (same as No. 59).

23. German translation of No. 21.

24. *Bible Study and Students' Helps.*

25. *The Only Name--A Criticism of Bishop Foster's New Gospel.*
    Jan. 1895, 16 pp.

26. Swedish translation of No. 21.

27. *A Dark Cloud and Its Silver Lining* (poem by John G.
    Whittier). April 1895, 4 pp. (same as Nos. 14, 54).

28. *Bringing Back the King.* Jan. 1903, 16 pp. (same as
    No. 60).

29. Dano-Norwegian translation of No. 21.

30. German translation of No. 28.

30-Extra. *Wait Thou Upon the Lord* (Poem by George M. Bills).
     Oct. 1895, 2 pp. (same as No. 51).

31. *Millennial Dawn* (Letter of withdrawal from Babylon).
     Nov. 1895, 2 pp.

32. *What Say the Scriptures About Hell?* 1896, 82 pp. (same
     as No. 55).

33. Dutch translation of No. 1, 1896.

34. German translation of No. 1, 1896.

35. Swedish translation of No. 28, 1896.

36. *Awake! Jerusalem, Awake!* Jan. 1897, 2 pp.

37. *How Readest Thou?* April 1897, 2 pp.

38. *The Hope of Immortality.* July 1897, 16 pp.

39. *What Say the Scriptures About Spiritism?* Oct. 1897,
     100 pp. (See p. 312 for reprint.)

40. *What Is the Soul?* Jan. 1898, 16 pp.

41. *Must We Abandon Hope of a Golden Age?* April 1898, 8 pp.

42. *Crosses True and False.* July 1898, 2 pp.

43. *The Bible versus the Evolution Theory.* Oct. 1898, 48 pp.

44. *Gathering the Lord's Jewels.* Jan. 1899, 16 pp.

45. *The Wonderful Story.* April 1899, 32 pp.

46. *The Good Shepherd and His Two Flocks.* July 1899, 8 pp.

47. (unknown)

48. *What Say the Scriptures About Our Lord's Return, His
     Parousia, Apokalupsis and Epiphania?* Jan. 1900, 80 pp.

49. *Which Is the True Gospel?* April 1900, 16 pp.

50. German translation of No. 49. Sept. 1900.

51. *Heathendom's Hope Future Therefore Wait Thou Upon the Lord.* Oct. 1900, 2 pp. (same as No. 30-Extra).

52. *Our Lord's Return: Its Object, The Restitution of All Things Spoken.* Jan. 1901, 16 pp. (printed both with and without a cover).

53. *Death Is the Wages of Sin.* April 1901, 32 pp. (same as No. 1).

54. *A Dark Cloud and Its Silver Lining.* July 1901, 4 pp. (same as Nos. 14, 27).

55. *What Say the Scriptures About Hell?* Oct. 1901, 82 pp. (same as No. 32).

56. *Epistle to the Hebrews* (Yiddish and some English). Jan. 1902, 64 pp.

57. *The Scripture Teaching on Calamities and Why God Permits Them.* April 1902, 16 pp. (same as Nos. 2, 73).

58. *Purgatory.* July 1902, 16 pp. (same as No. 17).

59. *The World's Hope.* Oct. 1902, 16 pp. (same as No. 22).

60. *Why Are Ye the Last to Welcome Back the King?* Jan. 1903, 16 pp. (same as No. 28).

61. *Protestants Awake!* April 1903, 16 pp. (same as No. 3).

62. *The Divine Plan of the Ages for Human Salvation: Why Evil Was Permitted.* July 1903, 15 pp. (same as Nos. 12, 74).

63. *Christ's Death Secured One Probation or Trial for Life Everlasting to Every Man.* Dec. 1903, 32 pp.

64. *Criticisms of Millennial Hopes and Prospects Examined.* Jan. 1904, 32 pp.

65. *Tabernacle Shadows of the Better Sacrifices.* Oct. 1904, 131 pp.

66. *Do You Know?* July 1904, 8 pp. (same as No. 21).

67. (Unknown)

68. *Increasing Influence of Spiritism.* Jan. 1905, 16 pp.
     (same as No. 75).

69. Pt. 1: *Christendom in Grave Danger!* April 1905, 4 pp.
     Pt. 2: *Study to Show Thyself Approved Unto God.* April
           1905, 4 pp.
     Pt. 3: *Refrain Thy Voices from Weeping.* April 1905, 4 pp.
     Pt. 4: *Hope for the Innumerable Non-Elect.* April 1905,
           4 pp.

70. Pt. 1: *Cheerful Christians!* July 1905, 4 pp.
     Pt. 2: *Divine Predestination in Respect to Mankind.*
           July 1905, 4 pp.

71. *"Thy Word Is Truth," An Answer to Robert Ingersoll's
     Charges Against Christianity.* Oct. 1905, 32 pp. (same
     as Nos. 15, 16).

72. *To Hell and Back! Who Are There. Hope for the Recovery
     of Many of Them.* Jan. 1906, 4 pp.

     Pt. 2: *The Oath-Bound Covenant.* Jan. 1906, 4 pp.
     Pt. 3: *Selling the Birthright.* Jan. 1906, 4 pp.
     Pt. 4: *The Great Prison-House.* Jan. 1906, 4 pp.

73. *Calamities--Why God Permits Them* (same as Nos. 2, 57).

74. *The Divine Plan.* July 1906, 8 pp. (same as Nos. 12, 62).

75. *Spiritism Is Demonism! It's Increasing.* Oct. 1906,
     8 pp. (same as No. 68).

76. Pt. 1: *Earthquakes in Prophecy.* Jan. 1907, 4 pp.
     Pt. 2: *"Tongues of Fire."* Jan. 1907, 4 pp.
     Pt. 3: *"In the Evil Day."* Jan. 1907, 4 pp. (also printed
           in *Pastor Russell's Sermons,* pp. 286-302 entitled
           "Wolves in Sheep's Clothing").
     Pt. 4: *Filthiness of Flesh and Spirit.* Jan. 1907, 4 pp.

77. Pt. 1: *Our Lord's Return.* 1900, 68 pp.

     Pt. 2: *What Would Satisfy Jesus for His Travail of Soul
           at Calvary?* Oct. 1907, 4 pp.

78. Pt. 1: *Are You of the Hopeful or of the Hopeless?* Jan.
           1908, 4 pp. (found in *Convention Report Sermons,*
           pp. 19-22).
     Pt. 2: *Seven Women Desire One Husband.* Jan. 1908, 4 pp.

Pt. 3: *The Millennial Morning Is Dawning! But a Night
of Awful Trouble Will Intervene.* Jan. 1908,
4 pp.

Pt. 4: *The Ransom Price Paid for Sinners Guarantees a
Millennial Age of Restitution.* Jan. 1908, 4 pp.

Pt. 5: *Word to the Watchers Update.* Jan. 1908, 4 pp.

Pt. 6: *A Lesson in Natures Distinct Purpose.* Jan. 1908.

79. *An Open Letter to a Seventh-Day Adventist.* 8 pp.

Miscellaneous Tracts

(series of tracts called *The Gospel Truth*;
late 1800s)

Once in Grace Always in Grace. N.d., 2 pp.

Self-Denial and Cross-Bearing Conditions. N.d., 2 pp.

"The Word Was Made Flesh"--Luke 2:1-16. N.d., 2 pp.

Other Miscellaneous Tracts

(listed according to date or approximate date)

Arp. B. 1886, 1 p. (advertisement for *The Plan of Ages*, a
commendation by C.T. Smith).

The Wonderful Story. 1891 (same as *Old Theology Quarterly*,
No. 7 with leatherette cover; contains 15 illustrations).

*"O Come Let Us Sing Unto the Lord: Let Us Make a Joyful Noise
Unto the Rock of Our Salvation."* N.d., 2 pp. (an advertisement for the book *Poems and Hymns of Millennial Dawn*).

*To Bible Students of All Denominations, and All Lovers of
Truth and Righteousness.* 1912, 1 p. (an open letter, dated
June 15, 1912, which criticizes Rev. I.M. Haldemann and his
views of C.T. Russell's teachings).

Report on Foreign Missions. 1917.

The Case of the International Bible Students Association.
4 pp. (about the Society's view of the imprisonment of seven
Watch Tower leaders by the U.S. government on June 21, 1918,
for sedition).

To Whom Work Is Entrusted. 1919.

Response to "Reconciliation Bulletin." London, England: Watchtower Press, Jan. 26, 1921, 4 pp.

Proclamation--a Challenge to World Leaders. 1922, 2 pp. (resolution of the International Bible Student Association
adopted at Cedar Point, Ohio, Sept. 10, 1922).

Proclamation--A Warning to All Christians. 1923, 2 pp. (resolution of the International Bible Student Association
adopted at Los Angeles, Cal., on Aug. 15, 1923).

Ecclesiastics Indicted--Civilization Doomed. 1924, 2 pp.

The Broadcaster. 1924, 4 pp.

Message of Hope--World Reconstruction. 1925, 2 pp. (resolution
of the International Bible Student Association adopted at
Indianapolis, Ind., on Aug. 29, 1925).

World Powers Addressed. 1926, 2 pp. (special edition of the
Golden Age; lecture given at London, England, on May 30,
1926).

Testimony to the Rulers of the World. 1926.

Do You Want to Know What's Wrong with the World? C. 1931,
2 pp.

Letters to Franklin D. Roosevelt. 1938, 4 pp. (open letters
to the President from Olin R. Moyle, legal counsel for the
WtBTS. The letters of Nov. 9 and Dec. 1, 1938, are critical
of the Catholic hierarchy).

It Must Be Stopped! 1940, 4 pp. (an exposé of the Canadian
government's persecution of the Jehovah's Witnesses; printed
in Toronto, Canada).

Resolution. 1941, 1 p. (adopted at 1941 Convention against
Olin R. Moyle for his anti-Watchtower activities).

"Now Let the People Hear." N.d., 2 pp.

Jehovah's Witnesses: Their Position. London, England: Watchtower Press, July 21, 1942, 4 pp.

Good-Will Letter No. 1. 1943, 2 pp. (letter to interested parties on Watchtower teachings, and a capsule review of the book *The New World*).

Good-Will Letter No. 2. 1943, 2 pp. (similar to Letter No. 1 with slight variations).

Good-Will Letter No. 3. 1943, 2 pp. (similar to Letter No. 1 with slight variations).

Good-Will Letter No. 4. 1943, 2 pp. (similar to Letter No. 1 with slight variations).

Quebec's Burning Hate for God and Christ and Freedom Is the Shame of All Canada. 1946, 4 pp. (similar to *It Must Be Stopped!*, 1940).

Quebec, You Have Failed Your People. 1946, 4 pp. (similar to *It Must Be Stopped!*, 1940).

Regret and Protest by American Convention-Hosts over Religious Discrimination Against Visiting Witnesses of Jehovah. 1950, 4 pp.

"Awake From Sleep!" 1951, 6 pp.

Hell Fire--Bible Truth or Pagan Scare? 1951, 6 pp.

Jehovah's Witnesses, Communists or Christians? 1951, 6 pp.

What Do Jehovah's Witnesses Believe? 1951, 6 pp.

Hope for the Dead. 1952, 6 pp.

The Trinity--Divine Mystery or Pagan Myth? 1952, 6 pp.

How Valuable Is the Bible? 1952, 6 pp.

Life in a New World. 1952, 6 pp.

The Sign of Christ's Presence. C. 1953, 6 pp.

Man's Only Hope for Peace. 1953, 6 pp.

Which Is the Right Religion? 1953, 6 pp.

Do You Believe in Evolution or the Bible? 1953, 6 pp.

How Has Christendom Failed All Mankind? 1958, 4 pp.

Blood Transfusion: Why Not for Jehovah's Witnesses? 1977, 4 pp. (written for members of the medical profession).

You Had a Visitor. C. 1977, 2 pp.

J. CATALOGS

Watch Tower Bible and Tract Society. 1932, 34 pp.; 1933, 35 pp.

Watch Tower Bible and Tract Society. 1938, 38 pp.; 1943, 16 pp.

Catalogue. 1946, 16 pp.

Watchtower Cost List. 1971, 48 pp.

K. BIBLES

The Watchtower Society has always stressed the distribution of the Bible, usually, until the early 1960s, the King James Version of 1611. When the Society was first incorporated in 1881, it took the name *Watch Tower Tract Society* and in 1896 *Watch Tower Bible and Tract Society* to emphasize its goal of distributing Bibles as well as publishing books and tracts on the Bible. Although the Society was not to print Bibles on its own presses for many years, in 1896 it commissioned the printing of Rotherham's New Testament, 12th Ed. Revised. In 1901 the Society commissioned a special printing of the Holman Linear Bible which contained the Authorized and Revised Versions of the Old and New Testaments, arranged to compare the readings of the two versions. In the margins were references to the five volumes of the *Studies in the Scriptures*, *Tabernacle Shadows*, and *Zion's Watchtower* 1895-1901. By April of 1902 the first 1,000 copies were shipped out of the Society's headquarters, and by 1903 the entire edition of 5,000 copies was sold.

In 1902 the Watch Tower Society obtained the plates for the *Emphatic Diaglott*, first published in 1864 by Benjamin Wilson, a newspaper editor from Geneva, Illinois. Although the Society owned the plates, it was not until December 21, 1926, that the *Emphatic Diaglott* was printed on the Society's own presses. On September 18, 1942, the first complete Bible printed on the Society's presses was released, the complete King James Version. Thirty-five thousand copies were distributed at the local assembly that year, and since then a total of 700,000 copies of the Watchtower edition have been sold.

After negotiation and final arrangement with the publishers of the American Standard Version in 1944, the Watchtower Society was able to purchase the use of the plates, and added an extensive, specially-prepared appendix written by the Society. This edition was for years the most popular Witness Bible, primarily because it used the name Jehovah in 6,823 places, or each time it was thought to occur in the original Hebrew Scriptures. This version was used until it was replaced by the New World Translation.

Since 1946 the president of the Society had been making arrangements to produce a new translation. On September 3, 1949, at Bethel headquarters the existence of a "New World Bible Translation Committee" was formally announced at the joint meeting of the Board of Directors of the Pennsylvania and New York operations. The committee had already turned its completed translation over to the control of the Watchtower Bible & Tract Society. On February 9, 1950, the translation committee completed its foreword, and the translation of the Greek Scriptures (New Testament) was immediately published. Subsequently, the Hebrew Scriptures were translated and published in five installments until the entire Bible was completed in 1960 (5 volumes). A large-type complete edition with footnotes was published in 1961, and later several revisions of the entire work were completed and released in small-print versions. This translation has drawn much criticism, primarily because of its rendering of various Scriptures which relate to doctrines such as trinity, hell-fire, immortality of the soul, etc., and the fact that it is somewhat awkward in places. The several revisions have corrected some of the grammatical and other problems, but the major problems remain.

In spite of the criticisms, the Society has endeavored to produce a workable, useful translation. When this writer was at Bethel in the mid-60s, during one of his many long days in the Bethel library, he uncovered several boxes of letters concerning the drafts of the translation between Fred W. Franz, the head of the translation committee, and the well-known university of Chicago translator Edgar J. Goodspeed. From these letters I concluded that Goodspeed and several other eminent scholars had greatly contributed to the final product. Subsequent attempts to obtain copies of these letters in the historical archives at the University of Chicago (where Good-speed deposited most of his letters, etc.) uncovered only a couple of vague letters. Subsequent attempts to obtain copies from the Watchtower Society have failed; my letters of inquiry were not answered.

Joseph B. Rotherham (translator). *The New Testament Newly Translated and Critically Emphasized*. Twelfth ed., revised, 1896. Printed commercially with Watch Tower imprint, Brooklyn, N.Y.: WtBTS. First printed in 1872.

Watchtower edition of *The Holy Bible* (King James Version) bound with *Berean Bible Teacher's Manual*. Brooklyn, N.Y.: WtBTS, 1901 (© by James Pott & Co.), other material useful for the Bible Students. (See *Berean Bible Teacher's Manual* for further details.) This edition was entitled *Bible Students Edition*.

Holman Linear. A.J. Holman Co., Philadelphia, Pa., and Allegheny, Pa.: WtBTS, 1902. The first Watchtower Bible with extensive notes by Russell and his followers; only 5,000 printed.

The Emphatic Diaglott (trans. by Benjamin Wilson). Brooklyn, N.Y.: WtBTS, 1902 (various eds., the latest in 1942). First published by Fowler and Wells in 1864. The first Watchtower printing was Dec. 21, 1926. The Society purchased the plates in 1902.

Concordant Version The Sacred Scriptures, ed. and trans. A.E. Knoch. Los Angeles, Ca.: Concordant Publishing Concern, 1919, 78 pp. This edition was specifically printed for Rutherford, and advertised as such in the *Watchtower*. When Rutherford found out that a number of prominent Bible Students had left his organization and joined Knoch's organization, he refused to fulfill his contract with Knoch. Thus Knoch was forced to sell this edition through his organization.

Authorized Version (King James Version). 1942; The Old Testament, 824 pp.; The New Testament and Concordance, 328 pp.; total pp. 1,152.

American Standard Version (© 1901 by Thomas Nelson and Sons). First printed by the Society with its own footnotes in 1944, the Old Testament, 1,002 pp.; the New Testament, 288 pp.; Concordance, 100 pp.; total pages are 1,390.

The New World Translation of the Christian Greek Scriptures.
1950 (revised ed. 1951), 800 pp. Translated into German,
French, Spanish, Portuguese, Italian, Dutch.

New World Translation of the Hebrew Scriptures. Vol. 1 (Genesis
to Judges), 1953, 864 pp.

New World Translation of the Hebrew Scriptures. Vol. 2 (Samuel
to Esther), 1955, 718 pp.

New World Translation of the Hebrew Scriptures. Vol. 3 (Job to
Ecclesiastes), 1957, 511 pp.

New World Translation of the Hebrew Scriptures. Vol. 4 (Isaiah
to Lamentations), 1958, 408 pp.

New World Translation of the Hebrew Scriptures. Vol. 5 (Ezekiel to Malachi), 1960, 480 pp.

New World Translation of the Holy Scriptures. 1961 (revised
ed. 1970, 1,468 pp.; large-print ed. with new footnotes,
1971, 1,371 pp.). This is the standard Witness Bible,
1,468 pp. Translated into Spanish, Japanese, German, Italian,
French, etc.

New World Translation of the Holy Scriptures. 1963, Vols. 1
through 5 of the Hebrew Scriptures and the Greek Scriptures
bound together in one volume, 3,646 pp.

Kingdom Interlinear Translation of the Greek Scriptures.
1969. Contains both the Greek and English.

The Bible in Living English, trans. Steven T. Byington.
1972, 1,596 pp. How the Society obtained this version is
unknown. Byington was very critical of the New World Translation.

*Comprehensive Concordance of the New World Translation of the
Holy Scriptures.* 1973, 1,275 pp.

L. MISCELLANEOUS

Special Supplement. July 1, 1879, 1 p.

Charter of Zion's Watchtower Tract Society. Nov. 12, 1884,
on file at the Recorder of Deeds, Allegheny County, Pa.,
6 pp. (handwritten by C.T. Russell).

Russell, C,T, Typed copy of sermon delivered at Bible House
Chapel, Arch St., Allegheny, Pa.
1. Sunday, June 1, 1902, 7 pp.
2. Saturday, Sept. 21, 1902, 7 pp.

The Messenger of Laodicea. 1919, 11 pp. (souvenir folder
with pictures of Charles T. Russell at different points
in his life; the pictures are also in the Watchtower reprints; the folder also gives Russell's background).

Radio Souvenirs. 1926.

Your Work with Transcription Machines. C. 1935, 4 pp.

M. INDEXES

(all published in Brooklyn, N.Y.)

Hardback Indexes

All indexes include a subject and scriptural
index for all of the official publications
published during the years the index covers.

Watch Tower Publications Index 1930-1960. 1961, 380 pp.

Watch Tower Publications Index 1961-1965. 1966, 254 pp.

Watch Tower Publications Index 1966-1970. 1971, 335 pp.

Watch Tower Publications Index 1971-1975. 1976, 201 pp.

Temporary Indexes

Since 1966, the Society has issued each
year an index covering all the previous
year's publications. After four or five
years these are usually replaced by hardbound
indexes covering several years (see above).
A list of these paperbound indexes follows.

1966 Index. 1967, 48 pp.

1967 Index. 1968, 48 pp.

1968 Index. 1969, 46 pp.

N. CONVENTION REPORTS

Chicago (World's Fair Convention). 1895. Published from 1901 to 1903; no known copies.

St. Louis, Mo. 1904, 20 pp.

Souvenir [notes from] Watch Tower Bible and Tract Society's Convention, Kingston, Jamaica. 1905.

Souvenir [notes from] Watch Tower Bible and Tract Society's Convention, Niagara Falls, New York. 1905, 34 pp.

Souvenir Report of the Asbury Park, New Jersey and St. Paul, Minnesota Conventions. 1906, 107 pp.

Souvenir Report of the Manchester Convention, Manchester, England. 1906-1907, 56 pp.

Souvenir Notes from Watchtower Bible and Tract Society's Conventions of Believers in the Atoning Blood of Christ,

*Indianapolis, Indiana; Niagara Falls, New York; and Norfolk,
Virginia.* 1907, Pt. I, 73 pp.; Pt. II, 206 pp.

Souvenir Notes of Watch Tower Convention at Cincinnati, Ohio.
1908, 152 pp.

*On to Victory: Watch Tower Bible Student's Convention, Put-In-
Bay Island, Ohio.* 1908, 168 pp.

Souvenir Report, Annotto Bay, Jamaica. 1908, 47 pp.

Souvenir Notes Bible Students' Convention, Nashville, Tennessee.
1908, 144 pp.

Souvenir Notes Bible Students' Convention, Various U.S. Cities.
1909, 256 pp. C.T. Russell and a number of Bible Students
traveled the south, west, and northwest by train. Conventions were held at each stop.

Glasgow, Scotland. 1909, 66 pp.

Souvenir Notes Bible Students' Conventions. Brooklyn, N.Y.,
1910, 299 pp.

*Souvenir Notes Bible Students' Conventions, Various U.S.
Cities.* 1911, 312 pp. A transcontinental tour by train of
the United States. The general convention was held at
Mountain Lake Park, Md.

*Souvenir Notes Bible Students' Conventions, Around the World
Tour.* 1912, 391 pp.

Souvenir Notes Bible Students' Conventions, Various Cities.
1913, 392 pp. The general conventions were held in Madison,
Wisc.; Springfield, Mass.; and Asheville, N.C. General
conventions in foreign countries were held in Toronto,
Canada; London, England; and Glasgow, Scotland.

Souvenir Notes Bible Students' Conventions, Various U.S. Cities.
1914, 272 pp. The general conventions were held in Clinton,
Iowa; Columbus, Ohio; and Asbury Park, N.J.

*Souvenir Notes Bible Students' Conventions, Oakland and San
Francisco, California.* 1915, 180 pp. This report includes
a 48-page supplement: The Rutherford-Troy Debate, Los
Angeles, California.

Supplement to the Souvenir Convention Report. 1915, 222 pp.

Souvenir Notes Bible Students' Conventions, Various U.S. Cities.
1916, 331 pp.

IBSA Souvenir Convention Report, Seattle, Washington. 1916,
65 pp.

Souvenir Report, Pittsburgh, Pennsylvania. 1919, 64 pp.

The Messenger. Toronto, Canada, July 18 to 26, 1927, 40 pp.
(four 8-page sections and a booklet on the Society's headquarters in Toronto, dated Feb. 19, 20, 22, 25).

The Messenger. Detroit, Mich., 1928, 40 pp. (five 8-page
sections dated July 31, Aug. 1, 4, 5, 6).

The Messenger. Columbus, Ohio, 1931, 40 pp. (five 8-page
sections dated July 25, 26, 28, 29, and 30).

*Supplement to Consolation: Report of the Convention of Jehovah's
Witnesses for the Northwest.* Vol. XIX, No. 491. Seattle,
Wash., 1938, 32 pp.

The Messenger. Various cities worldwide, 1938, 64 pp.

The Messenger. Various cities worldwide, 1939, 32 pp.

The Messenger. Various cities worldwide, 1940, 64 pp.

Report of the Jehovah's Witnesses Assembly, St. Louis, Missouri.
1941, 80 pp.

*Report of the New World Theocratic Assembly of Jehovah's Wit-
nesses.* Various cities worldwide; Cleveland, Ohio, key
city, 1942, 32 pp.

Supplement to Consolation. Various cities worldwide, 1943,
64 pp.

Consolation. Various cities worldwide; Buffalo, N.Y., key
city, 1944, 40 pp.

The Messenger. Cleveland, Ohio, 1946 (five 8-page sections
dated Aug. 5, 7, 9, 10, 11, and one 48-page section dated
Aug. 12), 88 pp.

*Report of the Theocracy's Increase Assembly of Jehovah's Wit-
nesses.* New York, 1950 (four 16-page sections dated Aug. 1,
2, 3, 6, and one 32-page section dated Aug. 8), 96 pp.

Report of the "Clean Worship" Assembly of Jehovah's Witnesses.
London, England, 1951, 32 pp.

Report of the New World Society Assembly of Jehovah's Witnesses,
New York City. New York, 1953 (four 16-page sections dated
July 21, 23, 25, and 26, and one 32-page section dated July
28), 96 pp.

Kongress, "Triumphierendes Konigreich." 1955, 8 pp. (German
Assembly).

1958 Report of the Divine Will International Assembly of
Jehovah's Witnesses. New York, 1958, 112 pp.

Report on "Everlasting Good News" Assembly of Jehovah's Wit-
nesses Around the World. Various cities worldwide, 1963,
192 pp.

Convention News. Vol. 1, No. 1. Toronto, Canada, 1966. 8 pp.

1969 Report "Peace on Earth" International Assembly of
Jehovah's Witnesses. Various cities worldwide, 1969, 32 pp.

Peace on Earth--International Assembly. 1969, 32 pp.

The Approaching Peace of a Thousand Years. 1969, 32 pp.

O. ARTICLES BY C.T. RUSSELL PRINTED IN
OVERLAND MONTHLY *(a monthly literature*
magazine printed in California).

All of the following have been reprinted in
What Pastor Russell Wrote by the Chicago
Bible Students (see below, p. 310).

"Battle of Armageddon." Vol. 62, Oct. 1913, pp. 402-411.

"Be Content with Your Wages." Vol. 60, July 1912, pp. 94-96.

"Bishop-Apostles' Costly Mistake." Vol. 67, March 1916, pp.
256-260.

"Changes of Creeds Necessary to Federation for Baptists, Adventists and Disciples." Vol. 61, March 1913, pp. 296-300.

"China's Prayer to One of Messiah's Kingdoms." Vol. 57, May 1911, pp. 548-551.

"Christendom in Great Danger." Vol. 63, March 1914, pp. 306-309.

"Church Militant's Surrender to the Church Triumphant." Vol. 59, April 1912, pp. 386-389.

"Church's Birth Due Now: World's Due Later--During Millennium." Vol. 66, Nov. 1915, pp. 456-460.

"Church's Hope--The World's Hope." Vol. 68, Oct. 1916, pp. 332-336.

"Civil Baptism in France." Vol. 58, Nov. 1911, pp. 429-431.

"Clean Thing Out of an Unclean." Vol. 58, July 1911, pp. 86-89.

"Conditions of Acceptable, Effective Prayer." Vol. 67, April 1916, pp. 344-348.

"Creed Smashings Necessary for Federation." Vol. 61, Feb. 1913, pp. 195-198.

"Divine Plan of the Ages." May 1917-April 1918: Vol. 69, pp. 425-430, 538-542; Vol. 70, pp. 90-94, 205-209, 300-305, 392-396, 495-499, 586-590; Vol. 71, pp. 87-97, 165-169, 252-256, 353-361.

"Divine Program." Feb. 1909-Jan. 1910: Vol. 53, pp. 85-88, 239-243, 349-354, 452-457, 548-554; Vol. 54, pp. 108-113, 193-199, 245-252, 400-405, 511-516, 567-569; Vol. 55, pp. 126-130.

"Episcopalian, Catholic, Lutheran: What These Creeds Surrender to Enter the Church Federation Proposed." Vol. 61, April 1913, pp. 400-404.

"Every Idle Word." Vol. 60, Sept. 1912, pp. 303-308.

"Exposition of the Justice of the Day of Vengeance." Vol. 65, March 1915, pp. 284-287.

"Famine in the Land." Vol. 62, Aug. 1913, pp. 201-204.

"Fatal Ambition--Noble Ambition." Vol. 63, June 1914, pp. 626-630.

"Financial, Ecclesiastical and Social Shakings." Vol. 65,
    Jan. 1915, pp. 95-98.

"Finished Mystery." Vol. 71, May 1918, pp. 447-451.

"God in the Home." Vol. 63, Feb. 1914, pp. 200-201.

"God's Chosen People." Feb. 1910-Jan. 1911: Vol. 55, pp. 227-
    231, 323-329, 414-420, 539-543, 622-627; Vol. 56, pp. 98-
    101, 238-244, 333-336, 427-432, 523-527, 615-618; Vol. 57,
    pp. 86-89.

"God's Justice and Love Perfectly Poised." Vol. 67, May
    1916, pp. 432-436.

"Golden Age at Hand." Vol. 66, Dec. 1915, pp. 542-545.

"Golden Rule." Vol. 61, Jan. 1913, pp. 89-93.

"Great White Throne: Day of Judgment Misunderstood." Vol. 62,
    July 1913, pp. 97-100 (reprinted in Vol. 64, July 1914, pp.
    102-104).

"Greatest Thing in the Universe." Vol. 58, Dec. 1911, pp.
    539-540.

"How and What to Fight." Vol. 64, Aug. 1914, pp. 216-220.

"Imminence of Christ's Kingdom." Vol. 64, Oct. 1914, pp.
    417-421.

"Immortality of the Soul." Vol. 57, April 1911, pp. 431-435.

"Infant One Hundred Years Old to Be Electrocuted." Vol. 57,
    March 1911, pp. 334-339.

"Is Christian Science Reasonable?" Vol. 66, Sept. 1915, pp.
    269-273.

"Is Christian Science Scriptural?" Vol. 66, Oct. 1915, pp.
    363-367.

"Japanese Complimented." Vol. 59, June 1912, pp. 580-583.

"Jehovah's Saintly Jewels." Vol. 68, Sept. 1916, pp. 262-264.

"Jesus Died a Human--Raised a Spirit Being." Vol. 65, May
    1915, pp. 482-485.

"Jews Not to Be Converted to Christianity." Vol. 58, Aug. 1911, pp. 171-175.

"Joyful Message for the Sin-sick." Vol. 59, Feb. 1912, pp. 174-178.

"Man's Fall from Divine Favor." Vol. 63, Jan. 1914, pp. 93-96.

"Messiah's Fast Approaching Kingdom." Vol. 64, Sept. 1914, pp. 316-319.

"Miraculous Birth of Jesus." Vol. 64, Nov. 1914, pp. 517-520.

"Nations Weighed in the Balances." Vol. 68, Nov. 1916, pp. 428-430.

"New Day Dawns." Vol. 65, April 1915, pp. 383-386.

"Observations on Conditions in the Orient." Vol. 60, Nov. 1912, pp. 503-506.

"Our Lord's Return." Vol. 60, Dec. 1912, pp. 600-606.

"Pains of Hell Explained to Us." Vol. 62, Sept. 1913, pp. 302-306.

"Paradise Better Than Honolulu." Vol. 59, March 1912, pp. 235-238.

"Pastor Russell and the Monitor." Vol. 58, Sept. 1911, pp. 261-267; Vol. 58, Oct. 1911, pp. 315-320.

"Pseudo Apostles of the Present Day." Vol. 67, June 1916, pp. 514-517; Vol. 68, July-August 1916, pp. 78-82, 174-176.

"Refrain Thy Voice from Weeping and Thine Eyes from Tears." Vol. 60, Oct. 1912, pp. 399-404.

"Reign of the Messiah." Vol. 59, May 1912, pp. 479-483.

"Reply to Cardinal Gibbons' Sermon." Vol. 57, Feb. 1911, pp. 186-191.

"Sabbath Day." Vol. 62, Nov. 1913, pp. 512-517.

"Satan the Murderer--Murderer to Die." Vol. 63, May 1914, pp. 521-524.

"Satan's Ambition--Jesus' Ambition." Vol. 63, April 1914,
    pp. 409-413.

"Songs of the Night." Vol. 59, Jan. 1912, pp. 78-80.

"Sowing to Self and Sin--Reaping Corruption." Vol. 67, Feb.
    1916, pp. 174-176.

"Three Men and Two Women Whom Jesus Loved." Vol. 64, Dec.
    1914, pp. 616-620.

"Thrust in Thy Sickle." Vol. 61, May 1913, pp. 509-512.

"True Church." Vol. 62, Dec. 1913, pp. 610-613.

"Twenty Billion Slaves to Be Freed." Vol. 67, Jan. 1916, pp.
    84-88.

"Two Escape from Hell--No Torment There!" Vol. 66, July 1915,
    pp. 87-91.

"Two Salvations." Vol. 61, June 1913, pp. 611-613.

"Value of Ideals to Church and World." Vol. 66, Aug. 1915,
    pp. 175-178.

"Weeping All Night." Vol. 60, Aug. 1912, pp. 189-193.

"What Is a Christian? What Are His Standards?" Vol. 65,
    June 1915, pp. 569-573.

"World That Was, Present Evil World and the World to Come."
    Vol. 57, June 1911, pp. 664-668.

"World-wide Theocracy." Vol. 65, Feb. 1915, pp. 190-194.

P. ARTICLES BY AND ABOUT C.T. RUSSELL
(Assistant Editor from Vol. 7, No. 1,
in HERALD OF THE MORNING, edited by N.H.
Barbour.

"The Prospect." Vol. 7, No. 1, July 1878, pp. 11-15.

Letter to C.T. Russell by Mrs. S.L. Slagle. Vol. 7, No. 2,
    Aug. 1878, p. 31.

"The Atonement." Vol. 7, No. 3, Sept. 1878, pp. 39–40.

"Holiness." Vol. 7, No. 4, Oct. 1878, pp. 62–63.

"The Prophetic Conference." Vol. 7, No. 6, Dec. 1878, pp. 83–84.

"Rich Man and Lazarus." Vol. 8, No. 1, Jan. 1879, pp. 9–10.

"The Sabbath." Vol. 8, No. 1, Jan. 1879, pp. 14–16.

"Your Vote Wanted." Vol. 8, No. 2, Feb. 1879, p. 40.

"The New Paper." Vol. 8, No. 3, March 1879, p. 42.

"Conversion and Holiness." Vol. 8, No. 4, April 1879, pp. 64–66.

Remarks by N.H. Barbour (about C.T. Russell's proposal of new paper). Vol. 8, No. 5, May 1879, pp. 83–87.

Q. ARTICLES BY C.T. RUSSELL
IN THE BIBLE EXAMINER,
Edited by George Storrs.

"Gentle Times: When Do They End?" Vol. 21, No. 1, Oct. 1876, pp. 27–29.

"Coming Events Cast Their Shadows Before." Vol. 21, No. 6, March 1877, pp. 181+.

R. ARTICLES BY JOHN H. PATON
(Assistant Editor of The Watchtower,
From Vol. 1, No. 1, to Vol. 8, No. 6)
In HERALD OF THE MORNING.

"Not of the World." Vol. 7, No. 2, Aug. 1878, pp. 25–26.

Extracts from Letters. Vol. 7, No. 2, Aug. 1878, p. 28.

"Euphrates." Vol. 7, No. 3, Sept. 1878, pp. 37–39.

"Light and Fellowship." Vol. 7, No. 4, Oct. 1878, pp. 54-55.

"The Atonement." Vol. 7, No. 4, Oct. 1878, p. 56.

"Atonement." Vol. 7, No. 6, Dec. 1878, pp. 89-91.

"Thoughts on Law." Vol. 8, No. 1, Jan. 1879, pp. 10-11.

"The Kingdom." Vol. 8, No. 2, Feb. 1879, pp. 31-32.

"Exhortation." Vol. 8, No. 6, June 1879, pp. 95-97.

SECTION TWO

MATERIAL ASSOCIATED WITH THE RUSSELL MOVEMENT

As a tremendous amount of early material influenced
Russell, it is difficult to compile an exhaustive list.
None of Russell's doctrines were original, and most of them
were openly accepted (or at least commonly discussed) by
the Millerites and the early Adventists, especially the
Second Adventists. For an index of some of these works see
*The Millerites and the Early Adventists; An Index to the
Microfilm Collection of Rare Books and Manuscripts* (University Microfilms, Ann Arbor, Michigan, 1978, 65 pp.). The
works listed below are either works by persons who were at
one time connected with Russell or works which Russell
openly and heavily relied upon. Some of the individuals such
as Barbour, Stetson, Wendell, Paton, and Storrs were at one
time close associates of Russell. It must be remembered,
however, that from the founding of the Watch Tower Bible and
Tract Society in 1879 until his death in 1916, Russell *was*
the Watch Tower Bible and Tract Society, and wrote virtually
all booklets and pamphlets produced by the Society, although
much of the *Watchtower* itself was also written by his wife,
Paton, and others. Russell had full authority in all doctrinal matters. However, he was heavily influenced by the
writings and personalities of George Storrs, Jonas Wendell,
Nelson Barbour, John Paton, George Stetson, Joseph A. Seiss,
and many others.

A. *IMPORTANT PRE-SOCIETY OR CONTEMPORARY LITERATURE*

(this material was highly influential in
the development of Russell's views).

Adams, A.P., ed. *The Spirit of the Word.* Vol. I (reprint of
the first 12 issues of the magazine, March 1885 to Feb. 1886).
Corona, Cal.: Scripture Studies Concern, n.d., 157 pp., hb.

Barbour, Nelson. *Evidences for the Coming of the Lord in 1873: or the Midnight Cry.* Rochester, N.Y.: D.T. Cooper, 1871, 99 pp.

————. *Washed in His Blood.* Rochester, N.Y.: Unique Book Co., 1907, 511 pp.

There are still some followers of Barbour living today; although, because Barbour left Russell in 1874, they were never associated with Russell's movement, the literature helps us understand the source of Russell's beliefs. Barbour was a major early influence on Russell. The modern Barbourite works are *A Review*, below, and Hobbs and Hobbs, p. 55.

A Review / God's Wisdom Versus Man's Wisdom. Dayton, Ohio: Christian Fellowship Associates, 1968, 81 pp.

Birks, T.R. *First Elements of Sacred Prophecy.* London: William Edward Painter, 1843.

Blain, Jacob. *"Death Not Life: or the Destruction of the Wicked (commonly called annihilation). Established, and Endless Misery Disproved, by a Collection and Explanation of All Passages on Future Punishment to Which Is Addenda Review of Dr. E. Beecher's Conflict of the Ages, and John Foster's Letter.* 7th ed. Buffalo: Pub. by author, 1857.

Brown, John Aquila. *The Even-Tide; or, The Last Triumph of the Blessed and Only Potentate, The King of Kings, and Lord of Lords; Being a Development of the Mysteries of Daniel and St. John.* London, England: J. Offer, 1823, 2 vols.

Dunn, Henry. *The Destiny of the Human Race, a Scriptural Inquiry.* England, 1863.

Elliott, E.B. *Horae Apocalyptical: or, A Commentary on the Apocalypse.* 5th ed. London, England: Seeley, Jackson and Halliday, 1862, 4 vols.

Farrar, Dr. F.W. *"Eternal Hope."* London, England: Macmillan, 1878.

————. *"Mercy and Judgment."* London, England: Macmillan, 1904.

Grant, Miles, ed. "The Crisis." N.d. (Opposition Journal, Advent Christian.)

Grew, Henry. *The Divine Testimony Concerning the Son of God.* Published by author, 1842.

————. *Future Punishment, Not Eternal Life in Misery but Destruction.* N.p., n.d.

————. *The Intermediate State.* Philadelphia: For sale by the author and H.L. Hastings, 1844.

Guinness, H. Grattan. *The Approaching End of the Age.* 2nd ed. London: Hodder and Stoughton, 1879, 695 pp.

Hobbs, A.E., and I.J. Hobbs. *Hope for All Mankind.* Auckland, New Zealand: Reliance Printing, 1920, 169 pp.

Jukes, Andrew. *The Restitution of All Things.* Pub. by author, 1867.

Martin, J.L. *The Voice of the Seven Thunders: or, Lectures on the Apocalypse.* 7th ed. Bedford, Ind.: James M. Mathes, 1874, 330 pp., hb.

Miller, William. *Evidence from Scripture and History of the Second Coming of Christ, About the Year 1843: Exhibited in a Course of Lectures.* Troy, N.Y.: Kember & Hooper, 1836. Also 1842 ed. Boston: Joshua Himes, 300 pp.

Moncrieff, Wm. Glen. *Dialogues on Future Probation.* C. 1840s.

————. *Dialogues on Future Punishment.* 1848.

Newton, Thomas. *Dissertations on the Prophecies.* Northampton, Mass.: William Butler, 1796.

Seiss, Joseph A., D.D. *The Parable of the Ten Virgins in Six Discourses.* Philadelphia, Pa.: Smith English and Co., 1862.

————. *The Last Times and Great Consummation.* Philadelphia, Pa., 1863.

————. *The Apocalypse.* Philadelphia, Pa.: Smith English and Co., 1865.

————. *A Miracle in Stone of the Great Pyramid of Egypt.* Philadelphia, Pa.: London Christian Office, 1877, 250 pp. Reprinted in 1973 by Multimedia Publishing Corp. of Blauvelt, N.Y. The reprint is titled *The Great Pyramid: A Miracle in Stone* and has a new introduction by Paul M. Allen.

————. *The Gospel in the Stars*. Philadelphia, Pa.: J.B. Lippincott, 1885.

Smith, Worth. *Miracle of the Ages: The Great Pyramid*. Holyoke, Mass.: The Elizabeth Towne Co., 1934, 160 pp., hb.

Smyth, Piazzi. *Our Inheritance in the Great Pyramid*. London, England: Daldy, Isbister & Co., 1877. A third ed. reprinted by Steiner Books of Blauvelt, N.Y., in 1977, 626 pp., hb. pb. A fourth ed. reprinted (under the title *The Great Pyramid: Its Secrets and Mysteries Revealed*) by Bell Publishing Co. of New York in 1978 with a new foreword, 676 pp., hb.

————. *The Glory of the Great Pyramid Found in England's Coming Glories* (fourth volume of the series "Identifications of the Anglo Saxons with Lost Israel"). Revised ed. by Edward Hine. New York: James Huggins, 1880, pp. 222-230.

Snow, S.S. *The Book of Judgment Delivered to Israel by Elijah the Messenger of the Everlasting Covenant*. New York: G. Mitchell, 1848, 432 pp., hb.

Wellcome, Isaac C. *History of the Second Advent Message and Mission, Doctrine and People*. Boston, Mass.: Advent Christian Publication Society, 1874, 707 pp.

Wendell, Rufus. *The New Testament of Our Lord and Savior Jesus Christ*. Albany, N.Y.: Pub. by author, 1882, c. 564 pp. This translation was by Jonas Wendell's brother. Jonas was the man who got Russell started in the Second Adventist movement.

B. PRE-SOCIETY OR CONTEMPORARY MAGAZINES WHICH WERE AN IMPORTANT PART OF RUSSELL'S MOVEMENT

Advent Chronicler and Tent Reporter. Buffalo, N.Y., 1843 to about 1844 (no known copies remain).

Barbour, Nelson H., ed. *The Midnight Cry*. 1871-1873 (a most important paper). From 1873 to 1874 this was called *The Midnight Cry and the Herald of the Morning*. In 1875 it was renamed *The Herald of the Morning* until 1903.

Fitch, Charles, ed. *Second Advent of Christ*. Cleveland, Ohio: c. 1843, 4 pp. (no known copies).

Gross, H.H., ed. *Sure Word of Prophecy.* Albany, N.Y., 1845.

Hek, C.W., ed. *The Bible Student's Monthly.* Vol. 1, No. 1, to Vol. VII(?), Jan. 1909-1916?

Himes, Joshua V., and S.S. Snow, eds. *True Midnight Cry.* Haverhill, Mass., 1844.

Himes, Joshua V., et al., eds. *Signs of the Times.* Boston, Mass.: 1840-1844 (continued as *Advent Herald*).

————. *Southern Midnight Cry.* New York, 1844 (no issues located).

————. *Advent Herald and Signs of the Times Reporter.* Boston, Mass., 1849 to 1873.

Hoskins, I.F., ed. *Watchers of the Morning* (no known copies).

Hutchinson, Richard, and C. Green, eds. *Voice of Elijah.* Montreal, Canada, semi-monthly, 1843-1844.

Jacobs, Enoch, ed. *The Coming of Christ.* New York, 1843.

Jones, A.D., ed. *Zion's Day Star* (later called *Day Star*). Oct. 1881-1894?. monthly. Jones worked closely with Russell for several years.

Jones, Henry, and C.D. Fleming, eds. *Second Advent Witness.* 1842, 32 pp. per issue (no known copies).

Litch, Josiah, ed. *Philadelphia Alarm.* 1844 (no known copies).

————. *Trumpet of Alarm.* Philadelphia, Pa., 1844-1845 (no known copies).

Lleming, L.D., ed. *The Kingdom at Hand.* Rochester, N.Y., 1843.

Marsh, Joseph, ed. *Christian Palladium.* Union Mills, N.Y., 1832-1846.

Paton, John H., ed. *The World's Hope.* 1880 to Aug. 15, 1916, semi-monthly, 16 pp. Paton was one of the founders of the Watchtower Society.

Rice, H.B., ed. *The Last Trump.* 1879.

Robertson, William, ed. *The Bible Student.*

Storrs, George, ed. *Bible Examiner.* Philadelphia, Pa., 1843-1853.

Thompson, John, ed. *Young Bible Students Messenger.* Great Britain.

C. THE WORKS OF GEORGE STORRS

George Storrs was born on December 13, 1796, in Lebanon, New Hampshire, and died December 28, 1879, at Brooklyn, New York. He published parts of his autobiography in his journal *The Bible Examiner*, and the final issue, published in March 1880 by his only daughter, Hattie Storrs with the assistance of his widow, gives a complete biography.
C.T. Russell evidently met Storrs through Jonas Wendell in about 1869. Rufus Wendell, a close associate of Storrs, was a relative of Jonas Wendell. George Storrs conducted a personal Bible study with Charles Russell who adopted many, if not most, of his views. Storrs was raised as a Calvinist and later involved himself with the Methodist Church, traveling, lecturing, and preaching (especially against slavery). His position on slavery (pro abolition) created conflicts (the Methodists were opposed to abolition work as they felt it was "radical," but were also opposed to slavery) and thus in 1840 under pressure he withdrew from the church. Eventually, partially because of a pamphlet written by Henry Grew, he came to believe that the soul was mortal (thus denying the doctrine of inherent immortality). In 1842 he heard the views of William Miller, which he accepted for a short time. In 1843 he began *The Bible Examiner*, which influenced C.T. Russell a great deal, and for which he wrote several articles.
In time, Storrs altered his ideas about the resurrection, the state of the unsaved, and other theological concepts and again had to change his religious association. He became president and editor of the Life and Advent Union but in 1871 he again went out on his own. He now held that Christ's ransom would benefit *all* mankind in that both the saved and the unsaved would be resurrected after Armageddon. Thus, because Russell was closely connected with the entire Adventist movement and highly influenced by George Storrs, a listing of some of Storrs's important works appears below. In fact, C.T. Russell, and Russell's father, Joseph Lytel Russell, supported

Storrs financially. When Storrs died, Russell states in the
January 1880 *Watchtower* "the news of Brother Storrs's death
(December 28, 1879) reached us too late for insertion in the
last issue ... he was ... a faithful servant ... we mourned
the loss of a friend and brother in Christ...." A number of
Storrs's followers felt that the "mantle" was passed from
Storrs to Russell in that Russell's magazine began just as
The Bible Examiner was ending. One major difference between
Storrs and Russell was that Storrs was definitely trinitarian
although he printed an article in *The Bible Examiner* which
indicated that the Holy Spirit was not a person but the power
of God. For an excellent review of the Miller movement from
which Storrs and C.T. Russell broke off, see Clara Endicott
Sears, *Days of Delusion* (Boston: Houghton Mifflin Co., 1927).

Storrs, George. *Mob Under Pretense of Law, or the Arrest and
	Trial of Rev. George Storrs at Northfield, N.H.* Concord,
	N.H.: E.G. Chase, 1835, 24 pp.

————. *Six Sermons of the Inquiry, Is There Immortality in
	Sin and Suffering?* New York, 1842, 167 pp. (200,000 copies
	were published from 1842 to 1861.)

————. *The Bible Examiner: Containing Various Prophetic
	Expositions.* Boston: Joshua V. Himes, 1843, 136 pp., hb.

————. *An Inquiry: Are the Wicked Immortal in Six Sermons.*
	Philadelphia, Pa.: Albany W. and A. White, 1847, 64 pp.

————. *The Gospel Hope.* New York, 1851, 85+ pp.

————. *The European War, or the Position and Prospects of
	the Papal Roman Power and the Napoleon Dynasty as Indicated
	in Scripture Prophecy.* New York, 1859, 34 pp.

————. *The French Empire.* N.p., 1859, 4 pp.

————. *The Unity of Man: or Life and Death Realities.* New
	York, n.d., 122 pp.

————. *Gospel Benefits.* New York, n.d., 12 pp.

————. *The Gospel Faith.* New York, n.d., 12 pp.

Magazine

The Bible Examiner. Vol. 1, No. 1, to Vol. 23, No. 10, 1843
to 1880. Suspended publication Jan. 1, 1858, to Jan. 1860
and from Aug. 1863, to Sept. 1871; 1843-1844 issued at
Brooklyn, N.Y., from 1845 to 1853 at Philadelphia, Pa.,
from 1853 on at Brooklyn, N.Y.

D. THE WORKS OF JOHN H. PATON

Probably one of the most influential Bible students was
John H. Paton. Paton, the son of David Paton and Christina
Woodburn, was born April 7, 1843, at Galston, Scotland, and
died on September 6, 1922, at Almont, Michigan. John and his
wife, Sarah Elizabeth Wilson, had six children.
Paton was involved in the Baptist Church until he encountered the ideas of the Adventists. His new ideas resulted in his disfellowshipping and he eventually affiliated
himself with C.T. Russell. He supplied much of the impetus
for the early Watchtower movement, and was highly influential
in formulating the doctrine of the early Watch Tower Society.
Paton had joined the Advent Christian Church with N.H. Barbour
in about 1873 and was Barbour's assistant editor until 1876.
At the time Russell became acquainted with Barbour, he also
became a close friend of Paton's.
Eventually Paton had a falling out with Russell. The
first edition of his book *Day Dawn* was accepted as an official
Watch Tower publication, but the second and third editions were
extensively revised and were *not* accepted by Russell, and his
followers were discouraged from buying or reading them. According to White (see Books about Witnesses), Russell arranged
for Paton to write *Day Dawn* and for Jones to publish it.
Paton continued to write for the Watch Tower Society (most
of his articles are signed J.H.P. and he was listed on the
inside cover as a regular contributor for a number of years)
until 1881 when he disagreed with Russell on the meaning of
Christ's ransom among other things.
Paton's leaving caused a great division for, aside from
Russell, he was the most prominent Bible student of the time.
Paton was to deviate even further from Russell's doctrine;
he even accepted the idea of universal salvation of all mankind, sometimes called "Universal Reconciliation" or "Universalism." After Paton broke with Russell (his last article was
published in the June 1881 *Watch Tower*) he began an ambitious
publishing career, producing numerous books, booklets, and a

monthly magazine for many years. Paton called his concern the Larger Hope Publishing Company ("larger hope" referring to his belief that many more were to be saved than most people believed). Although he was active in printing his literature and served as an itinerant preacher for a number of years (his diaries discuss his many activities in Michigan, Indiana, Ohio, and nearby states), he never built up a large organization, and his ministry stopped when he died. Today there are still a large number of Paton's relatives scattered around the United States, but few of them know much about his important contributions to the early Watch Tower Society. Most know only that he was a newspaper and book publisher and a minister. Paton was the last of Russell's five co-workers to break away (Jones, Adams, and Barbour had already split with Russell), and his work left an important mark on the Society, especially its chronology which concludes we are in the last days and basic theology, much of which is still accepted even today.

Publications by The Larger Hope Publishing Co.
in Almont, Mich.

Books

Paton, John H. *The Day Dawn or the Gospel in Type and Prophecy.* Pittsburgh, Pa.: A.D. Jones, 1880, 334 pp., hb. (4,000 copies printed). This was accepted as an official Watch Tower publication. The revised editions were regarded as heretical.

————. *The Day Dawn or the Gospel in Type and Prophecy.* 2nd ed. Almont, Mich.: The Larger Hope Publ. Co., 1882.

————. *Moses and Christ.* Almont, Mich.: The Larger Hope Publ. Co., 1888, 222 pp., hb. (3,000 copies printed).

————. *The Day Dawn or Gospel in Type and Prophecy.* 3rd ed. Almont, Mich.: The Larger Hope Publ. Co., 1890, 399 pp.

————. *Moses and Christ.* Almont, Mich.: The Larger Hope Publ. Co., 3rd ed.

————. *The Perfect Day.* Almont, Mich.: The Larger Hope Publ. Co., 1892, 240 pp., hb. (3,000 copies printed).

————. *Moses and Christ.* Almont, Mich.: The Larger Hope Publ. Co., rev. ed. 1896, 190 pp., hb. (Some copies bound with *The Great Revelation*, listed below.)

—————. The Great Revelation or God's Love, Purpose and
Plan. Almont, Mich.: The Larger Hope Publ. Co., 1896,
95 pp., hb.

—————. Souvenir of Our Visits to Scotland and England. 1897,
126 pp.

—————. Paton Family History. Almont, Mich.: privately
printed, 1905, 412 pp., hb.

—————. John H. Paton: Autobiography. Almont, Mich.: The
Larger Hope Publ. Co., 1915.

Stray, Ermina C. The Golden Link or The Shadow of Sin, A
Story of Our Times. Almont, Mich.: The Larger Hope Publ.
Co., 1891, 418 pp., hb.

Booklet

Paton, John H. The Atonement. Almont, Mich.: The Larger
Hope Publ. Co., 1898, 96 pp.

E. THE WORKS BY THE EDGAR BROTHERS
OF GLASGOW, SCOTLAND

The Edgar brothers were active Bible students who wrote
a great deal about the Great Pyramid. John Edgar was a
medical doctor (obstetrics and gynecology) and an associate
of Russell. He died on June 9, 1910, at the age of 48 (see
the Watchtower of July 15, 1910). The family later left the
Society. Their pre-c. 1920 publications were accepted as
semi-official.

Books

Edgar, John, and Morton Edgar. The Great Pyramid, Passages
and Chambers. Vol. 1. Glasgow, Scotland: Bone & Hulley,
1910, 1913, 1923, 410 pp., hb.; also quality pocket edition
(1910; 301 pp.). Reprinted by Berean Bible Students, see
below, p. 305.

—————. The Great Pyramid, Passages and Chambers. Vol. 2.
Glasgow, Scotland: Bone & Hulley, 1913, 329 pp., hb.; also

quality pocket edition; also London, England: The Marshall
Press, 1924, 310 pp., hb. Reprinted in 1976 by Berean Bible
Students, see below, p. 305.

Edgar, Morton. *The Great Pyramid, Its Scientific Features:
Part I of 1914 A.D. and the Great Pyramid.* Glasgow, Scotland: Maclure, Macdonald & Co., 1924, 217 pp., hb. Reprinted by Berean Bible Students in 1976, see below, p.
305.

————. *The Great Pyramid, Its Time Features: Part II of
1914 A.D. and the Great Pyramid.* Glasgow, Scotland: Bone
& Hulley, 1924, 180 pp., hb.

————. *The Great Pyramid, Its Spiritual Symbolism.* Glasgow,
Scotland: Bone & Hulley, 1924, 137 pp., hb.

Booklets

(Most of these were reprinted in 1976 by
the Berean Bible Students in one volume
[see below, p. 306].)

Edgar, John. *Where Are the Dead?* Glasgow, Scotland: Hay,
Nisbet and Co., Ltd., 48 pp.; another ed. c. 1909, 70 pp.,
hb., pb. (reprinted in 1949).

————. *Socialism and the Bible.* Glasgow, Scotland: Hay,
Nisbet and Co., Ltd., n.d. [c. 1908].

————. *A Tree Planted by the Rivers of Water.* Glasgow,
Scotland: Hay, Nisbet and Co. Ltd., c. 1909, 32 pp., hb.,
pb.

————. *The Preservation of Identity in the Resurrection.*
Glasgow, Scotland: Hay, Nisbet and Co. Ltd., c. 1909, 24
pp., hb., pb.

————. *Abraham's Life History: An Allegory.* Glasgow, Scotland: Hay, Nisbet and Co. Ltd., c. 1909, 42 pp., hb., pb.

Edgar, Minna. *Memoirs of Aunt Sarah.* Glasgow, Scotland,
n.d., 60 pp., hb., pb.

————. *Memoirs of Dr. John Edgar.* Glasgow, Scotland: Hay,
Nisbet and Co. Ltd., n.d., 60 pp., hb., pb.

Edgar, Morton. *Faith's Foundations, Also Waiting on God.*
Glasgow, Scotland: Hay, Nisbet and Co. Ltd., c. 1920,
66 pp., hb., pb.

————. *Prayer and the Bible.* Glasgow, Scotland: Hay, Nisbet
and Co. Ltd., c. 1920, 66 pp., hb., pb.

————. *The Great Pyramid and the Bible.* Glasgow, Scotland:
Hay, Nisbet and Co. Ltd., c. 1920, 50 pp., hb., pb.

————. *Mythology and the Bible.* Glasgow, Scotland: Hay,
Nisbet and Co. Ltd., n.d., 48 pp.

————. *1914 A.D., and the Great Pyramid.* Glasgow, Scotland:
Hay, Nisbet and Co. Ltd., n.d., 48 pp.

————. *Abraham's Life History—An Allegory Mythology and
the Bible Faith's Foundations.* Glasgow, Scotland: Hay,
Nisbet and Co. Ltd., n.d., 48 pp.

————. *The Restoration of Israel.* Glasgow, Scotland: Bone
& Hulley, c. 1920, 19 pp.

————. *The Pyramid Portrayal of Creation.* Glasgow, Scotland: Bone & Hulley, 1923, 64 pp.

————. *The Great Pyramid.* Glasgow, Scotland: Hay, Nisbet
and Co. Ltd., c. 1925, 8 pp.

————. *The Great Pyramid Witness and the Biblical Plan of
Salvation.* Glasgow, Scotland: Bone & Hulley, c. 1929,
19 pp., pb. (Swedish ed.: *Stora Pyramidens Vittnesbord och
Bibelns Fralningsplan*). Refutation of Rutherford's Nov. 15,
1928, *Watchtower.*

F. PAPERS AND MATERIAL RELATED TO THE
1917 ORGANIZATIONAL CRISIS
FOLLOWING PASTOR RUSSELL'S DEATH

Most of the papers concern problems related to the management of the Watchtower Society and the seventh volume of the
Studies in the Scriptures. This set of papers is an ongoing
set of charges, refutations, and countercharges, etc., from
1917 to 1919.

Pierson, A.N. Resolution of the Board of Directors of the Watchtower Bible and Tract Society. Brooklyn, N.Y., July 17, 1917. Signed by A.N. Pierson, W.E. Spill, W.E. Van Amburgh, J.A. Bohnet, A.H. MacMillan, Geo. H. Fisher. Later inserted on first page of *Harvest Siftings* (below).

Wright, J.D., A.I. Ritchie, I.F. Hoskins, and R.H. Hirsh. Circular. Brooklyn, N.Y., July 27, 1917, 4 pp. by J.D. Wright.

Rutherford, Joseph F. *Harvest Siftings.* Brooklyn, N.Y., August 1, 1917, 24 pp. by J.F. Rutherford.

Pierson, A.N., et al. "Open Letter to Boston Conventioners." Boston, Mass., Aug. 4, 1917, by A.N. Pierson, J.D. Wright, A.I. Ritchie, I.F. Hoskins, R.H. Hirsh. Reprinted on p. 23 of *Light After Darkness* (below).

Philadelphia Ecclesia. Letter to J.F. Rutherford, also "sent to each member of the Board." Philadelphia, Pa., Aug. 5, 1917. Published in *Light After Darkness* (below), p. 20.

Woodworth, C.J. *The Parable of the Penny.* Undated. Issued in the middle of Aug. 1917. (Tract), 6 pp.

McGee, Francis H. *An Open Letter to the Shareholders of the Society.* Freehold, N.J., Aug. 15, 1917. Published on pp. 15-19 in *Light After Darkness* (below), p. 10. Written to "Messrs. Pierson, Ritchie, Wright, Hoskins and Hirsh."

Fason, F.G. *Auditor's Letter to Shareholders.* 13 Cranberry St., Brooklyn, N.Y., Aug. 20, 1917. Published on p. 15 of *Light After Darkness* (below).

Cook, Frank F., and Charles R. Cox. Letter. Published *"In Behalf of the Truth and Christian Liberty."* Undated; later than Aug. 22, 1917, 2 pp.

Ritchie, A.I., J.D. Wright, I.F. Hoskins, and R.H. Hirsh. *Light After Darkness.* Sept. 1, 1917, 24 pp.

Rutherford, Joseph F. *Harvest Siftings, Part II.* Brooklyn, N.Y., Oct. 1, 1917, 8 pp.

————. "The Penny." *The Watchtower.* Brooklyn, N.Y., Oct. 1, 1917. Reprints, pp. 6149, 6150.

————. "Charges Answered." *The Watchtower.* Brooklyn, N.Y., Oct. 15, 1917. Reprints, p. 6154.

————. "The History and Operations of Our Society." *The Watchtower.* Brooklyn, N.Y., Nov. 1, 1917. Reprints, pp. 6161-6165.

Johnson, Paul S.L. *Harvest Siftings Reviewed.* Nov. 1, 1917, 20 pp. Later republished by the author in *Merariism* (1938), pp. 7-96. (See below, p. 264.)

Kuehn, E.O. "An Open Letter to the People of the Lord Throughout the World and a Petition to Bro. Rutherford and the Four Deposed Directors of the W.T.B. & T. Society." Undated; issued Nov. 1-15, 1917, 3 pp. Signed by 156 members of the Brooklyn, N.Y., Ecclesia. Sent to the public with *Facts for Shareholders* (below).

Ritchie, A.I., J.D. Wright, I.F. Hoskins, and R.H. Hirsh. *Facts for Shareholders.* Brooklyn, N.Y., Nov. 15, 1917, 16 pp.

Rutherford, J.F. "Some Reasons Why." *The Watchtower.* Brooklyn, N.Y., Nov. 15, 1917. Reprints, pp. 6166-6171.

————. "Questions Relating to Voting." *The Watchtower.* Brooklyn, N.Y., Nov. 15, 1917. Reprints, p. 6173.

————. "Privileges Now Great." *The Watchtower.* Brooklyn, N.Y., Dec. 1, 1917. Reprints, p. 6176.

————. "Important Notice." *The Watchtower.* Brooklyn, N.Y., Dec. 1, 1917. Reprints, p. 6181.

————. "Referendum Vote." *The Watchtower.* Brooklyn, N.Y., Dec. 15, 1917. Reprints, pp. 6184, 6185.

Pierson, Andrew. "Vice President's Statement." *The Watchtower.* Brooklyn, N.Y., Jan. 1, 1918. Reprints, pp. 6197, 6198.

Rutherford, J.F. "Annual Meeting of Shareholders." *The Watchtower.* Brooklyn, N.Y., Jan. 15, 1918. Reprints, pp. 6201-6204.

————. "Seeking to Cause Division" and "Our Reply." *The Watchtower.* Brooklyn, N.Y., Jan. 15, 1918. A published letter from "GMK" plus an official statement. Reprints, p. 6204.

————. "Two Classes in the Church." *The Watchtower*. Brooklyn, N.Y., Feb. 15, 1918. Reprints, pp. 6211-6215, 5 pp.

————. "Qualifications of Elders." *The Watchtower*. Brooklyn, N.Y., March 1, 1918. Reprints, p. 6220.

————. "A Warning to the Church." *The Watchtower*. Brooklyn, N.Y., March 1, 1918. Reprints, pp. 6222, 6223.

Wright, J.D., R.G. Jolly, P.S.L. Johnson, I.F. Hoskins, and R.H. Hirsh. "A Letter to International Bible Students." Brooklyn, N.Y., March 1, 1918, 4 pp.

Rutherford, J.F. "Sowers of Discord Among Brethren." *The Watchtower*. Brooklyn, N.Y., March 15, 1918. Reprints, pp. 6224, 6225. Subtitle of "The Great Shaking Now in Progress." March 15, 1918. Reprints, pp. 6223-6226.

————. "Resolution of Loyalty." *The Watchtower*. Brooklyn, N.Y., March 15, 1918. Reprints, pp. 6226, 6227, Philadelphia Ecclesia, Pa.

McGee, Francis H. "Not in Harmony." *The Watchtower*. Brooklyn, N.Y., March 15, 1918. Reprints, p. 6227.

The Bible Standard and Herald of Christ's Kingdom. Vol. 1, No. 1, Aug. 15, 1918, 16 pp. Only this sample issue. Limited distribution July 26, 1918. Members of the issuing committee were Wright, Jolly, Johnson, Hoskins, and Hirsh.

Resolution of the Philadelphia Church, Philadelphia, Pa. Aug. 18, 1918. Published in *Another Harvest Siftings Reviewed* (below), p. 11. Signed by the Philadelphia church (see below).

Johnson, Paul S.L. *Another Harvest Siftings Reviewed*. Philadelphia, Pa., Aug. 22, 1918, 12 pp. by Paul S.L. Johnson with endorsement of R.H. Hirsh and R.G. Jolly. Essentially republished by the author in *Gershonism* (1938), pp. 89-131. (See below, p. 264.)

Wright, J.D. *The Committee Bulletin*. No. 1, Aug. 1918, 8 pp. by J.D. Wright, I.F. Hoskins, P.L. Greiner, F.F. Cook, I.I. Margeson, F.H. McGee, H.C. Rockwell.

McGee, F.H. "A Brief Review of Brother Johnson's Charges." Undated; accompanied the Aug. 1918 *Committee Bulletin* (above), 4 pp.

Rutherford, J.F. "Interesting Questions." *The Watchtower*. Brooklyn, N.Y., Sept. 1, 1918. Reprints, p. 6322.

Wright, J.D., I.F. Hoskins, P.L. Greiner, F.F. Cook, I.I. Margeson, F.H. McGee, and H.C. Rockwell. *The Committee Bulletin*. No. 2, Sept. 1918, 8 pp.

McGee, Francis. "A Timely Letter of Importance to All the Brethren." Freehold, N.J., Sept. 10, 1918, 8 pp. Accompanied the Sept. 1918 *Committee Bulletin* (above).

Wright, J.D., I.F. Hoskins, P.L. Greiner, F.F. Cook, I.I. Margeson, F.H. McGee, and H.C. Rockwell. *The Committee Bulletin*. No. 3, Oct. 1918, 8 pp.

Wright, J.D. *Charter of Pastoral Bible Institute, Inc.* Signed by the Directors, Nov. 20, 1918; J.D. Wright, I.I. Margeson, P.L. Greiner, H.C. Rockwell, I.F. Hoskins, F.H. McGee, E.J. Pritchard. Published by Paul S.L. Johnson in *The Present Truth*, March 17, 1919, pp. 55, 56, and *Gershonism*, 1938, pp. 188-195. (See p. 264).

"Re-Election and Proxies." *The Watchtower*. Pittsburgh, Pa., Dec. 1, 1918. Reprints, p. 6366.

The Herald of Christ's Kingdom. No. 1, Dec. 1, 1918. The Pastoral Bible Institute. Editorial Committee of Five. First issue of regular monthly.

"Resolution." Dec. 1, 1918. The Philadelphia Ecclesia. Published by Paul S.L. Johnson in *The Present Truth*, Dec. 9, 1918 (below), p. 24.

Johnson, Paul S.L., ed. *The Present Truth and Herald of Christ's Epiphany*. Philadelphia, Pa., No. 1, Dec. 9, 1918, 24 pp.

Rutherford, J.F. "Varied Experiences a Blessing." *The Watchtower*. Pittsburgh, Pa., Dec. 15, 1918. Reprints, p. 6367, Dec. 15, 1918.

Johnson, Paul S.L., ed. *The Present Truth and Herald of Christ's Epiphany*. Philadelphia, Pa., No. 2, Dec. 24, 1918, 8 pp.

————. Letter to the Philadelphia Ecclesia. *The Present Truth*, March 17, 1919, pp. 59, 60, and *Gershonism*, 1938, pp. 215-217.

G. *PUBLICATIONS AND PAPERS BY ACTIVE WITNESSES*
PROTESTING PRACTICES AND DOCTRINES
OF THE WATCHTOWER SOCIETY

This is a group of papers by individuals protesting
various practices of the Society. Chris Christensen wrote
two "pronouncements" (1974-75) protesting the current harsh
disfellowshipping practices and calling for open meetings in
disfellowshipping cases (both allowing other Witnesses to be
present as well as changing the current system to be more like
the secular judicial system) among other organizational
changes. These papers were very well written and caused much
dissension in the Witness congregations in the United States,
Canada, Europe, and Australia. As a matter of fact, dozens
of disfellowshippings occurred as a result of these pronouncements.

Christensen, a highly respected younger Witness who had
made several contributions to the Society's publications before he wrote his tracts, was evidently disfellowshipped
because his research led him to question certain Watchtower
doctrines. He had been having a number of discussion meetings
with several Witnesses, and the Circuit Overseer and others
objected.

Christensen took the Society to court, claiming, among
other things, that the Society did not follow its own rules
of procedure and that he was unjustly disfellowshipped. The
courts, while acknowledging the validity of his claims, declined to rule in his favor, partly because they concluded
that the disfellowshipping occurred outside the court's juris-
diction.

The Olin Moyle letter is quite important in that it was
printed to protest certain allegedly immoral practices of the
Society, and it resulted in the Society's publishing several
articles against Moyle. Moyle brought suit for slander and
won $30,000 in damages (later on appeal reduced to $15,000;
see the section on Moyle).

The Walter Salter and Harvey Fink tracts are also important in that both Fink and Salter were well-known Witnesses,
and their leaving caused no little discussion. The booklets
by Weinz, Pawling, Gigliotti, etc., are primarily resignation
letters distributed to a large number of persons or printed
in semi-tract form and then distributed.

Alfandari, M. *We Bear Witness!* N.d., 2 pp., typed.

Amboy, Charles. *Response to the Pronouncements.* 1975, 13 pp.,
typed.

Bundy, Walter H., ed. *Studies in the Scriptures.* Los Angeles, Cal.: Concordant Publishing Concern, c, 1920, 160 pp., pb.

Christensen, Chris. *A Pronouncement: Concerning Justice for Jehovah's People.* 1974, 11 pp., typed and printed. Sent to thousands of Witnesses in the United States, Canada, Europe, and Australia.

————. *The Second Pronouncement Concerning Justice for Jehovah's People.* 1975, 20 pp., typed and printed. Sent to thousands of Witnesses in the United States, Canada, Europe, and Australia. This paper caused many persons to leave the Society and also caused many internal problems.

Fink, Harvey H. *An Open Letter to Jehovah's Witnesses.* 1940, 2 pp. Fink was a prominent Witness and a Zone servant. In this 2-page typeset tract, he briefly outlines why he left the Society.

Fleming, Harold. *Observation.* 1975, 4 pp. Attempts to resolve some of the problems raised by the pronouncements.

Gigliotti, Carman. *The Watchtower Society and Jehovah's Witnesses--The Big Lie.* N.d., 4 pp.

Gula, Michael. *Did the Watchtower Society Prophesy That Armageddon Would Occur in 1914?* N.d., c. 1978, 2 pp.

Inqui, Louis (Samuel). *Warning: Jehovah's Witnesses?* N.d., 1 p. The purpose of this letter, sent to thousands of Kingdom Halls in the United States, is not clear.

McGee, Ingram A. (pseudonym). "The Organizational Crisis in the Watchtower Society Following Russell's Death. Watchtower Presentations Corrected." March 1979, 38 pp., unpublished manuscript typed.

McKinney, Carlespie. *The Glorification of the Holy Ones--Its Timing & Nature.* 1975, 8 pp. A discussion which attempts to answer some of the questions raised in the Pronouncements.

Moyle, Olin R. *Information Vital to Jehovah's Witnesses.* 1940, 4 pp., typeset letter. See also publications and discussion under *The Bible Examiner,* in Section Four, below.

Pawling, James W. *Resignation Letter.* Jan. 1976, 18 pp., mimeo.

Questions. 1975, 20 pp. (by Randy Wysong et al.). Reprinted as *A Personal Letter from a Presiding Overseer, to All Jehovah's Witnesses in Good Standing.* 28 pp.; also as *Dear Brothers and Sisters,* 13 pp.

Reed, Joseph. *The Wild Beast.* 1977, 10 pp. A discussion of prophecy in the Book of Revelation and current Witness problems.

————. Untitled (about disfellowshipping). Rosedale, B.C., Canada, n.d. (c. 1977), 4 pp.

————. (about the situation in Malawi). N.d. (c. 1978), 3 pp.

————. *Daniel the Prophet, the "Two Witnesses" of Revelation and Jehovah's Witnesses on 1980, Where Do They All Fit In?* Rosedale, B.C., Canada: pub. by author, 1980, 8 pp.

————. *"The Great Tribulation" and "Kingdom Against Kingdom."* Part II. Rosedale, B.C., Canada: pub. by author, April 1981, 16 pp.

————. *Hello Richard* (about disfellowshipping). Rosedale, B.C., Canada, Oct. 1981, 8 pp.

————. *How Are the Dead to Be Raised Up? Yes, with What Kind of Body Are They Coming?* Rosedale, B.C., Canada: pub. by author, 1981, 12 pp.

Salter, Walter F. *Letter to J.F. Rutherford.* Toronto, Ont., Canada, 1937, 4 pp. (see also publications under Walter Salter directly below).

Weinz, John. *John Weinz to Jehovah's Witnesses.* 1941, 8 pp. Discusses why John Weinz left the Witnesses.

H. WALTER SALTER'S PUBLICATIONS

Walter Salter became a member of the International Bible Student Association in about 1913. In 1918, the President of the Society, J.F. Rutherford, asked him to take charge of the work in Canada as the Canadian general manager (today called the branch head or overseer). Disagreements occurred over continual changes in doctrine and the teachings of things such as "was it appropriate to 'lie' if the work of the

Watchtower Society could thereby be furthered," etc. In addition, Salter was somewhat independent; as his wife put it, "always he expressed his own convictions but not always were they letter perfect with the Watch Tower, though he was never really out of line with it." For a number of years, though, Salter was able to express his views without any problems.

In time, rumors circulated that Salter himself was somewhat autocratic and hard to get along with, and behaved "improperly" toward female Bethel members. These charges, however, were never proved. Finally, in the winter of 1935-36, unbeknown to Salter, Rutherford sent a number of persons to travel with him and "report on what he said in his lectures" (see letter from Mrs. Salter, Jan. 30, 1974; also *The Watchtower*, 1939, p. 120). On the basis of these reports, in May 1936, Rutherford "abolished the office of Canadian General Manager quite suddenly, which meant that Brother Salter was out of his position" (letter from Mrs. Salter). Rutherford then appointed Brother Chapman as head of the Canadian branch. For a period of nine months thereafter Salter continued as a "class worker" with the Toronto Bible class. But his continued study alienated him from the Witnesses and eventually, in February 1937, he wrote an article stating that Christ had not returned in 1874 as taught at that time by the Society.

At Rutherford's instigation, he was immediately disfellowshipped by the Toronto class (for, interestingly, holding beliefs that are accepted today by Witnesses). Most of his beliefs were summarized in his book, *Truth As I See It*.

Salter's leaving caused quite a commotion in the Watchtower Society, partly because he was well known and highly respected throughout Canada, and the Canadian branch was one of the largest branches of the Watchtower Society. It was evident that the situation affected Rutherford greatly, so much so that several *Watchtower* and *Golden Age* articles were written about the situation. These articles did not refer to Salter by name, but they unquestionably identified him. See *The Watchtower* (1937, pp. 159, 207; and 1939, pp. 117-126) and *Golden Age* (1937, pp. 498-507, 594-597) which directly or indirectly condemned Salter. After he left the Society, Salter spent the rest of his life doing Bible research and publishing various articles. Although he never formally started a group of his own, he did have many followers who agreed with his work and read his publications. He remained close to the Witness theology, but departed on some major points (he evidently embraced the theory of universal salvation). He died in April 1970 at the age of 86.

Book

Truth As I See It. Haliburton, Ont., Canada, 1959, 128 pp., pb.

Tracts

Letter to J.F. Rutherford. Toronto, Ont., Canada, April 1937, 4 pp. A typeset copy of a letter to Rutherford in which he explains why he left the Society. He discusses Rutherford's lavish spending on penthouses, his 16-cylinder automobiles, and his $75,000 mansion (a fortune in 1937). Salter also offers an excellent discussion of the failure of the prophecies for 1924 and 1925.

Our Lord's Return to Israel. Los Angeles, Cal.: Concordant Publishers Concern, n.d., 4 pp.

What Constitutes One a Christian? Haliburton, Ont., Canada, n.d., 1 p.

My Blind Servant. Haliburton, Ont., Canada, n.d., 1 p.

The Word of God. Haliburton, Ont., Canada, n.d., 1 p.

Christ the Seed of Promise. Haliburton, Ont., Canada, n.d., 1 p.

Christianity. Haliburton, Ont., Canada, n.d., 1 p.

Many False Christs; Matt. 24:11, 24. Haliburton, Ont., Canada, n.d., 1 p.

Israel, God's Chosen. Haliburton, Ont., Canada, n.d., 1 p.

The Kingdom of God Is at Hand--Jacob at War! Haliburton, Ont., Canada, n.d., 1 p.

Rightly Divide. Haliburton, Ont., Canada, n.d., 1 p.

Workers of Iniquity. Haliburton, Ont., Canada, n.d., 1 p.

Faith. Haliburton, Ont., Canada, n.d., 1 p.

Perilous Times Shall Come. Haliburton, Ont., Canada, n.d., 1 p.

G.J. Salter (Mrs. Walter Salter)

Booklet

A few Thoughts on the Scriptures. Haliburton, Ont., Canada, 1982, 51 pp.

Tracts

He As God Sitteth in the Temple of God. Haliburton, Ont., Canada, n.d., 1 p.

The Source and the Solution. Haliburton, Ont., Canada, n.d., 1 p.

Christ and Moses. Haliburton, Ont., Canada, n.d., 1 p.

Man's Destiny. Haliburton, Ont., Canada, n.d., 1 p.

Babylon. Haliburton, Ont., Canada, n.d., 1 p.

God. Haliburton, Ont., Canada, n.d., 1 p.

The Coming World Government. Haliburton, Ont., Canada, n.d., 1 p.

Hope and Expectation. Haliburton, Ont., Canada, n.d., 1 p.

Truth vs. Religion. Haliburton, Ont., Canada, n.d., 1 p.

Albert Rust

Booklet

The Human Paternity of Jesus Demonstrated. Haliburton, Ont., Canada: G.J. Salter Pub., 1983, 25 pp.

SECTION THREE

MATERIAL ABOUT JEHOVAH'S WITNESSES

This section is divided into books, dissertations, booklets, chapters of books, tracts, unpublished manuscripts,
court cases, and magazine articles. All of this material
specifically discusses Jehovah's Witnesses, although some works
may also discuss the offshoots of the Watch Tower, or related
groups. Aside from the literature issued by those organizations themselves, there is very little literature in print
about the offshoots of the Witnesses.

Although this section is not exhaustive, an effort has
been made to list all of the more important literature and
almost every work about the Witnesses from 1920 to 1983.

Most of the literature listed is in the compiler's personal
library. Some references, however, were obtained from secondary
sources, and for this reason the citations are sometimes incom-
plete. Much of this literature is rare and extremely difficult
to find. For example, fewer than one hundred copies of
Timothy White's classic, *A People for His Name*, were printed,
and this is one of the better scholarly books about the Witnesses. To obtain references for this bibliography, the
author visited dozens of large libraries throughout the United
States, Canada, and Europe and corresponded with over a score
of authors of books or articles about the Witnesses. He has
also consulted the Watchtower Society's libraries in Toronto,
Brooklyn, London, Paris, and the Netherlands.

A. *BOOKS ABOUT JEHOVAH'S WITNESSES*

Of the following books, almost all are either written by
former Witnesses or non-Witnesses, and the tone is basically
anti-Watchtower Society. Most of them concentrate on Witness
doctrine, and there is a great deal of repetition and over-
lapping in them. Only nine were authored by Witnesses who

were still active in the movement, the volumes by Anonymous,
Buckley, White, Penton, Macmillan, Cole, Zucher, and Blackwell,
and, therefore, these books are biased in favor of the Society.
Of these, all of the authors except Macmillan (who died shortly after he completed his book), Buckley, and Cole (actually
Cole's book was a joint effort with the Society, the Society
being the final authority) experienced a falling out with the
Watchtower Society. As discussed the Society manifests very
little tolerance toward those who write books, even if they
are extremely favorable to the Witness point of view and doctrinally correct.

The first Cole book, *Jehovah's Witnesses: The New World
Society*, was written as a pro-Society book to be placed in
libraries and sold to the public. The Society openly advertised and sold this book. Cole's second book was written on
his own, and even though it is also pro-Society, it was not
nearly as successful as the first, primarily because the
Society did not "authorize" or publicize it. The second book
created some difficulties for Cole with the Society, but he
is still an active Witness--he and Buckley are the only authors
who still are. In addition, Cole wrote a number of articles
in magazines such as *Nation*, *Color*, etc., which are highly pro-
Society and, interestingly, pro-education. Cole has taken
great pains in both his book *Triumphant Kingdom* and his other
writings to picture Witnesses as intelligent, informed, aware
persons, often well-educated, some who hold high positions in
secular society.

In this section are listed almost all the books about
Jehovah's Witnesses from their founding in 1879 to date.
Also included are most of the foreign-language books about
the Witnesses, including those published in Turkish, Russian,
Spanish, French, German, Swedish, and other languages. A
book is defined here as printed matter that is perfect bound
(glued, e.g., the phone book) or sewn (e.g., quality books)
and that generally has more than 90 pages. Both hardbound
and paperback books are included. Except those in other alpha-
bets, such as Russian and Chinese, the titles given in this
section are exactly as listed on the book cover. Other titles
were translated by the Library of Congress or the author.
Also, titles of most of the foreign-language books were translated into English, with the translated title given after the
publication data.

Some items are annotated, but in most cases the title is
indicative of the tone and scope of the work. About 80% of
the works are primarily theological, and although all of the
English-language books except those written by Witnesses mentioned above are essentially critical of the Watchtower Society,

the works by Beckford, Czatt, Felderer, Manwaring, and Rogerson are somewhat neutral, but more sociological and historical
than theological.
The theological works are often difficult for the layman
to follow. There are, however, many excellent academic studies,
mostly by sociologists. Recommended are the works by Manwaring,
Pike, Stevens, Rogerson, Harrison, Beckford, Stevenson, White,
and the 1945 classic by Stroup, which is still in print. Also
useful, especially for theological background, are the works
of Gruss and Sadlack and the classics by Schnell.
Several of the books listed here are excellent historical
studies of the Watchtower Society, but copies of many, the
works of White, for example, are rare. The most useful im-
partial works dealing with all aspects of the Witnesses are
by Stevens, Stevenson, Stroup, White, and Sterling. A pro-
Witness foreign-language work is that of Zucher, which discusses the Witnesses in World War II German concentration
camps; this work is available in German and French.

Algermissan, Konrad. *Die International Vereinigung Ernster
Bibleforscher.* Hanover: J. Giesel, 1928, 78 pp. (The
International Union of Serious Bible Researchers.)

Amaya, Ismael. *Los Falsos Profetas de Jehová: La Verdad Acerca
de los Testigos de Jehová.* Buenos Aires, Argentina: Metho-
press, 1964, 150 pp.

Anonymous. *1,000 Years Well Spent: 1942-1946.* 1947, 112 pp.,
pb. Jehovah's Witnesses in prison in Chillicothe, Ohio;
written by a Witness from a Witness viewpoint.

Arrinda, Donato, et al. *Testigos de Jehová.* Berriz, Vizcaya:
pub. by author, 1977, 157 pp. (Jehovah's Witnesses.)

Arzamazov, Vasilli Petrovich. *The True Face of Jehovah's
Witnesses.* Irkutsk: Siberian Publishing House, 1964, 160
pp. (Russian.)

Axup, Edward J. *The Jehovah's Witnesses Unmasked.* New York:
Greenwich Book Publishers, 1959, 77 pp., hb.

Barrett, Arthur, and Duane Magnani. *From Kingdom Hall to Kingdom Come.* Clayton, Cal.: Witness Inc., 1982, 79 pp., pb.

Barnett, Maurice. *Jehovah's Witnesses: History, Organization,
Doctrines and Deity of Christ.* Vol. I. Cullman, Ala.:
Printing Service, n.d. (c. 1975), 96 pp., pb.

——————. *Jehovah's Witnesses: Nature of Man, Death, Resurrection, Dual Classes, Eternal Punishment.* Vol. II. Cullman, Ala.: Printing Service, n.d'. (c. 1975), 91 pp., pb.

Barney, Dan. See Quidam, Roger

Barrett, Arthur, and Duane Magnani. *From Kingdom Hall to Kingdom Come.* Clayton, Cal.: Witness Inc., 1982, 79 pp., pb.

Bartoshevich, Eduard Mikhailovich. *In the Name of Jehovah God.* Moscow: State Publishing House of Political Literature, 1960, 158 pp. (Russian.)

——————. *Jehovah's Witnesses.* Moscow: Political Publishing House (Library of Contemporary Religions), 1969, 216 pp. (Russian.)

Beckford, James A. *The Trumpet of Prophecy.* Oxford, England: Basil H. Blackwell, 1975, 244 pp., hb.; New York: Halsted Press, 1975.

Beijer, Erik. *Falska Profeter: Ett ord om "Jehovas Vittnen."* Stockholm, Sweden: Bolm and Soner Baktryckeri AB, 1948, 84 pp. Reprinted by Svenska Kyrkans Diakonistyrelses Bokforlag of Stockholm, Sweden, 1955, 95 pp., pb. (False Prophets: A Word on "Jehovah's Witnesses.")

Bjornstad, James. *Counterfeits at Your Door.* Glendale, Cal.: A Division of G/L Publications, 1979, 160 pp. Discusses both Mormons and Jehovah's Witnesses; some good material but many inadequacies; basically discusses theology from an evangelical position.

Blackwell, Victor V. *O'er the Ramparts THEY Watched.* New York: Carlton Press, 1976, 246 pp., hb.

Bond, M.R. *Thy Word Is Truth.* Abington, Mass., 1905, 114 pp.

Bowser, Arthur. *What Every Jehovah's Witness Should Know.* Denver, Col.: B/P Publications, 1975, 65 pp., pb.

Bradley, M.C., ed. *Criticisms of Pastor Russell and the International Bible Students Association.* Elmhurst, Ill.: Elmhurst Press, Inc., 1914, 82 pp., pb. Written in support of Russell.

Bregning, Poul. *Jehovas Vidner Under Anklage.* Kobenhaven: Hans Reitzel, 1966, 248 pp. (Jehovah's Witnesses Under Pressure.)

Briem, Efraim. *Jehovas Vittnen.* Stockholm, Sweden: Bokforlaget Natur Och Kultur, 1944; 2nd ed. 1951, 79 pp., pb. (Jehovah's Witnesses.)

Brown, Jim. *Jesus Loves the Jehovah's Witness.* Scottsdale, Ariz.: Christian Communications, Inc., 1976, 86 pp., pb.

Buckley, J.A. *Second Century Orthodoxy.* Cornwall, Great Britain: pub. by author, 1978, 115 pp., hb. Buckley is a Witness.

Busch, Dr. Johannes. *Das Sektenwesen unter besonderer Beruchsichtigung der Ernsten Bibelforscher.* Hildesheim: Verlag Fr. Borgmeyer, 1929, 359 pp. (The Nature of Religious Sects with Special Consideration to the Jehovah's Witnesses.)

Cetnar, William, and Joan Cetnar. *Questions for Jehovah's Witnesses.* Phillipsburg, N.J.: Presbyterian and Reformed Pub. Co., 1983, 72 pp.

Cline, Ted. *Questions for Jehovah's Witnesses and Select Sermon Outlines.* Phoenix, Ariz.: Gospel Lighthouse Publ. Co., 1975, 74 pp., pb.

Coffey, John Francis. *The Gospel According to Jehovah's Witnesses.* Melbourne, Australia: The Polding Press, 1979, 173 pp., pb.

Cole, Marley. *Jehovah's Witnesses: The New World Society.* New York: Vantage Press, 1955, 229 pp., hb.

————. *Triumphant Kingdom.* New York: Criterion Books, 1957, 256 pp., hb.

Countess, Robert H. *The Jehovah's Witnesses New Testament.* Phillipsburg, N.J.: Presbyterian and Reformed Co., 1982, 136 pp.

Crocetti, Giuseppe. *I Testimoni de Geova un Dialogo e un Confronto Partendo dalla Biblia.* Bologna, Italy: EDB Publishers, 1978, 239 pp. (The Jehovah's Witnesses: A Dialogue of a Confrontation Based on the Bible.)

Czatt, Milton. *The International Bible Students: Jehovah's Witnesses.* Scottsdale, Pa.: Mennonite Press, 1933, 45 pp., No. 4, Yale Studies in Religion.

D'Amigo, G. *Dio e Geova: Confronto con i Testimoni de Geova.*
Revised by Giuseppe Sacino. Napoli, Italy. Edition
Dehoniane, 1975, 107 pp. (God and Jehovah: Confrontation
with the Jehovah's Witnesses.)

D'Angelo, Louise. *The Catholic Answer to the Jehovah's Witnesses: A Challenge Accepted.* Meriden, Conn.: Maryheart
Catholic Information Center, 1981, 177 pp.

Danyans, Eugenio. *Proceso a la "Biblia" de los Testigos de
Jehova.* Tarrasa, Spain: CLIE, 1971, 256 pp., pb. (The
Process of the Bible by Jehovah's Witnesses.)

Deberty, Leon. *Kitawala.* Elisabethville, Belgian Congo:
Editions Essor du Congo, 1953, 277 pp. A historical novel
about the Kitawala in Central Africa. The Kitawala is an
offshoot of the Watchtower and is indirectly connected with
it; also discusses the Watchtower itself. (French.)

Dencher, Ted. *The Watchtower Heresy versus the Bible.* Chicago: Moody Bible Institute, 1961, 160 pp., hb.

————. *Why I Left Jehovah's Witnesses.* Great Britain: C.
Tinling and Co., 1966, 222 pp., pb.; revised ed., Fort
Washington, Pa.: Christian Literature Crusade, 1980, 238
pp.

Doyon, Josy. *Hirten ohne Erbarmen (10 Jahre Irrweg mit den
"Zeugen Jehovas" Sonderausg.)* Zurich, Stuttgart, West
Germany: Zwingli Verlag, 332 pp. (Shepherds Without Mercy:
10 Years on the Wrong Path with Jehovah's Witnesses.)

————. *Ich War eine Zeugin Jehovas: Bericht uber einen
Irrweg.* 2nd ed. Hamburg, Germany: Siebenstern Teschenbuch
Verlag, 1975, 155 pp., pb. (I Was a Jehovah's Witness:
Account About a Wrong Way.) (Revised ed. of *Hirten ohne
Erbarmen,* 1966.)

Duggar, Gordon. *Jehovah's Witnesses--Not Just Another Denomination.* New York: Exposition, 1982, 124 pp.

Duncan, Homer. *Heart to Heart Talks with Jehovah's Witnesses.*
Lubbock, Texas: Missionary Crusader, 1972, 156 pp., pb.
(Spanish ed., *Los Testigos de Jehova ante la Biblia,* same
publisher, 1975, 118 pp., pb.)

Eaton, E.L. *The Millennial Dawn Heresy.* Cincinnati, Ohio:
Jennings and Graham, 1910, 153 pp. Reprint, Aberdeen,
Scotland: Impulse Publ., 1972, 119 pp., hb.

Engelland, Hans. *Die Zeugen Jehovas/Die Nevapostalischen.*
2nd expanded ed. Hamburg, Germany: Frieda Wiegand, 1969,
64 pp., pb. (The Jehovah's Witnesses/The New Apostles.)
The first 35 pages are about Jehovah's Witnesses. Discusses general beliefs and history.

Farr, Alfred Derek. *God, Blood and Society.* Aberdeen, Scotland: Impulse Publ., 1972, 119 pp., hb.

Felderer, Ditlieb. *The History of Jehovah's Witnesses.* Taby,
Sweden: pub. by author, 1971, 269 pp., pb.

Felipe del Rey, Pedro de. ¡*El reino de Dios empezo en 1914!*
(y el inminente fin del mundo en Armagedon) ¿*realidad o*
fraude? ¿*politica o religion?* Madrid: Felipe del Rey Pub.,
1974, 493 pp. (The Kingdom of God Began in 1914 (and the
Imminent End of the World in Armageddon) Reality or Fraud?
Politics or Religion?)

Fetz, August. *Weltvernichtung durch Bibelforscher und Juden.*
Munich: Deutscher Volksverlag, 1925, 164 pp. (World
Destruction through Bible Researchers [Jehovah's Witnesses]
and Jews.)

Forrest, James Edward. *Errors of Russellism: A Brief Examina-*
tion of the Teachings of Pastor Russell as Set Forth in His
"Studies of the Scriptures." Anderson, Ind., 1915, 277 pp.

Freyenwald, Jonak Von. *Die Zeugen Jehovas: Pioniere für*
ein Jüdisches Weltreich; die Politischen Ziele der Inter-
nationalen Vereinigung Ernster Bibelforscher. Berlin,
Germany, 1936, 104 pp., pb. (The Jehovah's Witnesses:
Pioneers for the Jewish World Kingdom: The Political Goals
of the International Union of Jehovah's Witnesses.)

Garcia, José Luis. *Los Testigos de Jehova: A la Luz de la*
Biblia. Tarrasa, Spain: Talleres Graficos de CLIE, 1976,
358 pp., pb. (Jehovah's Witnesses in the Light of the
Bible.)

Gazhos, V.F. *Peculiarities of the Ideology of Jehovahism*
and the Religious Consciousness of Sectarians. In materials
of the MSSR (Moldavian Soviet Socialist Republic). Under
the editorship of candidate of philosophical science V.N.
Yermuratsky. Kishinev, 1969, 92 pp. (Russian.)

Gebhard, Manfred. *Die Zeugen Jehovas: Eine Dokumentation*
über die Wachtturmgesellschaft. Schwerte, Ruhr (German

Democratic Republic): Verlag Hubert Freistühler, 1971,
317 pp., hb. (Jehovah's Witnesses: A Documentation about
the Watchtower Society.)

Gerard, Jacques E. *Les Fondements Syncretiques du Kitawala.*
Bruxelles, Belgium: Centre de Recherche et d'Information
Socio-Politiques C.R.I.S.P. (rue du Congress 35). Bruxelles,
Belgium: Le Livre Africain, 1969, 120 pp., pb. About the
Watchtower and its offshoots in Africa.

Gerasimenko, Vladimir Kuzmich, et al. *From an Alien Voice.*
Tavriia, USSR: Simferopol Pub. House, 1975, 104 pp.
(Russian.)

Geyraud, Pierre. *Les Petites Eglises de Paris.* Paris: Emile-
Paul Frères, 1937. (The Small Religions of Paris.)

Giron, José. *Los Testigos de Jehová y Sus Doctrinas.* Miami,
Fla.: Editorial Vida, 1954. 5th ed. 1972, 128 pp., pb.
(The Jehovah's Witnesses and Their Doctrines.)

Graebner, Theodore. *War in the Light of Prophecy, "Was It
Foretold?"* St. Louis, Mo., Concordia Pub. House, 1941, 143 pp.

Gregori, Aldo. *I Testimoni di Geova Dottrina ed Errori.*
Pesaro, Italy: STEP, 1967, 96 pp. (The Jehovah's Witnesses' Doctrine and Errors.)

Greschat, Hans-Jurgen. *Kitawala: Ursprung, Ausbreitung und
Religion der Watchtower-Bewegung in Zentralafrica.* Marburg,
Germany: Elwert, 1967, 126 pp., pb. (Jehovah's Witnesses:
Origin, Expansion, and Religion of the Watchtower Movement
in Central Africa.)

Grigg, David H. *Do Jehovah's Witnesses and the Bible Agree?*
New York: Vantage Press, 1958, 250 pp., hb.

Gruss, Edmond Charles. *Apostles of Denial: An Examination
and Exposé of the History, Doctrines and Claims of the
Jehovah's Witnesses.* Nutley, N.J.: Presbyterian and Reformed Publ. Co., 1970, 324 pp., hb., pb.

————. *The Jehovah's Witnesses and Prophetic Speculation.*
Nutley, N.J.: Presbyterian and Reformed Publ. Co., 1972,
131 pp., pb., 2nd ed. 1975.

————. *We Left Jehovah's Witnesses--A Non-Prophet Organization.* Nutley, N.J.: Presbyterian and Reformed Publ. Co.,

1974, 169 pp., pb. (reprinted by Baker Book House of Grand
Rapids, Mich., 1975).

Gustafsson, Axel. *Vittnar Jehovas Vittnen falskt? En Strids-
skrift.* Stockholm: Gummesson, 1955, 83 pp. (Are Jehovah's
Witnesses False Witnesses?)

Harrison, Barbara Grizzuti. *Visions of Glory: A History and
a Memory of Jehovah's Witnesses.* New York: Simon and
Schuster, 1978, 413 pp., hb., pb.

Hebert, Gerard, S.J. *Les Témoins de Jehovah.* Montreal: Les
Editions Bellarmin, 1960, 341 pp. (The Jehovah's Witnesses.)

Herrmann, Friedrich Wilhelm. *Bibelforscher oder Bibelfascher?*
Kassell: J.G. Oncken, 1925, 114 pp. (Bible Researchers or
Bible Falsifiers?)

Hewat, Elizabeth Glendinning Kirkwood. *Meeting Jehovah's Witnesses: A Study of Jehovah's Witnesses in Scotland and Elsewhere.* Edinburgh, Scotland: Saint Andrew Press, 1967, 93 pp.,
pb.

Hewitt, Joe. *I Was Raised a Jehovah's Witness.* Denver, Colo.:
Accent Books, 1979, 191 pp., pb.

Hoekema, Anthony. *Jehovah's Witnesses.* Grand Rapids, Mich.:
W.B. Eerdmans Publ. Co., 1972, 140 pp., pb.

Hudson, John Allen. *Russell-White Debate.* See Rowe, F.L.

Iarotski, Petro Lavrentiiovych. *The Anticommunism of the
Jehovah's Witnesses: Social and Political Doctrine.* Kiev,
USSR: Dumka Pub. House and the Academy of Sciences of the
Ukrainian S.S.R., 1976, 214 pp. (Ukrainian.)

————. *The Crisis of the Jehovah's Witnesses: A Critical
Analysis of the Ideology and Evolution of a Commonplace
Religious Confession.* Kiev, USSR: Dumka Pub. House and the
Academy of Sciences of the Ukrainian S.S.R., 1979, 301 pp.
(Ukrainian.)

————. *The Evolution of the Contemporary Jehovah's Witnesses.*
Kiev, USSR: Izdatelstvo Politicheskoi Literatury Ukrainy,
1981, 143 pp. (Ukrainian.)

Jabrah, Ibrahim. *The Truth About the Jehovah's Witnesses: An
Extension of the Jewish People.* Cairo, Egypt: Almahabbah
Library, 1976, 68 pp. (Arabic.)

Jaron, Pierre. *Les Témoins de Jehovah devant la Bible*. Dammarieles-Lys: France Editions S.D.T. (Signe des temps), 1969, 64 pp. (Jehovah's Witnesses Compared to the Bible.)

Jasmin, Damien. *Les Témoins de Jehovah*. Montreal, Canada: Les Editions Lumen, 1947, 189 pp. (The Jehovah's Witnesses.) Written from a Catholic viewpoint.

Kaufmann, Robert. *Millenarisme et Acculturation*. Bruxelles, Belgium: l'Université Libre de Bruxelles, 1964, 134 pp.

Kirban, Salem. *Jehovah's Witnesses: Doctrines of Devils*. No. 3. Chicago: Moody Press, 1972, 78 pp., pb.

Knaut, Horst. *Propheten der Angst: Berichte zu Psychopathology. Trends d. Gegenwart: ein Krit. Analyse*. Kempfenhausen Schultz Pub., 1975, 231 pp. (Prophets of Fear: Reports on Present Trends in Psychopathology: A Critical Analysis.)

Konik, Vasilii Vasilevich. *The "Truths" of the Jehovah's Witnesses*. Moscow: Politizdat Pub. House, 1978, 111 pp. (Russian.)

Lambert, O.C. *Russellism Unveiled*. Port Arthur, Texas: O.C. Lambert & Sons, 1940; reprinted by Firm Foundations Publ. House, Austin, Texas, n.d., 111 pp., pb.

Lanzoni, D. Giuseppe. *I Testimoni di Geova*. Faenza, Italy: Società Tipografica Taentina, Vol. I, 1952, 125 pp.; Vol. II, 1953, 143 pp.; Vol. III, 1953, 194 pp., pb. (The Jehovah's Witnesses.)

Lavaud, M. Benoit. *Sectes Modernes et Foi Catholique*. Paris: Aubier, 1954, pp. 15-198. (Modern Sects and Catholic Faith.)

Leech, Ken. *True Witness/The Amazing Story of British Detective Leech, Searching for the Truth, Escapes from the Clutches of "False Witness" into Glorious Liberty of Gospel*. Winona Lake, Ind.: Christian Witness Crusades, c. 1979, 152 pp.

Levnin, Viktor Nikolaevich. *The Brothers of the Brooklyn Apostles (Concerning the Jehovah's Witnesses and Their Activity in the Stavropol Region)*. Stavropol: Knizhno Izdatelstvo Pub. House, 1978, 87 pp. (Ukrainian.)

Long, Norman. *Social Change and the Individual*. Manchester, England: Manchester University Press, 1968, 262 pp.

Loofs, Friedrich. *Die "Internationale Vereinigung Ernster Bibelforscher."* Leipzig, Germany: J.C. Hinrichs'sche Buchhandlung, 1921, 60 pp. (The International Union of Serious Bible Researchers.)

Macmillan, A.H. *Faith on the March.* Englewood Cliffs, N.J.: Prentice-Hall, Inc., 1957, 243 pp., hb.

Magnani, Duane. *The Collector's Handbook of Watchtower Publications.* Clayton, Cal.: Jehovah's Witnesses Books, 1980, 165 pp., pb.

————. *Watchtowergate.* Clayton, Cal.: Jehovah's Witnesses Books, 1980, 345 pp., pb.

————. *Who Is the Faithful and Wise Servant?* Clayton, Cal.: Jehovah's Witnesses Books, 1981, 79 pp.

————, and Arthur Barrett. *Eyes of Understanding.* Clayton, Cal.: Witness Inc., 1980, 78 pp.; revised ed., 1981, 56 pp.

————. *Dialogue with Jehovah's Witnesses.* Clayton, Cal.: Witness Inc., 1983, 563 pp. (2 vols.).

Malik, Joseph, and Elizabeth Taze Malik. *Beyond the Watchtower.* New York: Vantage Press, 1982, 295 pp.

Mann, W.E. *Sect, Cult and Church in Alberta.* Toronto: University of Toronto Press, 1955.

Manwaring, David Roger. *Render unto Caesar: The Flag-Salute Controversy.* Chicago: The University of Chicago Press, 1962, 320 pp., hb.

Margot, Jean Claude. *Les Témoins de Jehovah.* Paris: Editions Delachaus et Niestle. (The Jehovah's Witnesses.)

Martin, Walter, and Norman Klann. *Jehovah of the Watchtower.* Grand Rapids, Mich.: Zondervan Publishing House, 1953, 201 pp., hb. (Revised and updated by Moody Press of Chicago, 1974, 221 pp., pb.) Several editions of this book were published; Italian edition, *Il Geova della Torre di Guardia*, Napoli, Italy: Edizione Centro Biblico, 1967, 250 pp.

Mason, Doug. *Witnessing to the Witnesses.* Australia: Pub. by author. (Pt. I), 63 pp., n.d. (c. 1974); *And All That* (Pt. II), 129 pp., n.d., *The Trinity* (Pt. III), 112 pp., n.d., pb.

McKinney, George D. *The Theology of the Jehovah's Witnesses.* Grand Rapids, Mich.: Zondervan Publishing House, 1962, 130 pp., hb.

————. *The Jehovah's Witnesses.* San Diego, Cal.: Production House, 1975.

Meffert, Franz. *Bibelforscher und Bibelforschung uber das Weltende.* 2nd ed. Freiburg: Caritasverlag, 1925, 149 pp. (The Jehovah's Witnesses on the End of the World.)

Melinder, J.O. *I Brytningstider, En Studie i Modern kattarforfoljelsa.* Harnosand: Berea-Forlaget, 1925, 144 pp. (In Difficult Times: A Study of Modern Heretics.)

Morey, Robert A. *How to Answer a Jehovah's Witness.* Minneapolis, Minn.: Bethany Fellowship, 1980, 109 pp.

Moskalenko, Aleksei Trofimovich. *Contemporary Jehovah's Witnesses.* Novosibirsk, USSR: "Science." Siberian Section, 1971, 227 pp. (Russian.)

Muller, Albert. *Meet Jehovah's Witnesses: Their Confusion, Doubts, and Contradictions.* Pulaski, Wisc.: Franciscan Publ., 1964, 115 pp., pb.

Munters, Quirinus J. *Rekrutering als raeping: Sociologische Overwegingen met Betrekking tot het Missionaire Handelen.* Meppel, Holland: J.A. Boom en Zoon, 1970, 216 pp., pb. (Recruiting as a Calling.)

Nelson, Wilton M. *Los Testigos de Jehová: Quienes son y lo que Creen.* Mexico: Casa Bavtista de Publicaciones, 1949. Revised ed., 1976, 130 pp., pb. (The Jehovah's Witnesses: Who They Are, and What They Believe.)

Nova, Alex. *Who's That Knocking at My Door.* Poughkeepsie, N.Y.: pub. by author, 1978, 108 pp., pb.

Nyman, Aaron. *Astounding Errors: The Prophetic Message of the Seventh-Day Adventists and the Chronology of Pastor C.T. Russell in the Light of History and Bible Knowledge.* Chicago: pub. by author, c. 1914, 419 pp. (especially pp. 3, 297-343.)

Oakley, Debbie, and Helen Ortega. *Mom and Me: Twenty Years Jehovah's Witnesses.* New York: Vantage Press, 1978, 82 pp., hb.

Paffrath, Tharsicius. *Die Sekte der Ernsten Bibelforscher.* Paderborn: Bonifacius-Druckerei, 1925, 176 pp. (The Sect of the Jehovah's Witnesses.)

Palotay, Sándor. *Tévedések útján: a Jehova Tanúi.* Budapest: Magyarországi Szabadegyházak Tanócsa (The Council of the Free Church of Hungary), 1977, 63 pp. (On the Road of Mistakes: Jehovah's Witnesses.)

Papa, Gunther. *Die Wahrheit uber Jehovas Zeugen: Problematik Dokumentation.* Rottweil, Germany: Neckar Verlag Aktuelle Texte, 1970, 190 pp., pb. (The Truth About Jehovah's Witnesses: Problem Documentation.)

————. *Ich War Zeuge Jehovas.* Aschaffenburg, West Germany: Paul Pattloch Verlag, 1961; 5th ed. 1975, 162 pp., pb. (I Was a Jehovah's Witness.)

Passantino, Robert, and Gretchen Passantino. *Answers to the Cultist at Your Door.* Eugene, Ore.: Harvest House Publishers, 1981, 200 pp.

Penton, M. James. *Jehovah's Witnesses in Canada.* Toronto, Canada: Macmillan, 1976, 388 pp., hb.

Pike, Royston. *Jehovah's Witnesses: Who They Are, What They Teach, What They Do.* New York: Philosophical Library; London: Watts Co., 1954, 140 pp., hb.

Platt, F.G. *A Chapter in My Life.* London, England: pub. by author, n.d., 75 pp., pb.

Potashov, Konstantin Ivanovich. *Why I Broke with the Jehovah's Witnesses̄.* Uzhgorod, USSR: Karpati Pub. House, 1978, 63 pp. (Ukrainian.)

Quidam, Roger D. (pseud. for Dan Barney). *The Doctrine of Jehovah's Witnesses: A Criticism.* New York: Philosophical Library, 1959, 117 pp., hb. Pp. 1-110 are poetry, pp. 110-117 are prose; this book requires a good knowledge of philosophy, but it is well worth the effort.

Robertson, William. *The I.B.S.A. or Russellites in Prophecy.* Edinburgh, Scotland: Bible Student Publishing Co., c. 1922, 128 pp.; 1923 ed., 192 pp.

Robinson, J.L. *The Truth About Jehovah's Witnesses.* New York: Carlton Press, 1969, 45 pp., hb. Very poor. The author has almost no knowledge of the Witnesses.

Rogerson, Alan Thomas. *Millions Now Living Will Never Die*. London, England: Constable and Co., 1969, 216 pp., hb. This is one of the best books ever written on the Witnesses. Rogerson (Ph.D., Oxford) was raised a Witness, and has done a great deal of research.

Roundhill, Jack. *Meeting Jehovah's Witnesses*. Guildford, London: Lutterworth Educational, 1973, 40 pp., pb.

Rowe, F.L., ed. *Russell-White Debate*. Cincinnati, Ohio: F.L. Rowe, 1908, 196 pp., hb. (reprinted by Campbell's Bookshelf of Magadore, Ohio, c. 1975). The transcript of a debate between Russell and White, a Church of Christ minister, on such topics as Hellfire, the Trinity, etc.

Sabiers, Karl. *Where Are the Dead?* Los Angeles, Cal.: Christian Pocket Books, 1959, 190 pp., pb. (Swedish ed.: *Var ar de doda?* Orebro, Sweden, 1970.) A book that primarily refutes the Witnesses' view of Hell. He quotes Rutherford a great deal.

Sadlack, Emil, and Otto Sadlack. *The Desolations of the Sanctuary*. St. Louis, Mo.: Pastoral Bible Institute, 1930 (1st English ed.--original edition in German), 314 pp., hb., pb.

Sagau, Antonio M. *Testigos de Quien?* Barcelona, Spain: Publicaciones Portavoz Evangelico, 1963. 4th ed. 1974, 108 pp., pb. (Witnesses of Whom?)

Saleeby, Abdallah Assed. *Truth Triumphant: or Falsehood Stripped of Its Mask*. Norfolk, Va.: pub. by author, 1919, 145 pp., hb.

Santos, José Estêvão dos. *A Verdada Sobre las Testemunhas de Jeova*. N.p.: pub. by author, 1975, 196 pp. (The Truth About Jehovah's Witnesses.)

Scheurlen, Paul. *Die Sekten der Gegenwart und neuere Weltanschauungsgebilde*. Stuttgart: Quell-Verlag der Evant. Gesellschaft, 4 Auflage, 1930, 440 pp. (The Sects of the Present and New World.)

Schlegel, Fritz. *Die Wahrheit über die Ernsten Bibelforscher*. Vol. I. Eckmann in Kehl a. Rh., 1922, 252 pp. (The Truth About the Serious Bible Researchers.)

————. *Die Teufelsmaske der Ernsten Bibelforscher, Propheten und Pioniere gewaltsamen Umsturzes.* Vol. II. Neckargemund, 1925, 217 pp. (The Devil's Mask of the Serious Bible Researcher: Prophets and Pioneer of the Violent Overthrow of the World.)

Schnell, William. *Thirty Years a Watchtower Slave.* Grand Rapids, Mich.: Baker Book House, 1956, 207 pp., hb., pb. (2nd ed. reprinted in 1973, pb.)

————. *Jehovah's Witnesses Errors Exposed.* Grand Rapids, Mich.: Baker Book House, 1959 (reprinted in 1976), pb.

————. *Into the Light of Christianity.* Grand Rapids, Mich.: Baker Book House, 1959, 211 pp., hb.

————. *Christians Awake!* Grand Rapids, Mich.: Baker Book House, 1969, 157 pp., pb.

————. *How to Witness to Jehovah's Witnesses.* Grand Rapids, Mich.: Baker Book House, 1975, reprint of *Christians Awake!*, 157 pp., pb.

Scott, Frank Earl. *Armageddon and You.* Portland, Ore.: Metropolitan Press, 1968, 184 pp., hb., pb.

————. *Revelation of Mysteries.* Portland, Ore.: Metropolitan Press, 1972, 124 pp., pb.

Segaud, Evelyne. *Confessions d'un ancien témoin de Jéhovah.* Paris: Pensée Universelle, 1976, 215 pp. (The Confessions of a Former Jehovah's Witness.)

Shields, T.T. *Russellism or Rutherfordism: The Teachings of the International Bible Students, Alias Jehovah's Witnesses, in the Light of the Holy Scriptures.* Grand Rapids, Mich.: Zondervan Publ. House, 1934, 106 pp. (2nd ed. 1942, 88 pp., pb.)

Skjerpe, Olav. *Jehovas Vitner--Hven laever de?* Oslo, Norway: Stavanger Nomi Forlag, 1970, 134 pp. (God's Witnesses: Who Are They?) Swedish ed., *Jehovas Vitten och vad de lar.* Stockholm, Sweden: Aktiebolaget Tryckmans, 1971, 125 pp., pb. (Jehovah's Witnesses and What They Teach.)

Spadafera, Francesco. *Testimoni de Geova, Avventisti, Millenaristi.* Rovigo: Istituto padano di arti grafiche, 1951, 123 pp. (The Jehovah Witness, Adventists, and Millennialists.)

————. *Pentecostali e Testimoni di Geova*. Rovigo: Ist. padano di arti grafiche, 1968, 298 pp. (Pentecostals and Jehovah's Witnesses.)

Spier, H.I. *De Jehovah's Getuigen en de Bijbel*. Kampen: J.H. Kok, 1971, 192 pp. (Jehovah's Witnesses Against the Bible.)

Sterling, Chandler. *The Witnesses: One God, One Victory*. Chicago: Henry Regnery Co., 1975, 198 pp., hb.

Stevens, Leonard. *Salute! The Case of the Bible vs. the Flag*. New York: Coward, McCann and Geohegan, Inc., 1973, 159 pp., hb.

Stevenson, W.C. *Year of Doom: 1975*. London: Hutchinson and Co., 1967, 209 pp., hb. (published in U.S. as *Inside Story of Jehovah's Witnesses*, Hart Publ. Co., 1968, 209 pp., hb.)

Stroup, Herbert Hewitt. *The Jehovah's Witnesses*. New York: Columbia University Press, 1945, 180 pp., hb. (reprinted in 1967 by Russell and Russell of New York.)

Tanyu, Hikmet. *Yehova Sahitleri*. Ankara, Turkey: ELIF Matbaacitite, 204 pp. (Jehovah's Witnesses.)

Thomas, Frank W. *Masters of Deception*. Grand Rapids, Mich.: Baker Book House, 1972, 158 pp., pb.

Thomas, Stan. *Jehovah's Witnesses and What They Believe*. Grand Rapids, Mich.: Zondervan Publishing House, 1967, 159 pp., hb.

Tomsett, Valerie. *Released from the Watchtower*. Birkenhead, England: Willmer Brothers, Ltd., 1971, 128 pp., pb.

————. *Watchtower Chaos*. London, England: Lakeland Publ., 1974, 112 pp., pb.

Trombley, Charles. *Bible Answers for Jehovah's Witnesses*. Broken Arrow, Okla.: Expositor Publications, 1966, 110 pp., pb.

————. *Kicked out of the Kingdom*. Monroeville, Pa.: Whitaker House, 1974, 184 pp., pb.

Trost, Alex, comp. *Jehovah's Witnesses: Alternatives to Blood Transfusion in Adults*. N.p.: pub. by compiler, c. 1972, 603 pp. A collection of articles from medical journals which relate to the blood transfusion issue.

———. *Jehovah's Witnesses: Alternatives to Blood Transfusions in Minors.* N.p.: pub. by compiler, c. 1972, 601 pp.

———. *Jehovah's Witnesses: Alternatives to Blood Transfusion.* N.p.: pub. by compiler, 1973, 603 pp. A selection of articles from the previous two volumes.

Twisselmann, Hans-Jurgen. *Vom, "Zeugen Jehovas" zum Zeugen Jesu Christi.* Giessen/Basil, Germany: Brunne-Verlag, 1961, 116 pp., pb.; 3rd ed. 1972. (*From Jehovah's Witnesses to Jesus Christ's Witnesses.*)

Van Buskirk, Michael. *The Sandcastle of the Jehovah's Witnesses.* Santa Ana, Cal.: Carts, 1975, 172 pp., pb.

Vaz, Antonio Luiz. *As Testemunhas de Jeová.* Braga, Portugal: Braga-Editora, 1967, 132 pp.

Verrier, Chanoine Henri. *L'Eglise devant les Témoins de Jehovah.* Raismes (Nord): Wattel, 1956, 230 pp. (Position of the Church on Jehovah's Witnesses.)

Walter, Paul H. *A Small Voice Crying in the Wilderness.* Los Angeles, Cal.: Great Western Book Publ. Co., 1962, 160 pp.

Watters, Randall. *Thus Said the Governing Body of Jehovah's Witnesses.* Manhattan Beach, Cal.: pub. by author, 1981, 107 pp.

Werge, Asger Dan. *Kirke Kontra Kaelter.* Kobenhavn, Denmark: Eget Forlag, 1952, 157 pp. (The Church Against the Cults.)

Whalen, William J. *Armageddon Around the Corner.* New York: John Day Co., 1962, 259 pp., hb.

White, Timothy. *A People for His Name: A History of Jehovah's Witnesses and an Evaluation.* New York: Vantage Press, 1967, 418 pp., hb.

Wisdom, William N., and L.W. Jones. *"The Laodicean Messenger": His Life, Works and Character.* Chicago: The Bible Student's Bookstore, 1923, 332 pp. About C.T. Russell. The only book written on his life and works.

Wright, Gerald. *New World Translation: Perversions and Prejudice.* Fort Worth, Texas: Star Bible and Tract Corp., 1975, 80 pp., pb.

Zurcher, Franz. *Kreuzzug gegen das Christentum.* Zurich-
New York: Europa Verlag, 1938, 214 pp. (Crusade Against
Christendom.) Translated into French as *Croisade contre
le Christianisme.* Paris: Editions Rieder, 1939, 210 pp.

Zygmunt, Joseph. *Jehovah's Witnesses.* Chicago: University
of Chicago Press, in press, [1983], 960 pp.

B. MASTER'S THESES AND PH.D. DISSERTATIONS ON JEHOVAH'S WITNESSES

Of all the works on the Witnesses, the most objective and
in many ways the most useful are the Ph.D. dissertations and
Master's theses. About half of these deal fairly objectively
with the Society's history or with various psychological and
sociological aspects of the movement. The most exhaustive
is Zygmunt's Master's and Ph.D. theses (his Ph.D. thesis is
three volumes (978 pages) and is the most complete history
available). Also highly recommended are Beckford's, Czatt's,
and Manwaring's (a 765-page discussion of the flag-salute
cases, it is the most extensive work ever done on this issue)
theses. Also very useful are the theses of Rogerson, Stroup,
and Sprague (an excellent history, it contains long discussions
of the Witnesses as personalities, and was submitted for a
Ph.D. in Sociology from Harvard in the 1940s). A number of
the theses are in political science (see Kernaghan, Kim, and
Richards). About half of the works are theological; the
theses of Curry, Morey, Gruss, Goodrich, and Lapides are all
excellent. Other extremely useful works are Cumberland (an
excellent history which contains much of the same information
that Zygmunt does, but is far briefer and more succinct), Elhard
(a good review of the flag-salute cases in America), and
Hellmund (an excellent review of the Witnesses in Germany).

Assimeng, John Maxwell. "A Sociological Analysis of the Impact
    and Consequences of Some Christian Sects in Selected African
    Countries." Oxford University, England, 1968; see especially
    pp. 97-214. (Ph.D. diss.)

Baron, Rev. Michael. "A Critical Examination, in the Light of
    the Catholic Doctrine, of the Key Teachings of the Jehovah's
    Witnesses." Catholic University of America, Washington,
    D.C., 1956. (Doctor of Sacred Theology, D.D. diss.)

Beckford, James A. "A Sociological Study of Jehovah's Witnesses in Britain." University of Reading, Reading, England, 1972, 892 pp. (Ph.D. diss.)

Brackenridge, Douglas. "A Study of the Jehovah's Witnesses' Interpretation of Scriptures Relevant to the Person of Jesus Christ in the Light of Historic Christianity." Xenia College, Pittsburgh, Pa., 1959, 81 pp. (Master's thesis.)

Burski, Ulrich von. "Die Zeugen Jehovas: Die Gewissensfreiheit und das Strafrecht. Freiburg im Breisgan, 1970, 181 pp. (Ph.D. diss.) (The Jehovah's Witnesses: Freedom of Conscience and the Criminal Law.) About the blood transfusion issue.

Cohn, Werner. "Jehovah's Witnesses as a Proletarian Sect." New School for Social Research, New York, 1954, 98 pp. (Master's thesis.)

Cross, Sholto. "The Watchtower Movement in South Central Africa." Oxford University, Oxford, England, 1975. (Ph.D. diss.)

Cumberland, William. "A History of Jehovah's Witnesses." University of Iowa, Iowa City, Iowa, 1958, 309 pp. (Ph.D. diss.)

Curry, Melvin Dotson. "A Linguistic and Theological Evaluation of the New World Translation." Wheaton College, Wheaton, Ill., 1963, 127 pp. (Master's thesis.)

————. "Jehovah's Witnesses: The Effects of Millennarianism on the Maintenance of a Religious Sect." Florida State University, Tallahassee, Fla., 1980, 317 pp. (Ph.D. diss.)

Czatt, Milton. "The International Bible Students Association: A Critical Study in Contemporary Religion." Yale University, New Haven, Conn., 1929, 356 pp. (Ph.D. diss.)

Dye, Elsa Maria. "Sectarian Protestantism: Another Dimension— The Case of Jehovah's Witnesses." The University of San Diego, San Diego, Cal., 1968, 132 pp. (Master's thesis.)

Elhard, D. Wayne. "The Brooks, Alberta, National Anthem Controversy." Baylor University, Waco, Texas, 1976, 150 pp. (Master's thesis.)

Goodrich, Arthur R. "Soteriology in Jehovah's Witnesses."
    Dallas Theological Seminary, Dallas, Texas, 1955. (Master
    of Theology thesis.)

Gruss, Edmond Charles. "Apostles of Denial." Talbot Theo-
    logical Seminary, Biola College, La Mirada, Cal., 1961,
    307 pp. (Master's thesis.)

Hellmund, Dietrich. "Geschichte der Zeigen Jehovas (In der
    Zeit von 1870 bis 1920) mit einem Anhang: Geschichte der
    Zeugen Jehovas in Deutschland (bis 1970)." University of
    Hamburg, Hamburg, Germany, 1972, 340 pp. (Ph.D. diss.)
    (The History of the Jehovah's Witnesses from 1870 to 1920
    with a History of the Jehovah's Witnesses in Germany to
    1970.)

Henson, Alan. "A Critique of the Doctrine of Hell in the
    Theology of the Jehovah's Witnesses." 59 pp.

Horrell, John Scott. "Isms versus a Biblical Doctrine of the
    Trinity." Dallas Theological Seminary, Dallas, Texas,
    1977. (Master of Theology thesis.)

Kernhagen, William. "Freedom of Religion in the Province
    of Quebec with Particular Reference to the Jews, Jehovah's
    Witnesses and Church-State Relations, 1930-1960." Duke
    University, Durham, N.C., 1966, 363 pp. (Ph.D. diss.)

Kim, Richard Chong Chin. "Jehovah's Witnesses and the Supreme
    Court—An Examination of the Cases Brought Before the
    United States Supreme Court Involving the Rights Claimed by
    Jehovah's Witnesses, from 1938-1960." University of Okla-
    homa, Norman, Okla., 1963, 395 pp. (Ph.D. diss.)

Klose, L.V. "The Cults and Sects in the Los Angeles Area."
    The University of Southern California, Los Angeles, 1940.
    (Master's thesis.)

Lapides, Louis S. "The Jehovah's Witnesses and Jesus Christ."
    Talbot Theological Seminary, Biola College, La Mirada, Cal.,
    1977, 45 pp. (Church History Course.)

Maeson, William August. "Jehovah's Witnesses Decisions in
    the United States Supreme Court as an Empirical Test In-
    volving Yinger's Application of the Iron Law of Oligarchy
    to Religious Movements." Indiana State University, Terre
    Haute, Ind., 1968, 58 pp. (Master's thesis.)

Manwaring, David Roger. "The Flag Salute Litigation." The
University of Wisconsin, Whitewater, Wisc., 1959, 765 pp.
(Ph.D. diss.)

McDowell, Joshlin. "An Examination of the Jehovah's Witnesses'
Doctrine of the Creation of Christ Based upon Proverbs
8:28, Colossians 1:15 and Revelation 3:14." Dallas Theological Seminary, Dallas, Texas, 1966, 90 pp. (B.A. thesis.)

McLean, David Leslie. "History of the Jehovah's Witnesses: A
Study in Biography, 1870-1962." McMaster University, Hamilton,
Ont., Canada, 1963, 155 pp. (B.A. thesis.)

Morey, Robert A. "How to Witness to a Jehovah's Witness."
Westminster Theological Seminary, Philadelphia, Pa., 1979,
c. 100 pp. (Ph.D. diss.)

Newman, Stephen Lee. "The Jehovah's Witnesses' Use of the
Greek New Testament in Relation to the Doctrine of the Deity
of Christ." Dallas Theological Seminary, Dallas, Texas,
1976. (Master's thesis.)

Richards, Claud Henry. "Jehovah's Witnesses: A Study in
Religious Freedom." Duke University, Durham, N.C., 1945,
166 pp. (Ph.D. diss.)

Rogerson, Alan Thomas. "A Sociological Analysis of the Origin
and Development of the Jehovah's Witnesses and Their
Schismatic Groups." Oxford University, Oxford, England,
1972, 302 pp. (Ph.D. diss.)

Salzman, Donald M. "A Study of the Isolation and Immunization
of Individuals from the Larger Society in Which They Are
Living." University of Chicago, Chicago, Ill., 1951,
244 pp. (Master's thesis.)

Schwartz, Miriam Elaine. "The Jehovah's Witnesses: A Sect in
Society." Liberal Arts College of the City of New York,
1954. (Honours Essay, B.A. thesis.)

Sprague, Theodore Wentworth. "Some Problems in the Integration of Social Groups with Special Reference to Jehovah's
Witnesses." Harvard University, Cambridge, Mass., 1942,
446 pp. (Ph.D. diss.)

Stroup, Herbert Hewitt. "The Jehovah's Witnesses." New
School for Social Research, New York, 1950, 256 pp. (Ph.D.
diss.)

Zygmunt, Joseph. "Social Estrangement and the Recruitment
Process in a Chiliastic Sectarian Movement." University of
Chicago, Chicago, Ill., 1953, 396 pp. (Master's thesis.)

————. "Jehovah's Witnesses: A Study of Symbolic and Structural Elements in the Development and Institutionalization
of a Sectarian Movement." University of Chicago, Chicago,
Ill., 1967, 978 pp. (Ph.D. diss.)

C. BOOKLETS ABOUT JEHOVAH'S WITNESSES

Works in this section are stapled, soft covered, have
fewer than 96 pages, and, except as noted, are completely
devoted to Jehovah's Witnesses. Booklets, being briefer than
books, are more limited in scope, often reflecting less research and investigation. Some are very poorly done. About
90% of the booklets in this section are theological in nature,
and about 90% of these were written specifically to denounce
the Witnesses, mostly concentrating on theological criticisms.
The Russian works (of which there are over a dozen in this
section) are generally critical not only of the Witnesses but
of religion in general, the Witnesses simply being one example of the shortcomings and inadequacy of organized religion.
The Soviet booklets contain excellent information although
they tend to rely heavily on secondary sources. They include
much material that is not found anywhere else although one
may doubt the accuracy of their sources (and in many cases
the source is not given).
    For the person not interested in extensive research, the
booklets are excellent, quick sources but are not as freely
available as the books. Most libraries will keep books longer
than booklets, and the same is true of individuals. Many
booklets give a good review of the Witnesses and their beliefs
and discuss the problems of these beliefs. Theological discussions highly recommended are those of Bale, Bruce, Kern,
and Kneedler. In this section the only contemporary booklets
written by Witnesses are the two by Bremer, which are quite
dated (published in the 1940s by the author) and two by Stockdale (one contains an excellent discussion of the approximately
5,000 Witnesses imprisoned during World War II; most were
imprisoned because of their "total objector" stand, i.e.,
they refused to perform either combat or noncombat duty in
the service).
    The only booklets in the Russell era printed in favor of
the followers of Russell are those by Bradford. Most of the

nonofficial booklets of this era are listed in the various
sections under Bible Students. All the other works are by
persons who are neutral toward or opposed to the Witnesses.
Excellent booklets for historical study are those published by the American Civil Liberties Union. Several excellent discussions of the controversial stand on blood
transfusions taken by the Witnesses appear in Bergman, Montague,
and the first work listed under Christadelphian Publications.
Extremely useful booklets for historical research, although
written primarily about Witness theology, include those by
Cook, Pollock, Wiley, Rideout, Ross, Shield, Shaddick, and
Swift. An excellent critique from a Seventh-Day Adventist's
view is the work by Price and from a Catholic view, those by
Rumble.
The foreign-language material is listed according to the
guidelines followed in the full-length section.
Two useful booklets are by the Dawn Book Supply, one in
favor of Russellism, the other opposed to modern-day Witnesses
(much of the literature by the offshoots either discusses the
offshoot itself or, if it discusses the Witnesses, tends to
be critical of certain teachings).

Abel, Ron W. *Christadelphianism: Of God or Men? A Christadelphian Reply to the August, 1962 Watchtower Article.*
Privately printed, c. 1963, 33 pp.

Ackland, Donald F. *False Witnesses: An Indictment of "Jehovah's
Witnesses."* Stirling, Scotland: Stirling Tract Enterprise,
1958, 24 pp.

Aldred, Guy Alfred. *Armageddon, Incorporated.* Glasgow,
Scotland: Strickland Press, 1941, 35 pp.

American Civil Liberties Union. *The Persecution of Jehovah's
Witnesses.* New York, 1941, 24 pp.

————. *Jehovah's Witnesses and the War.* New York, Jan.
1943, 36 pp.

————. *In Defense of Our Liberties.* New York, 1944.

————. *Liberty on the Home Front.* New York, July 1945.

————. *Liberty Is Always Unfinished Business, 36th Annual
Report, 1955/56.*

————. *Justice for All, 37th Annual Report, 1956/57.*

Andibur, Miron Vasil'evich. *Before the Judgment of the People.*
Abakan: Khakass Book Publishing House, 1963, 109 pp.
(Russian.)

Aydin, Ali Arslan, and Huseyin Atay. *Yehova Sahidlerinia.*
Ankara, Turkey, 1973, 55 pp. (Jehovah's Witnesses.)

Bales, James D. *Jehovah's Witnesses?* Dallas, Texas: Gospel
Teachers Publication, 1978, 96 pp.

Ballard, Frank. *Why Not Russellism?* London: Charles H. Kelly,
n.d.

Beck, William F. *A Dialog About the Jehovah's Witnesses'
Bible, "The New World Translation."* St. Louis, Mo.: Concordia Publishing House, 1965, 13 pp.

Beijer, Erik. *Jehovas Vittnen.* Stockholm: pub. by author,
1950. (Jehovah's Witnesses.)

Bergman, Jerry. *Jehovah's Witnesses and Blood Transfusions.*
St. Louis, Mo.: Personal Freedom Outreach, 1981. 20 pp.

Berry, Harold J. *Witnessing the Cults.* Lincoln, Neb.: Good
News Broadcasting Association, 1974, 14 pp. General discussion on cults.

Bezuglov, Anatoli Alekseevich. *Coming Out of the Darkness.*
Moscow: State Publishing House of Juridical Literature,
1960, 44 pp. (Russian.)

Bias, Rod. *"They Shall Know That a Prophet Was Among Them."*
Pub. by author, Jan. 1975, 8 pp. (also revised edition,
June 1975, slightly different).

————. *Jesus Christ: The Firstborn of All Creation.* Pub.
by author, March 1975, 8 pp. (also revised ed., slightly
different).

————. *Why Do Jehovah's Witnesses Have Complete Unity?*
Pub. by author, July 1975, 8 pp.

————. *Who Really Is the "Faithful and Discreet Slave?"*
Pub. by author, June 1976, 12 pp.

Biederwolf, William Edward. *Russellism Unveiled.* 1st ed.
Chicago: Glad Tidings Pub. Co., 1910, 28 pp. Reprinted by
Wm. B. Eerdmans Co., Grand Rapids, Mich., 1920 and 1949,
28 pp.

Bilz, Dr. Jakob. *Die Ernsten Bibelforscher und ihre Behauptungen.* In the 12th book of *"Hirt und Herd."* Freiburg: Beitrage zur zeitgemassen Seelsorge Verlags- buchandlung Herder & Co., 1924, 29 pp. (The Serious Bible Researchers and Their Contentions.)

B., J.H. *Pastor Russell's Position and Credentials.* New York: Loizeaux Bros., n.d.

Black, James, D.D. *New Forms of the Old Faith.* London, England: Nelson & Sons, 1948.

Blennow, Hugo. *Sanningen Om Jehovas Vittner.* Kallinge: Eginostiftelsens Forlag, 1956, 16 pp. (The Truth About the Jehovah's Witnesses.)

Bodine, Jerry, and Mariane Bodine. *Witnessing to the Witnesses.* Cal.: Christian Research Institute, 43 pp. Photostats covering false prophecy, doctrine of Trinity, deity of Christ, resurrection, hell.

Boiarskii, Fedor. *Prophets: A Sketch.* Alma Ata: Kazakh State Publishing House of Artistic Literature, 1960, 12 pp. (Russian.)

Bolchuk, Myroslav. *Who Are the Jehovah's Witnesses.* Kiev, 1957, 89 pp. (Russian.)

Bommert, Otto. *Wider Millennium-Tages-Anbruch oder wie C.T. Russell das kreuz Christi Vollstandig zunichte machte.* Westfalen: Verlagshaus der deutschen Zeitmission in Geisweid, 1924, 3 Auflage, 16 pp. (Against the Millennial Dawnites or How C.T. Russell Completely Destroyed the Cross of Christ.)

Bowser, Arthur. *Bible Study Course on Jehovah's Witnesses.* Denver, Colo.: Accent Books, 1975, 28 pp.

Bradford, W.H. *An Answer to Dr. Gray.* St. Paul, Minn.: St. Paul Enterprises, 1900(?), 47 pp. Bradford was a follower of Russell.

————. *The Rich Young Man Whom Jesus Loved and Another Rich Young Man, A Memorial Address for Pastor C.T. Russell.* St. Paul, Minn.: St. Paul Enterprises, 1916, 42 pp.

Brauenlich, P. *Die Ernsten Bibelforscher als Opfer bolschewistischer Religionsspotter.* Leipzig: Verlag M. Heinsius

Nachfolger Eger U. Sievers, 2nd ed., 1926, 40 pp. (The
Jehovah's Witnesses as Victims of Bolshevist Religious
Mockers.)

Branson, Ron. Jehovah's Witnesses (4 parts). North Hollywood,
Cal.: The Albert Sheet Publication Ministry #37-40, N.d.,
16 pp.

Bremer, J.C. In Defense of the Despised "Sect." Metropolis,
Ill.: J.C. Bremer Printing Service, Feb. 12, 1944, 14 pp.
Published by an active Witness.

————. By Their Fruits Ye Shall Know Them. 2nd ed. (revised).
Metropolis, Ill.: J.C. Bremer Printing Service, n.d., 25 pp.
Published by an active Witness.

Brooks, Keith L. The Spirit of Truth and the Spirit of Error.
Los Angeles, Cal.: Christian Fundamentals League, n.d.

————. Prophetic Program of Judge Rutherford. Los Angeles,
Cal.: American Prophetic League, Inc., n.d., 12 pp.

————. Prophetic Program of Jehovah's Witnesses. Los Angeles,
Cal.: American Prophetic League, Inc., n.d., 12 pp.

Brown, C.H. Jesus Is Jehovah. Bible Truth Publishers, 1963.

Brown, Jim. Jesus Loves the Jehovah's Witnesses. Scottsdale,
Ariz.: Christian Communications, 1976, 86 pp.

Bruce, F.F., and J.W. Martin. The Deity of Christ. Manchester,
England: North England Evangelical Trust, 1964, 24 pp.

Bruder-dienst. Wir Wollen Wahrheit und Klarheit. Itzehoe,
Germany, 8 pp. (We Want Truth and Clarity.)

Bunzel, Ulrich. Die Ernsten Bibelforscher. Nos. 14 and 15
of the series of booklets "In alle Wahrheit." Berlin:
Kranzverlag des Christlichen zeitschriftenvereines, 1928,
32 pp. (The Jehovah's Witnesses.)

Bureau of Legal Medicine & Legislation. Blood Transfusion:
Court's Right to Order, People v. Labrenz. 104 N.E. (2d)
769 (Illinois, 1952).

Burganger, Karl (pseud.). The Watchtower Society and Absolute
Chronology. Lethbridge, Alberta, Canada: Christian Fellowship International, 1981, 28 pp.; revised ed. 1982, 28 pp.

Burrell, Rev. Maurice C. *Jehovah's Witnesses*. London, England: Church Book Room Press, Ltd., 1960, 20 pp. (also 1968 ed.).

————. *The Person and Work of Christ in Two Modern Deviationist Religions—-Jehovah's Witnesses and Christadelphians.* Bristol, England, 1962.

Burridge, J.H. *Pastor Russell's Date System and Teaching on the Person of Christ.* New York, c. 1911, 30 pp.

————. *Pastor Russell's Position and Credentials and His Methods of Interpretation.* New York, c. 1911, 32 pp.

————. *Pastor Russell's Teaching on the Coming of Christ.* New York, c. 1911, 31 pp.

Caris. *Examining the Watchtower Society: The New World Translation, A Perfect Score of 64, Why?* Santa Ana, Cal., n.d., 8 pp.

————. *Examining the Watchtower Society: 1975 Yearbook of Jehovah's Witnesses "Something Special?"* Santa Ana, Cal., n.d., 8 pp.

Carty, Charles. *Freak Religion: An Expose of the Witnesses of Jehova.* Pub. by author, 1939.

Catalfamo, Margaret. *From Jehovah's Witness to Witness for Christ Jesus.* Victoria, Australia: Standfast Pub. Co., 1980, 56 pp.

Central Board for Conscientious Objectors Bulletin. London, England, July 1941–Sept. 1946.

Chery, H. Ch. *L'Offensive des Sectes.* Paris: Les Editions du Cerf, 1954. (The Position of the Sects.)

Christadelphian Publications. "Blood Transfusion Does Not Violate Bible Teaching." *Herald of the Coming Age*, Vol. 16, No. 2, Aug. 1965 (revised ed. Vol. 24, No. 5, June 1974), 16 pp.

————. *Who Are God's True Witnesses?* Erith, England, n.d., 20 pp.

————. "Jehovah's Witnesses Refuted by the Bible." *Herald of the Coming Age*, Vol. 20, No. 3. Victoria, Australia:

The Clyde Press, Oct. 1969, 48 pp. Revised, and printed as
Vol. 31, No. 2, Aug. 1982, 16 pp.

Clyne, Harold W. *A Word About Jehovah's Witnesses.* Palmerton
North, New Zealand: Argosy Industrial Photos (1st ed. 1971),
1975, 30 pp.

Colinon, Maurice. *Faux Prophets et Sectes d'aujourd'hui.*
Paris: Librairie Plon, 1953. (False Prophets and Sects of
Today.)

————. *Le Phenomène des Sectes au XX Siècle.* Paris: Librairie
Artheme Fayard, n.d. (The Phenomenon of Sects in the 20th
Century.)

Conner, W.T. *The Teachings of "Pastor" Russell.* Nashville,
Tenn.: Sunday School Board of the Southern Baptist Convention Publishers, 1926, 68 pp.

Cook, Charles C. *More Data on "Pastor Russell."* New York:
pub. by author, n.d., 32 pp.

————. *All About One Russell.* Philadelphia, Pa.: Philadelphia School of the Bible, n.d., 24 pp. (republished by
Bible Institute of Los Angeles, Los Angeles, Cal., n.d.,
48 pp.).

Cooke, A.E. *Jehovah's Witnesses.* Toronto, Canada: United
Church Publishing House, 1948.

Cooksey, N.B. *Russellism Under the Searchlight.* Cincinnati,
Ohio: Abingdon Press, 1916, 68 pp.

Cooper, G.H. *Millennial Dawnism or Satan in Disguise.*
Swengel, Pa., n.d., 10 pp.

Coveney, Maurice. *Jehovah's Witnesses: Do They Have the
Truth?* Kelowna, B.C., Canada: pub. by author, n.d., 7 pp.

————. *"Are You Truly Making Sure of All Things?"* Kelowna,
B.C., Canada: Goodwill Printers, 1980, 64 pp.

Crain, C. *"Millennial Dawn" Teaching on the Person of Christ.*
New York: Loizeaux Brothers, Bible Truth Dept., n.d., 15 pp.

Crawford, William. *"Battle" of Armageddon Not Biblical.* Sun
City, Cal.: pub. by author, n.d., 55 pp.

Cross, P.G. *Russellism.* Cincinnati, Ohio: Standard Publishing, n.d.

Curran, Edward Lodge. *Judge "for four Days" Rutherford.* Brooklyn, N.Y.: International Catholic Truth Society, 1940, 32 pp.

Custer, Stewart. *Do Jehovah's Witnesses Contradict the Bible?* Greenville, S.C.: Bob Jones University Press, 1975, 12 pp.

Cutting, C.R. *Why I Left Jehovah's Witnesses.* Minneapolis, Minn.: Osterhaus Publishing House, n.d., 19 pp.

Dagon, Gerard. *Petites Eglises et Grandes Sectes.* Paris, 1962. (Small Religious Groups and Large Sects.)

————. *Petites Eglises de France Saverne.* 1969. (Small Religions of France.)

————. *Les Sectes en France.* N.d. (Sects in France.)

Davidson, J.L. *Debunking "Jehovah's Witnesses": A Written Discussion with the Cult of Jehovah's Witnesses.* Conroe, Texas: pub. by author, n.d., 50 pp.

Davies, Rupert Eric. *Is [sic] Their Witnesses True?* London, England: Epworth (Foundery Pamphlets No. 11), Aug. 1958.

Dawn Book Supply, The. *When Pastor Russell Died.* 1951, 53 pp.

————. *The Teaching of Jehovah's Witnesses Examined.* London, England, c. 1971, 16 pp.

Demchenko, Mykola Stepanovych. *Who Are Jehovah's Witnesses?* Moscow, 1958. (Russian.)

Dencher, Ted. *Jehovah's Witnesses and John 8:58.* Sharon, Pa.: pub. by author, n.d., 8 pp.

————. *Should I Become a Jehovah's Witness?* Sharon, Pa.: pub. by author, n.d., 16 pp.

————. *An Alarming Situation for Jehovah's Witnesses.* Fort Washington, Pa.: Christian Literature Crusade, 1974, 28 pp.

————. *I Wouldn't Believe in the "Trinity" If It Wasn't for the Watchtower Bible.* Sacramento, Cal.: Alpha-Media, 1977, 11 pp.

———. *Is This an "Aid to Bible Understanding?"* Sharon, Pa.: pub. by author, n.d., 8 pp.

Der Ernste Bibelforscher. Zürich: NZN-Verlag, 1922, 30 pp. (The Jehovah's Witnesses.)

Deutsch, Martin. *Die Sekte der Ernsten Bibelforscher.* Heidelberg: Evangelischer Verlag, 1925, 55 pp. (The Sect of the Jehovah's Witnesses.)

D'Haene, Daniel. *Praise the Lord, I Am Saved.* Sacramento, Cal.: Ted Dencher Publications, n.d. (c. 1976), 32 pp.

Diaz, Edwin. *¿Testigos de Jehová o Testigos de Satanas?* West New York, N.J.: Alex Books, 39 pp. (Witnesses of Jehovah or Witnesses of Satan?)

Diocese Anglican de I'LL, Maurice, Port Louis. *Les Témoins de Jehovah un court récit de l'histoire des croyances ainsi que des méthodes d'une secte étrange*, traduit de l'anglais. Port Louis, Mauritius: Almadina Press, n.d. (Brief Review of the History, Beliefs, Methods of a Foreign Sect.)

Dixon, A.C. *"Russell" Under the Searchlight.* London, England: Marshall, 1935.

Doev, Azgirel Batcherievich. *Under the Cover of Religion.* Frunze, USSR: Kirghizia (Atheists Library), 1964, 43 pp. (Russian.)

Doherty, J.E. *Jehovah's Witnesses.* Liguori, Mo.: Liguorian Pamphlets, 1961, 22 pp.

Dollinger, Ingo. *Die Zeugen Jehovahs und das Zeugnis der Heiligen Schrift.* Donauworth, W. Germany: Verlag Ludwig Auer Cassianeum Donovworth, 1965, 64 pp. (The Jehovah's Witnesses and the Witness of the Holy Scripture.)

Dönges, Emil. *Wider die Irrlehren der Ernsten Bibelforscher.* Dillenburg: Verlag der Geschwister Donges, 1925, 22 pp. (Against the False Teachings of the Jehovah's Witnesses.) From a Roman Catholic viewpoint.

Dorosh, Ievmen Kykrylovych. *Types of Brooklyn Corporations.* 1966, 117 pp. (Ukrainian.)

Downie, Henry. *The Annihilation of Jesus Christ or "Millennial Dawnism" Unveiled.* London, England: 14 Paternoster Row, A. Holness, n.d.

Duncan, Homer. *A Concise History of the Jehovah's Witnesses.*
Lubbock, Texas: Missionary Crusader, n.d., 8 pp.

————. *Armageddon in 1975?* Lubbock, Texas: Missionary
Crusader, n.d., 12 pp.

————. *Did Jesus Return in 1914?* Lubbock, Texas: Missionary
Crusader, n.d., 60 pp.

————. *Doctrines of Jehovah's Witnesses.* Lubbock, Texas:
Missionary Crusader, n.d.

————. *Five Themes That Transcend the Range of Human Understanding.* Lubbock, Texas: Missionary Crusader, n.d., 23 pp.

————. *Is It Not Strange That....* Lubbock, Texas: Missionary
Crusader, n.d. 7 pp.

————. *Jehovah's Witnesses and the Deity of Christ.* Lubbock,
Texas: Missionary Crusader, n.d., 54 pp.

————. *Maliciously Misrepresenting the Holy Spirit.* Lubbock,
Texas: Missionary Crusader, c. 1965.

————. *On the Wrong Train.* Lubbock, Texas: Missionary
Crusader, n.d., 18 pp.

————. *Questions the Jehovah's Witnesses Cannot Answer.*
Lubbock, Texas: Missionary Crusader, n.d., 8 pp.

————. *Satan's Strategy.* N.d.

————. *The Doctrines of the Jehovah's Witnesses Compared
with the Holy Scriptures.* Lubbock, Texas: Missionary Crusader, c. 1973, 64 pp.

————. *The Jehovah's Witnesses and the Second Coming of
Christ.* C. 1976, 45 pp. A revision of *Did Jesus Christ
Return in 1914?*

————. *The Jehovah's Witnesses Are Right!* Lubbock, Texas:
Missionary Crusader, n.d., 8 pp.

————. *Who Is Your Teacher?* Lubbock, Texas: Missionary
Crusader, n.d.

————. *Why I Love Jehovah's Witnesses.* Lubbock, Texas:
Missionary Crusader, 1972, 23 pp.

Elliott, Philip. *Jehovah's Witnesses in the First and Twentieth Centuries.* Stirling, Scotland: Stirling Tract Enterprises, n.d., 24 pp.

Engelder, Th. *Popular Symbolics.* St. Louis, Mo., 1934.

Ernste Bibelforscher, Die. *Katholische Antwort auf verschiedene Bibelfragen.* Zurich: N3N-Verlag, n.d., 30 pp. (The Catholic Answer to Different Bible Questions.)

Fardon, A.H., and A.J. MacFarland. *Jehovah's Witnesses: Who Are They? What They Teach.* Chicago, Ill.: Moody Bible Institute, 1941, 23 pp.

Felix, Rev. Richard. *Rutherford Uncovered.* Pilot Grove, Mo.: Our Faith Press, 1937, 35 pp.

Fellowship Baptist Church. *Who are Jehovah's Witnesses?* Lexington, Ky.: 1975, 22 pp.

Fennell, W.G. "Reconstructed Court and Religious Freedom." New York Univ. Law Quarterly, 1942 (paper).

Fetz, August. *Der grosse Volks- und Weltbetrug.* 4th ed. Hamburg: Verlag Arthur Gotting, 1924, 40 pp. (The Great Deception of a People and the World.)

F.F.B. and W.J.M. *The Deity of Christ.* Manchester, England: North of England Evangelical Trust, 1964, 24 pp.

Fiebig, Paul. *Die Bibelauslegung der Internationalen Vereinigung Ernster Bibelforscher.* 2nd ed. Berlin: Wiehem-Verlag, 1925, 32 pp. (The Bible of the International United Serious Bible Researchers.)

Fisch, Rudolf. *Die Ernsten Bibelforscher entlarvt.* Elberfeld: Licht-und Leben Verlag, 1925, 32 pp. (The Jehovah's Witnesses Exposed.)

Fisk, Samuel. *Confronting "Jehovah's Witnesses."* Brownsburg, Ind.: Biblical Evangelism, 1975, 24 pp.

Floyd, Shelby G. *An Examination of the Jehovah's Witnesses.* Greenwood, Ind.: Pulpit Publications, 1977, 76 pp.

Gardiner, Ronald. *I Was a Jehovah's Witness.* Santa Ana, Cal.: CARIS, 1978, 12 pp.

Gascoin, E. *Les Religions Inconnues.* Paris: Librairie Gal-
    limard, 1928. (The Little Known Religion.)

Gaskill, Bonnie, and Toni Jean Alquist Meneses. *We Left the
    Watchtower for Jehovah!* Seattle, Wash.: Trinity Printing,
    1979, 47 pp.

Gauss, J.H. *God's Truth v. Man's Theories.* St. Louis, Mo.:
    Faithful Words Publishing Co., 1948.

Gazhos, V.F. *The Characteristics of J.W. Ideology and the
    Religious Conscience of the Sect's Members Based on the
    Material in the M.S.S.R.* Ed. V.N. Ermuratski. Keshenev,
    1969, 92 pp. (Russian.)

Gerasimets, Aleksei Sergeevich. *The Truth About the Organiza-
    tion of Jehovah's Witnesses.* Irkutsk: Irkutsk Book Pub-
    lishing House, 1960, 52 pp. (Russian.)

————. *For Us Not According to the Path of the Jehovists.*
    Ed. I.P. Pentykhov. Irkutsk, 1960, 67 pp. (Russian.)

————. *A Criticism of the Ideology of Contemporary Jehovah
    Witness Faith.* Scientific Leader N.A. Reshetinikov.
    Irkutsk: 1965, 20 pp. (Russian.)

Gerecke, Karl. *Die Gotteslasterungen der Ernsten Bibelforscher.*
    Leipzig: Verlag Adolf Klein, 1931, 51 pp. (The Blasphemy
    of the Jehovah's Witnesses.)

Gerstner, John H. *The Teachings of the Jehovah's Witnesses.*
    Grand Rapids, Mich.: Baker Book House, 1960, 31 pp.
    Originally appeared as Chapter 3 in *The Theology of the
    Major Sects.*

Gilbert, Dan. *Spiritual Bolshevism: The Truth About the
    Teachings of Jehovah's Witnesses.* Washington, D.C.:
    Christian Press Bureau, 1945, 75 pp. Revised and published
    as *Jehovah's Witnesses.* Grand Rapids, Mich.: Zondervan
    Printing Co., 1946, 75 pp.

Gillentine, E.C. *Russellism or Jehovah's Witnesses vs.
    Christianity and the Bible.* Arkansas: Sunday School and
    Training Course Literature of the American Baptist Associa-
    tion, 1954, 32 pp.

Giselsson, Emanuel. *Sen till vad I horen! En Varning fur
    Jehovas Vittnens Propaganda.* Hasselholm, Sweden, 1958.

(Pay Attention to What May Be Heard: A Warning About the Propaganda of the Jehovah's Witnesses.)

Godbey, William B. *Russellism.* Zarephath, N.J.: Pillar of Fire, 1918, 38 pp.

Good News Publishers. *Do You Know ... What These Religions Teach?* Chicago, Ill., n.d., pp. 10-11. (Jehovah's Witnesses....)

Gray, James M. *The Errors of "Millennial Dawnism."* Chicago, Ill.: The Bible Institute Colportage Association, 1920, 24 pp.

Greaves, Arnold E. *That Servant.* New York: privately published, 1932, 32 pp. A booklet about C.T. Russell.

Grieshaber, Erich, and Jean Grieshaber. *The Watchtower Doors Begin to Open.* Santa Clara, Cal.: pub. by authors, 1976, 10 pp.

————. *Redi-Answers on Jehovah's Witnesses Doctrine.* Santa Clara, Cal.: pub. by authors, 1979, 51 pp.

————. *Expose of Jehovah's Witnesses.* Santa Clara, Cal.: pub. by authors, n.d., 90 pp.

————. *False Prophecy Packet.* Santa Clara, Cal.: pub. by authors, n.d. Photocopies of Watchtower coverups.

Grudinin, Nikolai Nikolaivich. *The Jehovah Witness Faith and Children.* Irkutsk: Eastern-Siberian Book Publishing House, 1965, 50 pp. (Russian.)

Guindon, Kenneth, and David Nicholas. *Why a New World Translation of the Holy Scriptures? A Frank Analysis of Jehovah's Witnesses.* Minnesota, c. 1977, 39 pp.

Gustafsson, Axel. *Vittnar Jehovas Vittnen falskt?* Falkoping, Sweden, 1955, 82 pp. (Are Jehovah's Witnesses False Witnesses?)

Gustafsson, Ingemar. *Tro på villovägar.* Falkoping, Sweden, 1975, 48 pp. (Belief in Freewill; Jehovah's Witnesses, Transcendental Meditation, and the Scientology Church.)

Gutfleisch, Richard. *Der internationale Verein Ernster Bibelforscher.* Karlsruhe: Badenia-Verlag, 1922, 22 pp. (The International Society of Bible Researchers.)

Haack, Friedrich-Wilhelm. *Jehovas Zeugen.* München, Germany:
Evangelischer Presseverband für Bayern, 1975, 44 pp.
(Jehovah's Witnesses.)

Haldeman, Isaac Massey. *Millennial Dawnism: The Blasphemous
Religion Which Teaches the Annihilation of Jesus Christ.*
New York: Charles C. Cook Publications, c. 1910, 80 pp.

—————. *The New Religion or Athenian Culture and Christianity.*
New York: Charles C. Cook Publications, 1910, 30 pp.

—————. *What Russellism or Millennial Dawnism Teaches.*
Chicago: Bookstall, n.d., 11 pp.

—————. *The History of the Doctrine of Our Lord's Return.*
New York: pub. by author, n.d., 40 pp.

—————. *Two Men and Russellism.* New York, c. 1915, 63 pp.

—————. *A Great Counterfeit or the False and Blasphemous
Religion Called Russellism.* New York: Charles C. Cook,
1915.

Hammund, T.C. *What Is Millennial Dawn Theory?* London:
Charles J. Thynne, n.d.

Harding, William. *Cults, No. 1: Jehovah's Witnesses.* Faith
Theological Seminary, n.d., 18 pp.

Hart, Alf. A. *Notes on the Finished Mystery.* Adelaide,
Australia: pub. by author, 1919, 42 pp. Objections to the
7th vol. from a Bible Student point of view.

Hartzler, J.E. *Heresy of Russell and Russellism.* Scottsdale, Pa.: Mennonite Publ. House, n.d.

Haug, Karl. *Die Ernsten Bibelforscher, auch Millenniumsleute
oder Russellianer genannt.* Lorch: Verlag Karl Rohm, 1923,
16 pp. (The Serious Bible Researchers, Also Called Millennial Dawnites or Russellites.)

Haynes, Carlyle B. *Why I Am Not a Russellite.* Warburton,
Victoria, Australia: Signs Publication Co., 1920, 8 pp.

Hearn, Roy J. *Handbook on Materialism. A Discussion of the
Question: Does Man Have an Immortal Spirit?* Crossville,
Tenn.: (Box 211), n.d.

Hedegard, David. *Adventistes, Russellianer och Efraims bud-parak*. Stockholm: Svenska Missionsforbundet Forlag, 1929, 47 pp. (Adventists, Russellites and Ephraim's Messenger.)

————. *Jehovas Vittnen (Kring Jehovas Vittnen?)*. 1930?, 1958. (Jehovah's Witnesses.)

Heimbucher, Dr. Max. *Was sind denn die Ernsten Bibelforscher für leute*. Regensburg: G.J. Manz, 3rd ed 1927, 85 pp. (What Kind of People Are the Jehovah's Witnesses?)

Help Jesus. *The False Prophet*. Kent, England: Help Jesus, n.d., 10 pp.

————. *The 144,000: Who Are These?* Kent, England: Help Jesus, n.d., 10 pp.

Hewitt, P.E. *Russellism Exposed*. Grand Rapids, Mich.: Zondervan Publishing Co., 1941, 60 pp.

Heydt, Henry J. *Jehovah's Witnesses and Their Translation*. New York: American Board of Missions, n.d., 19 pp.

Hickethier, C. Robert. *Are Jehovah's Witnesses Really His Witnesses?* Darby, Pa.: pub. by author, n.d., 16 pp.

Hingston, W.H. *"Jehovah's Witnesses" Exposed*. Toronto, Canada: Garden City Press Co-Operative, n.d., 49 pp.

Hobbs, A.G. *False Testimony of "Jehovah's Witnesses."* Fort Worth, Texas: Hobbs Publications, 1955, 20 pp.

Hodd, Eugene V. *L'Eglise et les Sectes*. Paris: Société Centrale d'Evangelisation, 1941. (The Church and the Sects.)

Hodges, Tony. *Jehovah's Witnesses in Central Africa*. Report No. 29. London, England: Minority Rights Group, 1976, 16 pp.

Hohenberger, Adam. *Christus und Sein Reich nach der Entstellung durch die Ernsten Bibelforscher*. Leipzig: Sonderabdruck aus "Pastor Iblatter," herausgegeben von Lich. E. Strange 68, Jahrgang Heft 5, Kommissionsuerlag C.L. Ungelenk in Dresden, 1926, 20 pp. (Christ and His Kingdom after the Creation According to the Serious Bible Researchers.)

Holmlund, W.A. *A Substitute Gospel*. Vancouver, B.C., Canada, 1965, 23 pp.

Hoornstra, Jean, ed. *The Millerites and Early Adventists: An
    Index to the Microfilm Collection of Rare Books and Manu-
    scripts.* Ann Arbor, Mich.: University Microfilms Inter-
    national, 1978, 65 pp.

Hopkins, Dick. *A Letter to the Watchtower Society.* Dublin,
    Cal.: pub. by author, 1981, 54 pp.

Hopkins, L.H.C. *I.B.S.A. or Russellism.* Toronto, Canada:
    Ryerson Press, United Church, n.d.

Hunt, Marion Palmer. *The Exposure of Millennial Dawnism.*
    Louisville, Ky.: Pentecostal Publishing Co., 1934, 62 pp.

Iatsenko, Borys Ivanovych. *Servant of the Yellow Devil.* N.p.,
    1963, 56 pp. (Ukrainian.)

Il'in, Viktor Andrilovych. *The Prophets of Armageddon.* Kiev,
    1961, 36 pp. (Ukrainian.)

Jackson, Dennis R. *From Darkness to Light: The Testimony of
    a Converted Jehovah's Witness.* Lubbock, Texas: Missionary
    Crusader, 1972, 21 pp.

Jackson, Wayne. *Jehovah's Witnesses and the Doctrine of the
    Deity of Christ.* Stockton, Cal.: pub. by author, 1979,
    24 pp.

————. *The Battle of Armageddon.* Stockton, Cal.: pub. by
    author, c. 1978, 12 pp.

Jacquemin, Suzanne. *Les Prophètes des Derniers Temps.* Paris:
    Editions du Vieux Colombier, 1958. (The Prophets of the
    Last Days.)

James, H.H. *Blood Transfusion: Is It an Unscriptural Prac-
    tice?* Reprint. Hastings, New Zealand, 1961, 14 pp.

Jehovah's Witness, Are You Free? N.p., n.d., 22 pp.

Jehovah's Witnesses. Port Louis, Mauritius, France: n.p.,
    n.d.

Johnson, Andrew E. *Jehovah's Witnesses--Witnesses with False
    Evidence.* Lincoln, Neb.: Good News Broadcasting Co., 1973,
    15 pp.

Johnson, B. *Nagot om Jehovas Vittnen*. Lund, Sweden, 1975.
(Something About the Jehovah's Witnesses.)

Johnson, Maurice. *8 Kinds of Death*. N.p.: pub. by author,
n.d., 13 pp.

Johnson, Thos. Cary. *Russellism*. Richmond: Presbyterian
Commission of Publications, c. 1920, 64 pp.

Jolly, Raymond G. *The Teachings of Jehovah's Witnesses Examined in the Light of the Scriptures*. Philadelphia, Pa.:
Laymen's Home Missionary Movement, n.d., 36 pp.

————. *A Message for "Jehovah's Witnesses."* Philadelphia,
Pa.: Laymen's Home Missionary Movement, n.d., 7 pp.

Judah, J. Stillson. *Jehovah's Witnesses*. Philadelphia, Pa.:
Westminster Books, 1967, 11 pp.

Kaiser, Fr. *Wer sind die sogenannten Ernsten Bibelforscher?*
Witten-Ruhr: Bundesverlag, 3rd ed. 1924, 40 pp. (Who Are
the So-Called Serious Bible Researchers?)

Kaufmann, Robert. *Millenarisme et Acculturation*. Bruxelles,
Belgium: L'Institut de Sociologie de l'Université de
Bruxelles, 1, 1964. (Millenarianism and Acculturation.)

Kaul, Arthur O. *Are Jehovah's Witnesses God's Witnesses?* St.
Louis, Mo.: Concordia Tract Mission, n.d., 9 pp.

Kern, Herbert. *How to Respond to the Jehovah's Witnesses*.
St. Louis, Mo.: Concordia Publishing House, 1977, 38 pp.

Kim, Kwan Suk. *A Critical Evaluation on the "Jehovah's Witnesses."* Korea: Christian Literature Society of Korea,
1963, 34 pp.

Kirby, Gilbert Walter. *Jehovah's Witnesses*. London, England:
Crusade Reprints, 1957, 12 pp.

Kneedler, William Harding. *Christian Answers to Jehovah's
Witnesses*. Chicago: Moody Bible Institute, 1953, 64 pp.
(Italian edition: *Risposte dei Cristiani ai Testimoni di
Geova*. Napoli, Italy: Edizioni Centro Biblico, 1966, 32
pp.)

Knights of Columbus. *Some Bible Beliefs Have to Be Wrong!*
St. Louis, Mo.: Knights of Columbus, 1963, 28 pp.

Köhler, Ludwig. *Was sagen Wir zu den Ernsten Bibelforschern?*
Zurich: En Vortrag. Art Institut Ovell, Fussli, 1924, 24
pp. (What Do We Say About the Jehovah's Witnesses?)

Krawielitzki, Martin. *Die Internationale Vereinigung Ernster
Bibelforscher.* Bad Blankenburg: Verlag Harfe, 1930, 16 pp.
(The International Association of Bible Researchers.)

Kuptsch, Julius. *Aufklärung über die Ernsten Bibelforscher.*
Tilsit: J. Reylaender v. Sohn, 1927, 47 pp. (Enlightenment
About the Serious Bible Researchers.)

Lackner, O.; J. Meister; and H. Hagenau. *Die Bibel und die
sogenennten Ernsten Bibelforscher.* Kassel: Christliche
Traktatgesellschaft, 1924, 15 pp. (The Bible and the So-
called Serious Bible Researchers.)

La Haye, Tim F. *Jesus, Who Is He? An Open Letter to Jehovah's
Witnesses.* San Diego, Cal.: Scott Memorial Baptist Church,
c. 1965, 16 pp.

Langrehr, Wilhelm. *Die Ernsten Bibelforscher und Wir.* Witten-
Ruhr: Evang. Pressverlag, 1925, 16 pp. (The Serious Bible
Researchers and Us.)

Lanzoni, Giuseppe O. *I Testimoni di Geova (errori-confuta-
zione).* Faenza: Biblioteca "S. Carlo Borromeo" del Seminari
di Faenza, 1952. (The Jehovah's Witnesses--Errors and Con-
fusions.)

Lash, Gustav. *Die Internationale Vereinigung Ernsten Bibelforscher und die Evangelische Kirche.* Strassburg: Evang.
Gesellschaft, 1921, 20 pp. (The Serious Bible Researchers
and the Protestant Church.)

Lenfest, Edna T. *Charles Taze Russell 1852-1916.* Acton,
Maine, n.d., 8 pp.

Lewis, Gordon R. *The Bible, the Christian, and Jehovah's
Witnesses.* Philadelphia, Pa.: Presbyterian and Reformed
Publishing Co., 1966, 30 pp.

Lienhardt, Hans. *Ein Riesenverbrechen am deutschen Volk und
die Ernsten Bibelforscher.* Weissenberg: Grossdeutscher
Verlag, 2nd ed. 1921, 46 pp. (The Colossal Crime Upon the
German People and the Jehovah's Witnesses.)

Lindsay, Gordon. *What About Jehovah's Witnesses?* Dallas, Texas: Christ for the Nations, 1974, 66 pp.

Lockyer, Herbert. *Jehovah's Witnesses Exposed.* Grand Rapids, Mich.: Zondervan Publishing Co., 1954, 32 pp.

Loofs, Friedrich. *Die Internationale Vereinigung Ernsten Bibelforscher.* Leipzig: J.C. Hinrich'sche Buchhandlung, 1921, 60 pp. (The International Union of the Serious Bible Researchers.)

MacCarty, William. *1914 and Christ's Second Coming.* Washington, D.C.: Review and Herald Publishing Assoc., 1975, 64 pp.

MacGregor, Keith, and Lorri MacGregor. *The Watchtower Fairy Tale of Jesus Christ.* Vancouver, B.C., Canada: MacGregor Ministries, 1980, 10 pp.

Magnani, Duane. *Eyes of Understanding: Watchtower Armageddon Prophecies Examined.* Clayton, Cal., 1972, 36 pp.; 2nd ed. 1977.

————. *Who Is the Faithful and Wise Servant? A Study of Authority over Jehovah's Witnesses.* Clayton, Cal.: Witness, Inc., 1979, 33 pp.

————, and Arthur Barrett. *Witnessing to Jehovah's Witnesses: How to Lead a JW to Christ in One Meaning.* Clayton, Cal.: Witness, Inc., 1979, 66 pp.

Main, C.F. *Notes on "The Finished Mystery."* Melbourne, Australia: Bible Students Tract Society, 1919, 43 pp.

Mansfield, H.P., ed. *Blood Transfusion Does Not Violate Bible Teaching* (West Beach, S. Australia, 5024). *The Herald of the Coming Age*, Vol. 24, No. 5, June 1974.

————, ed. *"Jehovah's Witnesses" Refuted by the Bible.* Victoria, Australia: The Clyde Press, n.d., 16 pp. (reprint of *Herald of the Coming Age*, Vol. 20. No. 3, October 1969, pp. 33-48).

Martin, Walter R. *The Jehovah's Witnesses.* Grand Rapids, Mich.: Zondervan Publishing House, 1957.

————. *Jehovah's Witnesses and the Trinity.* N.p., n.d., 11 pp.

————. *What About Jehovah's Witnesses?* N.d., n.p., 32 pp.

Martin Sanchez, Benjamin. *¿Quienes son los Testigos de Jehova?* Zamora, Monte Casino, 1971, 47 pp. (Who are the Jehovah's Witnesses?)

Mayer, F.E. *Jehovah's Witnesses.* St. Louis, Mo.: Concordia Publishing House, 1942 (revised 1957), 52 pp.

Maynard, John Albert. *"Russellism."* London: S.P.C.K., 1926, 31 pp.

McCluskey, Neil G. *Who Are Jehovah's Witnesses?* New York: The American Press, 1956, 17 pp. (reprinted from *America Magazine*, Nov. 19, 1955, pp. 204-208).

McLean, W.T. *Isms, "Heresies, Exposed by the Word of God."* Grand Rapids, Mich.: Zondervan Publishing House, n.d., 29 pp.

Mellows, F. *Russellism, the Latest Blasphemy, or "Millions-now-living-will-never-die-ism."* London: C.J. Thynne, 1921, 24 pp. (Vol. 4 of *Substitutes for Christianity.*) This is extremely rare—the only known copy is at Princeton University.

Metzger, Bruce M. *The Jehovah's Witnesses and Jesus Christ.* Princeton, N.J.: Theological Book Agency, n.d., 21 pp. (reprinted from *Theology Today*, April 1953, pp. 65-85).

Meyenberg, Albert. *Über die sogenannten Ernsten Bibelforscher.* Luzern: Räber u. Cie, 1924, 19 pp. (About the So-called Serious Bible Researchers.)

Miksch, L. *Die Ernsten Bibelforscher.* Lorch: Verlag Karl Rohm, 1925, 40 pp. (The Serious Bible Researchers.)

Miller, C. John. *Witnessing to Jehovah's Witnesses.* Philadelphia, Pa.: Westminster Theological Seminary, n.d., 4 pp.

Moffitt, Jerry, ed. *"Jehovah's Witnesses."* Thrust (Austin, Texas: Southwest Church of Christ), Vol. 1, No. 1, 1979, 40 pp.; Vol. 1, No. 2, 1980, pp. 41-90.

Montague, Havor. *Watchtower Congregations: Communion or Conflict?* Santa Ana, Cal.: CARIS, 1978, 8 pp.

————. *Jehovah's Witnesses and Blood Transfusions.* Santa Ana, Cal.: CARIS, 1979, 21 pp.

Moskalenko, Aleksei Tromfimovich. *Who Are Jehovah's Witnesses?*
Moscow: "Knowledge" (The All-Union Society for the Propaga-
tion of Political and Scientific Knowledge) (Editions, Series
2, No. 29), 1959, 80 pp. (Russian.)

————. *The Sect of Jehovah's Witnesses and Reactionary Substance (Essence)*. Moscow: "University," 1961, 76 pp.
(Russian.)

Moyer, Robert L. *The Rich Man in Hell and the Blasphemous
Trinity*. Minneapolis, Minn.: Osterhus Publishing House,
1946, 29 pp.

Müller, Anton. *Die Ernsten Bibelforscher und die letzten
Dinge*. 12th vol. of the series *"Hirt und Herde."* N.d.,
23 pp. (The Serious Bible Researchers and the Last Things.)

Munro, W. Fraser. *The Facts About Jehovah's Witnesses*.
Toronto, Canada: The Board of Evangelism and Social Service,
The United Church of Canada, n.d.

Murray, Wm. W., M.D. *Millennial Hopes and Prospects*. Richmond, Va.: The Williams Printing Co., 1903, 16 pp.

National Service Board for Religious Objectors. *Statements
of Religious Bodies on the Conscientious Objector*. Dec.
1951; revised Aug. 1953.

Nelson, Wilton. *Jehovah's Witnesses*. Chicago: Moody Press,
c. 1955, 15 pp.

Nielsen, John R. *An Open Letter to the Jehovah's Witnesses*.
St. Louis, Mo.: Concordia Tract Mission, n.d., 9 pp.

O'Brien, John A. *Light on Jehovah's Witnesses*. Huntington,
Ind.: Sunday Visitor, Inc., n.d., 29 pp.

O'Hair, J.G. *Millions Now Dying Will Never Live, A Scriptural
Investigation of Russellism*. Chicago: pub. by author, n.d.,
21 pp.

On the Watch (Australia). *What the Watchtower Does Not Tell
You*. 19 pp.

Othmalm, E. *Bibelns lara om Gud*. Orebro, Sweden, 1975. (The
Bible's Teaching on God.)

Our Hope Publication Office. *How Pastor Russell Died*. New
York, n.d.

————. *How Russellism Subverts the Faith.* New York, n.d.

————. *Date System and Teaching on Christ.* New York, n.d.

Parkinson, James B. *The Bible Student Movement.* Glendale, Cal.: pub. by author, 1975.

————. *Bible Students' Fragments in Brief.* Glendale, Cal.: pub. by author, 1976, 30 pp.

————. *On Resolving the Chronological.* Glendale, Cal.: pub. by author, 1977.

Personal Freedom Outreach. *Jehovah's Witnesses: The Christian View.* St. Louis, Mo., 1978, 19 pp. This booklet accompanies the slide set produced by *Personal Freedom Outreach.*

Petersen, Mark E. *Some Helps Regarding Jehovah's Witnesses.* Salt Lake City, Utah: Mormon Missionary Manuals, n.d., 8 pp.

————. *Christ, Jehovah and the "Witnesses."* Salt Lake City, Utah: Mormon Missionary Manuals, n.d., 32 pp.

————. *"Questions About the Jehovah's Witnesses," in Peter and "The Rock."* Salt Lake City, Utah: Mormon Missionary Manuals, n.d., pp. 12-26.

Pfeil, Carl. *Jesus, Jehovah, and "The New World Translation": A Study of the Deity of Christ in the Jehovah's Witness Translation of the Bible.* Renton, Wash.: Family Bible Fellowship, 1976, 20 pp. (2nd ed. 1978, 20 pp.).

Pile, William. *Mistakes Jehovah's Witnesses Make.* Los Angeles, Cal.: Good News Publishers, 1968 (packet of 13 tracts--total of 56 pp.).

Pollock, A.J. *Examination of Judge Rutherford's Books.* New York, n.d., 15 pp.

————. *How "Pastor" Russell Died.* New York, n.d.

————. *"Jehovah's Witnesses" and Judge Rutherford's Books.* London: The Central Bible Truth Dept., n.d., 16 pp.

————. *Millennial Dawnism: Briefly Tested by Scripture.* London, England: Central Bible Truth Dept., 1917, 23 pp.

118 Section Three

————. *Jehovah's Witnesses and Judge Rutherford's Books: An Exposure.* London, England: Central Bible Truth Dept., 1942, 16 pp.

Power, Pearl A. *The Paton-Williams Debate on Universal Salvation and the Destiny of the Wicked.* Chicago, Ill.: Advocate Publishing House, c. 1910, 35 pp.

Prakh'ie, Borys Semenovych. *The Jehovah's Witnesses.* Odessa, USSR: Library of Atheism, 1959, 13 pp. (Ukrainian.)

Price, E.B. *God's Channel of Truth--Is It the Watchtower?* Mountain View, Cal.: Pacific Press Publishing Assoc., 1967, 112 pp.

————. *Our Friends: The Jehovah's Witnesses.* Victoria, Australia: Lay Activities Department of Victorian Conference of Seventh-Day Adventists, n.d., c. 87 pp.

————. *What the Watchtower Does Not Tell You.* Victoria, Australia: Lay Activities Department of Victorian Conference of Seventh-Day Adventists, n.d., 17 pp.

Proctor, W.C. *An Answer to Latest Slogan of Russellism, Pamphlets on the Second Advent.* London: Thynne and Jarvis, 1926 or 1925.

Putnam, C.E. *Jehovah's Witnesses: Russellism, Rutherfordism-- Are They God's Prophets?* Randleman, N.C.: n.p., n.d., 6 pp.

Reed, David. *Radio Free Watchtower.* Stoughton, Mass.: Christians, 1981, 12 pp.

Reid, R.J. *How Russellism Subverts the Faith.* New York, n.d. (c. 1920), 69 pp.

Rekemchuk, Aleksandr Evseevich. *A Double-Depth--Documentary Novel.* Moscow: Siktivkar Komi Book Publishing House, 1958, 53 pp. (Russian.)

————. *The Double Depths of "Jehovah's Witnesses," A Documentary Story.* Moscow: State Publishing House for Political Literature, 1959, 43 pp. (Russian.)

Ridout, George Whitefield. *The Deadly Fallacy of Russellism or Millennial Dawnism.* Louisville, Ky.: Pentecostal Publishing Co., n.d., 20 pp.

Riley, W.B. *Mistakes of Millennial Dawn.* Los Angeles, Cal.:
Bible Institute of Los Angeles, Biola Book Room, n.d.

Rinman, John. *"Russellianism" Sken och Verklighet.* Stockholm:
Evang. Fosterlands Stiftelsens Forlags, 1915, 32 pp. (Truth
and Light on Russellism.)

Ripley, Francis J. *The Witnesses of Jehovah.* London, England:
Catholic Truth Society, n.d., 24 pp.

Rockwood, Perry. *Jehovah's Witnesses Examined in the Light of
the Word of God.* Halifax, N.S., Canada, n.d., 21 pp.

Rogozniak, Nikolai. *We Cannot Be Silent. An Open Letter,
Published in the Newspaper "Eastern Siberian Truth," No. 22
from 26 January, 1963, to Members of the Organization,
"Jehovah's Witnesses"* (Nikolai Rogozniak, Nikolai Khamei,
Vasilii Pron.). Irkutsk, 1963, 14 pp. (Russian.)

Rohkohl, Pastor. *Wer hat recht?* Berlin: Evang. Presseverband,
1928, 34 pp. (Who Is Right?)

Ross, Edward Eugene. *Jehovah's Witnesses: A Study and Analysis.*
N.d., 94 pp.

Ross, Rev. J.J. *Some Facts and More Facts About the Self-
styled "Pastor" Charles T. Russell.* Philadelphia, Pa.:
Philadelphia Presbyterian Board; Los Angeles, Cal.: Bible
Institute of Los Angeles, 1912, 50 pp.

————. *Some Facts About the Self-styled "Pastor" Russell.*
New York: C.C. Cook, n.d.

Ross, K.N. *Jehovah's Witnesses.* London, England: S.P.C.K.,
1954 (2nd ed. 1962), 10 pp.

Rowell, J.B. *The Death of Our Lord.* N.p., n.d., 60 pp.

————. *The Deity of Jesus Christ Our Lord.* Victoria, B.C.,
Canada: Hebden Printing Co., n.d., 39 pp.

Ruiz, Agustin. *Los Testigos de Jehova Coleccion de Doctrinas
Modernas.* 1966 (1976 ed.). (The Jehovah's Witnesses: A
Collection of Modern Doctrines.)

Rule, Andrew K. "Jehovah's Witnesses" in *The Church Faces the
Isms,* ed. Arnold B. Rhodes. Nashville, Tenn.: Abingdon
Press, 1958, pp. 80-87.

Rumble, Leslie. *The Anti-Immortals: A Reply to the Rational-
ists, Jehovah Witnesses, Adventists, and Christadelphians.*
St. Paul, Minn.: Fathers Rumble and Carty, n.d., 32 pp.

————. *The Incredible Creed of Jehovah's Witnesses.* St.
Paul, Minn.: Fathers Rumble and Carty, c. 1963, 31 pp.
British ed., London, England: Catholic Truth Society, 1963,
24 pp.

————. *Jehovah Witness.* St. Paul, Minn.: Fathers Rumble
and Carty, n.d., 32 pp.

Russell, O.B. *The Errors of Russellism.* N.p., 1934.

Sanders, E.L. *A Critique of the Jehovah's Witnesses.* Langley,
B.C., Canada: Apostolic Church of God., n.d., 40 pp.

Sanders, J. Oswald, and J. Stafford Wright. *Some Modern Religions.* London, England: The Tyndale Press, 1956, 72 pp.

Sandt, George W. *Another Pious Fraud or The Story of Russellism.* Philadelphia, Pa.: General Council Publication House,
1913, 31 pp.

Scheurlen, Paul. *Die Sekten der Gegenwart und neuere Weltan-
schauungsgebilde.* Stuttgart: Quell-Verlag des Evang.
Gesellschaft, 1923. (The Present Sects and Their New
World View.)

Schevchenko, Vladimir Ivanovich. *The Prophets of Fire and
Doom.* Moscow: "Knowledge" (Read, Comrades! series), 1961,
34 pp.

Schmiedel, Paul. *Pilatus über Jesus bei den Ernsten Bibelforschern.* Zurich: Art Institute Ovell Füssli, 1924, 15 pp.
(Pilatus on Jesus by the Jehovah's Witnesses.)

Schnell, William J. *Another Gospel.* Seattle, Wash.: The
Life Messengers, n.d., 32 pp.

————. *Who Are Jehovah's Witnesses?* Youngstown, Ohio:
Expositer, n.d., 8 pp.

Scott, Frank Earl. *Son of Man Revealed.* Wallace, Ind.: pub.
by author, 1973, 32 pp.

Shadduck, B.H. *The Seven Thunders of Millennial Dawn.* Ashta-
bula, Ohio: Homo Publishing Co., n.d., 32 pp.

Sheldon, Henry Clay. *Russell's Ventures in Adventism.* New
   York: Methodism Book Concern, 1921, 31 pp.

Shields, T.T. *Russellism, Rutherford: The Teachings of the
   International Bible Students in the Light of Holy Scripture.*
   Grand Rapids, Mich., 1934, 106 pp.

————. *Russellism or Rutherfordism in the Light of the Holy
   Scriptures.* Toronto, Canada: The Gospel Witness, 1946,
   72 pp.

Sinhung, Chonggyo Munje Yon'guso. *Research Report of Jehovah's
   Witnesses.* Seoul, Korea: New Religious Research Institute,
   1978, 25 pp. (Korean.)

Skjerpe, Olav. *Jehovas Vittnen och Vad de Lär.* Stockholm,
   Sweden, 1971, 125 pp.

Smith, R.T. *Jehovah's Witnesses: Millennial Dawnism or Russellism and Rutherfordism--What Do They Teach?* Philadelphia,
   Pa.: n.d., 8 pp.

Smith, W.A. *The Search for Truth--A True Life Story.* Melbourne, Australia: Berean Bible Institute, n.d., 35 pp.

Soldiers of Christ. *The Doctrines of the Jehovah's Witnesses
   Contrasted to the Bible and the Historic Christian Faith.*
   Six Lakes, Mich.: The Soldiers of Christ, 1976, 60 pp.

Sprung, Renate. *Gefangnis ohne Mauern: Wir waren Zeugen Jehovas.*
   Ostfildern: Schwabenverlag, 1977, 71 pp. (Prison Without
   Walls: We Were Jehovah's Witnesses.)

Staehelin, Ernst. *Was haben wir von den Ernsten Bibelforscher
   zu halten?* Basel: F. Reinhardt, 1925, 32 pp. (What Do We
   Think About the Serious Bible Researchers?)

Stallmann, Heinrich. *Die International Vereinigung Ernster
   Bibelforscher.* Zwickau: Verlag des Schriftvereins, 2nd
   ed., 1925, 32 pp. (The International Union of Serious
   Bible Researchers.)

Starkes, M. Thomas. *Armageddon's Army: The Jehovah's Witnesses.* Atlanta, Ga.: Home Mission Board, 1976, 12 pp.
   Reprinted from *Home Missions Magazine,* March 1975.

Stephens, Carl. *Light on the Tower: Are They Really Jehovah's
   Witnesses?* Texarkana, Texas: Bogard Press, 1977, 54 pp.

Stevens, Edward. *The Watchtower Society: Its Origin, Doctrine and Destiny*. Riverside, Cal.: c. 1960, 18 pp.

Stevens, Grover. *Jehovah's Witnesses Answered*. Lubbock, Texas: Stevens Publications, n.d., 37 pp.

Stevens, W.C. *Arraignment of Millennial Dawn*. Los Angeles, Cal.: Biola Book Room, Bible Institute of Los Angeles, n.d.

————. *Why I Reject the Helping Hand of Millennial Dawn*. N.d., 121 pp.

Stilson, Max. *How to Deal with Jehovah's Witnesses*. Grand Rapids, Mich.: Zondervan Publishing House, 1962, 61 pp.

Stockdale, William. *Jehovah's Witnesses in American Prisons*. Putnam, Conn.: The Wilda Press, 1946, 27 pp.

————. *The Government Is the Criminal*. Putnam, Conn.: The Wilda Press, 1947, 79 pp. Written by an active Witness and highly sympathetic to the Witness situation.

Stover, Gerald L. *"Ye Shall Know the Truth"--An Expose of "Jehovah's Witnesses."* Ontario, Canada: Kitchener Printing Service, 1945, 50 pp.

Strauss, Lehman. *An Examination of the Doctrine of "Jehovah's Witnesses."* New York: Loizeaux Brothers, 1942, 47 pp. (also titled *An Examination of the Teachings of Jehovah Witnesses*).

Stuermann, Walter. *The Jehovah's Witnesses and the Bible*. Tulsa, Okla.: Univ. of Oklahoma, 1955, 31 pp.

Stump, J. *Russellism*. Philadelphia, Pa.: United Lutheran Publishing, 1923.

Suarez, Fernandez. *Los Falsos Testigos de Jehova*. Mexico: Casa Bautista de Publicaciones, 1962 (1975 ed.), 46 pp. (The False Witnesses of Jehovah.)

Sundstrom, Erland. *Jehovas Vittnen pa fammersch, Religions-sociologiska Institute*. Forsknings-rapport, No. 133 (1976:5), Oct. 1976, 25 pp. (Jehovah's Witnesses on the March.) (Swedish.)

Swartz, Frank. *A Close Look at the Jehovah's Witness Bible*. Little Rock, Ark.: The Challenge Press, 1974, 32 pp.

Swift, John McIntosh. *Jehovah's Witnesses: A Brief Account of the History, Beliefs, and Methods of a Strange and Widespread Organization.* Oxford, England: A.R. Mowbray & Co., 1942, 16 pp.

Talbot, Louis T. *Jehovah's Witnesses and the Bible.* Findlay, Ohio: Dunham Publishing Co., 1957, 48 pp.

————. *What's Wrong with Jehovah's Witnesses.* Findlay, Ohio: Dunham Publishing Co., n.d., 48 pp.

Tanis, Edward J. *What the Sects Teach.* Grand Rapids, Mich.: Baker Books, 1958, 89 pp.

Target, G.W. *The Black Plague--Russellism.* Great Britain: Holiness, n.d.

Thomas, Fred W. *The Bible Answers: Jehovah's Witnesses' Ridicule of Hell.* Minneapolis, Minn.: Osterhus, n.d., 30 pp.

————. *Should Jehovah's Witnesses Ridicule or Fear Hell?* Vancouver, B.C., Canada: pub. by author, n.d., 24 pp.

Thorell, Folke. *Lögn Profeter: En Saklig undersökning angående Jehovas Vittnen och deras lära.* Stockholm, Sweden: Normans Förlag, n.d., 40 pp. (False Prophets: A Factual Research About the Jehovah's Witnesses and Their Doctrines.)

————. *Tio religionssurrogat: Folke, Thorell Forlay.* Orebro, 1973, 49 pp. (Ten Religious Surrogates.)

Tipton, S.R. *The Jehovah Witnesses Versus the Bible.* N.p., n.d.

Tolle, James M. *An Expose of Jehovah's Witnesses.* Fullerton, Cal.: Tolle Publ., c. 1957, 29 pp. (earlier ed. San Fernando, Cal., 19 pp.).

Torhorst, Arnold. *Die Ernsten Bibelforscher als Propheteten des Weltendes.* Potsdam: Stiftungsverlag, 1925, 12 pp. (The Jehovah's Witnesses: Prophets of the World's End.)

Tovarystvo, Diia Poshyrennia. *The Society for the Spread (Development) of Political and Scientific Knowledge in the Ukraine.* Chernivetske, 1959, 42 pp. (Ukrainian.) Revised as: *The Society of Znannia (knowledge) in the Ukraine RSR: Who Do Jehovah's Witnesses Follow?* Ed. E. Cherozok and O. Guber. 1959, 42 pp.

Tucker, W. Leon. *What Is Russellism? Commonly Called Millennial Dawn*. Los Angeles, Cal.: Serial Tract Publishing Co., c. 1910, 28 pp.

Tweisselmann, Hans-Jurgen. *Die "Zeugen Jehovas" Erwahlte oder Verfuhrte?* Witten (Ruhr), West Germany: Bundes-Verlag, 1967, 32 pp. (The Jehovah's Witnesses: Chosen or Misled?)

————. *Als Zeugen Jehovas Erlebt Erutten und Erzalt*. Witten Ruhr, West Germany, n.d. (As Jehovah's Witnesses Experienced and Suffered.) Letters, reports, and confessions.

————. *"Zengen Jehovas" Brauchen Antwort*. N.p., n.d. (Jehovah's Witnesses Need Answers.)

————, ed. *Alles--nur Kein Blut! Menschenleben opfern um religioser Grundsatze willen? Verlangt das ner Christliche Glaube?* Itzehoe, Germany, n.d., 23 pp. (All--But No Blood. To Sacrifice for the Sake of Religious Principles? Does the Christian Creed Require That?)

Valisevich, Ivan Stepanovich. *The Religious Sects--Baptists and Jehovah's Witnesses*. 2nd supplemental ed. Irkutsk: Irkutsk Book Publishing House, 1958, 84 pp. (Russian.)

Van Buskirk, Michael. *The Scholastic Dishonesty of the Watchtower*. Santa Ana, Cal.: CARIS, 1975, 22 pp. (revised 1976 ed., 48 pp.).

Van Sommers, Tess. *Religions in Australia*. Adelaide, Australia: Rigby Ltd., 1966.

Verrier, Chanoine Henri. *L'Eglise devant les Témoins de Jehovah*. Raismes, France: Les Editions Polyglottes, 1957. (The Position of the Church and Jehovah's Witnesses.)

Voke, Rogerd. *Be Not Deceived*. Roodeport, Transvaal, South Africa: Transo Press, n.d., 36 pp.

Walkem, Charles William. *Jehovah's Witnesses: An Expose*. Los Angeles, Cal.: pub. by author, 1943, 32 pp.

Walker, C.C. *Has Christ Come? The Truth About the Parousia, Apokalupsis, and Epiphaneia, as Against Some Errors of Russellism*. Birmingham, England: "The Christadelphian," 1915, 16 pp.

————. *"A Ransom for All"*: *The Bible Doctrine of Ransom or Redemption in Opposition to the Errors of Universalism and Russellism.* Birmingham, England: "The Christadelphian," 1937, 24 pp.

Wallace, William. *To the Jehovah's Witness Caller.* Athens, Ala.: C.E.I. Pub. Co., n.d., 18 pp.

Walters, Wesley, and M. Kurt Goedelman. *Jehovah's Witnesses.* Downers Grove, Ill.: Inter-Varsity Press, 1983, 32 pp.

Warren, Thomas B., ed. *"Jehovah's Witnesses"* in the *Spiritual Sword* (Memphis, Tenn.: Getwell Church of Christ), Vol. 6, No. 1, Oct. 1974, 48 pp.

Wassink, A. *The Bible and Jehovah's Witnesses.* Grand Rapids, Mich.: Faith, Prayer and Tract League, n.d., 16 pp.

Watchtower Bible Studies. *What Jehovah Wants His Witnesses to Know in the Watchtower Translations: New World Interlinear Translation of the Greek Scriptures.* Cleveland, Tenn.: 1977, 56 pp.

Welsh, Harold E. *Do Jehovah's Witnesses Have a Personal Relationship with Jesus Christ?* South Gate, Cal.: Christian Publications, n.d., 25 pp.

Westby, Wayne. *Christ's Witnesses.* Rose Valley, Saskatchewan, Canada: privately printed, n.d., 8 pp.

Westwood, Tom. *Jehovah's Witnesses the True and the False.* Glendale, Cal.: pub. by author, n.d., 32 pp.

Whalen, William J. *Jehovah's Witnesses.* Chicago: Claretian Publications, 1975, 25 pp. (revised ed. 1978, 32 pp.)

————. *What About the Jehovah's Witnesses?* N.p., n.d., 32 pp.

Wheeler, Gerald. *Is God a Committee?* Nashville, Tenn.: Southern Publishing Association, 1975, 47 pp.

Whittaker, Harry. *"Jehovah's Witnesses"* in *People We Meet.* Birmingham, England: the Christadelphians, 1976, pp. 10-11.

————. *Why I Am Not a Jehovah's Witness.* Birmingham, England: Christadelphian Auxiliary Lecturing Society, n.d., 8 pp.

Whyte, Lloyd. *Witnessing to the Witness*. Atlanta, Ga.: Home Mission Board, Southern Baptist Conv., 1973, 16 pp.

Williams, Thomas. *Russellism Refuted*. Chicago: Advocate Publishing House, n.d., 48 pp.

Wimbish, John S. *What Is a Jehovah's Witness?* Murfreesboro, Tenn.: Sword of the Lord Publishers, 1956, 22 pp.

Windle, Charles P. *The Rutherford Racket*. Chicago, Ill.: Iconoclast Publishing Co., 1937.

Winnipeg Free Press. *Constitutional Freedom in Peril: The Jehovah Witnesses' Case*. Winnipeg, Canada, 1954, 23 pp.

————. *Rights and Citizenship: The Threat to Our Freedom*. Winnipeg, Canada, 1954, 8 pp.

Wolff, Richard. *Do Jehovah's Witnesses Follow the Bible?* Lincoln, Neb.: Back to the Bible Broadcast, 1959.

Woods, A. *Tremendous Truth from the New World Translation*. Phoenix, Ariz.: pub. by author, n.d., 31 pp.

Wright, Gerald. *Perversions and Prejudices of the New World Translation*. Fort Worth, Texas: Star Bible Tract Society, 80 pp.

Zellner, Herold T. *Behold, He Cometh*. Nazareth, Pa.: pub. by author, n.d., 20 pp.

————. *Each Day for a Year*. N.d., 4 pp.

————. *57 Reasons Why I Believe in the Bodily Resurrection of Jesus Christ*. Nazareth, Pa.: pub. by author, n.d., 16 pp.

————. *The Church of God*. Nazareth, Pa.: pub. by author, n.d., 8 pp.

————. *The Gateway into God's Kingdom*. Nazareth, Pa.: pub. by author, n.d., 15 pp.

————. *Who Is That Faithful and Wise Servant?* Nazareth, Pa.: pub. by author, n.d., 19 pp.

D. CHAPTERS AND SECTIONS OF BOOKS
ABOUT JEHOVAH'S WITNESSES

All works in this section are full-length chapters or book sections about Witnesses. This excellent material is generally inaccessible, as most standard indexes and bibliographies do not tap this source. This list was compiled through extensive library research of indexes, fellow researchers, and the various books written on the Witnesses. About half of these entries discuss theological issues; often these books contain a full chapter on the Witnesses, plus discussion elsewhere in the text. The other entries contain information relative to the Witnesses' influence on various governments (mainly in Africa, America, and Europe) and various political involvements of the Witnesses, mostly relative to personal freedoms (especially freedom of the press, of speech, to not salute the flag, and to proselytize from door to door, in parks, and with the use of loudspeakers).

Although only a fraction of the material about Witnesses in books is included here, an attempt has been made to utilize some of the more common references as well as some of the lengthier references. Almost all the works in this section are in English although some important chapters in other languages are also included. Thus, this section is far less exhaustive than any other in this book. Some of the sections about Witnesses are very short but are included because of their significance. A number of these works include extremely extensive discussions of the Witnesses. For example, Margrete Buber's *Under Two Dictators* is about her experiences with Witnesses in the concentration camps of the Soviet Union and Germany. Other references which deal with the concentration camps are those by Luchterhand, Kogan, and Bettelheim. Buber, not a Witness herself, discusses extensively her experiences with them and her observations of those she met in the camps during World War II.

Books that are recommended for a general understanding of the Witnesses include those by Braden, Clark, Kolarz (expertly discusses the Witnesses in Russia), Davies, Gardner (an excellent discussion and criticism of the Witnesses' belief, held until the late 1920s, that the Great Pyramid of Giza is a "Bible in stone," God's hidden communication about the end of the age—our time in history—and various important events in history, which are easily interpreted in retrospect), and Gerstner (a very useful review of the Witnesses' theology). Also very useful are the works by Gruss (an excellent review of the Witnesses' theology), and Hoekema (a detailed discussion of some of the problems of the Witnesses' doctrines of Jesus, hellfire, etc.).

Several of the references included were written by active Witnesses, for example, Henschel and Knorr (most of Knorr's references are in various encyclopedias). Another excellent source is Hoffman, who includes a chapter in his book, *Jungle Gods*, about "Thomas, son of God," an early Watchtower convert who caused havoc in Africa and left several score dead. Concerning the African situation in general, the most useful references are Shepperson and Rotburg. From a sociological perspective the works by Bryan Wilson, Yinger, Zaretsky, Beckford, La Fave, Maesen, and Lanternari are the most useful and the most often quoted.

Abel, Ron W. *Wrested Scriptures*. Pasadena, Cal.: Geddes Press, c. 1974, pp. 57-67, hb.

Abrams, Ray H. *Preachers Present Arms*. New York: Round Table Press, Inc., 1933, pp. 135, 182-185, 218-219, hb.

Adair, James, and Ted Miller, eds. *We Found Our Way Out*. Grand Rapids, Mich.: Baker Book House, 1964 (reprinted in 1975).

Alexander, David, ed. *Eerdman's Handbook to the Bible*. Grand Rapids, Mich.: William B. Eerdman's Publ. Co., 1973, p. 79.

Algermissen, Konrad. *Konfessionskunde*. Hanover: J. Giesel, 1930, 845 pp. (Study of Denominations.)

————. *Christian Denominations*. St. Louis, Mo.: B. Herder Book Co., 1945, pp. 875-880.

————. *The Christian Sects*. London: Burns and Oates, 1962.

The Australian Encyclopaedia. Vol. V. Sydney, Australia: Halstead Press, c. 1958, pp. 125-126.

Bach, Marcus. *They Have Found a Faith*. Indianapolis, Ind.: Bobbs-Merrill Co., 1946, Chapter 2, "Jehovah's Witnesses," pp. 22-56.

————. *Faith and My Friends*. New York: Bobbs-Merrill, 1951, 302 pp. About the small American sects including several similar to the Witnesses.

————. *Strange Sects and Curious Cults*. New York: Dodd, Mead and Co., 1961, pp. 3, 114-124.

Backman, Milton V. *American Religions and the Rise of Mormonism*. Salt Lake City, Utah: Deseret Book Co., 1970, pp. 377-387.

————. *Christian Churches of America: Origins and Beliefs*. Provo, Utah: Brigham Young University Press, 1976, Chapter 16, "The Watchtower Bible and Tract Society," pp. 175-184.

Ball, Howard. *Judicial Craftsmanship or Fiat?* Westport, Conn.: Greenwood Press, 1967, Chapter 4, "The Flag Salute Cases," pp. 66-102.

Barber, Hollis W. "Religious Liberty v. Police Power: Jehovah's Witnesses" in *Outside Readings in Sociology*, ed. E.W. Schuler, pp. 439-442, Reading 53.

Barker, A.J. *Prisoners of War*. New York: Universe Books, 1975, p. 116.

Barker, Lucius. *Freedom, Courts, Politics: Studies in Civil Liberties*. Englewood Cliffs, N.J.: Prentice-Hall, Inc., 1965, pp. 220-221.

Barrett, David. *Schism and Renewal in Africa*. Oxford, England: Oxford University Press, 1968, pp. 25, 57-58.

Barth, Alan. *Prophets with Honor*. New York: Alfred A. Knopf, 1974, Chapter V, "Freedom of Mind and Spirit Must Be Preserved," pp. 108-130 and "Minersville School District," Appendix D, pp. 224-228.

Bartoshevich, E.M. "Jehovah's Witnesses" in *The Great Soviet Encyclopedia*. New York: Macmillan, Inc., 3rd ed., Vol. 10, 1976, p. 523.

Bates, Ernest Southerland, ed. "Russell, Charles Taze" in *Dictionary of American Biography*, Vol. VIII. New York: Charles Scribner & Sons, 1935, 1963, p. 240.

Beckford, James A. "The Embryonic Stage of a Religious Sect's Development: The Jehovah's Witnesses" in *Sociological Yearbook of Religion in Great Britain*, ed. Michael Hill, Vol. 5, pp. 11-32. London: SCM Press Ltd., 1972.

————. "The Contrasting Types of Sectarian Organization" in *Sectarianism: Analysis of Religious and Non-Religious Sects*, ed. Roy Wallis. London: Peter Owen Ltd., 1975, pp. 70-85; New York: John Wiley & Sons, 1975.

Beesley, Winfield. *Evangelism Unmasked*. N.J.: Independent
    Publications, n.d., p. 31.

Benoit, Jean Paul. *Denominations et Sectes*. Paris: Librairie
    Protestante, n.d. (Denominations and Sects.)

Benson, Purnell Handy. *Religion in American Culture*. New
    York: Harper & Bros., 1960, pp. 120-121, 614, 615, 669,
    671, 691.

Benware, Paul N. *Ambassadors and Armstrongism*. Nutley, N.J.:
    The Presbyterian and Reformed Publishing Co., 1975, pp.
    30-32.

Berkouner, G.C. *The Person of Christ*. Grand Rapids, Mich.:
    Wm. B. Eerdmans Pub. Inc., 1954, "The Deity of Christ," pp.
    155-192.

Berry, Harold. *Examining the Cults*. Lincoln, Neb.: Back to
    the Bible Pub., 1977, 1979, Chapter 4, "Jehovah's Witnesses:
    A Twisted Testimony," pp. 45-59.

Bestic, Alan. *Praise the Lord and Pass the Contribution*.
    London, England: Cox and Wyman, Ltd., 1971, pp. 217-237,
    251 and p. x (Chapter 12, "The End of the World Is Nigh").

Bettelheim, Bruno. *The Informed Heart*. Glencoe, Ill.: The
    Free Press of Glencoe, Illinois, 1960, pp. 20, 119, 122-
    123, 182, 190, 280.

Bickel, Alexander. *The Supreme Court and the Idea of Progress*.
    New York: Harper Torchbooks, 1970, pp. 105-106.

Bills, Alex V. "The History of the English Bible: Studies of
    Translation and Translators, Versions and Publications."
    Unpublished manuscript, Garden City, Kans., n.d.

Blanshard, Paul. *God and Man in Washington*. Boston, Mass.:
    Beacon Press, 1960, pp. 21, 51, 53, 57, 62-63, 67-69.

————. *Religion and the Schools: The Great Controversy*.
    Boston, Mass.: Beacon Press, 1963, p. 21.

Blessing, William L. *Outer Space People and Inner Earth
    People*. Colo.: House of Prayer for All People, 1965, 1973,
    p. 146.

Bloesch, Donald G. *The Reform of the Church.* Grand Rapids, Mich.: William B. Eerdmans Publishing Co., 1970, p. 139.

Boa, Kenneth. *Cults, World Religions and You.* Wheaton, Ill.: Victor Books, 1972 (reprinted in 1977), Chapter 12, "Jehovah's Witnesses," pp. 73-80.

Bociurkiw, Bohdan R., and John W. Strong, eds. *Religion and Atheism in the U.S.S.R. and Eastern Europe.* Toronto, Canada: University of Toronto Press, pp. 60, 74, 85, 89, 126, 130, 146, 147, 361.

Bodensieck, Julius. *Isms New and Old.* Columbus, Ohio: The Book Concern, 1939. 111 pp. One chapter on Russellism.

Boehm, Eric H. *We Survived: Fourteen Histories of the Hidden and Hunted of Nazi Germany.* Santa Barbara, Cal.: CLIO Press, 1966, pp. 27, 137, 208.

Booth, Joseph. *Africa for the African.* Baltimore, Md., 1897. Booth was a follower of Russell for several years.

Bourdeaux, Michael. *Religious Ferment in Russia.* London, England: Macmillan, 1968, pp. 148-149; New York: St. Martin's Press, 1968.

Braden, Charles S. *These Also Believe.* New York: Macmillan, 1949, 1960, Chapter 10, "Jehovah's Witnesses," pp. 358-384.

————. "Jehovah's Witnesses" in *Twentieth Century Encyclopedia of Religious Knowledge,* Vol. 1, pp. 444-445.

Breese, Dave. *Know the Mark of Cults.* Wheaton, Ill.: Victor Books, 1975, pp. 37, 41, 47, 48, 83, 113, pb., 128 pp.

Brock, Peter. *Pacifism in the United States.* Princeton, N.J.: Princeton Univ. Press, 1968, pp. 18, 860-866, 918, 948.

————. *Twentieth-Century Pacifism.* New York: Van Nostrand Reinhold Co., 1970, pp. 34, 45, 111, 165, 175, 180, 199-207.

Brooks, Keith. *The Trinity: Must We Believe It?* Chicago: Moody Press, n.d., p. 2.

Brown, A.C. *Translations of the English Bible: Revisions and Versions--A Reference Guide.* Oak Park, Ill., c. 1970, pp. 41-42, 51.

Brown, W. Gordon. *Pagan Christianity*. Toronto, Canada:
   Toronto Baptist Seminary (first ed. Aug. 1933), revised ed.
   Jan. 1946, pp. 170-180.

Bruce, F.F. *The English Bible: A History of Translations*.
   New York: Oxford Univ. Press, 1961, 1970, p. 184.

Buber, Margarete. *Under Two Dictators*. London, England:
   Gollancz, 1940 (also published by Dodd, Mead & Co. in New
   York, n.d.), pp. 185-186, 201, 204, 213, 218-238, 246-249,
   255, 256, 259, 261-262, 265, 271, 274, 277, 279, 280, 317-
   318.

Buell, Raymond Leslie. *The Native Problem in Africa*, Vol. 1.
   New York: Macmillan Co., 1928, pp. 242-243, 246-249.

Burrell, Maurice, and J. Stafford Wright. *Some Modern Faiths*.
   London, England: Inter-Varsity Fellowship, 1974, pp. 19-36
   and 58-69.

————. *Whom Then Can We Believe?* Chicago: Moody Press,
   1976, pp. 16-34, 66-67, pb.

Butter, Stephen H. *Legal Rights to Draft Deferments*. Cleveland, Ohio: Centre House Publishing, Inc., 1971, pp. 92-93,
   122-123.

Butterworth, George. *Churches, Sects and Religious Parties*.
   London, England: Society for Promoting Christian Knowledge,
   1936, Part III, Chapter 6, "Judge Rutherford," pp. 137-141.

Buzzard, Lynn, and Samuel Ericsson. *The Battle for Religious
   Liberty*. Elgin, Ill.: David Cook Pub. Co., 1982, pp. 65-
   68, 72, 100, 251-252.

Cantor, Norman L. "A Patient's Decision to Decline Life-
   saving Medical Treatment: Bodily Integrity Versus the
   Preservation of Life." Chapter 27 in *Ethics in Medicine*,
   ed. Stanley Joel Reiser et al. Cambridge, Mass.: MIT
   Press, pp. 156-168, 199.

Case, Shirley Jackson. *The Millennial Hope: A Phase of War-
   Time Thinking*. Chicago: The University of Chicago Press,
   1918, p. 253.

Cawley, Clifford C. *The Right to Live: The Position of the
   Law When Religious Dogma Opposes Medicine*. South Brunswick,
   Canada: A.S. Barnes and Co., 1969, 303 pp. Deals with
   Jehovah's Witnesses, Christian Science, and other religions.

Chamberlin, Eric Russell. *Antichrist and the Millennium.* New York: Saturday Review Press/E.P. Dutton Co., 1975, "October 1975," pp. 167-95.

Chapman, Antony J., and Hugh C. Foot. *Humour and Laughter: Theory, Research and Applications.* London, England: Wiley, 1976, p. 73.

The Christadelphians. *People We Meet.* N.d., pp. 10-11. Partly by Harry Whittaker.

Clark, Elmer. *The Small Sects in America.* Nashville, Tenn.: Abingdon Press (revised ed. 1965), pp. 45-47, 256 pp., hb., pb.

Colson, Elizabeth, and Max Gluckman, eds. *Seven Tribes of British Central Africa.* Manchester, England: Manchester University Press, 1959, p. 235.

Concordia Cyclopedia. "Russellism" (1927 ed.).

Congressional Record, May 4, 1918, p. 6052, Senator Overman, Vol. 56, Part 6, pp. 6050-6054.

Conway, J.S. *The Nazi Persecution of the Churches: 1933-1945.* London, England: Weidenfeld and Nicolson, n.d., pp. 195-199, 200-201, 371, 373, 413 n. 61, 450.

Cornell, Julien. *Conscience and the State.* New York: John Day Co., 1944, pp. 67, 68, 135. Reprinted New York: Garland Pub. Inc., 1973.

Craig, Samuel. *Christianity, Rightly So Called.* Philadelphia, Pa.: Presbyterian and Reformed Publishing Co., 1957, pp. 6, 252.

Creighton, Helen. *Law Every Nurse Should Know.* Philadelphia, Pa.: W.B. Saunders Co., 1975, pp. 145-149.

Cross, Sholto. "A Prophet Not Without Honour: Jeremiah Gondwe" in *African Perspectives*, ed. Christopher Allen and R.W. Johnson. Cambridge, Mass.: Cambridge University Press, 1970, pp. 171-184, 187.

Cunha, Silva E. *Movimentos Associativas no. Africa Negra, Ministero do Ultramar Lisboa.* 1956 (one chapter on the Watchtower Society).

Current Biography. "Knorr, Nathan H(omer)." Ed. Marjorie Candee. New York: H.W. Wilson Co., pp. 310–312.

Cushman, Robert E. *Civil Liberties in the U.S.* Ithaca, N.Y.: Cornell University Press, 1956.

Davies, Horton. *The Challenge of the Sects.* Philadelphia, Pa.: The Westminster Press, 1961, pp. 99–110, pb.

————. *Christian Deviations* (revision of *Challenge of the Sects*). Philadelphia, Pa.: Westminster Press, 1961, pp. 64–73, pb. British edition of SCM Press Ltd., London.

Dedek, John F. *Contemporary Medical Ethics.* New York: Sheed and Ward, Inc., 1975, pp. 13, 17.

De Moor, U. *Leur Combat.* Paris, n.d. (Their Struggle.) One chapter on Kitawala.

Dennett, H. *A Guide to Modern Versions of the New Testament.* 1966, "The New World Translation," pp. 111–113.

Dicks, Henry V. *Licensed Mass Murder.* New York: Basic Books, Inc., 1972, pp. 228–229.

Douty, Norman F. *Another Look at Seventh-day Adventism.* Grand Rapids, Mich.: Baker Book House, 1962, pp. 62, 70, 182, hb.

Drinan, Robert. *Religion, the Courts and Public Policy.* 1963, pp. 20, 76–77, 190–193.

Drury, Robert L., and Kenneth C. Ray. *Essentials of School Law.* New York: Appleton-Century-Crofts, 1967, pp. 147–148.

Duncan, Homer. *The King Is Coming.* Lubbock, Texas, n.d., p. 14.

Einbinder, Harvey. *The Myth of the Britannia.* New York: Grove Press, 1964, p. 67.

Eisenhower, Dwight D. *At Ease: Stories I Tell to Friends.* Garden City, N.Y.: Doubleday and Co., Inc., 1967, pp. 305–306.

Emerson, Thomas I. *Toward a General Theory of the First Amendment.* New York: Vintage Books, 1963, pp. 65, 136, 137–141.

Encyclopedia of Russia. "Jehovah's Witnesses." New York: Macmillan, 1972, Vol. 10, p. 244.

Encyclopedia of World Biography. "C.T. Russell" by Charles Wetzel. New York: McGraw-Hill, 1973, Vol. 9, p. 332.

Ferguson, Charles W. *The Confusion of Tongues.* Garden City, N.Y.: Doubleday, Doran & Co., 1928, pp. 63–88, 464 pp., hb.

Field, G.C. *Pacifism and Conscientious Objection.* Cambridge, Mass.: Cambridge University Press, 1945, pp. 16–17, 98.

Fisher, C. William. *Why I Am a Nazarene.* Kansas City, Mo.: Nazarene Publishing House, 1958, pp. 70–90, pb. Revised ed., 1969.

Flint, David. *The Hutterites: A Study in Prejudice.* Toronto, Canada: Oxford University Press, 1975, p. 66.

Franz, Frederick W. "Jehovah's Witnesses" in *Britannica Book of the Year,* 1978, pp. 127, 610. The same article was revised each year to date: 1979, pp. 600–601; 1980, p. 600; 1981, p. 598; 1982, pp. 599, 606.

Freeman, Hobart E. *Every Wind of Doctrine.* Claypool, Ind.: Faith Publications, 1974, pp. 91–94, hb.

Friedman, Phillip. "Was There an 'Other Germany' During the Nazi Period?" in *Yivo Annual of Jewish Social Science,* Vol. 10. New York: Yivo Institute for Jewish Research, 1955, pp. 111–113.

————, and Tadeusz Holvj. *Oswiecim.* Warsaw: Spolka Wydawnicza "Ksiazke," 1946. Summaries in French, Russian, and English, pp. 291–308. Pages 163–164 contain documents both in their original German and in a Polish translation. On pp. 179 to 186 is the letter written on July 15, 1943, by Ernst Kaltenbrunner regarding Nazi policies concerning Jehovah's Witnesses.

Gaebelein, A.C. *The Work of Christ.* New York: Our Hope, 1913, pp. 60–61.

Gann, L.H. *A History of Northern Rhodesia.* London, England: Chatto and Windus, 1964, pp. 168–170, 230–237, 300–303.

Gardner, Martin. *Fads and Fallacies in the Name of Science* (originally published in 1952 under the title *In the Name of Science*). New York: Dover, 1957, pp. 181–182; also Chapter 15, "The Great Pyramid," mostly about Russell's ideas.

Garrison, Winfred. *Unassimilable Varieties of Religious Expression*. New York: Harper and Brothers, 1933, p. 293.

Gaustad, Edwin Scott. *Dissent in American Religion*. Chicago: Univ. of Chicago Press, 1973, pp. 114–117.

——————. *Historical Atlas of Religion in America*. New York: Harper and Row, 1969, pp. 115–118.

——————, ed. *The Rise of Adventism*. New York: Harper and Row, 1964, pp. 200, 204.

Gaylin, Willard. *In the Service of Their Country: War Resisters in Prison*. New York: Viking Press, 1970, pp. 179, 192, 269–273, 315, 327.

Gerstner, John H. *The Theology of the Major Sects*. Grand Rapids, Mich.: Baker Book House, 1960, pp. 11, 13, 29–39, 130–134, 153–169, pb.

Goode, Erich. *Deviant Behavior*. Englewood Cliffs, N.J.: Prentice-Hall, 1978, p. 78.

Gorovitz, Samuel, ed. *Moral Problems in Medicine*. Englewood Cliffs, N.J.: Prentice-Hall, Inc., 1976, pp. 196, 230–241.

Graebner, Theodore. *War in the Light of Prophecy, "Was It Foretold?"* St. Louis, Mo.: Concordia Publishing House, 1941, pp. 8, 13–14, 20–21, 35–36, 73, 99–102, 103–113, 130–133, hb. About Russell's predictions and those of others about 1914 and World War I.

Gray, James M. *Satan and the Saint: The Present Darkness and the Coming Light*. Chicago, Ill., 1909. One chapter on Jehovah's Witnesses.

Great Soviet Encyclopedia, Vol. 10. New York: Macmillan, Inc., c. 1970, p. 523. An American translation of Russian edition entitled *Bol'shaia Sovetskaia Entsiklopediia*, ed. A.M. Prokhorov.

Gruss, Edmond. *Cults and the Occult in the Age of Aquarius*. Nutley, N.J.: The Presbyterian and Reformed Publishing Co., 1974, pp. 5, 7–13, 131–132, pb.; 2nd ed. 1980, Revised, pp. 5, 9–16.

————. *The Ouija Board: Doorway to the Occult.* Chicago: Moody Press, 1975.

Gwatkin, H.M. *The Arian Controversy.* New York: Longmans Green & Co., Inc., n.d. (about 1890).

Hardon, John A. *The Protestant Churches of America.* Westminster, Md.: The Newman Press, 1956, pp. 297-302, hb.

Hasselgrave, David. *Dynamic Religious Movements.* Grand Rapids, Mich.: Baker Book House, 1978, Chapter 9, "Jehovah's Witnesses" by Wilton Nelson and Richard Smith, pp. 137-199.

Hayes, Denis. *Challenge of Conscience: The Story of the Conscientious Objectors of 1939-1949.* Reprint of original, New York: Garland Publishing, 1972, pp. 25-27, 48, 54, 83, 107-111, 170-175, 242-245, 254-256, 268-269, 274-275, 353, 374.

Hayward, Max, and William Fletcher, eds. *Religion in the Soviet State.* London, England: Pall Mall Press, 1969.

Hebert, Gerard. "Jehovah's Witnesses" in *The New Catholic Encyclopedia*, Vol. 7. New York: McGraw-Hill Book Co., 1967 ed., pp. 864-865.

Heley, A. "Jehovah's Witnesses' Worship" in *A Dictionary of Liturgy and Worship*, ed. J.G. Davis. New York: Macmillan Co., 1972, pp. 206-207.

Henschel, Milton G. "Who Are Jehovah's Witnesses?" in *Religion in America*, ed. Leo Rosten. New York: Simon and Schuster, 1963.

Hershey, L.B. *Legal Aspects of Selective Service.* Jan. 1, 1963. Rev. ed., pp. 21-23; Jan. 1, 1969. Rev. ed., pp. 24-27. Washington, D.C.: U.S. Government Printing Office.

Hills, Margaret T. *The English Bible in America.* New York: The American Bible Society, 1962, pp. 410, 416-417.

Hochhuth, Rolf. *The Deputy.* Trans. Richard and Clara Winston. New York: Grove Press, Inc., 1964, pp. 152, 305-306.

Hoekema, Anthony A. *The Four Major Cults.* Grand Rapids, Mich.: William B. Eerdmans Co., 1963, pp. 223-360, 432-435, hb.

Höess, Rudolf. *Commandant of Auschwitz*. Trans. Constantine
    Fitz-Gibbon. New York: Popular Library, 1951, pp. 61, 78–
    82, 126, 201; London: Weidenfeld and Nicolson, 1959; New
    York: World Pub. Co., 1959, pp. 75, 95–99, 149–151, 237.

Hoffman, Carl von. *Jungle Gods*. New York: Henry Holt and
    Co., 1929, pp. 42–67, 283, 284, hb. Much information about
    the work of Russell in early 1900 Africa.

Hook, Sidney. *Religion in a Free Society*. Lincoln, Neb.:
    Univ. of Nebraska Press, 1967, pp. 95–97.

Hopkins, Joseph. *The Armstrong Empire*. Grand Rapids, Mich.:
    William Eerdmans, 1974, pp. 98, 109, 127, 129, 184, 207,
    220–221.

Hudson, Winthrop S. *Religion in America*. New York: Charles
    Scribner's Sons, 1965, 1973, pp. 347–350.

Huestis, Douglas W.; Joseph Bove; and Shirley Busch. *Practical
    Blood Transfusion*. Boston, Mass.: Little, Brown and Co.,
    1969, pp. 363–364.

Hutten, Kurt. *Iron Curtain Christians*. Trans. Walter Till-
    manns of *Christen hinter dem Eiserner Vorhang*. Minneapolis,
    Minn.: Augsburg Publ. House, 1967, pp. 81–83, 255.

Ingham, Kenneth. "Korea" in *Britannica: Book of the Year, 1974,*
    pp. 397–398.

————. "Malawi" in *Britannica: Book of the Year, 1974,*
    p. 444.

————. "Malawi" in *Britannica: Book of the Year, 1976,* p.
    500.

Irvine, William C. *Heresies Exposed*. New York: Loizeaux
    Brothers, 12th ed., 1942, pp. 149–153, pb. First ed.:
    Timely Warnings, 1917; 2nd ed.: *Modern Heresies Exposed*,
    1919; 3rd ed.: *Heresies Exposed*, 1921, revised 1927, 1929,
    1930, 1935.

Johnson, Thomas Cary. *Some Modern Isms*. Richmond, Va.:
    Presbyterian Committee on Publ., 1919, "Russellism, One of
    the Most Insidious of the Modernisms," pp. 96–156.

Kahle, Paul E. *The Cairo Geniza*. London, England: Oxford
    Univ. Press, 1947.

Kauper, Paul C. *Religion and the Constitution.* Baton Rouge: Louisiana State Univ. Press, 1964, pp. 15, 26, 32, 88, 92.

Keen, Clarence. "Jehovah's Witnesses" in *Darkness vs. Light.* Hayward, Cal.: The Regular Baptist Press, 1953, pp. 63-67.

Kellett, Arnold. *Isms and Ologies, A Guide to Unorthodox and Un-Christian Beliefs.* London, England: Epworth, 1965; New York: Philosophical Library, 1965, p. 10, and Chapter 6, "Jehovah's Witnesses," pp. 53-62 in both editions.

Knorr, Nathan Homer. "Jehovah's Witnesses of Modern Times" in *Religion in the Twentieth Century* by Vergilius Ferm. New York: The Philosophical Library, 1948, pp. 380-392.

————. "Jehovah's Witnesses" in *Britannica: Book of the Year,* *1974*, p. 588.

————. "Jehovah's Witnesses" in *Britannica: Book of the Year,* *1975*, p. 591.

————. "Jehovah's Witnesses" in *Britannica: Book of the Year,* *1976*, pp. 590-591.

————. "Jehovah's Witnesses" in *Britannica: Book of the Year,* *1977*, pp. 500, 530, 570.

————. "Jehovah's Witnesses" in *Colliers Encyclopedia.* New York: Macmillan Ed. Corp., 1979, pp. 534-535 (updated by Herbert Stroup).

————. "Jehovah's Witnesses" in *Encyclopedia Americana,* Vol. 16, 1977 ed., p. 11; and Vol. 16, 1981 ed., p. 11. Danbury, Conn.: Grolier, Inc.

Kogan, Eugene. *The Theory and Practice of Hell.* New York: Farrar, Straus and Cudahy, Inc., 1950, pp. 41-45, 55, 122, 123, 273, hb., pb.

Kolarz, Walter. *Religion in the Soviet Union.* New York: Macmillan, 1966, pp. 338-344.

Konefsky, Samuel J. *Chief Justice Stone and the Supreme Court.* New York: Macmillan Co., 1946, pp. 215-234, 270-272.

Kubo, Sakae, and Walter Specht. *So Many Versions.* Grand Rapids, Mich.: Zondervan Publ. Co., 1975, pp. 88-106.

Kurland, Philip B. *Religion and the Law.* Chicago: Aldine
Publ. Co., 1961; 2nd ed. 1962, pp. 41-74.

La Fave, Lawrence. *Psychology of Humor: Humor Judgments as
a Function of Reference Groups and Identification Classes.*
New York: Academic Press, Inc., 1972, pp. 195-210.

Landis, Benson Y. *Religion in the United States.* New York:
Barnes & Noble, Inc., 1965, pp. 31-32, 82, 105.

Lanternari, Vittorio. *The Religions of the Oppressed: A
Study of Modern Messiah Cults.* New York: Alfred A. Knopf,
1963, pp. 11, 28-31, 35, 44-45, 54-55, 73, 134, 164, 195,
307, 309, 311 (original Italian edition, 1960).

Larson, Martin A., and C. Stanley Lowell. *Praise the Lord for
Tax Exemption: How the Churches Grow Rich--While the Cities and
You Grow Poor.* New York: Robert B. Luce, Inc., 1969, pp. 68,
192.

————. *The Religious Empire: The Growth and Danger of Tax-
Exempt Property in the United States.* New York: Robert B.
Luce, Inc., 1976, pp. 124, 192, 237-238.

Lee, Charles M. *The Vatican, the Kaiser and the World War.*
Aurora, Mo.: Menace Publ Co., 1918, p. 67. Quotation from the
Oct. 15, 1898, *Watchtower*, p. 302.

Leinwand, Gerald. *The Draft.* New York: Pocket Books, 1970,
pp. 33, 35.

Lewis, Gordon. *Confronting the Cults.* Nutley, N.J.: Presbyterian and Reformed Publ. Co., 1966.

Lewy, Guenter. *The Catholic Church and Nazi Germany.* New
York: McGraw-Hill Book Co., 1964, p. 43.

Lincoln, C. Eric. *The Black Muslims in America.* Boston:
Beacon Press, 1961, p. 13.

Littell, Franklin Hamlin. *From State Church to Pluralism.*
New York: Anchor Books, 1962, pp. 90-92.

Luchterhand, Elmer. "Social Behavior of Concentration Camp
Prisoners: Continuities and Discontinuities with Pre- and
Post-camp Life." Chapter 10 in *Survivors, Victims, and
Perpetrators: Essays on the Nazi Holocaust*, ed. Joel E. Dims-
dale. Washington, D.C.: The Hemisphere Pub. Corp., c. 1980.

Maesen, William, and Lawrence La Fave. "The Jehovah's Witnesses Today: A Study by Participant Observation" in *Pro-
ceedings of the Southwestern Sociological Society*, Dallas,
Texas, 1960, pp. 102-104.

Malachy, Yona. "Jehovah's Witnesses and Their Attitude Toward
Judaism and the Idea of the Return to Zion" in *Herzl Year
Book*, Vol. 5, ed. Raphael Patai. New York: Herzl Press,
1963, pp. 175-208.

Mann, Brenda J. "The Great Crowd: Ethnography of Jehovah's
Witnesses" in *The Cultural Experience: Ethnography in Complex
Society*, ed. James P. Spradley. Chicago: Science Research
Associates, 1972, pp. 151-168.

Mann, W.E. *Sect, Cult and Church in Canada*. Toronto, Canada:
Univ. of Toronto Press, 1955.

Marnell, William H. *The First Amendment: The History of Religious Freedom in America*. Garden City, N.Y.: Doubleday &
Co., Inc., 1964, pp. 152, 173-183.

Martin, Walter R. *The Christian and the Cults*. Grand Rapids,
Mich.: Zondervan Publ. House, 1956, pp. 62-66.

――――. *The Kingdom of the Cults*. Minneapolis, Minn.:
Bethany Fellowship, Inc. Publishers, 1965, revised 1968,
Chapter 4 on Jehovah's Witnesses and the Watchtower, pp.
34-110, 325-332, 335.

――――. *The Rise of the Cults*. Grand Rapids, Mich.: Zondervan Publ. House, 1955, revised and enlarged in 1957, 1977,
and 1980, Chapter 2, "Jehovah's Witnesses and the Dawn Bible
Students," pp. 19-33, and pp. 11-17, 73, 105-106.

Marty, Martin E. "The Jehovah's Witnesses" in *Our Faiths*,
ed. Martin E. Marty. New York: Pillar Books, 1976, pp.
224-228.

Mason, Alpheus Thomas. *Harlan Fiske Stone: Pillar of the Law*.
New York: Viking Press, 1956, pp. 525-535, 598-601.

――――, and William M. Beaney. *American Constitutional Law*.
Englewood Cliffs, N.J.: Prentice-Hall, Inc., 1954; 3rd ed.,
1964, pp. 535-544.

Mathis, J.J.W. *A Review of Russellism and Other Sects*.
Arlington, Texas: pub. by author, 1916, pp. 1-43.

Mathison, Richard R. *Faith, Cults and Sects of America.* In-
    dianapolis, Ind.: Bobbs-Merrill, 1960; reprinted as *God Is
    a Millionaire* in 1962, pp. 44-49, 60-65, 278. Chapter 9
    entitled "Jehovah's Witnesses," pp. 61-64.

Maxey, Chester C., and Robert Fluno. *The American Problem of
    Government.* New York: Appleton-Century-Crofts, Inc., 1934;
    5th ed. 1949, pp. 491-492, 494.

Mayer, F.E. *The Religious Bodies of America.* St. Louis, Mo.:
    Concordia Publ. House, 1956, pp. 457-471.

McDowell, Josh, and Don Stewart. *Understanding the Cults.*
    San Bernardino, Cal.: Here's Life Pub. Co., 1983, Chapter 5,
    "Jehovah's Witnesses," pp. 55-82.

McGrath, John J., ed. *Church and State in American Law: Cases
    and Materials.* Milwaukee, Wisc.: The Bruce Publ. Co.,
    1962, pp. 218-236, 274-314, hb.

McLean, W.T. *Isms, "Heresies" Exposed by the Word of God.*
    Grand Rapids, Mich: Zondervan Publ. House, 1951, Chapter 2,
    "Millennial Dawnism," pp. 12-15.

McLintock, A.H., ed. *An Encyclopaedia of New Zealand.* Well-
    ington, New Zealand: R.E. Owen, Government Printer, 1966,
    Vol. 2, p. 460; Vol. 3, p. 64.

McLoughlin, William, ed. *Religion in America.* Boston:
    Houghton-Mifflin Co., 1968, pp. 45-46, 50, 57, 128, 345
    (Winter 1967 *Daedalus*).

McPherson, Aimee Semple. *That Is That--Personal Experiences
    and Writings: The Watchtower.* N.p., n.d., pp. 566-567.

Mead, Frank S. *Handbook of Denominations in the United States.*
    Nashville, Tenn.: Abingdon, 1980, 7th ed., pp. 145-148.

Miller, Edith Starr. *Occult Theocrasy*, Vol. II. Hawthorne,
    Cal.: The Christian Book Club of America, 1933, pp. 539-540
    (reprinted in 1968).

Miller, George W. *Moral and Ethical Implications of Human
    Organ Transplants.* Springfield, Ill.: Charles C. Thomas,
    1971, p. 5.

Minority Rights Group. *Religious Minorities in the Soviet
    Union*, 1960-70, Report No. 1, 1970.

Mitscherlich, Alexander, and Fred Mieke. *Doctors of Infamy: The Story of Nazi Medical Crimes.* Trans. Heinz Norden. New York: Henry Schuman, 1949.

Moberg, David O. *The Church as a Social Institution.* Englewood Cliffs, N.J.: Prentice-Hall, Inc., 1962, pp. 79, 91-92, 403, 455, 458-459, 474.

Molland, Einar. *Christendom.* New York: Philosophical Library, 1959, "Jehovah's Witnesses," pp. 341-347.

Mollison, P.L. *Blood Transfusion in Clinical Medicine.* Oxford, England: Blackwell Scientific Publications, 1972, p. 140.

Morgan, Richard E. *The Politics of Religious Conflict.* New York: Pegasus, 1968, pp. 36, 78, 130.

————. *The Supreme Court and Religion.* New York: The Free Press, 1972, pp. 58-74, 126, 146-147, 158.

Morris, R.B. *Encyclopedia of American History.* New York: Harper & Row, 1965, pp. 499, 586.

Myers, Gustavus. *History of Bigotry in the United States.* New York: Random House, 1943, pp. 490-493.

National Cyclopaedia of American Biography, Vol. XII, "Russell, Charles Taze." New York: James T. White & Co., 1904, pp. 317-318.

Neve, J.L. *Churches and Sects of Christendom.* Burlington, Iowa: The Lutheran Literary Board, 1940, pp. 581-584; reprinted, Blair, Neb.: Lutheran Publ. House, 1952.

Newsweek Editors. *Religion in Action.* Silver Springs, Md.: Dow Jones & Co., 1965, "Jehovah's Witnesses," pp. 108-111.

Niemoller, Wilhelm. "The Niemoller Archives" in *The German Church: Struggle and the Holocaust,* ed. Franklin H. Littell. Detroit, Mich.: Wayne State Univ. Press, 1974, p. 41.

Norman, E.R. *The Conscience of the State in North America.* Cambridge, Mass.: Cambridge Univ. Press, 1968, pp. 89+.

Nyman, Aaron. *Astounding Errors: The Prophetic Message of the Seventh Day Adventists and the Chronology of Pastor*

C.T. Russell in the Light of History and Bible Knowledge.
Chicago: pub. by author, c. 1914, pp. 3, 297-343. An
excellent, but very rare, book.

O'Donnell, Thomas. *Medicine and Christian Morality.* New
York: Alba House, 1975, pp. 45, 58-71.

Olmstead, Clifton. *History of Religion in the United States
of America.* Englewood Cliffs, N.J.: Prentice-Hall, 1960,
pp. 522-523.

Osborn, R.E. *The Spirit of American Christianity.* New York:
Harper & Bros., 1958, p. 42.

Parkinson, James. *New Testament Manuscript and Translation
Studies.* Los Angeles, Cal.: pub. by author, 1970, pp. 24,
28.

Pfeffer, Leo. *Church, State and Freedom.* Boston, Mass.:
Beacon Press, 1968, pp. 650-706.

————. *The Liberties of an American.* Boston, Mass.: Beacon
Press, 1956, 2nd ed. 1963, pp. 50-55, 64, 79, 89, 107,
138-139, 246, 282-283.

————. *The Religious Situation.* Boston, Mass.: Beacon
Press, 1968, pp. 360-361.

Pike, Royston. *Encyclopedia of Religion and Religions.* New
York: Meridian Books, 1958, pp. 207-208.

Pinson, Roppel S. *Modern Germany: Its History and Civiliza-
tion.* New York: Macmillan Co., 1966, p. 513.

Pollock, J.C. *The Faith of the Russian Evangelicals.* New
York: McGraw-Hill, 1964.

Poovey, William. *Your Neighbor's Faith.* Minneapolis, Minn.:
Augsburg Publ. House, 1959, pp. 107-113, pb. (student edition, pp. 112-118).

Powles, L.N. *The Faith and Practice of Heretical Sects.*
1962.

Prewitt, Kenneth, and Sidney Verba. *Principles of American
Government.* 2nd ed. New York: Harper & Row, 1977, pp.
267-268.

Price, Ira M. *The Ancestry of Our English Bible.* New York: Harper & Row, 1956, p. 304.

Prosser, C.E. *Interesting Data on Biblical Subjects.* Los Gatos, Cal.: P.O. Box 989, n.d., 30 pp.

Qualben, Lars P. *A History of the Christian Church.* New York: Thomas Nelson & Sons, 1933, p. 465.

Rall, Harris Franklin. *Modern Premillennialism and the Christian Hope.* New York: Abingdon Press, 1920, pp. 16, 109-168.

Redeker, Charles F. *A Confirmation of the True Bible Chronology.* 1971, 93 pp.

Reich, Warren T., ed. *Encyclopedia of Bioethics.* Vols. 1-4. New York: The Free Press, 1979, pp. 133, 271, 1026, 1361, 1365, 1373, 1377, 1426, 1512, 1514, 1885.

Renker, Z. *Unsere Brüder in den Sekten.* Limburg, Germany: Lahn-Verlag, 1964. (Our Brothers in the Sects.)

Reumann, J. *Four Centuries of the English Bible.* 1961, p. 53.

Reutter, E. Edmund. *Schools and the Law.* Reston, Va.: Nat. Ass. of Secondary School Principals, 1981, pp. 31, 40-41.

Rhodes, Arnold Black, ed. *The Church Faces the Isms.* New York: Abingdon Press, 1958, pp. 31, 69-71, 80-87, pb.

Rice, John R. *Some Serious, Popular False Doctrines Answered from the Scriptures.* Murfreesboro, Tenn.: Sword of the Lord Publ., 1970, chapter on Jehovah's Witnesses by John Wimbush, pp. 293-316, hb.

Richards, Claud Henry. "Religion and the Draft: Jehovah's Witnesses Revisited" in *Law and Justice: Essays in Honor of Robert S. Rankin,* ed. Carl Beck. Durham, N.C.: Duke University Press, 1970, pp. 47-75.

Ridenour, Fritz. *So What's the Difference?* Glendale, Cal.: G/L Publications, 1967, pp. 130-143, pb.

Robertson, D.B. *Should Churches Be Taxed?* Philadelphia, Pa.: Westminster Press, 1968, pp. 36-37, 212-213, 223.

Robertson, Irving. *What the Cults Believe*. Chicago: Moody
    Press, 1966, pp. 47-62, 120, 121, 125, 126, hb.

Robertson, Roland. *The Sociological Interpretation of Re-*
    ligion. New York: Schocken Books, 1970, pp. 119, 134-135,
    148, 166.

Robinson, Jacob, and Philip Friedman. *Guide to Jewish History*
    under Nazi Impact. Joint Documentary Projects Bibliographical
    Series No. 1. New York: KTAV Publishing House, 1973, p. 22.

Roche, John. *The Quest for the Dream*. New York: Macmillan
    Co., 1963, pp. 147, 200-202.

Rohr, John. *Prophets Without Honor: Public Policy and the*
    Selective Conscientious Objector. New York: Abingdon Press,
    1971, pp. 30-32, 76-77.

Roll, William G. *The Poltergeist*. New York: New American
    Library, 1972, pp. 134-142.

Rosten, Leo. *Religions in America*. New York: Simon &
    Schuster, 1952, pp. 96-102, 347-351, 356, 358, 361-362.

Rotberg, Robert I. *The Rise of Nationalism in Central Africa:*
    The Making of Malawi and Zambia 1873-1964. Cambridge,
    Mass.: Harvard Univ. Press, 1965, pp. 66-71, 135-155, 162-
    169, 172-175.

————, and Ali A. Mazrui. *Protest and Power in Black Africa*.
    New York: Oxford Univ. Press, 1970, pp. 478-479, 486-489,
    520-523, 530-531, 536-537, 544-549, 558-559, 566-568, 996-
    997, 1002-1003.

Roy, Ralph, Lord. *Apostles of Discord*. 1953, pp. 20, 21.

Rumble, Leslie, et al. *Radio Replies*. St. Paul, Minn.:
    1939, Vol. I, pp. 312, 325-326; 1940, Vol. II, pp. 299,
    327, 331-336; 1942, Vol. III, pp. 62, 84, 237.

Rusling, Geoffrey W. "Jehovah's Witnesses" in *Chamber's Ency-*
    clopedia. London: International Learning Systems, Inc.,
    Vol. 8, p. 70.

St. John-Stevas, Norman. *Life, Death and the Law*. Blooming-
    ton: Indiana Univ. Press, 1961, p. 47.

Salisbury, W. Seward. *Religion in American Culture: A Sociological Interpretation*. Homewood, Ill.: The Dorsey Press, 1964, pp. 10, 34, 97, 177, 195–202, 240–243, 313, 329–332, 335, 454.

Sanders, J. Oswald. *Cults and Isms, Ancient and Modern*. Grand Rapids, Mich.: Zondervan Publ. House (first ed. titled *Heresies, Ancient and Modern*, 1948; new revised and enlarged ed. 1962), pp. 74–87, pb.

Schwartz, Gary. *Sect Ideologies and Social Status*. Chicago: The University of Chicago Press, 1970, p. 20.

Scott, F.R. *Civil Liberties and Canadian Federalism*. Toronto, Canada: Univ. of Toronto Press, 1959.

Sears, Clara Endicott. *Days of Delusion: A Strange Bit of History*. Boston: Houghton Mifflin Co., 1924, pp. 202–265.

Seldes, George. *The Catholic Crisis*. New York: Julian Messner, Inc., 1939, pp. 116–117.

Shepperson, George, and Thomas Price. *Independent African*. Edinburgh, Scotland, 1958, pp. 18–69, 92, 109–121, 147–161, 185, 210, 226, 323–355, 402, 411–417, 431, 458–460, 498, 539.

Shuster, George N. *Religion Behind the Iron Curtain*. New York: Macmillan Co., 1954, pp. 38–39, 149.

Sibley, Mulford Q., and Philip E. Jacob. *Conscription of Conscience: The American State and the Conscientious Objector, 1940–47*. Ithaca, N.Y.: Cornell Univ. Press, 1952.

Sire, James. *Scripture Twisting: 20 Ways Cults Misread the Bible*. Downers Grove, Ill.: Intervarsity Press, 1981.

Skilton, J.H. *The Translation of the New Testament into English 1881–1950*. 2 vols. Ann Arbor, Mich.: University Microfilms, Inc., 1961, pp. xxxii, 125, 323–325, 327–329, 337, 343–345, 348, 350, 352.

Smart, Ninian. *The Religious Experience of Mankind*. New York: Charles Scribner's Sons, 1969, pp. 22, 487, 488.

Smith, Chard Powers. *Yankees and God*. New York: Hermitage House, n.d.

Smith, Elwyn. *Religious Liberty in the United States*. Philadelphia, Pa.: Fortress Press, 1972, pp. 251, 264-269, 286-287, 290-293, 302-303, 336-337.

Smith, H.S.; R.T. Handy; and L.A. Loetscher. *American Christianity*. New York: Scribner's Sons, 1963, Vol. II, pp. 315, 332-336, 623.

Smith, Paul B. *Other Gospels*. London, England: Marshall, Morgan and Scott, 1970.

Smith, Wilber Morehead. *Egypt in Bible Prophecy: The Strange Cult of the Pyramidists*. Boston: W.A. Wilde Co., 1957, pp. 210, 213.

Spittler, Russell P. *Cults and Isms*. Grand Rapids, Mich.: Baker, 1962.

Stanley, Manfred. *Jehovah in the City of Mammon: On the Sociology of Anti-thetical Worlds in Urbanism, Urbanization and Change*, ed. H. Mizruchi and P. Meadows. Boston: Addison-Wesley, 1969.

Starkes, M. Thomas. *Confronting Popular Cults*. Nashville, Tenn.: Broadman Press, 1972, Chapter 2, "Jesus Is Second Best," pp. 33-43, 118, pb.

Stedman, Murray S. *Religion and Politics in America*. New York: Harcourt, Brace & World, Inc., 1964, pp. 5, 37, 74-77, 123.

Strommen, Merton, ed. *Research on Religious Development: A Comprehensive Handbook*. New York: Hawthorn Books, Inc., pp. 624.

Stroup, Herbert H. "The Attitude of the Jehovah's Witnesses Toward the Roman Catholic Church" in *Religion in the Making*, Vol II, Jan. 1942, pp. 148-163.

————. "Rutherford, Joseph Franklin" in *Dictionary of American Biography*, Supplement 3, 1941-1945. New York: Charles Scribner & Sons, 1973, pp. 678-679.

Strout, Cushing. *The New Heavens and New Earth*. New York: Harper & Row, 1974, pp. 286-289, 311-312.

Struve, Nikita. *Christians in Contemporary Russia*. London, England: Harvill Press, 1967, pp. 240-243 (also published by Charles Scribner & Sons in New York).

Stuber, Stanley. *Denominations, How We Got Them.* New York: Association Press, 1958, pp. 110, 111.

Target, G.W. *Under the Christian Carpet: A Study of Minority Christian Sects.* London, England: Clifton Books, 1969, "Millions Living Will Never Die," pp. 139-148.

Tatum, Arlo, ed. *Handbook for Conscientious Objectors.* Philadelphia, Pa.: Larchwood Press, 1967, pp. 22, 36, 37, 39, 41.

Taylor, J.V. *Christianity and Politics in Africa.* London, England: Penguin, 1957.

————, and Dorothea Lehmann. *Christians of the Copperbelt.* London, England: S.C.M., 1961.

Thomas, Frank W. *Kingdom of Darkness.* Plainfield, N.J.: Logos International, 1973, pp. 35-39.

Thomas, Norman M. *The Conscientious Objector in America.* New York: Huebsch Inc., 1923.

————. *Is Conscience a Crime?* New York: Vanguard Press, 1927. Reprinted by Garland Publishing, Inc., 1972, pp. 33-34.

Thrupp, Sylvia, ed. *Millennial Dreams in Action.* New York: Schocken Books, 1970, pp. 32, 48-52, 148-155.

Toch, Hans. *The Social Psychology of Social Movements.* Indianapolis, Ind.: Bobbs-Merrill Co., 1965, pp. 132, 152, 220.

Tomlinson, Lee Glen. *Churches of Today in the Light of Scripture.* Cincinnati, Ohio: Christ Leader Corp., 1927, "Russellism," pp. 97-109. Reprinted by Gospel Advocate, Nashville, Tenn., 1950, 1977.

Tussman, Joseph, ed. *The Supreme Court on Church and State.* New York: Oxford Univ. Press, 1962, pp. 72-181, 205.

U.S. Government Printing Office. *Conscientious Objection: Special Monograph No. 11,* Vol. 1, 1950, pp. 9, 18-19, 26, 149-150, 153, 261-265, 269-272, 318, 320, 322-323, 326, 328, 338.

————. *Enforcement of the Selective Service Law: Special Monograph No. 14, 1950,* pp. 80-81, 93-96, 98, 100, 110.

——————. *Industrial Deferment: Special Monograph No. 6*, Vol. 1, 1947, pp. 269-270.

——————. *Legal Aspects of Selective Service, revised Jan. 1, 1963*, pp. 8-13, 19-23. (Jan. 1, 1969, ed., pp. 10-15, 23-27.)

——————. *Selective Service: 2nd Report, 1943*, p. 265.

——————. *Selective Service and Victory: 4th Report 1944-1945*, printed 1948, pp. 186, 265.

——————. *Selective Service as the Tide of War Turns: 3rd Report 1943-1944*, printed 1945, p. 178.

——————. *Selective Service Circular No. 3461, Supplement No. 9*, Sept. 28, 1943, pp. 1-4.

——————. *Selective Service in Peacetime Washington, U.S., 1942*, p. 197.

——————. *Trials of War Criminals Before the Nuremberg Military Tribunal, Vol. III* (about a Jehovah's Witness, August Dickmann, who was executed by the German government). Washington, D.C., 1951, pp. 331-332.

Valisevich, Ivan Stepanovich. *Religious Sects*. Irkutsk: Irkutsk Book Publishing House, 1957, 37 pp. (Russian.)

Van Baalen, Jan K. *Our Birthright and the Mess of Meat: Isms of Today Analyzed and Compared with the Heidelberg Catechism*. Grand Rapids, Mich.: Wm. B. Eerdmans Publ. Co., 1919, one chapter on Jehovah's Witnesses.

——————. *The Gist of the Cults*. Grand Rapids, Mich.: Wm. B. Eerdmans Publishing Co., 1938 (revised 1951, 1962), pp. 257-276, hb. Trans. into Spanish as *El Caos de las Sectas*, 1969, pp. 239-261, pb. Reprinted as *The Chaos of the Cults*.

Van Buren, James G. *Cults Challenge the Church*. Cincinnati, Ohio: Standard Pub. Co., 1965, Chapter 5, "Jehovah's Witnesses," pp. 45-56.

Van Sommers, Tess. *Religions in Australia*. Adelaide: Rigby Limited, 1966, "Jehovah's Witnesses," pp. 87-93.

Vorspan, Albert, and Eugene J. Lipman. *Justice and Judaism*. New York: Union of American Hebrew Congregations, 1959, pp. 141-142.

Walker, Allen. *Last-Day Delusions.* Nashville, Tenn.: Southern Publishing Association, 1957, pp. 49-64, 108-128.

Walker, Eric A. *A History of Southern Africa.* New York: Longmans, n.d., p. 667.

Walker, Luisa Jeter de. *¿Cual Camino? Estudio de religiones y sectas.* Miami, Fla.: Editorial Vida, 1968 (2nd ed. 1972), pp. 250-272, pb.

Wallechinsky, David, and Irving and Amy Wallace. *The Book of Lists.* New York: Bantam, 1978, p. 222.

Wallis, Roy. *Sectarianism: Analyses of Religious and Non-Religious Sects.* London: Peter Owen Ltd., 1975, pp. 9-11, 39-40, 43, 70-86, 197, 211, hb.; New York: John Wiley and Sons, 1975.

Warner, Charles W. *Quacks.* Jackson, Miss.: Charles Warner Publ., 1941, pp. 11, 13, 49, 55, 57-58, 189-190.

Washington, J.R., Jr. *Black Religion.* Boston, Mass.: Beacon Press, 1964, p. 117.

Watson, William. *Tribal Cohesion in a Money Economy: A Study of the Mambwe People of Northern Rhodesia.* N.p., n.d., pp. 84, 197-202.

Wellcome, Isaac C. *History of the Second Advent.* Boston, Mass.: Boston Advent Christian Publ., 1874.

Whalen, William J. *Faith's for the Few.* 1963.

————. "Jehovah's Witnesses" in *Encyclopedia Britannica.* Chicago, 1980, Vol. 10, pp. 131-132 (15th ed.).

————. *Minority Religions in America.* Staten Island, N.Y.: Society of St. Paul, 1972, pp. 1, 3, 5, 9, 11, 37, 85-95, 99, pb.

————. *Separated Brethren: A Survey of Non-Catholic Christian Denominations.* Milwaukee, Wisc.: The Bruce Pub. Co., 1958, pp. 174-184, hb.

Wilhite, J. Potter. *Modern Churches and the Church.* Oklahoma: Telegram Book Co., 1956.

Williams, J.P. *What Americans Believe and How They Worship*. New York: Harper & Brothers, 1952 (2nd ed. 1962), pp. 439-441.

Williamson, A.E. "Millennial Dawn," *The New Schaff-Herzog Encyclopedia of Religious Knowledge*, 1910 ed., Vol. 7, p. 374. Grand Rapids, Mich.: Baker Book House, 1954 reprint.

Wilson, Bryan. *Religion in Secular Society: A Sociological Comment*. London: C.A. Watts and Co., Ltd., 1966, pp. 182, 190, 196, 211.

———. *Religion in Sociological Perspective*. Oxford, England: Oxford Univ. Press, 1982, pp. 92, 109, 110, 111, 114, 132, 135, 143.

———. *Religious Sects*. London: World University Library, 1970, pp. 10-17, 34, 98-99, 110-117, 170, 193, 194, 230, 237-239, pb.

———. *Sects and Society*. Berkeley: University of California Press, 1961, pp. 3, 94, 116, 264, 294-295, 319, hb.

Wilson, John. *Introduction to Social Movements*. New York: Basic Books, 1973, pp. 118-119, 128-129, 171, 307, 318.

Words and Phrases, Vol. 1923, "Jehovah's Witnesses." St. Paul, Minn.: West Publishing Co., 1967, p. 9.

Wormser, Migot. *Le Système Concentrationnaire Nazi, 1933-1945*. Paris: Presses Universitaires de France. (The Nazi Concentration Camp System, 1933-1945.)

Wright, J. Stafford. "Jehovah's Witnesses" in *The New International Dictionary of the Christian Church*, ed. J.D. Douglas. Grand Rapids, Mich.: Zondervan Pub. House, 1974, pp. 527-528.

Wyrick, Herbert. *Seven Religious Isms*. Grand Rapids, Mich.: n.d., 99 pp. (one chapter on Jehovah's Witnesses.)

Yinger, J. Milton. *Religion in the Struggle for Power: A Study in the Sociology of Religion*. Durham, N.C.: Duke Univ. Press, 1946, pp. 23, 209-210, 212.

———. *Sociology Looks at Religion*. New York: Macmillan Co., 1961, 1963, pp. 46-48.

Zahn, Gordon C. *War, Conscience and Dissent.* New York: Hawthorn Books, Inc., 1967, p. 102.

Zaretsky, Irving I., and Mark P. Leone, eds. *Religious Movements in Contemporary America.* Princeton, N.J.: Princeton Univ. Press, 1975, pp. 17-20, 27-35, 41, and the chapter entitled "'Publish' or Perish: Negro Jehovah's Witnesses Adaptation in the Ghetto," by Lee Cooper, pp. 700-721.

Zeigler, Harmon. *Interest Groups in American Society.* Englewood Cliffs, N.J.: Prentice-Hall, 1964, pp. 316, 326. Discusses social status, and the flag issue.

E. TRACTS ABOUT JEHOVAH'S WITNESSES

This section consists of tracts published by religious houses, mostly of an evangelical or fundamentalist orientation. Almost all of them are about doctrine; most discuss the Witnesses' denial of the Trinity, immortality, hellfire, and similar issues. They are sometimes difficult to follow unless the reader has a theological background or training. Unfortunately, many are also inaccurate polemics that do not always reflect the Witness position, telling more about the writer than the Witnesses. Some are printed by local print shops and are filled with mistakes. Many are articles reprinted from religious magazines. Some are a personal history of someone who was at one time involved with the Watchtower Society. Many, however, are still very useful in a study of the Witnesses and their opposition.

Acts 17. *Jehovah's Witnesses vs. The Bible.* La Mesa, Cal., n.d., 2 pp.

Adler, Kathie. *Biblical Christianity vs. the Cults.* Holbrook, N.Y.: Narrow Way Ministries, n.d., 3 pp.

————. *Jesus Answered, Watch Out That No One Deceives You. For Many Will Come in My Name, Claiming "I Am the Christ" and Will Deceive Many.* Holbrook, N.Y.: Narrow Way Ministries, n.d., 2 pp.

————. *Narrow Way Ministries.* Holbrook, N.Y.: Narrow Way Ministries, n.d., 1 p.

————. *The Common Traits of Cultism.* Holbrook, N.Y.: Narrow Way Ministries, n.d., 7 pp.

————. *Who Is Jesus That the Angels Worship Him?* Holbrook, N.Y.: Narrow Way Ministries, n.d., 8 pp.

Ahlen, A.C.M. *Sincerity Is Not Enough! Facts Worth Knowing About Jehovah's Witnesses.* Minneapolis, Minn.: Tract Mission, n.d., 6 pp.

Allman, Brad, *The Double Jeopardy of Jehovah's Witnesses.* Gadsden, Ala.: J.W. Ministry, n.d., 2 pp.

Armstrong, Arthur. *There Is a Worldwide Family! Are You a Member?* Detroit, Mich.: pub. by author, n.d., 4 pp. (revised and enlarged c. 1976, 6 pp.).

————. *Twelve Scriptural Reasons Why I Am Not a Jehovah's Witness!* Detroit, Mich.: pub. by author, n.d., 4 pp. Revised, retitled: *Are You Awake to the Personal Visible Return of Jesus Christ to Jerusalem in the Land of Israel?* 1981, 6 pp.

Bias, Rodney. *They Shall Know a Prophet Was Among Them; Jesus Christ, the Firstborn of All Creation; Why Do Jehovah's Witnesses Have Complete Unity?* Scottsdale, Ariz.: pub. by author, c. 1974.

Brooks, Keith L., comp. *The Spirit of Truth and the Spirit of Error.* Chicago: Moody Press, 1969, 12 pp.

Brown, Dorothy M. *A Challenge to Jehovah's Witnesses.* Minneapolis, Minn.: Osterhus Publ. House, n.d., 4 pp. Also published by Pilgrim Tract Society in Randleman, N.C.

Cameron, Neil D. *The Analyst.* North Syracuse, N.Y.: The Book Fellowship, n.d., 7 pp.

————. *The Curse of the Cults.* North Syracuse, N.Y.: The Book Fellowship, n.d., 5 pp.

Cheshire, John. *Witnessing to Jehovah's Witnesses.* Toronto, Canada: Midnight Cry Crusade, n.d., 3 pp. Later revised and retitled *Witnessing to Jehovah's False Witnesses.*

Christian Literature for Jehovah's Witnesses. *A Recorded Message for Jehovah's Witnesses--269-2882.* Scottsdale, Ariz., c. 1976, 1 p.

A Christian Messenger. *Warning: Beware of Religious Door-knockers*. Western Australia: A Christian Messenger, 1983, 6 pp. About blood.

Coleridge, W.J. *Whose Witnesses?* Los Angeles, Cal.: John Ferguson, n.d. 4 pp.

Concordant Publisher's Concern. *Pastor Russell Writes.* Los Angeles, Cal.: c. 1925, 4 pp.

Danger: Jehovah's Witnesses (Russellites). Oak Park, Ill.: Brotherhood of St. Mark of Ephesus, n.d., 6 pp.

Dencher, Ted. *From the Watchtower Society to God.* North Syracuse, N.Y.: The Book Fellowship, n.d., 4 pp.

E.J.T. *A Letter to a Millennial Dawnist.* London: pub. by author, c. 1928, 4 pp.

Emmanuel Gospel Center. *Questions for Readers.* Boston, Mass., n.d., 7 pp.

Faith, Prayer & Tract League. *Jehovah's Witnesses Refuted.* Grand Rapids, Mich.: n.d., 2 pp.

Fisk, Rev. Samuel. *Judge Rutherford and Jehovah's Witnesses.* Manila, Philippine Islands, n.d., 4 pp.

Gigliotti, Carmen. *The Watchtower ... the Big Lie.* Santa Clara, Cal., 1977, 4 pp.

Gospel, Jack. *The Bible and the Watchtower--Do They Agree?* Roseville, Mich.: pub. by author, n.d., 8 pp.

Gospel Tract Distributors. *"Jehovah's Witnesses": The True and the False.* Portland, Ore.: n.d., 7 pp.

Gruss, Edmond C. *Is the Watchtower Society God's Channel?* Brewerton, N.Y., n.d., 4 pp. (later entitled *Who Is "the Channel" to God?* and published by Help Jesus Ministry of Kelowna, B.C., Canada).

————. *Delivered from the Jehovah's Witnesses.* Newhall, Cal.: Los Angeles Baptist College and Theological Seminary, 1972, 3 pp. (reprinted from *Challenge*, July 2, 1972).

————. *Jehovah's Witnesses: A Survey.* Newhall, Cal.: Los Angeles Baptist College and Theological Seminary, n.d., 2 pp.

————. *Why a Witness of Jesus Christ—Not a Jehovah's Witness?* Newhall, Cal.: Los Angeles Baptist College and Theological Seminary, n.d., 5 pp.

————. *Jehovah's Witnesses: The Watchtower Society and Prophetic Speculation*, reprinted from *The Discerner*, Jan.-March 1972 issue, 3 pp.

Gudel, Joe. *Prophecy & the Watchtower*. Kent, Ohio: Bible & Tract Society, n.d., 4 pp.

————. *Is Jesus Really Michael the Archangel?* Kent, Ohio, n.d., 3 pp.

Guindon, Kenneth R. *New Birth Brings Freedom*. Van Nuys, Cal.: Van Nuys Baptist Church, 1974, 5 pp.

————. *How to Witness to Jehovah's Witnesses*. Gadsden, Ala.: J.W. Ministry, n.d., 1 p.

Guinness, H. Gratton. *Light for the Last Days*. London, England: Morgan & Scott, 1917.

Hadley, S. *Do "Jehovah's Witnesses" Follow Jehovah?* Danville, Ill.: Grace & Truth, Inc., n.d., 8 pp.

Hammond, Rev. T.C. *What Is Millennial Dawn Theory?* London, England: Charles J. Thynne, n.d.

Hatton, Max. *The New World Translation of the Bible*. Australia: pub. by author, c. 1967, 4 pp. Hatton is an ex-Witness and now a Seventh Day Adventist pastor.

————. *Jesus Christ—The Firstborn of Creation*. Australia: pub. by author, n.d., 2 pp.

Help Jesus Ministry (all probably written by Maurice Coveney). All published in Kelowna, B.C., Canada.

————. *... Are You Ready for Him?* N.d., 3 pp.

————. *Dear Jehovah's Witness: Can You Accept His Challenge?* N.d., 4 pp.

————. *Fact Sheet for Jehovah's Witnesses*. N.d., 2 pp.

————. *Help Jesus: World Crusade to Help Jehovah's Witnesses Meet Christ*. N.d., 4 pp.

————. *Jehovah's Witnesses, Can You Accept the Challenge?* N.d., 4 pp.

————. *Jesus Christ the Firstborn of All Creation.* Whittier, Cal.: n.d., 4 pp. (reprinted from *Watchout*, March 30, 1975).

————. *Mr. Jehovah's Witness ... "Whom Can You Trust?"* C. 1976, 4 pp.

————. *Mr. J.W. ... Read This Reply to a W.T. Overseer, and "You Be The Judge!"* C. 1979, 4 pp.

————. *Some Definite and Indisputable Mistranslations Found in the Watchtower's Own "New World Translation" of the Bible.* N.d., 2 pp.

————. *Some Helpful Hints.* N.d., 2 pp.

————. *The Balance of Life Is in Christ.* 1975.

————. *The 144,000.* 1975.

————. *The Prophet Who Presumes to Speak in My Name....* N.d., 4 pp.

————. *Warning!* N.d., 4 pp.

————. *Was He Around Recently? Beware of False Prophets at Your Door!* N.d., 4 pp.

————. *The Watchtower or God ... Who Is Telling the Truth?* N.d., 4 pp. (also entitled *The Watchtower or God ... Who Is Lying?*).

————. *The Way Out of the Fog ... Christ!* 1975.

————. *Were You Told the Truth About 1975?* N.d., 4 pp.

————. *Whatever Has Happened to One-Quarter of a Million Jehovah's Witnesses?* C. 1979, 3 pp.

————. *What Greek Scholars Really Think!* N.d., 3 pp.

————. *Who Is Jehovah? ... The Mystery of God.* N.d., 4 pp.

————. *The World's Most Dangerous Book!!* N.d., 4 pp.

————. *You Have Been Warned!* N.d., 4 pp. (also revised issue entitled *Beware! You Have Been Warned!*).

————. *"You Must Be Born Again."* N.d., 4 pp.

Hickethier, C. Robert. *There Is a Way That Seemeth Right.* Darby, Pa., n.d., 3 pp.

Hill, William F. *Are "Jehovah's Witnesses" Really Witnessing for Jehovah?* Independence, Iowa: Calvary Evangelistic Center, 1974, 7 pp.

Jackson, J.L. *When Is the Firstborn Not the Firstborn?* New Hyde Park, N.Y.: pub. by author, n.d., 3 pp.

————. *Is It Right to Worship Jesus?* New Hyde Park, N.Y.: pub. by author, n.d., 7 pp.

Jackson, Wayne N. *Are Jehovah's Witnesses True to the Bible?* Saltillo, Miss.: Barber Pub., 1978, 8 pp.

Kaul, Arthur O. *Are Jehovah's Witnesses God's Witnesses?* St. Louis, Mo.: Concordia Tract Mission, n.d.

Kenner, Forrest L. *"Jehovah's Witnesses?" or Satan's Salesmen?* Lawton, Okla.: Bethel Baptist Church, n.d., 5 pp.

Knoch, A.E. *Pastor Russell Writes Concerning the Universal Reconciliation* (Pastor Russell's letter printed with reply). Los Angeles, Cal.: n.d., 4 pp.

Laymen's Home Missionary Movement. *A Message for "Jehovah's Witnesses."* Chester Springs, Pa., n.d., 6 pp.

Linenmann, K. *Russellism.* St. Louis, Mo., c. 1900, 2 pp.

MacGregor, Keith. *Beth-Sarium and the Watchtower Coverup.* Vancouver, B.C., Canada, n.d., 4 pp.

Mantey, Julius Robert. *A Grossly Misleading Translation.* Chicago, Ill.: pub. by author, n.d., 4 pp.

Martin, Walter R. *Jehovah's Witnesses and the Deity of Jesus Christ.* Oradell, N.J.: American Tract Society, n.d., 3 pp.

————. *Jehovah's Witnesses and the Resurrection of Jesus Christ.* Oradell, N.J.: American Tract Society, n.d., 5 pp.

————. *Jehovah's Witness and the Trinity.* Oradell, N.J.: American Tract Society, n.d.

Mason, Doug. *Anointed by the Spirit--How Is It Manifest?*
Kilsyth, Victoria, Australia, n.d., 4 pp.

————. *What the Watchtower Does Not Tell You.* Kilsyth,
Victoria, Australia, n.d., 19 pp.

Massalink, E.J. *So You Are a Jehovah's Witness?* Colton,
Cal.: Colton Comm. Church, c. 1970, 4 pp.

Mavis, Jeanne M. *I Found the Truth When I Left the Watchtower.* Seattle, Wash.: pub. by author, c. 1980, 4 pp.

Maynard, R.W. *Are Jehovah's Witnesses in Error?* Minneapolis,
Minn.: Osterhus Publ. House, n.d., 4 pp.

Mignard, Robert B. *Fifteen Reasons Why I Cannot Be a Jehovah's
Witness.* Largo, Fla.: Evangel Missionary Fellowship, c.
1965, 6 pp., reprinted by *Independent Fundamental Churches
of America* in Westchester, Ill., 1966, 3 pp.

Miller, C. John. *Witnessing to Jehovah's Witnesses.* Philadelphia, Pa.: Westminster Theological Seminary, n.d., 4 pp.

Moorhead, W.G. *Remarks on "Millennial Dawn."* New York:
Loizeaux Brothers, c. 1891, 4 pp.

Murley, T.R. *Who in the Skies Can Be Compared to Jehovah?*
Orangevale, Cal., n.d., 8 pp.

Nielsen, Rev. John R. *An Open Letter to the Jehovah's Witnesses.* St. Louis, Mo.: Concordia Tract Mission, n.d.,
9 pp.

Orr, William W. *Do You Know What These Religions Teach?*
Minneapolis, Minn.: Religion Analysis Service.

Palmer, Rev. R.F. *What to Say to Jehovah's Witnesses at the
Door.* Cambridge, Mass.: The Society of Saint John the
Evangelist, n.d., 2 pp.

Personal Freedom Outreach. *Whom Can You Trust?* St. Louis,
Mo., 1980, 4 pp.

————. *Why the Name Jehovah's Witnesses?* St. Louis, Mo.,
1980, 4pp.

————. *The World's Most Dangerous Book!!: New World Translation of the Holy Scriptures.* St. Louis, Mo., n.d., 4 pp.

Peters, G. *Theocratic Kingdom.*

The Philippian Fellowship. *Jehovah's Witnesses on Trial: Is This a United Body of True Christians?* North Syracuse, N.Y., n.d., 4 pp.

————. *A Message to Friends of the "Watchtower."* North Syracuse, N.Y., n.d., 7 pp.

Pilgrim Tract Society. *Man Is a Soul: False Doctrines of Russellism and Seventh Day Adventism in the Light of God's Word.* Randleman, N.C., n.d., 4 pp.

————. *A Present-Day "Ism."* Randleman, N.C., n.d., 4 pp.

Pont, Charles E. *"Jehovah's Witnesses" Do Not Believe.* Minneapolis, Minn.: Religion Analysis Services Inc., n.d., 6 pp.

Price, E.B. *Jehovah's "Prophet"?* Pub. by author, n.d., 4 pp.

Questions for Jehovah's Witnesses. Gadsden, Ala.: J.W. Ministry, n.d., 2 pp.

Rockstad, Ernest B. *Questions for "Jehovah's Witnesses."* Andover, Kans.: Faith and Life Publications, n.d., 3 pp. Also published by Osterhus Publ. House of Minneapolis, Minn., n.d., 4 pp.

Russellism or the International Bible Students' Association: The Teachings of Demons. Toronto, Canada, c. 1920, 2 pp.

Salt Publications. *Jehovah's Witnesses/Do They Have the Truth?* Escondido, Cal.: n.d., 8 pp.

Schnell, William J. *How to Witness to a "Jehovah's Witness."* North Syracuse, N.Y.: The Book Fellowship, n.d., 6 pp.

————. *Who Are Jehovah's Witnesses?* Minneapolis, Minn.: Osterhus Publ. House, n.d., 8 pp.

————. *Witnessing for Christ to Jehovah's Witnesses.* Randleman, N.C.: Pilgrim Tract Society, n.d., 4 pp.

Scott, Frank Earl. *Letter to Mr. Kaika.* Wallace, Idaho: pub. by author, 1973, 8 pp.

Smith, Jami. *Dear Brothers and Sisters.* Cal.: pub. by author, 1978, 2 pp.

————. *Regarding That Year 1975.* Cal.: pub. by author, 1979, 2 pp.

Smith, Oswald J. *The Error of Jehovah's Witnesses.* Minneapolis, Minn.: Osterhus Publ. House, n.d., 4 pp.

Sowers, Ivan. *Asleep? How to Counteract Brainwashing by the Jehovah's Witnesses.* Youngstown, Ohio: Berean Baptist Church, n.d., 6 pp.

Staiger, William. *Questions Which Move the Jehovah's Witnesses.*

Storz, Peter. *Witnessing to the "Witnesses."* St. Louis, Mo.: Concordia Tract Mission, n.d., 5 pp.

Stromberg, D.E. *If Christ Is Not God....* Minneapolis, Minn.: Osterhus Publ. House, n.d., 3 pp.

Thomas, Fred W. *Are Jehovah's Witnesses Christians?* Vancouver, B.C., Canada: pub. by author, n.d., 8 pp.

————. *Are Jehovah's Witnesses Deceivers?* Vancouver, B.C., Canada: pub. by author, n.d., 8 pp. (revised ed. entitled *Who Are These Deceivers?*; also entitled *Are Jehovah's Witnesses Deceived?*).

————. *Beware of False Prophets.* Vancouver, B.C., Canada: pub. by author, n.d., 8 pp.

————. *Beware of Their Deception.* Vancouver, B.C., Canada: pub. by author, n.d., 8 pp.

————. *Christianity and Jehovah's Witnesses Contrasted.* Vancouver, B.C., Canada: pub. by author, n.d., 8 pp.

————. *Is It Wrong to Worship Christ as Jehovah's Witnesses Teach?* Minneapolis, Minn.: Osterhus Publ. House, n.d., 8 pp.

————. *Jehovah's Witnesses Deny Worship to Christ.* Vancouver, B.C., Canada: Faith Contenders Guild, n.d., 8 pp.

————. *Kingdom of Darkness.* Vancouver, B.C., Canada: pub. by author, n.d.

————. *Masters of Deception.* Vancouver, B.C., Canada: pub. by author, n.d., 4 pp.

————. *Peddlers of Deception.* Vancouver, B.C., Canada: pub. by author, n.d., 8 pp.

————. *So You're Annoyed.* Vancouver, B.C., Canada: pub. by author, n.d., 2 pp.

————. *The Horrors of Hell.* Vancouver, B.C., Canada: pub. by author, n.d., 8 pp.

————. *Unmasking the Deceivers.* Vancouver, B.C., Canada: pub. by author, n.d., 8 pp.

————. *Victims of Deception.* Vancouver, B.C., Canada: pub. by author, n.d., 8 pp.

Trombley, Charles. *Dear Jehovah's Witnesses, Please Consider These Things.* San Francisco, Cal., n.d., 1 p.

————. *Dialogue on the Christian Cross.* Clayton, Cal., n.d., 4 pp.

————. *Discerning the Body.* Clayton, Cal., n.d., 4 pp.

————. *Eyes of Understanding: Examining Watchtower Armageddon Prophecies.* Clayton, Cal., 1978, 2 pp.

————. *Introducing Witness Inc.* Clayton, Cal., n.d., 8 pp.

————. *Is Jesus Christ Worthy of Worship?* Clayton, Cal., n.d., 4 pp.

————. *Is Jesus Coming Again?* San Francisco, Cal., c. 1976, 4 pp.

————. *Jehovah's Witnesses and the Second Coming of Jesus.* Sarasota, Fla., n.d., 4 pp.

————. *Jesus, Spirit or Man?* Clayton, Cal., n.d., 3 pp.

————. *Keep Testing Whether You Are in the Faith.* San Francisco, Cal., c. 1976, 4 pp.

————. *Theocratic War Strategy or Lying to the Public.* Clayton, Cal., n.d., 4 pp.

————. *To Marry, or Not to Marry?* Clayton, Cal., n.d., 4 pp.

————. *Watchtower Authority over Jehovah's Witnesses.* Clayton, Cal., n.d., 4 pp.

————. *What About 1975?* Clayton, Cal., 1975, n.d., 4 pp.

————. *What Happened in 1925?* Clayton, Cal., n.d., 4 pp.

Twisselmann, Hans-Jurgen. *Bei Jehovas Zeugen--Nur Draussen Eine Klinke?* Itzehoe: Bruder-dienst, c. 1976, 4 pp. (In the Case of Jehovah's Witnesses ... Only a Door Knob on the Outside?)

————. *Der Wachtturm und der Staat.* Itzehoe: Bruder-dienst, c. 1976, 4 pp. (The Watchtower and the State.)

————. *Falsche Propheten unter uns.* Itzehoe: Bruder-dienst, c. 1976, 4 pp. (False Prophets Among Us.)

————. *Jehovas Zeugen und das Jahr 1975.* Itzehoe: Bruder-dienst, c. 1976, 4 pp. (Jehovah's Witnesses and the Year 1975.)

————. *Wer ist der Kluge und treue Knecht von dem Jesus sprach?* Itzehoe: Bruder-dienst, c. 1976, 4 pp. (Who Is the Faithful and Discreet Servant of Whom Jesus Spoke?)

Walhem, Charles William. *Jehovah's Witnesses.* N.p., n.d., 4 pp.

Watters, Randall. *Don't Read Your Bible!* Manhattan Beach, Cal.: Bethel Ministries, 1983, 6 pp.

————. "The Good News of the Kingdom." Manhattan Beach, Cal.: pub. by author, 1981, 8 pp.

————. *What Happened at the World Headquarters of Jehovah's Witnesses in the Spring of 1980?* Manhattan Beach, Cal.: pub. by author, 1981, 8 pp.

Westby, Wayne. *A Message for a Mess-Age.* Vancouver, B.C., Canada: pub. by author, n.d., 1 p.

————. *Christ's Witnesses.* Rose Valley, Saskatchewan, Canada: pub. by author, n.d., 8 pp.

————. *The Clocktower.* Vancouver, B.C., Canada: pub. by author, n.d., 2 pp.

————. *False Religion.* Vancouver, B.C., Canada: pub. by

————. *Help the Blind.* N.d., 1 p.

————. *Spirit Hijackers.* Vancouver, B.C., Canada: pub. by author, n.d., 2 pp.

————. *Watchtower Watergate.* Vancouver, B.C., Canada: pub. by author, n.d., 2 pp.

————. *Which Witness Is Right?* Vancouver, B.C., Canada: pub. by author, n.d., 2 pp.

Wheatley, H.A. *Jehovah's Witnesses vs. the Witness of Jehovah.* Camden, N.J.: Grace Bible Institute, n.d., 6 pp.

Whittaker, Harry. *Why I Am Not a Jehovah's Witness.* Birmingham, England: Christadelphian Auxiliary Lecturing Society.

Witness, Inc. (Most of these are written by Duane Magnani.) *Do You Make Sure of All Things?* Clayton, Cal., 1978, 8 pp.

WtBTS—*Jehovah's Witnesses: Their Position.* London, England.

WtBTS—*British Branch.* 37 Craven Terrace, London, England.

Yuille, Glenn. *Doctrines of Devils.* Pontiac, Mich.: pub. by author, n.d., 3 pp.

Zellner, Harold T. *Each Day for a Year.* Nazareth, Pa.: pub. by author, n.d., 4 pp.

Zions Tower of the Morning Tract Publications. *Food for Thinking Jehovah's Witnesses.* Detroit, Mich, n.d., 4 pp.

Zuck, Roy B. *Letter to a Jehovah's Witness.* Chicago: Moody Bible Institute, 1974, 6 pp. (reprinted from March 1973 issue of *Moody Monthly*).

F. UNPUBLISHED MANUSCRIPTS ABOUT JEHOVAH'S WITNESSES

The following are papers which were presented at professional conventions (such as Maesen, Aguirre, Rogerson) or were circulated among Witnesses. Papers written specifically

to protest various practices of the Watchtower Society are
listed in another section.

Aguirre, Benigno E. "Social Upheaval, Organizational Change,
and Religious Commitment: The Jehovah's Witnesses in Cuba
1938-1965." Presented at the 54th Meeting of the Southwestern Sociological Association.

Alston, Jon P., and David G. Johnson. "Cross-Cultural Analyses
of Missionary Success Among the Mormons, Jehovah's Witnesses,
and Seventh-Day Adventists." Presented at the Society for
Scientific Study of Religion meeting in Oct. 1979, 33 pp.
Mimeo.

Anonymous. "Fight for Freedom." N.d., 6 pp. Mimeo.

————. "History of Jehovah's Witnesses in Canada (1958-1959)."
N.d., 17 pp. Mimeo.

Brills, Alexander. "Discussion of the New World Translation--
Jehovah's Witnesses." P. 23.

Guindon, Kenneth, and David Nicholas. "Why a New Translation
of the Holy Scriptures? (A Frank Analysis of the Bible of
Jehovah's Witnesses)." N.d., 39 pp. Mimeo.

H.L.P. "Should We Salute the Flag?" N.d., 2 pp. Mimeo.

Hook, Roy A. "Memoirs of the Hook Family." Feb. 1970, 13 pp.
Mimeo.

Hupalo, Joseph. "History of the Wkaw Congregation." Oct.
1968, 5 pp. Mimeo.

Maesen, William August. "Cryptic Ambiguity and Belief-System
Formulation: An Exploratory Study Viewing Watchtower Influ-
ence Upon Black Muslim Eschatology." Presented at the
Michigan Sociological Association in Kalamazoo, Mich., on
Nov. 21, 1969, 15 pp. Mimeo.

————, and Lawrence La Fave. "Conflict Resolution as Empirical Refutation of the Iron Law of Oligarchy." Presented at the annual meeting of the Southeastern Psychological Association, Louisville, Ky., April 24, 1970, 9 pp.
Mimeo.

Melin, Arnie G. "My History with the Watchtower Society."
46 pp. Mimeo.

Naish, George P. "The Early Years." Saskatoon, Sask.,
   Canada, 45 pp. Mimeo.

Penton, M.M. "Debate Between M.M. Penton and William Petreman"
   (Pentecostal Preacher). June 1916, 25 pp.

Rogerson, Alan Thomas. "A Study of Educational Theory and
   Practice in the Sect of Jehovah's Witnesses Since 1945 with
   Special Reference to Education Beyond High School Age." Univ.
   of Cambridge, 1970.

Wainwright, Frank. "Appreciating Years of Joyful Service."
   15 pp. Mimeo.

Wainwright, Isabel. "My History with the Watchtower Society."
   Toronto, Canada, 1971, 29 pp. Mimeo.

G. NEWSLETTERS AND MAGAZINES
PRIMARILY ABOUT JEHOVAH'S WITNESSES

   The following are newsletters and magazines which discuss
primarily Jehovah's Witnesses; many of them are no longer
in existence. The only one printed by Witnesses is the *Ham
Association Newsletter*, which contains useful information
about the Witnesses as a movement. Probably the most useful
are William Schnell's (no longer published) and E.B. Price's
papers (also no longer published).

Christen. Ed. Werner Wetter. Wurtt, West Germany, 1975 (?),
   Vol. 1, pp. 3, 5-8, 13-19, Vol. 2, pp. 19-29.

Christian Apologetics Project News. Ed. Bill Warner. Vol. 1,
   No. 1, to Vol. 3, No. 1 (Jan. 1983), published quarterly,
   each 8-12 pp. long. Discusses cults in general.

*Christian Apologetics: Research and Information Service News-
letter*. Ed. Mick Van Buskirk. Vol. 1, No. 1, Dec. 1976/
   Jan. 1977 to Vol. 3, No. 2, Third Quarter 1979, published
   occasionally (about four times a year), each about 8-12
   pp. long.

The Christian Research Institute Newsletter. Ed. Jack Beisner,
   later Gretchen Passantino, and currently Howard Pepper.
   Vol. 1, No. 1, Winter 1979 to date, published quarterly,

usually 8-12 pp. long. Discusses cults as a whole. Name changed to *Forward* with Vol. 2, No. 1 issue.

Christliche Verantwortung. Ed. Willy Müller. Founded 1959, 81 issues as of April 1976. Published bi-monthly.

The Converted Jehovah's Witness Expositor. Ed. William J. Schnell. Vol. 1, No. 1, 1957 to Vol. 8, No. 7, 1969, usually published bi-monthly; most issues about 12 pp. long.

The Expositor. Ed. Charles Trombley. Vol. 1, No. 1, First quarter 1963 to c. 1975, published quarterly, each about 24 pp. long. Charles Trombley was an active Witness for 20 years until about 1964 when he left the movement.

Jehovah's Witnesses HAM Association. A newsletter published monthly, each 2-4 pp. long; first issue probably May 1969. Primarily contains information about HAM radio operation, but also discusses Witness activities and persons.

Personal Freedom Outreach. Ed. Keith Morse. St. Louis, Mo., Vol. 1, No. 1 (April-June 1972) to date, 6 pp. each.

Pros Aponolian. Ed. Ken Guindon. Vol. 1, No. 1, Sept.-Oct. 1974 to Vol. 3, No. 4, Oct.-Dec. 1976, usually published bi-monthly, each about 4-8 pp. long.

Rhema: Sword of the Spirit. Ed. Charles Trombley. Vol. 1, No. 1, Aug. 1976 to date, usually published monthly, some issues combined, usually 4 pp. long. This newsletter deals less and less with the Witnesses. Later issues deal largely with Trombley's charismatic ministry.

Watchman Fellowship Newsletter. Ed. David Henke. Columbus, Ga., May/June 1980 to date, 3 pp.

Witness. Ed. E.B. Price. Vol. 1, No. 1, March-April 1975 to date, published quarterly, usually 16-30 pp. in length. A magazine published by the Lay Activities Dept. of Victorian Conference of Seventh-Day Adventists of Victoria, Australia.

H. REVIEWS OF THE NEW WORLD TRANSLATION

For minor reviews or comments,
see the previous sections.

Byington, Steven T. "N.W.T." *The Christian Century*, 67
(Nov. 1, 1950), pp. 1295-1296.

————. "How Bible Translators Work." *The Christian Century*,
68 (May 9, 1951), pp. 587-589.

————. "Jehovah's Witnesses' Version of the O.T." *The
Christian Century*, 70 (Oct. 7, 1853), pp. 1133-1134.

————. "New World Old Testament." *The Christian Century*,
72 (Oct. 5, 1955), p. 1146.

Countess, Robert H. "The Translation of THEOS in the New
World Translation." *Bulletin of the Evangelical Theological
Society*, 10 (Summer 1967), p. 160.

Gruss, Edmond C. *Apostles of Denial*. Presbyterian and Reformed Publishing Co., 1970, pp. 196-214.

————. "The New World Translation of the Holy Scriptures."
The Bible Collector, 7 (July-Dec. 1971), pp. 3-8.

Haas, Samuel S. "The New World Translation of the Hebrew
Scriptures." *Journal of Biblical Literature*, 74 (March
1955), pp. 282-283.

Heydt, Henry J. "Jehovah's Witnesses: Their Translation."
American Board of Missions to the Jews. N.d., pp. 1-19.

Lewis, Jack P. "The New World Translation of the Holy Scriptures." *The Spiritual Sword*, 6 (Oct. 1974), pp. 32-36.

Light, Dennis W. "Some Observations on the New World Translation." *The Bible Collector*, 7 (July-Dec. 1971), pp. 8-10.

McCoy, R.M. "Jehovah's Witnesses and Their New Testament."
Andover Newton Quarterly, 3 (Jan. 1963), pp. 15-31.

Martin, Walter R., and Norman H. Klann. *Jehovah of the Watch
Tower*. Grand Rapids, Mich.: Zondervan Publ. House, 1956,
pp. 142-161.

Mattingly, J.F. "Jehovah's Witnesses Translated the New Testament." *Catholic Biblical Quarterly*, 13 (Oct. 1951), pp. 439-443.

Metzger, Bruce M. "Jehovah's Witnesses and Jesus Christ." *Theology Today*, 10 (April 1953), pp. 65-85.

————. "Book Review: The New World Translation of the Christian Greek Scriptures." *The Bible Translator*, 15 (July 1964), pp. 150-152.

Rowley, H.H. "How Not to Translate the Bible." *Expository Times*, 65 (Nov. 1953), pp. 41-42.

————. "Jehovah's Witnesses' Translation of the Bible." *Expository Times*, 67 (Jan. 1956), pp. 107-108.

Steadman, Ray C. "The New World Translation of the Christian Greek Scriptures." *Our Hope*, 60 (July 1953), pp. 29-39.

Sturmann, Walter E. "The Bible and Modern Religions: III. Jehovah's Witnesses." *Interpretation*, 10 (July 1956), pp. 339-346.

Sturz, Harry A. "Observations on the New World Translation." *The Bible Collector*, 7 (July-Dec. 1971), pp. 11-16.

Thomson, Alexander. "An Interesting New Version." *The Differentiator*, 14 (April 1952), pp. 52-57.

————. "An Interesting New Version." *The Differentiator*, 16 (June 1954), pp. 131-136.

————. "An Interesting New Version." *The Differentiator*, 17 (Dec. 1955), pp. 257-262.

————. "Jehovah's Theocratic Organization." *The Differentiator*, 21 (June 1959), pp. 98-104.

Further Comments on the New World Translation

Bruce, F.F. *The English Bible: A History of Translations*. London, England: Lutterworth Press, 1961, p. 184.

Dennett, Herbert. *A Guide to Modern Versions of the New Testament*. Chicago: Moody Press, 1966, p. 111.

Guindon, Kenneth R. *Why a New World Translation of the Holy Scriptures?* Unpublished, pp. 1-41.

I. COURT CASES INVOLVING JEHOVAH'S WITNESSES

The following court cases are all either Supreme Court cases or State and Canadian court cases. Witnesses have been taken before the courts thousands of times in the United States, Canada, and many other countries of the world. Thus, the cases listed here are all Supreme Court and the more important State court cases. It would be impossible to locate all of the cases Witnesses have fought, especially as most of them were in local courts.

I. Supreme Court Cases (all in
Supreme Court Reporter, listed according to
general topics.

1. SOLICITATION AND STATE ORDINANCE CASES

Lovell v. City of Griffin, 303 U.S. 444 (1938), pp. 444-453.

Schneider v. Irvington, N.J., 308 U.S. 147 (1939), pp. 147-165.

Largent v. Texas, 318 U.S. 418 (1943), pp. 418-422.

Jamison v. Texas, 318 U.S. 413 (1943), pp. 413-417.

Martin v. City of Struthers (Ohio), 319 U.S. 141 (1943), pp. 141-157.

Prince v. Massachusetts, 321 U.S. 158 (1944), pp. 158-178.

2. PERMIT, PARK, AND PARADE CASES

Cox v. New Hampshire, 312 U.S. 569 (1941), pp. 569-578.

Niemotko v. Maryland, 340 U.S. 268 (1951), pp. 268-289.

Fowler v. Rhode Island, 345 U.S. 67 (1953), pp. 67-70.

Poulos v. New Hampshire, 345 U.S. 395 (1953), pp. 395-426.

3. SOUND DEVICES AND "FIGHTING WORDS" CASES

Cantwell et. al. v. Connecticut, 310 U.S. 296 (1940), pp. 296-311.

Chaplinsky v. New Hampshire, 315 U.S. 568 (1942), pp. 568-574.

Saia v. New York, 334 U.S. 588 (1948), pp. 558-572.

4. *LIFE, LIBERTY, AND LICENSE TAXES CASES*

Jones v. Opelika, 316 U.S. 584 (1942), pp. 584-624.

Murdock v. Jeannette, Pennsylvania, 319 U.S. 105 (1943), pp. 105-140.

Douglas v. City of Jeannette, 319 U.S. 157 (1943), pp. 157-181.

Busey et al. v. District of Columbia, 319 U.S. 579 (1943), pp. 579-583.

Follett v. Town of McCormick, 321 U.S. 573 (1944), pp. 573-581.

5. *FLAG SALUTE CASES (Students)*

Minersville School District v. Gobitis, 310 U.S. 586 (1940), pp. 586-607.

Taylor v. Mississippi, 319 U.S. 583 (1943), pp. 583-590.

West Virginia State Board of Education v. Barnette, 319 U.S. 624 (1943), pp. 624-671.

Mathews v. Hamilton, 320 U.S. 707 (1943).

6. *PEDDLING AND PRIVATE PROPERTY CASES*

Marsh v. Alabama, 326 U.S. 501 (1946), pp. 501-517.

Tucker v. Texas, 326 U.S. 517 (1946), pp. 517-521.

7. *CONSCRIPTION AND CONSCIENCE (C.O.) CASES*

Falbo v. United States, 320 U.S. 549 (1944), pp. 549-561.

Estep v. United States, Smith v. United States, 327 U.S. 114 (1946), pp. 114-146.

Gibson v. United States, Dodez v. United States, 329 U.S. 338 (1946), pp. 338-361.

Sunal v. Large, Alexander, Warden v. United States ex. rel. Kulick, 332 U.S. 174 (1947), pp. 174-193.

Cox v. United States, 332 U.S. 442 (1947), pp. 442-459.

Dickinson v. United States, 346 U.S. 389 (1953), pp. 389-401.

Gonzales v. United States, 348 U.S. 407 (1955).

Witmer v. United States, 348 U.S. 375 (1955), pp. 375-384.

Sicurella v. United States, 348 U.S. 385 (1955), pp. 385-396.

Simmons v. United States, 348 U.S. 397 (1955), pp. 397-406.

Bates v. United States, 348 U.S. 966 (1955).

Simon v. United States, 348 U.S. 967 (1955).

De Moss v. United States, 349 U.S. 918 (1955).

Patteson v. United States, 351 U.S. 215 (1956).

Johnston v. United States, 351 U.S. 315 (1956), pp. 215-224.

Gonzales v. United States, 364 U.S. 59 (1960), pp. 59-75.

Cases Listed in the Federal Reporter *or* Supreme
Court Reporter *involving Jehovah's Witnesses.*

1. CONSCRIPTION AND CONSCIENCE (C.O.) CASES

United States v. Grieme, Same v. Sadlock, 128 F. 2d 811 (1942),
   pp. 811-815.

Base v. United States, 129 F. 2d 204 (1942), pp. 204-210.

Goff v. United States, 135 F. 2d 610 (1943), pp. 610-613.

United States ex. rel. Hull v. Stalter, 151 F. 2d 633 (1945),
   pp. 633-639.

United States ex. rel. Arpaia v. Alexander, 68 F. Suppl. 820
   (1946), pp. 820-823.

Knox v. United States, 200 F. 2d 398 (1952), pp. 398-402.

Dickinson v. United States, 74 S. Ct. 152 (1953), pp. 152-160.

Jewell v. United States, Thoman v. United States, 208 F. 2d
   770 (1953), pp. 770-772.

United States v. Lowman, 117 F. Suppl. 595 (1954), pp. 595-
   598.

United States v. Edmiston, 118 F. Supp. 238 (1954), pp. 238-
   240.

White v. United States, 215 F. 2d 782 (1954), pp. 782-791.

Tomlinson v. United States, 216 F. 2d 12 (1954), pp. 12-18.

Hacker v. United States, 215 F. 2d 575 (1954), pp. 575-576.

Brown v. United States, 216 F. 2d 258 (1954), pp. 258-260.

Campbell v. United States, 221 F. 2d 454 (1955), pp. 454-460.

Witmer v. United States, 75 S. Ct. 392 (1955), pp. 392-397.

Sicurella v. United States, 75 S. Ct. 403 (1955), pp. 403–409.

Gonzales v. United States, 75 S. Ct. 409 (1955), pp. 409–415.

Simmons v. United States, 75 S. Ct. 397 (1955), pp. 397–402.

United States v. Diercks, 223 F. 2d 12 (1955), pp. 12–15.

United States v. Ransom, 223 F. 2d 15 (1955), pp. 15–19.

Olvera v. United States, 223 F. 2d 880 (1955), pp. 880–884.

Rowton v. United States, 229 F. 2d 421 (1956), pp. 421–422.

United States v. Kahl, 141 F. Supp. 161 (1956), pp. 161–166.

United States v. Capehart, 141 F. Supp. 708 (1956), pp. 708–719.

Capehart v. United States, 237 F. 2d 388 (1956), pp. 388–390.

Pate v. United States, 243 F. 2d 99 (1957), pp. 99–108.

United States v. Cheeks, 159 F. Supp. 328 (1958), pp. 328–330.

Manke v. United States, 259 F. 2d 518 (1958), pp. 518–524.

Wiggins v. United States, 261 F. 2d 113 (1958), pp. 113–119.

Rogers v. United States, 263 F. 2d 283 (1959), pp. 283–287.

United States v. Tettenburn, 186 F. Supp. 203 (1960), pp. 203–212.

2. FLAG SALUTE CASES (Teachers fired)

Palmer v. Board of Ed. of City of Chicago, 466 F. Supp. 600 (1979), pp. 600–605. Teacher who was fired for not saluting upheld. Brief submitted to Supreme Court Oct. Term, 1979, printed in booklet form, typeset, No. 79-738. The Supreme Court refused to hear the case, thus letting the lower court decision stand. For EEOC decision, see Vol. 22, *Employment Practices Decisions*, ¶30,692–30,694, pp. 14,638–14,644.

3. BLOOD TRANSFUSION CASES

People v. Labrenz, 104 North Eastern Reporter (2d) (Illinois, 1952), pp. 769–774.

Powell v. Columbia Presbyterian Medical Center, 49 misc. 2d 215, 216, 267 N.Y.S. 2d. 450, 451 (Sup. Ct. 1965).

United States v. George, 239 F. Supp. 752 (1965), pp. 752+

Jehovah's Witnesses v. Kings County Hospital, 278 F. Supp. 488
(1967), pp. 488-502.

John F. Kennedy Memorial Hospital v. Heston, 47 Notre Dame
Law 571 (1972).

4. EMPLOYMENT CASES (loss of job because of Witness faith
    or practice)

Lincolin vs. True, U.S. District Court, Kentucky, June 3, 1975,
No. C74-483 L(A), reprinted in *Fair Employment Practice
Cases*, Washington, D.C., The Bureau of National Affairs,
Inc., Vol. 13, 1977, pp. 199-200.

Redmond vs. GAF Inc., U.S. Court of Appeals, Seventh Circuit
(Chicago), April 10, 1978, No. 76-1839, reprinted in *Fair
Employment Practice Cases*, Washington, D.C., The Bureau of
National Affairs, Inc., Vol. 17, 1978, pp. 208-213.

Gavin, Charles R. vs. Peoples Natural Gas Co. In *Employment
Practice Decisions*, Chicago, Commerce Clearing House, Inc.,
1979, Vol. 19, pp. 6431-6440, Para. 9033.

*Thomas vs. Review Board of the Indiana Employment Security
Division*, 79-952 (April 6, 1981), 21 pp.; also 450 U.S. 707
(1981).

II. American Court Cases—Other Than
Supreme Court (miscellaneous)

Nicholson v. Merstetter, 68 Missouri Appeal Reports, Oct. Term
1897, Vol. 68, pp. 441-447. In this case J.F. Rutherford
was accused of illegally taking possession of a cash register.

Moyle v. Rutherford, 261 App. Div. 968, 26 N.Y.S. 2d 860.

Moyle v. Franz et al., 267 App. Div. 423, 46 N.Y.S. (2d) 667,
aff'd, pp. 666-677, 293 N.Y. 842, 59 N.E. (wd) 437 (1944).
The printed transcript is 3 volumes of almost 2000 pages.
Moyle was an attorney for the Society but left because of
what he perceived as un-Christian practices at Bethel.
The Society twice printed an announcement regarding his
leaving and Moyle sued for slander and won. 60 Sup. Ct.
Reporter 1010, Vol. 60, No. 15, June 15, 1940.

Rutherford v. United States, U.S. District Ct., Eastern District of New York, June Term of 1918 (June 20, 1918;
District Judge Harland S. Howe). Rutherford and several
board members were convicted of sedition.

Rutherford et al. v. United States, 258 Fed. Rep. 855 (1919), pp. 855-867. An appeal to reverse the decision of the District Court of United States for the Eastern District of New York. Rutherford won the appeal, 2 to 3. The case was later dismissed and the charges dropped.

John v. Arizona, 319 U.S. 103 (1943).

Watchtower Bible & Tract Soc. v. Metropolitan Life I. Co., 69 N.Y.S. 2d 385 (1947), pp. 385-394. This is a "right to proselytize" court case.

People v. Mastin, 80 N.Y.S. 2d 323 (1948), pp. 323-329. The Watchtower Society tried to gain tax-exempt status partly because a large amount of products of the farms were sold to the public.

People ex. rel. Watchtower Bible and Tract Society v. Haring, 8 N.Y. 2d, pp. 350-358, Nov. 17, 1960; also in 207 *New York Supplement 2nd Series*, pp. 673-679.

COURT CASES INVOLVING CHARLES TAZE RUSSELL

Marie F. Russell v. Charles T. Russell. No. 202 April Term, 1908. Appeal C. P. No. 1 Allegheny Co. filed Oct. 19, 1908, 8 pp.

Marie F. Russell v. Charles T. Russell. No. 459 June Term, 1903. Court of Common Pleas No. 1, Allegheny Co. Summary filed Sept. 1908, 4 pp. This is the famous Russell divorce case.

Marie F. Russell v. Charles T. Russell. No. 459 June Term, 1903. Application for trial by jury filed Dec. 7, 1903.

Response (on the above case) by C.T. Russell, 3 pp.

Opinion (on the above case against Russell) by J. Macfarlane, 5 pp.

Response by C.T. Russell, 3 pp.

F.I. F.A. Nov. 30, 1908, 3 pp.

Answer to sheriff's interpleader, 1 p.

Charles T. Russell v. Brooklyn Eagle Defendant, No. 12, 462, c. 1904, pp. 188-236.

Russell v. Wash. Post Co., April Term 1907, No. 1781, pp. 21-22; 10-11. (Court of Appeals of the District of Columbia.)

Russell v. Russell, 37 Pa. Superior Ct. 348 (1908), pp. 348-354. Mrs. Russell went back to court to insure Russell's payment of her alimony.

Marie F. Russell v. Charles T. Russell. No. 202 April Term, 1908. Appeal C. P. No. 1 Allegheny Co. filed Oct. 19, 1908, 8 pp.

III. Canadian Cases

Rex v. Kinler et al., St. Francais, 1925, Sept. 10. From *Quebec Official Law Reports (Superior Court)*, Vol. 63, 1925 (p. 483), 2 pp.

Robert Donald v. Board of Education for the City of Hamilton, A.S. Morris and C.B. Hoyce, Trial at Hamilton, delivered Sept. 12, 1944, 9 pp.

Robert Donald v. Board of Education for the City of Hamilton, et al. Court of Appeal, delivered June 6, 1945, 9 pp.

Robert Donald v. Board of Education for the City of Hamilton, A.W. Morris, and C.B. Hoyce, The Supreme Court of Ontario, June 6, 1945.

Walter Lloyd Evans v. The King, The County Court of the County of Simcoe, Nov. 8, 1945, 4 pp.

Greenless v. Attorney General for Canada, Court of Appeal, delivered Dec. 26, 1945, 7 pp.

Eustice W. Kite v. Rex, The County Court of Manaimo, Holden at Manaimo, June 7, 1949, 8 pp.

His Majesty the King on the Information of Joseph Mackie v. George Naish, Police Magistrate's Court, Saskatoon, Sask., Feb. 18, 1950, 13 pp.

Esymier v. Edmond Romain, Province of Quebec, District of Pontiac, No. 5201, Superior Court, Campbell's Bay, June 10, 1952, 7 pp.

Esymier Chaput v. Edmond Romain et al., Province of Quebec, District of Montreal, No. 4873, Court of Queen's Bench (in Appeal), 6 pp. Appeal side, 1 p., July 1954.

Cajeten Chabot v. Les Commissaires d'Ecoles de la morandiens and The Honourable Attorney General for the Province of Quebec, Province of Quebec, District of Quebec, No. 5156, Court of Queen's Bench (Appeal Side), n.d., 11 pp.

Frank Grundy v. The King, 12 pp. (Appendix "A." 10 pp.).

Mario Furlan v. La Cité de Montréal, Province de Quebec, District de Montréal, No. 164 (m), Cour du Banc du Roi (Juridiction d'Appel), 5 pp.

J.B. Duval et al. v. His Majesty the King, Province of Quebec,
   District of Montreal, No. 232, Court of King's Bench (Appeal
   Side), 12 pp.

J. MAGAZINE ARTICLES

This section is divided into the following topics: (1) the
blood issue, (2) court cases, (3) theology and doctrine,
(4) the flag issue, (5) history, and (6) sociological and
psychological studies. Many articles fall into the news
category, i.e., reporting of a specific court trial or a
discussion of some blood transfusion cases. Those in professional journals, such as the *American Political Science
Review* and the *American Journal of Sociology*, tend to be the
most accurate, and those in popular magazines such as the
Saturday Evening Post tend to be the least accurate, sometimes
openly incorrect. Articles in the popular religious magazines
discuss primarily theological matters, and, unfortunately,
many of the writers have a poor understanding of the religious
beliefs, doctrines, faith, and practice of the Witnesses.
Magazine and journal articles are extremely useful because
they report events as they happen, and thus strongly reflect
the *zeitgeist*. One can glean a flavor of how the Witnesses were
received in the past by the public, and especially the press,
by reviewing the articles printed in the 1930s and 1940s in
Newsweek, *Time*, *Saturday Evening Post*, etc. While the Witnesses are not always treated much more courteously in the
public press today, in the 1930s and 1940s they were seen as
the lunatic fringe, attracting only misfits and oddballs.
It is apparent that the Witnesses are slowly becoming much
more respectable, more middle class, well organized, wealthier,
and a permanent part of the American religious scene.
Book reviews are listed under the name of the author of
the book, not the reviewer, since in a number of cases the
reviewer is not known, and generally one is more likely to
be aware of the name of the author of the book being reviewed
than of the reviewer's name.
A large number of authors are unknown (often in the case
of short, one-page news articles). These articles are listed
under their titles.

Blood Transfusion

Ackerman, Terrance. "The Limits of Beneficence: Jehovah's
    Witnesses and Childhood Cancer." *The Hastings Center Report*,
    Vol. 10, No. 4, Aug. 1980.

"Adult Jehovah's Witnesses and Blood Transfusion." *Journal
    of the American Medical Association*, Vol. 219, No. 11,
    1972, pp. 273-274.

"Adult Patient Compelled to Take Blood Transfusion Contrary
    to Religious Belief." *Catholic Lawyer*, Vol. 10, Summer
    1964, pp. 260-263.

"The All Writs Statute and the Injunctive Powers of a Single
    Appellate Judge." *Michigan Law Review*, Vol. 64, pp. 324-335.

Amonic, Robert, et al. "Hyperbaric Oxygen Therapy in Chronic
    Hemorrhagic Shock." *Journal of the American Medical Associa-
    tion*, Vol. 208, No. 11, June 16, 1969, pp. 2051-2054.

Andreassen, M. "Transfusion and Jehovah's Witnesses."
    Ugeskr Laeger, Vol. 138, No. 30, July 19, 1976, pp. 1847-
    1848.

Annexton, May. "Autotransfusion for Surgery: A Comeback."
    Journal of the American Medical Association, Vol. 240, No.
    25, Dec. 15, 1978, pp. 2710, 2711.

"Authorization of Involuntary Blood Transfusion for Adult
    Jehovah's Witness Held Unconstitutional." *Michigan Law
    Review*, Vol. 64, Jan. 1966, pp. 554-561.

"Autotransfusion and Jehovah's Witnesses: Abstract." *Linacre
    Quarterly*, Vol. 31, Nov. 1964, p. 222.

Bach, B., et al. "Surgery of the Esophagus under Hemodilution
    and Autotransfusion in a Jehovah's Witness." *Anesthesia
    Analgesie Reanimatologiia*, Vol. 33, No. 1, Jan.-Feb. 1976,
    pp. 133-145.

Bailey, Charles. "Management of the Major Surgical Blood
    Loss Without Transfusion." *Journal of the American Medical
    Association*, Vol. 198, No. 11, Dec. 12, 1966, pp. 1171-1174.

——————. "Open Heart Surgery Without Blood Transfusion."
    Vascular Diseases, Vol. 5, No. 4, Dec. 1968, pp. 179-187.

————. "Electrolyte Solution in Surgical Patients Refusing Transfusion." *Journal of the American Medical Association*, Vol. 215, No. 13, March 29, 1971, pp. 2077-2083.

Barnard, Jim. "Artificial Blood: Medical Breakthrough That Will Save Thousands--Doctors Claim Miracle Blood Has No Type--Anyone Can Use It." *National Examiner*, Jan. 8, 1980, p. 3.

Barnikel, W. "Blood Transfusion and Patient's Consent." *Deutsche Medizinische Wachen-Schrift*, Vol. 104, No. 13, March 26, 1979, pp. 330-331.

Barton, Frank. "The Battle over Blood." *Today's Health*, Feb. 1966, pp. 46, 79, 80.

Beall, Arthur C., et al. "Physiological Studies during Cardio-pulmonary Bypass Eliminating Hepernized Blood." *Diseases of the Chest*, Vol. 47, No. 1, Jan. 1965, pp. 7-16.

————. "Open Heart Surgery Without Blood Transfusion." *Archives of Surgery*, Vol. 94, April 1967, pp. 567-570.

Begley, Grant F. "Religion Affects Practice of Medicine." *Texas Medicine*, Vol. 66, Dec. 1970, pp. 25, 26.

Benfield, D.G. "Giving Blood to the Critically Ill Newborn of Jehovah's Witness Parents: The Human Side of the Issue." *Legal Aspects of Medical Practice*, Vol. 6, No. 6, June 1978, pp. 33-36.

"Birthright (About Blood Transfusions and the Unborn)." *Church and State*, Vol. 17, No. 8, Sept. 1964, p. 9.

Blomdahl, Rune. "Swedish Conscientious Objectors Win Blood-less Battle." *Liberty*, Vol. 67, Nov.-Dec. 1978, pp. 18, 19.

"Blood for a Baby." *Newsweek*, April 30, 1951, p. 25.

"Blood Transfusion and Jehovah's Witnesses." *Nouvelle Presse Medicale*, Vol. 4, No. 20, May 1975, pp. 1513-1518.

"Blood Transfusion Court Case." *Church and State*, Vol. 16, No. 1, Jan. 1963, p. 13.

"Blood Transfusion Does Not Violate Bible Teachings." *Herald of the Coming Age*, Vol. 24, No. 5, June 1974, p. 16.

"Blood Transfusion--Jehovah's Witnesses." *Journal of the American Medical Association*, Feb. 23, 1957, pp. 660-661.

"Blood Transfusion Refused on Religious Grounds." *Anesthesia and Analgesia*, Vol. 52, July-Aug. 1973, pp. 529-530.

"Blood Transfusions--Jehovah's Witnesses." *Medicine and the Law*, Vol. 163, No. 8, Feb. 23, 1975, pp. 660, 661.

Bloodwell, D.R., et al. "Aortic Valve Replacement and Correction of Fetralogy of Fallot with Double Outlet Right Ventricle in a Jehovah's Witness: Case Report." Submitted for publication.

Boba, Antonio. "Support of Blood Volume During Operation Without Blood Transfusion." *Surgical Forum*, Vol. 17, Oct. 1966, pp. 61-63.

Bolooki, H. "Treatment of Jehovah's Witnesses: Example of Good Care." *Miami Medicine*, Vol. 51, 1981, pp. 25-26.

Bonakdar, M.I., et al. "Major Gynecologic and Obstetric Surgery in Jehovah's Witnesses." *Obstetrics and Gynecology*, Vol. 60, No. 5, Nov. 1972, pp. 587-590.

Bortolotti, V., et al. "Open Heart Surgery in Jehovah's Witnesses." *Giornale Italiano de Cardiologia*, Vol. 9, No. 9, 1979, pp. 996-1000.

Bosomworth, Peter. "Replacement of Operative Blood Loss of More Than 1 Liter with Hartmann's Solution." *Journal of the American Medical Association*, Vol. 203, No. 6, Feb. 5, 1968, pp. 399-402.

Breig, J. "Tough to Be a Justice: Refusal of Blood Transfusions." *Ave Maria*, Vol. 98, No. 15, Nov. 2, 1963.

Bricker, D.L., et al. "Repair of Acute Dissection of the Ascending Aorta, Associated with Coaretation of the Thoracic Aorta in a Jehovah's Witness." *Journal of Cardiovascular Surgery*, Vol. 21, No. 3, May-June 1980, pp. 374-378.

Brown, Howard G. "Opinions of Trial Judges: Parental Right to Refuse Medical Treatment." *Crime and Delinquency*, 1965, pp. 377-385.

Brown, Tom. "The Courageous Last Days of Wife Who Sacrificed Her Life to Save Our Unborn Child." *National Enquirer*, July 15, 1980, p. 3.

Byrne, M.P. "Abdominal Aortic Aneurysm Surgery in the Jehovah's Witnesses." *Illinois Medical Journal*, Vol. 150, No. 1, July 1976, pp. 87-90.

Cantor, Norman L. "A Patient's Decision to Decline Life-saving Medical Treatment: Bodily Integrity vs. the Preservation of Life." *Rutgers Law Review*, Vol. 26, 1973, pp. 228-264.

Celenza, Marlo. "Blood Transfusion and Jehovah's Witnesses and the Bible." *The New Creation*, Vol. 35, No. 10, pp. 10-15.

Clancy, Leo. "Enquirer Story of Bloodless Operation Helped Crippled Reader 'Walk Tall' Again." *National Enquirer*, Jan. 20, 1974, p. 6.

Clapp, Rodney. "The Jehovah's Witnesses Are a 'Killer Cult' Says a Defector." *Columbia Law Review*, Vol. 25, No. 20, Nov. 20, 1981.

Cleveland, S.E. "Jehovah's Witnesses and Human Tissue Donation." *Journal of Clinical Psychology*, Vol. 32, No. 2, 1976, pp. 453-458.

Cockett, Abraham, et al. "Hyperbaric Oxygen Therapy in Chronic Hemorrhagic Shock." *Journal of the American Medical Association*, Vol. 208, No. 11, June 16, 1969, pp. 2051-2054.

Cole, Bill. "Blood Specialist Claims ... Half of All Blood Transfusions in America Are Unnecessary." *National Enquirer*, March 6, 1975.

"Compulsory Medical Treatment and a Patient's Free Exercise of Religion." *Medical Legal Bulletin*, Vol. 24, No. 3, March 1975, pp. 1-10.

Connolly, J.R., et al. "Total Hip Replacement in a Jehovah's Witness Using Hypotensive Anesthesia." *Nebraska Medical Journal*, Vol. 62, No. 8, Aug. 1977, pp. 287-290.

Cooley, Denton, et al. "The Anesthesiologist and the Cardiac Surgeon." *Anesthesiology*, Vol. 33, No. 2, Aug. 1970, pp. 126-127.

————. "Cardiac Valve Replacement Without Blood Transfusion." *American Journal of Surgery*, Vol. 112, Nov. 1966, pp. 743-751.

————. "Open Heart Surgery in Jehovah's Witnesses." *The American Journal of Cardiology*, Vol. 13, No. 6, June 1964, pp. 779–781.

————. "Physiologic Studies during Cardiopulmonary Bypass Eliminating Hepernized Blood." *Diseases of the Chest*, Vol. 47, No. 1, Jan. 1965, pp. 7–16.

————. "Vascular Surgery in Jehovah's Witnesses." *Journal of the American Medical Association*, Vol. 213, No. 6, Aug. 10, 1970, pp. 1032–1034.

"Court Orders Blood Transfusions for Twins over Mother's Objection." *Liberty*, Vol. 67, Jan.–Feb. 1979, p. 30.

"Court Orders Transfusion." *Church and State*, Vol. 19, No. 3, March 1966, p. 9.

"Court Refuses Ruling in Transfusion Dispute." *Hospital Progress*, Vol. 45, Aug. 1974, p. 12.

Cowart, Virginia Snodgrass. "Can 'Artificial Blood' Live Up to Public Billings?" *The Journal of the American Medical Association*, Vol. 247, No. 8, Feb. 26, 1982, pp. 1104–1105.

Dalenius, E. "Blood Transfusion and Jehovah's Witnesses." *Lakartidningen* (Stockholm), Vol. 67, Jan. 14, 1970, pp. 206–207.

DeTouzalin, H. "Refusal to Consent to a Treatment by the Parents of a Minor Child in Danger of Dying." *Nouvelle Presse Medicale*, Vol. 4, No. 20, May 17, 1975, pp. 1515–1517.

Dixon, J.L. "Jehovah's Witnesses and Blood Transfusion." *Connecticut Medicine*, Vol. 39, No. 7, July 1975, pp. 433–437.

Dixon, Lowell. "The Reason Why." *Ethicon*, Vol. 10, No. 7, Jan. 1973, pp. 14, 15.

————, and Gene Smalley. "Jehovah's Witnesses: The Surgical/Ethical Challenge." *The Journal of the American Medical Association*, Nov. 27, 1981, pp. 2471–2472. Reprinted in *Awake!*, June 22, 1982, pp. 25–27.

Doll, P.J. "Refusal of a Life-saving Transfusion: To What Extent May This Refusal by a Traffic Accident Victim Influence the Increase in Damages and Benefits Solicited by Those with a Right to Them?" *Nouvelle Presse Medicale*, Vol. 4, No. 26, May 17, 1975, pp. 1517-1518.

Dor, V., et al. "Value of Extra-corporeal Circulation in Autoperfusion. Technical and Laboratory Problems in More Than 800 Cases Including 52 Jehovah's Witnesses." *Annales de Chirurgie-Thoracique et Cardiovasculaire* (Paris), Vol. 16, No. 4, Oct. 1977, pp. 276-284.

Dornette, W.H.L. "Jehovah's Witnesses and Blood Transfusion: The Horns of a Dilemma." *Anesthesiology Analogues*, Vol. 542, 1973, pp. 272+.

Drew, N.C. "The Pregnant Jehovah's Witness." *Journal of Medical Ethics*, Vol. 7, No. 3, Sept. 1981, pp. 137-139.

Dumitru, A.P. "The Anesthesiologist and the Jehovah's Witnesses." *Anesthesia and Analgesia*, Vol. 44, March-April 1965, pp. 197-198.

"Faith and Blood." *Time*, Vol. 59, May 12, 1952, p. 55.

Fatteh, M.M. "Jehovah's Witnesses, How Can We Help Them?" *Journal of the Medical Association of Georgia*, Vol. 69, No. 12, Dec. 1980, pp. 977-979.

Fernstrom, V. "Blood Transfusion: Religious Faith Versus Medical Ethic." *Lakartidningen* (Stockholm), Vol. 66, Nov. 19, 1969, pp. 4834-4835.

Fishbein, Morris, ed. "What Does a New Heart Do to the Mind?" *Medical World News*, Vol. 10, No. 21, May 23, 1969, pp. 17-18.

Fitts, William, et al. "Blood Transfusion and Jehovah's Witnesses." *Journal of Surgery, Gynecology and Obstetrics*, Vol. 108, No. 3, 1959, pp. 502-507.

Foley, W.J., et al. "Jehovah's Witnesses and the Question of Blood Transfusion." *Postgrad Medicine*, Vol. 53, 1973, pp. 109+.

Folk, F.S., et al. "Open Heart Surgery Without Blood Transfusion." *Journal of the National Medical Association*, Vol. 61, 1969, pp. 213-218.

Ford, J.C. "Refusal of Blood Transfusions by Jehovah's Witnesses." *Linacre Quarterly*, Vol. 22, Pt. I, February 1955, pp. 3-10; Pt. II, May 1955, pp. 41-50. Reprinted in *Catholic Lawyer*, Vol. 10, Summer 1964, pp. 212-226.

Frankel, L.A. "Childhood Cancer and the Jehovah's Witness Faith." *Pediatrics*, Vol. 60, No. 6, 1977, pp. 916-921.

Frey, R. "Refusal of Blood Transfusion for Religious Reasons." *Anaestheist*, Vol. 21, July 1972, p. 316.

Garner, Carl B., et al. "The Jehovah's Witnesses and Blood Transfusion." *Thrust*, Vol. 1, No. 2, 1980, pp. 89, 90.

————. "Major Surgery in Jehovah's Witnesses." *New York State Journal of Medicine*, Vol. 76, May 1976, pp. 765-767.

Gill, G. "Adenotonsillectomy in a Jehovah's Witness with Blood Dyscrasia." *Archives of Otolaryngology*, Vol. 101, No. 6, June 1975, pp. 392-394.

Goetsch, C. "Aspects of Refusal of Blood Transfusion." *American Journal of Obstetrics and Gynecology*, Vol. 101, Jan 1, 1968, pp. 390-396.

Gollub, Seymour, et al. "Electrolyte Solution in Surgical Patients Refusing Transfusion." *Journal of the American Medical Association*, Vol. 215, No. 13, March 29, 1971, pp. 2077-2083.

————. "Management of Major Surgical Blood Loss Without Transfusion." *Journal of the American Medical Association*, Vol. 198, No. 11, Dec. 12, 1966, pp. 1171-1174.

Gonzalez, Elizabeth Rasche. "The Saga of 'Artificial Blood': Fluosol a Special Boon to Jehovah's Witnesses." *The Journal of the American Medical Association*, Vol. 243. No. 8, Feb. 22, 29, 1980, pp. 719-720, 724.

Gordon, M.E., et al. "Peptic Ulcer Hemorrhage: Vasopressin for a Jehovah's Witness." *Annals of Internal Medicine*, Vol. 79, Sept. 1973, pp. 451-452.

"Guides to the Judge in Medical Orders Affecting Children." *Crime and Delinquency*, Vol. 14, No. 2. April 1968, pp. 107-120.

Haenische, G. "Transfusion Refusal for Religious Reasons." *Deutsche Medizinische Wochenschrift*, Vol. 100, No. 51, Dec. 19, 1975, p. 2622.

Hall, George. "Blood Transfusions and Jehovah's Witnesses."
  The New Physician, Vol. 13, May 1964, pp. A-81, A-83.

Hallman, Grady. "Vascular Surgery in Jehovah's Witnesses."
  Journal of the American Medical Association, Vol. 213, No.
  6, Aug. 10, 1970, pp. 1032-1034.

Handel, K. "Correction of Double-Outlet, Right Ventricle with
  Pulmonary Stenosis and Aortic Insufficiency in a Jehovah's
  Witness." *The Annals of Thoracic Surgery*, Vol. 11, No. 5,
  May 1971, pp. 472-478.

————. "Court Decision on the Refusal to Permit a Blood
  Transfusion." *Oeffentliche Gesundheits-Wesen*, Vol. 28,
  Dec. 1966, pp. 536-538.

Hargest, Robert F. "Lifesaving Treatment for Unwilling
  Patients." *For Biblical Faith*, Vol. 36, May 1968, pp.
  695-706.

Harvey, J.P. "A Question of Craftsmanship." *Contemporary
  Orthopaedics*, Vol. 2, 1980, p. 629.

"Health Matters: Refusing Transfusing." *Today's Health*,
  Feb. 1979.

"Heart Surgery Without Transfusion." *Reader's Digest*, Jan.
  1978, p. 152.

Hecker, W.C. "Jehovah's Witnesses: The Free to Die." *M.M.W.
  Muenchener Medizinische Wachenschrift*, Vol. 120, No. 9,
  March 3, 1979, p. 257.

Herbsman, H. "Treating the Jehovah's Witness." *Emergency
  Medicine*, Vol. 12, 1980, pp. 73-76.

Hirose, Tervo. "Electrolyte Solution in Surgical Patients
  Refusing Transfusion." *Journal of the American Medical
  Association*, Vol. 215, No. 13, March 29, 1971, pp. 2077-
  2083.

Holloway, J.S., Jr. "Blood Transfusion--Jehovah's Witnesses."
  Journal of the American Medical Association, Vol. 163,
  Feb. 23, 1957, p. 660.

Horty, J.F. "Liability Nightmares, Patient Refuses Transfusion." *Modern Hospital*, Vol. 117, Oct. 1971, pp. 78-80.

How, W. Glen. "Blood Transfusion." *Canadian Doctor*, Dec.
    1960, pp. 37–58. Reprinted in *Canadian Law Journal*, Fall
    1960, as "Religion, Medicine and Law," pp. 365–421.

Jacob, Harry, et al. "The Scientific Mind at Work (and Play)."
    Journal of the American Medical Association, Vol. 246, No. 1,
    July 3, 1981, pp. 25–29.

"Jehovah's Witness Dies for Faith." *Insight*, Vol. 6, Feb. 11,
    1975, p. 23.

"Jehovah's Witnesses and Transfusions" (Congress of U.S.--Dear
    Readers). *Spinal Column*, June 5, 1967, p. 1.

"Jehovah's Witnesses Due in Federal Court in State of Washing-
    ton to Restrain Forced Transfusions." *Journal of the Indiana
    State Medical Association*, Vol. 59, No. 8, 1966, pp. 958,
    960.

Kamat, R.V., et al. "Open Heart Surgery in Jehovah's Wit-
    nesses: Experience in a Canadian Hospital." *Annals of
    Thoracic Surgery*, Vol. 23, No. 4, 1971, pp. 367+.

Kaplan, R.F., et al. "Transfusions for Jehovah's Witnesses."
    Anesthesia and Analgesia, Vol. 62, No. 1, 1983, p. 122.

Kearney, D.J. "Leukemia in Children of Jehovah's Witnesses--
    Issue and Priorities in a Conflict of Care." *Journal of
    Medical Ethics*, Vol. 4, No. 1, 1978, pp. 32–35.

Kelly, A.D. "Aequanimitas." *Canadian Medical Association
    Journal*, Vol. 96, 1967, p. 432.

Kevorkian, Jack. "Our Unforgivable Trespass." *Clinical
    Pediatrics*, Vol. 5, No. 12, Dec. 1966, pp. 40A, 41A.

Lang, M., et al. "Sequential Triple-valve Replacement in a
    Jehovah's Witness." *Canadian Medical Association Journal*,
    Vol. 122, No. 4, Feb. 23, 1980, pp. 433–435.

Lapin, R. "Major Surgery in Jehovah's Witnesses." *Contem-
    porary Orthopedics*, Vol. 2, 1980, pp. 647–654.

Larson, S.J. "Blood Transfusion, Religious Beliefs and
    Medical Ethics." *Ugeskr Laeger*, Vol. 138, No. 30, July 19,
    1976, pp. 1844–1847.

"The Law and the Life." *Time*, Vol. 57, April 30, 1951, pp.
    84, 85.

Lebeaupin, B. "Blood Transfusion and Jehovah's Witnesses." *Anesthesie Analgesie Reanimation* (Paris), Vol. 18, April-June 1961, pp. 371-381.

Levin, M. "Religious Objection to Transfusion." *Military Medicine*, Vol. 130, Oct. 1965, pp. 1023-1024.

Levinsky, L., et al. "Intracardiac Surgery in Children of Jehovah's Witnesses." *Johns Hopkins Medical Journal*, Vol. 148, No. 5, May 1981, pp. 196-198.

Lichtiger, B. "Hemotherapy During Surgery for Jehovah's Witnesses: A New Method." *Anesthesia and Analgesia*, Vol. 61, No. 7, July 1982, pp. 618-619.

Lorhan, Paul. "Anesthesia for a Jehovah's Witness with a Low Hematocrit." *Anesthesiology*, Vol. 29, No. 4, July-Aug. 1968, pp. 847-848.

————, et al. "Hyperbaric Oxygen Therapy in Chronic Hemorrhagic Shock." *Journal of the American Medical Association*, Vol. 208, No. 11, June 16, 1969, pp. 2051-2054.

McDonald, R.T., et al. "Blood, the Jehovah's Witness and the Physician." *Arizona Medicine*, Vol. 24, Oct. 1967, pp. 969-973.

Macklin, Ruth. "Consent, Coercion, and Conflicts of Rights." *Perspectives in Biology and Medicine*, Vol. 20, No. 3, Spring 1977, pp. 360-371.

"'Medical Alert' for Witnesses." *Journal of the American Medical Association*, Vol. 246, No. 1, July 3, 1981, p. 19.

"Medicolegal Aspects of Blood Transfusion." *Journal of the American Medical Association*, Vol. 151, 1953, p. 1435.

Milhollin, G. "The Refused Blood Transfusion: An Ultimate Challenge for Law and Morals." *National Law Review*, Vol. 10, 1965, pp. 202-214.

Minuck, Max, et al. "Anesthesia and Surgery for Jehovah's Witnesses." *Canadian Medical Association Journal*, Vol. 84, May 27, 1961, pp. 1187-1191.

Moore, J.L. "Religion and Blood Transfusions." *Journal of the Medical Association of Georgia*, Vol. 53, Sept. 1964, p. 304.

Morgan, Paul. "New Jersey Supreme Court Orders Pregnant
  Jehovah Witness to Consent to Blood Transfusion to Save
  Unborn Child" (Case: *Memorial Hospital v. Anderson*). *For
  Biblical Faith*, Vol. 23, Oct. 1964, pp. 80-86.

Morikawa, S. "Refusal of Blood Transfusion and the Jehovah's
  Witness." *Japanese Journal of Anesthesiology*, Vol. 23,
  No. 11, Oct. 1974, pp. 1130-1132.

Nelson, C.L., et al. "Total Hip Replacement Without Transfusion." *Contemporary Orthopaedics*, Vol. 2, 1980, pp.
  655-658.

Neptune, W.B., et al. "Clinical Use of a Pump-Oxygenator Without Donor Blood for Priming or Support During Extracorporeal
  Perfusion." *Circulation*, Vol. 20, 1960, p. 745.

Nixon, Robert W. "Beliefs Cost Mother Her Children." *Liberty*,
  Vol. 67, May-June 1972, pp. 6, 7.

O'Donnell, T. "Jehovah's Witness and the Problem of Blood
  Transfusion." *Linacre*, Vol. 32, May 1965, pp. 169-172.

"On the Side of Life." *Time*, Feb. 21, 1964, pp. 76, 78.

Orloff, Marshall. "Blood Transfusion and Jehovah's Witnesses."
  Journal of Surgery, Gynecology and Obstetrics, Vol. 108,
  1959, pp. 502-507.

Ott, David, and Denton Cooley. "Cardiovascular Surgery in
  Jehovah's Witnesses." *Journal of the American Medical
  Association*, Vol. 238, No. 12, Sept. 19, 1977, pp. 1256-
  1258.

Paris, J. "Forced Medications: By Whose Right?" *America*,
  Vol. 133, Nov. 15, 1975, pp. 323-325.

————. "Compulsory Medical Treatment and Religious Freedom:
  Whose Law Shall Prevail?" *University of San Francisco Law
  Review*, Vol. 10, 1975, pp. 1035.

"Physical Welfare vs. Religious Liberty." *Church and State*,
  Vol. 21, No. 6, June 1968, p. 14.

Pierre-Louis, C. "The Refusal of Transfusion for Religious
  Reasons." *Bulletin of the Association of Medicine in Haiti*,
  Vol. 12, Oct. 1972, pp. 78-82.

Posnikoff, Jack. "Cure of Intracranial Aneurysm Without Use of Blood Transfusion." *California Medicine*, Feb. 1967, pp. 124-127.

Quenu, L., et al. "Is It Possible to Consider a Refusal of Blood Transfusion Because of Religious Convictions?" *Nouvelle Presse Medicale*, Vol. 3, Nos. 41-43, Nov. 14-Dec. 1974, pp. 2575-2576.

Raleigh, Fitkin. "New Jersey Supreme Court Orders Pregnant Jehovah Witness to Consent to Blood Transfusion to Save Unborn Child" (Case: *Memorial Hospital vs. Anderson*). *For Biblical Faith*, Vol. 33, Oct. 1964, pp. 80-86.

Rector, Milton. "Guides to the Judge in Medical Orders Affecting Children." *Crime and Delinquency*, Vol. 14, No. 2, April 1968, pp. 107-120.

"Recycling Blood." *Time*, Vol. 117, No. 11, March 16, 1981.

"Refusal of Parental Consent to Blood Transfusion." *British Medical Journal*, Vol. 2, No. 5476, Dec. 1965, p. 1494.

Rieger, H.J. "Refusal of Blood for Religious Reasons." *Deutsche Medizinische Wachenschrift*, Vol. 100, No. 12, March 12, 1975, pp. 172-173.

Rigor, Benjamin. "Replacement of Operative Blood Loss of More Than 1 Liter with Hartmann's Solution." *Journal of the American Medical Association*, Vol. 203, No. 6, Feb. 5, 1968, pp. 399-402.

Roen, P.R., and F. Velcek. "Extensive Urologic Surgery Without Blood Transfusion." *New York State Journal of Medicine*, Vol. 72, 1972, pp. 2524-2527.

Roth, A.B., et al. "When the Patient Refuses Treatment: Some Observations and Proposals for Handling the Difficult Case." *St. Louis Law Review*, Vol. 23, 1979, pp. 429+.

Rottlander, W. "Refusal of Blood Transfusion on Religious Grounds." *Medizinische Klinik*, Vol. 61, June 30, 1966, pp. 1049-1051.

Rozovsky, Lorne. "Jehovah's Witnesses and the Law." *Canadian Hospital*, March 1971, pp. 41-42.

Rush, Benjamin. "Replacement of Operative Blood Loss of More Than 1 Liter with Hartmann's Solution." *Journal of the American Medical Association*, Vol. 203, No. 6, Feb. 5, 1968, pp. 399-402.

"St. Thomas, Ontario: Blood Transfusions." *Church and State*, Vol. 12, No. 3, March 1959, p. 5.

Sandiford, F.M., et al. "Aorto-coronary Bypass in Jehovah's Witnesses: Report of 36 Patients." *Journal of Thoracic/Cardiovascular Surgery*, Vol. 68, 1974, pp. 1-7.

————. "Aortocoronary Bypass in Jehovah's Witnesses: Review of 46 Patients." *American Surgeon*, Vol. 42, No. 1, Jan. 1976, pp. 17-22.

Schaefer, Clara. "Electrolyte Solution in Surgical Patients Refusing Transfusion." *Journal of the American Medical Association*, Vol. 215, No. 13, March 29, 1971, pp. 2077-2083.

Schechter, D.C. "Problems Relevant to Major Surgical Operations in Jehovah's Witnesses." *American Journal of Surgery*, Vol. 116, 1968, pp. 73-80.

Sharpe, David. "Lifesaving Treatment for Unwilling Patients." *Fordham Law Review*, Vol. 36, No. 4, May 1968, pp. 695-706.

Simmons, Wilton, et al. "Vascular Surgery in Jehovah's Witnesses." *Journal of the American Medical Association*, Vol. 213, No. 6, Aug. 10, 1970, pp. 1032-1034.

Smith, Earl Belle. "General Surgery in Jehovah's Witnesses Personal Experience: A 22 Year Analysis." *Journal of the National Medical Association*, Vol. 22, July 1980, pp. 657-660.

Sneierson, H. "Autotransfusion for Massive Hemorrhage Due to Ruptured Spleen in Jehovah Witness." *New York Journal of Medicine*, Vol. 67, June 15, 1967, pp. 1769-1771.

Spencer, J.D. "The Witnesses Could Win." *Legal Aspects of Medical Practice*, Vol. 6, No. 6, 1978, pp. 45-49.

Sureau, C. "Can a Refusal of Blood Transfusion for Religious Convictions Be Accepted?" *Nouvelle Presse Medicale* (Paris), Vol. 3, No. 34, Oct. 12, 1974, pp. 2188-2190.

"Surgery Without Blood Transfusions." *Journal of the Iowa Medical Society*, Vol. 68, No. 1, Jan. 1978, pp. 19-20.

Svigals, Robert. "Electrolyte Solution in Surgical Patients Refusing Transfusion." *Journal of the American Medical Association*, Vol. 215, No. 13, March 29, 1971, pp. 2077-2083.

"Terry and the Parents." *Newsweek*, Vol. 77, Jan. 18, 1971, p. 43.

Testas, P. "Acute Hemodilution in Normouplemia. Possibilities of Major Surgical Operations Without Transfusion: Apropos of an Esogastrectomy in a Jehovah's Witness." *Chirugie*, Vol. 161, No. 4, March 12-19, 1975, pp. 266-271.

Thomas, George, et al. "Some Issues Involved with Major Surgery on Jehovah's Witnesses." *The American Surgeon*, Vol. 34, No. 7, July 1968, pp. 538-543.

Thompson, Anthony. "She May Die If She Chooses." *Liberty*, Vol. 67, Jan.-Feb. 1977, p. 25.

Thompson, James. "Hyperbaric Oxygen Therapy in Chronic Hemorrhagic Shock." *Journal of the American Medical Association*, Vol. 208, No. 11, June 16, 1969, pp. 2051-2054.

"Transfusion for Minor Patient Despite Parents' Religious Objections." *Anesthesia and Analgesia*, Vol. 52, May-June 1973, pp. 462-463.

"Transfusion Friction." *Church and State*, Vol. 34, No. 10, Nov. 1981, p. 22.

"Transfusion to Unwilling Witness Ruled Illegal." *Pentecostal Evangelical*, Jan. 16, 1966.

"Unscientific Christian Creeds Doom Millions to Needless Death." *Muhammad Speaks*, Sept. 2, 1966, pp. 7, 8.

Weinberger, Morris; William M. Tierney; James Y. Green; and P. Albert Studdard. "The Development of Physician Norms in the United States; The Treatment of Jehovah's Witness Patients." *Social Science and Medicine*, Vol. 16, 1982, pp. 1719-1723.

Williamson, Willie P. "Life or Death--Whose Decision?" *Journal of the American Medical Association*, Vol. 197, No. 10, Sept. 5, 1966, 139-141.

Winter, R.B., et al. "Jehovah's Witnesses and Consent." *Journal of Legal Medicine*, Vol. 2, No. 9, 1974, p. 9.

"Without Transfusion." *Inside Baylor Medicine*, No. 2, 1968, pp. 2-4.

"Witnesses' Campaign Will Stress Position on Blood Transfusions." *Liberty*, Vol. 67, Nov.-Dec. 1977, p. 30.

Woloski, Rosalie. "As God Was Their Witness." *Maclean's*, Sept. 21, 1981, pp. 24, 26.

————. "Blood, Toil, Tears and Death." *Maclean's*, Vol. 94, April 20, 1981, p. 33.

Wong, K.C. "Hemodilution and Induced Hypotension for Insertion of a Harrington Rod in a Jehovah's Witness." *Clinical Orthopaedics and Related Research*, Vol. 152, Oct. 1980, pp. 237-240.

Zaorski, J.R., et al. "Open Heart Surgery for Acquired Heart Disease in Jehovah's Witnesses: A Report of 42 Operations." *American Journal of Cardiology*, Vol. 29, 1972, pp. 186-189.

Zaremski, M.J. "Blood Transfusions and Elective Surgery: A Custodial Function of an Ohio Juvenile Court." *Cleveland State Law Review*, Vol. 23, No. 2, pp. 231-244.

Witness Court Cases, Law Problems
and Related Issues (see also Flag Salute Cases)

"The All Writs Salute and the Injunctive Power of a Single Appellate Judge." *Michigan Law Review*, Vol. 64, Dec. 1965, pp. 324-335.

Balter, Harry G. "Freedom of Religion Interpreted in Two Supreme Court Decisions." *The State Bar Journal of the State Bar of California*, Vol. 15, No. 6, June 1940, pp. 160-165.

"Bearing Witness." *Time*, Vol. 117, No. 11, April 20, 1981, p. 51. About a witness who quit his job after he was transferred to a defense plant.

Bourdin, Louis B. "Freedom of Thought and Religious Liberty under the Constitution." *Lawyers Guild Review*, Vol. 4, No. 3, June 7, 1944, pp. 9-24.

Butler, W.J. "Right of Free Listening." *Catholic World*,
    Vol. 168, Dec. 1948, pp. 200-201.

"Civil Rights vs. Property." *The New Republic*, Vol. 114,
    Jan. 21, 1946, p. 69.

"Constitutional Law--Due Process Under the Fourteenth Amend-
    ment--Freedom of Religion, Speech and Assembly." *Minnesota
    Law Review*, Vol. 32, No. 5, April 1948, pp. 498-502.

Eliff, Nathan. "Jehovah's Witnesses and the Selective
    Service." *Virginia Law Review*, Vol. 31, 1945, pp. 811-
    834.

Fraser, R.B. "How Will Supreme Court Weigh Duplessis' Power?"
    Macleans, Canada's National Magazine, Vol. 71, July 7, 1958,
    p. 2.

"Freedom to Proselyte." *Newsweek*, Vol. 25, March 12, 1945,
    p. 88.

Green, J.R. "Liberty Under the Fourteenth Amendment." *Wash-
    ington University Law Quarterly*, Vol. 27, Summer 1942,
    pp. 497-562.

Howerton, Huey B. "Jehovah's Witnesses and the Federal Con-
    stitution." *Mississippi Law Journal*, Vol. 17, No. 1,
    March-May 1946, pp. 347-371.

Hunter, Ian A. "Would This Couple Make Good Citizens of
    Canada?" *United Church Observer*, Nov. 1976, pp. 27, 28.

"In Re Jehovah's Witnesses." *The Fortnightly Law Journal*,
    Vol. 16, Feb. 15, 1947, pp. 221, 222.

"Jehovah's Witnesses and the Supreme Court." *The Sign*, Vol.
    22, June 1943, p. 645.

"Jehovah's Witnesses and the Supreme Court." *Social Service
    Review*, Vol. 17, June 1943, p. 226.

"Jehovah's Witnesses: Persecution, Past and Present." *The
    Wiener Library Bulletin*, Vol. 5, 1951, p. 8.

King, R.C.C. "Constitutional Legacy of the Jehovah's Wit-
    nesses." *Social Science Quarterly*, Vol. 45, Sept. 1964,
    pp. 125-134.

"Konzentrations Lager." *Sunday Mirror* (Magazine Section),
    Feb. 9, 1941, pp. 2, 12. (Concentration Camp.)

Lunny, Rev. W.J., and Ethel Douglas. Letters (in response to
    the Nov. 1976 article "Would This Couple Make Good Citizens
    of Canada?"). *United Church Observer*, Jan. 1977, p. 2.

MacGowan, Gault. "Jehovah's Witnesses." *Catholic Digest*,
    Vol. 3, Jan. 1938, pp. 71–76.

Munters, Quirinus J. "Recruitment as a Vocation: The Case of
    Jehovah's Witnesses." *Sociologia Neerlandica*, Vol. 7, No.
    2, 1971, pp. 88–100.

O'Brien, Kenneth R., and Daniel O'Brien. "Freedom of Re-
    ligion in Restatement of Inter-Church-and-State Common Law."
    The Jurist, Vol. 6, Oct. 1946, pp. 503–523.

Owen, Ralph Dornfield. "Jehovah's Witnesses and Their Four
    Freedoms." *University of Detroit Law Journal*, Vol. 14,
    No. 3, March 1951, pp. 111–113.

Pound, Roscoe. "Constitutional Law--Jehovah's Witnesses."
    Notre Dame Lawyer, Vol. 22, Nov. 1946, pp. 82–94.

"Recent Jehovah's Witnesses Cases." *International Judicial
    Association Bulletin*, Vol. 10, July 1941, pp. 5–7.

"Religious Freedom and the Jehovah's Witnesses." *Virginia
    Law Review*, Vol. 34, Jan. 1948, pp. 77–83.

"Religious Liberty under the Constitution of the United States."
    Michigan Law Review, Vol. 39, Nov. 1940, pp. 149–152.

"Religious Liberty under the Constitution of the United
    States." *Southern California Law Review*, Vol. 14, Nov.
    1940, pp. 57–58, 73–76. Not the same as above.

"Religious Liberty under the Constitution of the United
    States." *University of Detroit Law Journal*, Vol. 4, Nov.
    1940, pp. 38–41. Not the same as above.

Schur, Morris J. "The Theology of the Jehovah's Witnesses
    and Its Conflict with Earthly Governments." *Western
    Political Quarterly*, Vol. 17, 1967, p. 101.

"The Sources and Limits of Religious Freedom." *Illinois Law
    Review*, Vol. 41, No. 1, May-June 1946, pp. 53–80.

"Supreme Court Comes to Order." *Collier's Magazine*, June 12, 1943, p. 78.

"Supreme Court Decision Allows Local Limitation of Free Press." *Publishers Weekly*, Vol. 141, June 20, 1942, p. 2266.

"Supreme Court Reverses Convictions of Jehovah's Witnesses." *Publishers Weekly*, Vol. 149, Feb. 16, 1946, p. 1137.

"Supreme Court Reverses Decision in Jehovah's Witnesses Case." *Publishers Weekly*, Vol. 143, May 8, 1943, p. 1820.

"Supreme Court Reverses Stand on Anti-Peddling Ordinances." *Public Management*, Vol. 25, June 1943, p. 179.

Tietz, J.B. "Jehovah's Witnesses: Conscientious Objectors." *Southern California Law Review*, Vol. 28, Feb. 1955, pp. 123-137.

"Two Liberal Opinions from the Federal Courts." *Social Service Review*, Vol. 16, Dec. 1942, p. 672.

"Victory without Peace." *Extension*, Vol. 38, Aug. 1943, p. 19.

Votaw, Herbert H. "Jehovah's Witnesses and Freedom of Speech." *Life*, Vol. 43, 4th Quarter 1948, pp. 16-20.

Wright, H. "Religious Liberty under the Constitution of the United States." *Virginia Law Review*, Vol. 27, Nov. 1940, pp. 75-87.

The Flag Salute Issue
(see also Court Cases)

A., J.S. "Religious Freedom, Flag Salute in Public Schools." *Washington Law Review*, Vol. 15, Nov. 1940, pp. 265, 266.

Anderson, P.H. "Religious Freedom, Flag Salute in Public Schools." *Georgia Bar Journal*, Vol. 2, May 1940, pp. 74-76.

B., W.C. "The Supreme Court Hands Down an Educationally Significant Decision." *School and Society*, Vol. 57, No. 1487, June 26, 1943, pp. 696, 697.

Baldus, S.A. "Saluting the Flag." *Extension*, Vol. 35, Dec. 1940, pp. 18, 19.

Bergman, Jerry. "Witnesses to a New Area of Book Collecting."
    Book Collector's Market, Vol. 4, No. 3, May-June 1979, pp.
    1-9.

Blakely, P.L. "Omnipotent Schoolboards: Enforced Flag Salute."
    America, Vol. 63, June 22, 1940, p. 286.

——. "Flag Salute vs. Oregon Case." *America*, Vol. 63,
    June 15, 1940, pp. 259-260.

"Breeding Peace Martyrs in Cradle: Children of Jehovah's Wit-
    nesses Refuse to Salute the Flag." *Literary Digest*, Vol.
    21, May 2, 1936, p. 18.

Chambers, M.M. "Flag Salute Before the Bench." *Nations Schools*,
    Vol. 23, June 1939, p. 62.

——. "You Can't Come to School." *Nations Schools*, Vol. 20,
    Dec. 1937, pp. 33, 34.

"Chief Justice Hughes Interrupts." *Ave Maria*, Vol. 54, April
    20, 1940, p. 483.

"Children Must Salute the Flag." *The New Republic*, June 17,
    1940, p. 810.

"Compulsory Flag Salute." *Journal of Education*, Vol. 120,
    Dec. 1937, p. 195.

"Constitutional Law—Due Process Under the Fourteenth Amend-
    ment—Freedom of Religion, Speech, and Assembly." *Minnesota
    Law Review*, Vol. 32, 1948, pp. 498-502.

"Constitutional Law—Freedom of Religion—Public Schools—
    Compulsory Flag Salute." *Minnesota Law Review*, Vol. 27,
    No. 5, April 1943, 471, 472.

"Constitutional Law—Freedom of Worship—Salute to the Flag."
    St. John's Law Review, Vol. 13, Nov. 1938, pp. 144-147.

"Court and the Flag." *Newsweek*, June 21, 1943.

Coutts, Mary T. "How the Flag Pledge Originated." *Journal
    of Education*, Vol. 125, Oct. 1942, pp. 225, 226.

Cunningham, Juanita. "Our American Flag." *The Grade Teacher*,
    Vol. 54, Feb. 1937, pp. 64, 65.

Cupples, H.L. "Protection of Personal Liberties Under the Fourteenth Amendment: The Flag Salute." *George Washington Law Review*, Vol. 8, May 1940, pp. 1094-1097.

Dilliard, Irving. "Salute to the Court: Jehovah's Witnesses Cases." *The New Republic*, Vol. 108, March 1, 1943, pp. 276, 277.

"Education: 'Devil's Emblem.'" *Time*, Nov. 18, 1935, p. 59. About Jehovah's Witnesses who refuse to salute flag.

F., J.F. "Religious Freedom. Flag Salute in Public Schools." *New York University Law Quarterly Review*, Vol. 18, Nov. 1940, pp. 124-127.

Fennell, W.G. "The Reconstructed Court and Religious Freedom; the Gobitis Case in Retrospect." *New York University Law Quarterly Review*, Vol. 19, Nov. 1941, pp. 31-48.

"The Flag Ritual." *Journal of Education*, Vol. 124, Jan. 1941, p. 25.

"The Flag Salute." *Journal of the National Education Association*, Vol. 32, No. 9, Dec. 1943, pp. 265, 266.

"Flag Salutes and Food." *Social Service Review*, Vol. 14, Sept. 1940, pp. 574, 575.

"Flag Saluting Case." *Extension*, Vol. 37, Aug. 1942, pp. 19, 20.

Frankfurter, F. "Religious Freedom." *The New Republic*, Vol. 102, June 24, 1940, pp. 843, 852-855. Contains the complete text of dissent with editorial comment on the flag salute case.

"Freedom of Religion--Compulsory Flag Salute." *Michigan Law Review*, Vol. 42, Aug.-Oct. 1943, pp. 186, 187, 319-321.

"Freedom of Religion--Compulsory Flag Salute." *Minnesota Law Review*, Vol. 28, Jan. 1944, p. 133.

"Freedom of Religion--Flag Salute--Duty of Lower Federal Court to Follow Unreversed Decisions of Supreme Court." *Columbia Law Review*, Vol. 43, Jan. 1943, pp. 134, 135.

"Freedom of Religion--Flag Salute--Duty of Lower Federal Court to Follow Unreversed Decisions of Supreme Court." *George Washington Law Review*, Vol. 11, Dec. 1942, pp. 112-114.

Fuller, Helen. "Section 52 Is News." *The New Republic*, Feb. 15, 1943, p. 204.

H., W.T. "Freedom of Religion--Compulsory Flag Salute." *Temple University Law Quarterly*, Vol. 17, Aug. 1943, pp. 465, 466.

H., W.W. "Religious Freedom. Flag Salute in Public Schools." *Temple University Law Quarterly*, Vol. 14, July 1940, pp. 545-547.

Hodgdon, Daniel R. "Flag-Salute Issue Settled." *Clearing House*, Vol. 19, Nov. 1944, pp. 192, 193.

————. "No More Compulsory Salutes Allowed." *Clearing House*, Vol. 21, April 1947, pp. 499, 500.

Howard, F.L. "Civil Liberties, Freedom of Religion, Compulsory Flag Salute." *Montana Law Review*, Vol. 6, Jan. 1941, pp. 106-111.

"I Pledge a Legion." *Journal of Education*, Vol. 120, March 1, 1937, pp. 122, 123. Not the same as the article by Moser below.

"Jehovah Reversal." *Newsweek*, May 10, 1943, pp. 40, 42.

"Jehovah's Witnesses and Supreme Court." *Sign*, Vol. 22, June 1943, p. 645.

"Jehovah's Witnesses Convicted." *Ave Maria*, Vol. 53, Feb. 22, 1941, p. 227.

"Jehovah's Witnesses. The American Flag and the Courts." *Social Service Review*, Vol. 14, Sept. 1940, pp. 574, 575.

"Judiciary 4 to 5; 5 to 4." *Time*, May 17, 1943, p. 21.

Kearney, J.J. "Supreme Court Abdicates as Nation's School Board." *Catholic Educational Review*, Vol. 38, Oct. 1940, pp. 357-360.

Kim, Richard C.C. "The Constitution, the Supreme Court, and Religious Liberty." *Journal of Church and State*, Vol. 6, 1964, pp. 333-343.

Levene, L. "Religious Freedom, Flag Salute in Public Schools." *Cornell Law Quarterly*, Vol. 26, Dec. 1940, pp. 127-130.

"Lynn, Mass. Schoolboy Refuses to Salute the Flag." *America*, Vol. 53, Oct. 5, 1935, p. 615.

Manwaring, David. *Render Unto Caesar: The Flag-Salute Controversy*. Reviewed by Joseph Andrews. *Library Journal*, Vol. 87, June 15, 1962, p. 2387.

——. *Render Unto Caesar*. Reviewed by Harold Stahmer. *Political Science Quarterly*, Vol. 78, March 1963, pp. 159, 160.

Moser, A.C., and Bert David. "I Pledge a Legion." *Journal of Educational Sociology*, Vol. 9, March 1936, pp. 436-440.

Nesbitt, J.S. "Civil Liberties, Freedom of Religion, Compulsory Flag Salute." *Georgia Bar Journal*, Vol. 3, Nov. 1940, pp. 66, 67.

Olander, Herbert T. "Children's Knowledge of the Flag Salute." *Journal of Educational Research*, Vol. 35, No. 4, Dec. 1941, pp. 300-305.

"Our Pledge of Allegiance--A Task for Tomorrow." *Ohio Schools*, Vol. 21, Oct. 1942, pp. 306, 307, 327.

"Parents' Rights." *Newsweek*, Feb. 14, 1944, p. 86.

Punke, Harold H. "The Flag and the Courts in Free Public Education." *Journal of Religion*, Vol. 24, April 1944, pp. 119-130.

"Religious Freedom and the Jehovah's Witnesses." *Virginia Law Review*, Vol. 34, Jan. 1948, pp. 77-83.

"Religious Freedom, Flag Salute in Public Schools." *St. John's Law Review*, Vol. 15, November 1940, pp. 95-97.

"Religious Freedom, Flag Salute in Public Schools." *International Juridical Association Bulletin*, Vol. 9, No. 1, July 1940, pp. 10-12.

Remmlein, M.K. "Freedom of Religion--Compulsory Flag Salute." *George Washington Law Review*, Vol. 12, Dec. 1943, pp. 70-80.

"A Reporter at Large: Love of Country." *The New Yorker*, July 13, 1973, pp. 35-46. An important article which discusses a case history of a teacher who refused to salute the flag for personal reasons. The teacher was not a Jehovah's Witness.

Ruediger, W.C. "Saluting the Flag." *School and Society*, Vol.
    49, June 26, 1943, pp. 696, 697.

S., D.E. "Religious Freedom, Flag Salute in Public Schools."
    University of Cincinnati Law Review, Vol. 14, May-Nov. 1940,
    pp. 444-447.

Shenk, Phil M., ed. "Fire Unpatriotic School Teacher." *So-
    journers*, March 1980, p. 6.

Slade, T.B. "Freedom of Religion--Compulsory Flag Salute."
    Georgia Bar Journal, Vol. 6, Feb. 1944, pp. 249, 250.

Stone, H.F. "Religious Freedom." *The New Republic*, Vol. 102,
    June 24, 1940, pp. 843, 852-855. Flag salute case: complete
    text of majority opinion and of dissent with editorial
    comment.

"Supreme Court Reversal." *Ave Maria*, Vol. 57, May 22, 1943,
    p. 644.

Waite, Edward F. "The Debt of Constitutional Law to Jehovah's
    Witnesses." *Minnesota Law Review*, Vol. 28, No. 4, March
    1944, pp. 209-246.

"Weight of Witnessing." *America*, Vol. 83, Aug. 19, 1950,
    p. 507.

Wilthy, J. "Jehovah's Witnesses Before the Supreme Court."
    America, Vol. 63, April 20, 1940, pp. 35-36.

Wingerd, S. "Civil Liberties, Freedom of Religion, Compulsory
    Flag Salute." *Journal of the Bar Association of Kansas*,
    Vol. 9, 1941, pp. 276-280.

"Witnesses of Jehovah." *Sign*, Vol. 25, Dec. 1945, pp. 27-28.

Sociological and Psychological Studies

Aguirre, Benigno. "Organizational Change and Religious Commit-
    ment of Jehovah's Witnesses and Seventh-Day Adventists in
    Cuba, 1938-1965." *Pacific Sociological Review*, Vol. 23,
    No. 2, April 1980, pp. 171-179.

Aiken, James M. "I Was Brainwashed by the Jehovah's Witnesses."
    Power for Living, Oct. 18, 1964.

Alston, Jon P. "Congregational Size and the Decline of Sectarian Commitment: The Case of the Jehovah's Witnesses in South and North America." *Sociological Analysis*, Vol. 40, No. 1, Spring 1979, pp, 63-70.

————. "Organizational Change and Religious Commitment of Jehovah's Witnesses and Seventh-Day Adventists in Cuba, 1938-1965." *Pacific Sociological Review*, Vol. 23, No. 2, April 1980, pp. 171-179.

Andre, J. "Religious Group Value Patterns and Motive Orientations." *Journal of Psychology and Theology*, Vol. 8, No. 2, 1980, pp. 129-139.

Assimeng, John Maxwell. "Jehovah's Witnesses: A Study in Cognitive Dissonance." *Universitas* (Pub. by the Univ. of Ghana), Vol. 92, Sept. 1943, pp. 103-105.

Beckford, James A. "Organization, Ideology and Recruitment: The Structure of the Watchtower Movement." *The Sociological Review*, Vol. 23, No. 4, Nov. 1975, pp. 893-909.

————. "Sociological Stereotypes of the Religious Sect." *The Sociological Review*, Vol. 26, No. 1, Feb. 1978, pp. 109-123.

————. "Structural Dependence in Religious Organizations: From 'Skid-Row' to Watchtower." *Journal for the Scientific Study of Religion*, Vol. 15, No. 2, June 1976, pp. 169-175.

————. *The Trumpet of Prophecy.* "On the Doorstep: Review of *The Trumpet of Prophecy: A Sociological Study of Jehovah's Witnesses*" by Bryan Wilson. *New Statesman and Nation*, Vol. 90, Sept. 19, 1975, p. 340.

————. *The Trumpet of Prophecy: A Sociological Study of Jehovah's Witnesses.* Reviewed by J.P. Alston. *Social Forces*, Vol. 55, No. 1, 1976, p. 211.

————. *The Trumpet of Prophecy: A Sociological Study of Jehovah's Witnesses.* Reviewed by Val Clear. *Review of Religious Research*, Vol. 19, No. 2, Winter 1978, p. 215.

————. *The Trumpet of Prophecy: A Sociological Study of Jehovah's Witnesses.* Reviewed by William Kaeson. *Journal for the Scientific Study of Religion*, Vol. 16, No. 1, March 1977, pp. 106-109.

————. *The Trumpet of Prophecy: A Sociological Study of Jehovah's Witnesses*. Reviewed by M.G. Taylor. *Contemporary Sociology--A Journal of Reviews*, Vol. 5, No. 6, 1976, p. 804.

————. *The Trumpet of Prophecy: A Sociological Study of Jehovah's Witnesses*. Reviewed by John Whitworth. *Times Literary Supplement*, June 4, 1976, p. 679.

————. *The Trumpet of Prophecy: A Sociological Study of Jehovah's Witnesses*. Reviewed by Bryan Wilson. *Encounter*, Vol. 45, Oct. 1975, p. 77.

————. *The Trumpet of Prophecy: A Sociological Study of Jehovah's Witnesses*. Reviewed by K.M. Wulff. *International Review of Modern Sociology*, Vol. 6, No. 2, 1976, pp. 418-420.

————. *The Trumpet of Prophecy: A Sociological Study of Jehovah's Witnesses*. Reviewed by J.F. Zygmunt. *Sociological Analysis*, Vol. 37, No. 4, 1976, pp. 353-354.

Biebuych, Daniel. "La Société Kumu Face au Kitawala." *Zaire*, Vol. 11, No. 1, Jan. 1957, pp. 7-40. (Kuma Society in Relation to Jehovah's Witnesses.)

Bram, Joseph. "Jehovah's Witnesses and the Value of American Culture." *Transactions of the New York Academy of Sciences*, Vol. 19, 1956, pp. 47-53.

Brausch, G. "Intégration des institutions coutumieves dans l'action sociale en Afrique centrale." *Problèmes d'Afrique Centrale*, No. 33, 1956, p. 4.

Campbell, Roger F. (Told by Shirley Lyon). "Jehovah's Witnesses Built a Wall Between My Husband and Me." *Voice*, Feb. 1971, pp. 4, 5.

Cohn, Werner. "Jehovah's Witnesses and Racial Prejudice." *The Crisis*, Vol. 63, Jan. 1956, pp. 5-9.

Cole, Marley. "Jehovah's Witnesses--Religion of Racial Integration." *The Crisis*, April 1953, pp. 205-211, 253-255.

Coleman, James S. "Social Cleavage and Religious Conflict." *Journal of Social Issues*, Vol. 12, No. 3, 1956, pp. 44-56.

Cowley, Susan C. "Persecution in Malawi." *Newsweek*, May 10, 1976, pp. 106, 107.

Dericquebourg, Regis. "Les Témoins de Jehovah dans le nord de la France: implantation et expansion" (intro. in English and article in French). *Social Compass*, Vol. 24, No. 1, 1977, pp. 71-82. (Jehovah's Witnesses in Northern France—Establishment and Expansion.)

Dewing, Kathleen. "Some Characteristics of the Parents of Creative Twelve-Year-Olds." *Journal of Personality*, Vol. 41, No. 1, March 1973, pp. 71-85. Found children of Jehovah's Witnesses were rated "highly creative" more often than non-Witness children.

"Did Yahshua Die to Save the House of Kyrious?" *World Today Analyzed in Prophecy's Spotlight*, April 1976, pp. 10, 11.

Drake, Betty. Letter from Mrs. L. Robinson, Baltimore, Md., in the section titled "Speak Out America." *National Examiner*, Jan. 15, 1980.

"Hare Krishnas in the Dock." *Newsweek*, Sept. 29, 1980, p. 83.

Harris, Richard. "A Reporter at Large; I'd Like to Talk to You for a Minute." *The New Yorker*, Vol. 32, June 16, 1956, pp. 72-80.

Harrison, Barbara Grizzuti. "Life with Jehovah." *Ms.*, Vol. 4, No. 6, Dec. 1975, pp. 56-59, 89-92.

————. "The Way We Live Now: Papa Mia." *Ms.*, Vol. 5, No. 12, June 1977, pp. 30, 32.

————. "Estranged from Joy." *McCall's Magazine*, Dec. 1977, pp. 111, 188, 190, 191.

"How God Changed Teresa Graves' Life!" *Movie Mirror*, Vol. 19, No. 1, Nov. 1974, pp. 28, 60.

Janner, Von J. "Die Forensisch-Psychiatrische und Sanitats-dienstliche Beurteilung von Dienstuerweigerern." *Schweizerische Medizinische Wochenschrift*, Vol. 93, No. 23, 1963, pp. 819-826.

Jefferson, Marge. "Touch of the Poet." *Newsweek*, Oct. 29, 1975, p. 51. About Patti Smith.

"Jehovah's Vittnen på Frammarsch." *Religions Sociologiska Institute*, No. 133, Oct. 1976, 25 pp. (Jehovah's Witnesses on the Move.)

Jubber, Ken. "The Persecution of Jehovah's Witnesses in
   Southern Africa" (intro. in French and article in English).
   Social Compass, Vol. 24, No. 1, 1977, pp. 121-134.

Kater, Michael K. "Die Ernsten Bibelforscher im Dritten
   Reich." *Vierteljahrhefte für Zeitgeschichte*, 17 Jahrgang,
   1 Heft/Jan. 1979, pp. 181-218. (The Jehovah's Witnesses
   in the 3rd Reich.)

Knoch, Adolph Ernst. *Unsearchable Riches*, Vol. 56, No. 3,
   p. 13.

————. "An Appeal to the I.B.S.A." *Unsearchable Riches*,
   Vol. 23, 1932, pp. 327-330.

La Farge, Christopher. "Mickey Spillane and His Bloody Hammer."
   Saturday Review, Vol. 37, Nov. 6, 1954, pp. 11, 12. Spillane
   was a Witness for many years.

Lamping, Severin. "Mister Rutherford." *Sodalist*, Feb. 1938.
   Condensed in *Catholic Digest*, Vol. 2, April 1938, pp. 5-7.

Larson, Charles R. "Invitation to a Wedding." *McCall's
   Magazine*, Aug. 1977, pp. 128, 191-193.

"Les Cuites Syncretiques Ont Fait l'Objet de Plusieurs Publications il Est Fait Occasionnelment Allusion au Kitawala
   ou à des Mouvements Analogues dans Certaines d'Entre Elles--
   Paris." *Sociologie Actuelle de l'Afrique Noire*, 1954.

Letters. *Ms.*, April 1976, pp. 4, 6.

Lockwood, Robert. "How Jehovah's Witnesses Attack Catholicism."
   Sunday Visitor, Dec. 2, 1973, pp. 1, 12, 13.

"The Lost Word of Jehovah's Witnesses." *Power for Living*,
   Dec. 24, 1972.

"Lying Lips Abomination to the Lord." *Zion's Herald*, May
   1976, p. 234.

Lyon, Shirley. "Jehovah's Witnesses Built a Wall Between My
   Husband and Me." *Voice*, Feb. 1971, pp. 4-5.

Maesen, William A. "Abstract of 'An Empirical Refutation of the
   Iron Law of Oligarchy: United States Supreme Court Decisions Re
   the Jehovah's Witnesses." *Sociological Abstracts*, Vol. 17,
   No. 5, p. 103. Abstract number 09041.

————. "Watchtower Influence on Black Muslim Eschatology." *Journal for the Scientific Study of Religion*, Vol. 9, No. 4, Winter 1970, pp. 321-325.

Mason, Joni. Letter in response to "Invitation to a Wedding" (Aug. 1977). *McCall's Magazine*, Nov. 1977, p. 10.

Mellor, Steven. "Religious Group Value Patterns and Motive Orientations." *Journal of Psychology and Theology*, Vol. 8, No. 2, 1980, pp. 129-139.

Montague, Havor. "The Pessimistic Sect's Influence on the Mental Health of Its Members: The Case of Jehovah's Witnesses" (intro. in French and article in English). *Social Compass*, Vol. 24, No. 1, 1977, pp. 135-147.

"Mother Denied Custody After Change in Religion." *Liberty*, Vol. 77, No. 1, Jan.-Feb. 1982, p. 27.

Munters, Quirinus J. "Abstract of 'Recruitment as a Vocation: The Case of Jehovah's Witnesses.'" *Sociological Abstracts*, 1973, p. 1178.

————. "Recruitment et candidats en puissance" (intro. in English and article in French). *Social Compass*, Vol. 24, No. 1, 1977, pp. 59-69. (Recruitment of Jehovah's Witnesses and Potential Candidates.)

Nichol, Francis D. "The Editor's Mailbag." *Review and Herald*, April 9, 1964.

"Nudie Housing Idea Takes Off." *Moneysworth*, Feb. 28, 1977, p. 1. About a former Witness.

Palmer, Phillip G. "Reply--Witnesses." *New Society*, July 26, 1973, p. 231.

Phillips, Wayne. "What Impels Jehovah's Witnesses." *New York Times Magazine*, Aug. 10, 1958, pp. 15, 48, 49.

"Photos." *Oui*, Oct. 1974, p. 14. Discusses *Watchtower* magazine.

Redekop, Calvin. "Decision Making in a Sect." *Review of Religious Research*, Vol. 2, No. 2, Fall 1960, pp. 79-86.

————. "The Sect Cycle in Perspective." *Mennonite Quarterly Review*, Vol. 36, No. 2, April 1962, pp. 155-161.

————. "The Sect from a New Perspective." *Mennonite Quarterly Review*, July 1965, pp. 204-217.

Regehr, Ernie. "Jehovah's Witnesses in Africa." *Christian Century*, Vol. 93, Jan. 7, 1976, pp. 17, 18.

Religion och Kulture, Vol. 47, No. 4, 1976, pp. 1-20. Complete issue on the Witnesses.

Russell, Gordon, et al. "The Perception of Judeo-Christian Religion." *Canadian Journal of Behavioral Science*, Vol. 11, No. 2, 1979, pp. 140-152.

Rylander, Gosta. "En Medicinsk-psykiatrisk-socialogisk undersokning av Jehovahs Vittnen." *Nordisk Medicin*, Vol. 29, No. 1, Jan.-March 1946, pp. 526-533. (A Psychological and Sociological Study of Jehovah's Witnesses.)

Salholz, Eloise. "Are They False Witnesses?" *Newsweek*, July 20, 1981, p. 75.

"Short Takes." *Time*, Feb. 28, 1972, p. 46. Playmate studying to be a Jehovah's Witness. See also *Playboy Magazine*, Nov. 1971, cover and p. 94.

Smith, Patti. "Penthouse Interview." *Penthouse*, Vol. 7, No. 8, April 1976, pp. 124-126, 150. Smith was raised a Witness.

Sprague, Theodore W. "Some Notable Features in the Authority Structure of a Sect." *Social Forces*, Vol. 21, March 1943, pp. 344-350.

Stevenson, W.C. "Big Brother Knorr: Review of Year of Doom 1975." *Times Literary Supplement*, March 7, 1968, p. 234.

Stroup, Herbert. "The Attitude of Jehovah's Witnesses Toward the Roman Catholic Church." *Religion in the Making*, Vol. 2, No. 2, Jan. 1942, pp. 148-163.

————. "Class Theories of the Jehovah's Witnesses." *Social Science*, Vol. 19, No. 2, April 1944, pp. 94-97.

————. *The Jehovah's Witnesses*. Reviewed by S.K. Ratcliffe. *Spectator*, Vol. 175, Oct. 5, 1945, p. 316.

Student Action Committee. "Sister Dies as a Result of Rape." *Obsidian*, Oct. 30, 1978, p. 3.

Whalen, William J. *Armageddon Around the Corner: A Report on Jehovah's Witnesses.* Reviewed by Theodore W. Sprague. *Journal for the Scientific Study of Religion,* Vol. 3, No. 1, Fall 1963, pp. 137, 138.

———. *Armageddon Around the Corner.* Reviewed by Charles C. Braden. *Review of Religious Research,* Vol. 5, No. 2, Winter 1964, pp. 120, 121.

Whitbread, Jane. "Poor Boy's Rich Life." *Look,* Vol. 17, Sept. 6, 1966, pp. m8–m10+.

Wilson, Bryan. "Aspects of Kinship and the Rise of Jehovah's Witnesses in Japan" (intro. in French and article in English). *Social Compass,* Vol. 24, No. 1, 1977, pp. 121–134.

———. "The Debate over Secularization: Religion, Society and Faith." *Encounter,* Vol. 45, Oct. 1975, pp. 77–83.

———. "Jehovah's Witness in Africa." *New Society,* Vol. 25, No. 562, July 17, 1973, pp. 73–75.

———. "Jehovah's Witnesses in Kenya." *Journal of Religion in Africa,* Vol. 5, 1974, pp. 128–149.

———. "When Prophecy Failed." *New Society,* Vol. 26, Jan. 26, 1978, pp. 183, 184.

"Wise Up! Is God a 'Dope'?" *National Lampoon,* Dec. 1974, pp. 57–59.

"Witnesses Expelled." *The Christian Century,* April 7, 1982, p. 402.

Woefkin, C. "The Religious Appeal of Premillenarianism." *Journal of Religion,* Vol. 1, pp. 255–260.

Woodward, Kenneth L. "Are They False Witnesses?" *Newsweek,* July 20, 1981, p. 75.

"You Can Win a Soul for Christ." *Our Sunday Visitor,* Oct. 2, 1955.

Younghusband, Peter. "Persecution in Malawi." *Newsweek,* May 10, 1976, pp. 106, 107.

"Zoning Hits Minority Church." *Church and State*, Vol. 35, No. 3, March 1982, p. 17.

History of the Watchtower Society
and Jehovah's Witnesses

Amidon, Beulah. "Can We Afford Martyrs?" *Survey Graphic*, Vol. 29, Sept. 1940, p. 457.

"Anti-Zionist 'Watchtower' Movement Betrayed 'Founder's' Prophetic Call." *United Israel Bulletin*, Vol. 34, No. 2, Summer 1977, pp. 1, 4.

"Argentina's Military Government Has Abolished a Decree That Banned Jehovah's Witnesses." *Christianity Today*, Vol. 25, No. 4, Feb. 20, 1981, pp. 49, 50.

Armstrong, Herbert W. "No! I Never Was a Jehovah's Witness, or a Seventh-Day Adventist!" *Plain Truth*, Nov. 1970, pp. 106, 107.

Assimeng, John Maxwell. "Sectarian Allegiance and Political Authority: The Watchtower Society in Zambia 1907-35." *Journal of Modern African Studies*, Vol. 8, No. 1, 1970, pp. 97-112.

Beatty, Jerome. "Peddlars of Paradise." *Reader's Digest*, Jan. 1941, pp. 78-81.

Beckford, James A. "Les Témoins de Jehovah à travers le monde" (in French, intro. in English). *Social Compass*, Vol. 24, No. 1, 1977, pp. 5-31. (Jehovah's Witnesses Worldwide.)

Berger, Doris. "The Acid Test." *U.S. Week*, Vol. 1, No. 6, April 19, 1941, p. 23.

"Besynnerliga men anda beundransvarda." *En Ny Varld*, Vol. 5, May 1946, p. 17. (Strange, But Also Wonderful.)

"Bible Teaching Banned in Liberia." *Church and State*, Vol. 22, No. 6, June 1969, p. 10.

"Big Week for Witnesses" (Annual Convention, St. Louis, Mo.). *Newsweek*, Aug. 18, 1941, p. 50.

Binsse, Harry L. "Religion and a Liquor License." *Commonweal*, Jan. 10, 1947, pp. 317, 318.

Blandre, Bernard. "Russell et les Etudiants de la Bible 1870-1916." *Revue de l'Histoire des Religions*, Vol. 187, 1975, pp. 181-199.

Blessing, William L. "Jehovah's Witnesses." *Showers of Blessing*, Vol. 690, June 1978, pp. 14, 15. Reprinted in *Blessing Letter*, June 1978, pp. 1-4.

"Brother Bundy's Journey." *Unsearchable Riches*, Vol. 30, 1939, p. 263.

Brozan, Nadine. "Case of Self-Sufficiency." *Harper's Magazine*, Vol. 246, March 1973, p. 7.

Bryant, Delmar H. "When Futurism Failed." *Christ Is the Answer*, March 1973, pp. 16-18.

"California Cults." *Time*, Vol. 15, No. 13, March 31, 1930, pp. 60-61.

Calzon, Frank. "Report: Jehovah's Witnesses in Cuba." *Worldview*, Vol. 19, No. 12, Dec. 1976, pp. 13, 14.

Cameron, Gail. "Mickey Spillane Is at It Again--The Soft Side of a Hard Egg." *Life*, Vol. 51, No. 10, Sept. 8, 1961, pp. 127-129. Spillane was a Witness for many years.

"Canada: Le Chef Is Dead." *Time*, Vol. 74, Sept. 14, 1959, pp. 38, 41. About Duplessis, a government antagonist of the Witnesses.

Carr, A.M. "Witnesses of What?" *Columbia*, Vol. 38, Nov. 1958, pp. 4+.

"Cartoon about Jehovah's Witnesses." *Crucible*, July 1979, p. 4.

Clapp, Rodney. "The Watchtower Cracks Again." *Christianity Today*, Vol. 26, No. 4, Feb. 19, 1982, pp. 27, 32.

"Cloud of Witnesses." *Time*, July 27, 1953, p. 72.

Cole, Marley. "Inside the Witnesses: Review of *Jehovah's Witnesses, The New World Society*." *Nation*, Vol. 181, Oct 1, 1955, p. 290.

————. "Jehovah's Witnesses." *Herald Tribune Book Review*, July 31, 1955, p. 9.

————. "Jehovah's Witnesses: God's Army on the March." *Color*, Aug. 1953, pp. 24-28.

————. "Jehovah's Witnesses--Religion of Racial Integration." *Crisis*, Vol. 60, April 1953, pp. 205-211.

————. "Mob Rule in Crossville." *Nation*, Vol. 172, June 9, 1951, pp. 539-541.

————. "Speaking of Trailerists: They're Rolling Toward Heaven." *Trailer Life*, May 1953.

————. "Theocratic Trailer City." *Trailer Topics*, April 1953, pp. 19, 70, 72, 74, 77.

————. "Training Africans for Better Life" as told by George Brumley. *Color*, April 1953, pp. 18-21.

————. "World's Fastest Growing Religion." *Color*, Dec. 1952, pp. 30-35.

Collison, James W. "By Leaps and Bounds--A Report on Jehovah's Witnesses." *Voice of St. Jude*, Vol. 25, July 1959, pp. 24-28.

"Conscientious Objectors and Jehovah's Witnesses." *DePaul Law Review*, Vol. 4, Spring-Summer 1955, pp. 296-306.

"Convert's Husband Loses Damage Suit." *Moody's Monthly*, Vol. 83, No. 3, Nov. 1982, p. 134.

"The Crime of Airman Cupp." *Commonweal*, Dec. 21, 1956, pp. 301, 302.

Cross, Sholto. "Social History and Millennial Movements: The Watchtower in South Central Africa" (intro. in French and article in English). *Social Compass*, Vol. 24, No. 1, 1977, pp. 83-95.

Cunnisen, Ian. "A Watchtower Assembly in Central Africa." *International Review of Missions*, Vol. 40, Oct. 1951, pp. 456-569.

————. "Jehovah's Witnesses at Work: Expansion in Central Africa." *The British Colonies Review*, Vol. 29, 1st Quarter 1958, p. 13.

Dahlin, John E. "An Exodus from the Jehovah's Witnesses." *The Discerner*, Vol. 11, No. 1, Jan. 2, 1983, p. 10.

Dailey, K. "Jehovah's Witnesses." *Information*, Vol. 69, Dec. 1955, pp. 25-30.

Davidson, Bill. "Jehovah's Traveling Salesmen." *Collier's Magazine*, Vol. 118, No. 18, Nov. 2, 1946, pp. 12, 13, 72-77. Reprinted in *Reader's Digest*, Jan. 1947, pp. 77-80.

Davis, Larry L. "Larry L. Davis Reports on 1971 Colorado Bible Students Convention at Fort Collins." *United Israel Bulletin*, Vol. 28, No. 3, Nov. 1971, pp. 1, 3.

"Departing Leaders Reveal Cracks in the Watchtower." *Christianity Today*, Vol. 24, No. 21, Dec. 12, 1980, pp. 68-71.

Dilliard, Irving. "About-Face to Freedom." *The New Republic*, Vol. 108, May 24, 1943, pp. 693-695. Discusses Supreme Court reversal in Jehovah's Witnesses flag case.

Doherty, J.E. "Jehovah's Witnesses." *Liquorian*, Vol. 41, March 1953, pp. 151-157.

"Efforts to Curb Jehovah's Witnesses." *Church and State*, Vol. 27, No. 5, May 1974, p. 16.

"800 Baptisms an Hour." *Newsweek*, Aug. 19, 1946, p. 78.

"Eine schleichende Heresie." *Zentral-Blatt*, Vol. 30, June 1937, p. 106. (A Creeping Heresy.)

"The End Is Near (cont'd)." *Time*, Vol. 110, July 11, 1977, pp. 64, 65.

"Eutychus and His Kin: A Case of Conversion from the Jehovah's Witnesses." *Christianity Today*, Vol. 9, 1964, p. 305.

"Ex-Jehovah's Witnesses Gathered." *Christianity Today*, Vol. 24, Dec. 7, 1979, p. 52.

Fecher, R.J. "Made in U.S.A." *Nuntius Aulae*, Vol. 43, 1961, pp. 169-177.

Felix, R. "Fight Fire with Fire." *Catholic Mind*, Vol. 37, Aug. 8, 1939, p. 788.

"Fighting Fire with Fire Activities of Judge Rutherford."
    America, Vol. 61, Aug. 12, 1939, p. 424.

"Founder of Anti-Zionist J.-Witnesses Hailed Zionism as Being
    Biblically Prophetic." *United Israel Bulletin*, Vol. 28,
    No. 1, March 1971, pp. 1, 4.

Furlong, Monica. "Nuts in April." *Spectator*, Vol. 204,
    April 29, 1960, p. 609.

Gdovia, G. "Jehovah's Witnesses: Hard Sell Converting."
    Information, Vol. 73, Aug. 1959, pp. 3-11.

"God's in His Heaven...." *Newsweek*, July 5, 1943, pp. 81, 82.

"God's New World: Jehovah's Witnesses Surprise the World with
    Their Unusual Beliefs and Steadfast Courage." *Our World*,
    Vol. 8, No. 11, Nov. 1953, pp. 17-24.

"Greeks Arrested for Proselytizing." *Church and State*, Vol.
    12, No. 10, Nov. 1959, p. 3.

"Greeks Execute Objector; Britain Releases Green." *News
    Notes of the Central Committee for Conscientious Objectors*,
    Vol. 1, No. 2, Feb. 1949, p. 1.

"Growth Arrested." *Time*, Feb. 13, 1978.

Harrison, Barbara G. *Visions of Glory: A History and a
    Memory of Jehovah's Witnesses*. Reviewed by E.C. Dennis.
    Library Journal, Vol. 103, Aug. 1978, p. 1501.

————. *Visions of Glory: A History and a Memory of Jehovah's
    Witnesses*. Reviewed in *Saturday Review*, Vol. 5, Sept. 16,
    1978, p. 47.

————. *Visions of Glory: A History and a Memory of Jehovah's
    Witnesses*. Reviewed in *New York Review of Books*, Vol. 25,
    Oct. 26, 1978, p. 53.

————. *Visions of Glory: A History and a Memory of Jehovah's
    Witnesses*. Reviewed by Catharine R. Stimpson. *Ms.*, Oct.
    1978, pp. 43-45.

————. *Visions of Glory: A History and a Memory of Jehovah's
    Witnesses*. Reviewed by Vivian Gornick. *New York Times
    Book Review*, Nov. 19, 1978, p. 9.

————. *Visions of Glory: A History and a Memory of Jehovah's Witnesses.* Reviewed in *The Worldview*, Vol. 21, No. 10, Oct. 1978.

————. *Visions of Glory: A History and a Memory of Jehovah's Witnesses.* Reviewed by Jack Miles. *Commonweal*, Vol. 105, Dec. 22, 1978, p. 818.

————. *Visions of Glory: A History and a Memory of Jehovah's Witnesses.* Reviewed by Lisa Gubernick. *Nation*, Vol. 228, Jan. 1979, p. 22.

"He Was Present at Historic Hippodrome Meeting in 1910." *United Israel Bulletin*, Vol. 28, No. 3, Nov. 1971, p. 3.

Henderson, R.E. "Pastor Russell." *Overland Monthly*, Vol. 69, Jan. 1917, p. 56. A poem.

Higgins, J. "Jehovah's Witnesses at Your Door." *Liquorian*, Vol. 60, Oct. 1972, pp. 16-19.

High, Stanley S. "Armageddon, Inc." *Saturday Evening Post*, Vol. 213, Sept. 14, 1940, pp. 18, 19, 50, 54, 58.

Holt, R. "What on Earth Is Jesus Waiting For?" *These Times: Special Issue*, July 1, 1975, p. 7.

"Homecoming (Malawi)." *Time*, Dec. 1, 1975, p. 6.

Hooker, J.R. "Witnesses and Watchtower in the Rhodesias and Nyasaland." *Journal of African History*, Vol. 6, No. 1, Jan. 1965, pp. 91-106.

Hopkins, Joseph M. "Religious Freedom for All—Except Jehovah's Witnesses." *Columbia Law Review*, Vol. 25, No. 4, Feb. 20, 1981, pp. 46-48.

How, Glen. "A Portrait." *MacLean's; Canada's National Magazine*, Vol. 77, Jan. 4, 1964, p. 12.

Hubbard, J. Glen. "I Examine a Book Published by Jehovah's Witnesses." *Two Worlds*, March 1969, pp. 80-84.

Hutchinson, Paul. "The President's Religious Faith." *Christian Century*, March 24, 1954, pp. 362-369. Published simultaneously in *Life*, Vol. 36, March 22, 1954, pp. 151-170. About Eisenhower, who was raised a Witness.

"In Memoriam: Fredrick Homer Robison." *Unsearchable Riches*, Vol. 23, 1932, pp. 292-297.

"Italian Military Court." *Christianity Today*, Vol. 18, April 27, 1973, p. 48.

Jeavons, Art. "Letter to the Editor." *The Plain Truth*, April 19, 1975, p. 13.

"Jehovah's Witness Sues Disney World." *Church and State*, Vol. 35, No. 11, Dec. 1982, p. 19.

"Jehovah's Witnesses." *Time*, Vol. 25, No. 23, June 10, 1935, pp. 34-36.

"Jehovah's Witnesses" (Editorial). *Liberation*, Vol. 3, Summer 1958, p. 3.

"Jehovah's Witnesses Arrested in Spain." *Church and State*, Vol. 22, No. 9, Oct. 1969, p. 10.

"Jehovah's Witnesses: CIA Cover?" *Muhammad Speaks*, June 12, 1970, p. 12.

"Jehovah's Witnesses Convicted of Proselytizing." *Church and State*, Vol. 27, No. 1, Jan. 1974, p. 19.

"Jehovah's Witnesses: Hard Sell Converting." *Information*, Vol. 73, Aug. 1959, pp. 3-11.

"Jehovah's Witnesses: Holding Doomsday at Hand, Sect Steps up Propaganda." *Newsweek*, Vol. 13, June 26, 1939, p. 29.

"Jehovah's Witnesses Prosecuted by Orthodox Church." *Church and State*, Vol. 12, No. 2, Feb. 1959, p. 3.

"Jehovah's Witnesses Push 'Creationism' in Schools." *Church and State*, Vol. 35, No. 5, May 1982, p. 17.

"Jehovah's Witnesses Sentenced to Death in Greece." *Church and State*, Vol. 19, No. 9, Oct. 1966, p. 10.

"Jehovah's Witnesses Sentenced to Jail." *Church and State*, Vol. 19, No. 3, March 1966, p. 10.

"Jehovah's Witnesses Threatened with Expulsion." *Church and State*, Vol. 26, No. 1, Jan. 1973, p. 21.

"Jehovah's Witnesses: U.S.-Born Religious Society Attracts
Increasing Number of Negro Converts." *Ebony*, Vol. 6, Oct.
1951, pp. 98-104.

"Jehovah's Witnesses Who Refuse to Salute U.S. Flag, Hold
Their National Convention." *Life*, Vol. 9, Aug. 12, 1940,
pp. 20, 21.

"Jehovas Vitten i Finland retireade inte." *En Ny Varld*, Vol.
5, March 1946, p. 17. (Jehovah's Witnesses in Finland Don't
Give Up.)

Johnston, Richard W. "Death's Fair-Haired Boy: Sex and Fury
Sell 13 Million Gory Books for Mickey Spillane." *Look*,
Vol. 17, Aug. 28, 1953, pp. 79-95. Spillane was a Witness.

"Judge Declined Jehovah's Witnesses' Citizenship." *Church
and State*, Vol. 22, No. 5, May 1969, p. 11.

Kennedy, J.S. "I Admire the Jehovah's Witnesses." *Columbia*,
Vol. 22, Jan. 1943, pp. 7+. Reprinted in *Catholic Mind*,
Vol. 41, May 1943, pp. 39-45.

"Kenya Has Banned Missionaries." *Christianity Today*, Vol. 17,
No. 9, Sept. 28, 1973, p. 57.

King, Christina E. "Strategies for Survival: An Examination
of the History of Five Christian Sects in Germany 1933-1945."
Journal of Contemporary History, Vol. 14, No. 2, April
1979, pp. 211-234.

Lawson, W. "How Do You Explain the Rapid Growth of Jehovah's
Witnesses?" *Church Order*, Vol. 5, Nov. 1964, p. 690.

"Letter from Walter Salter." *Unsearchable Riches*, Vol. 30,
1939, p. 198.

Lewis, Richard Warren. "Then Time Out for Bible Study."
TV Guide, Vol. 22, No. 48, Nov. 30, 1974; Vol. 22, No. 49,
Dec. 6, 1974, pp. 20-23, cover.

Lobsenz, Norman M. "The Embattled Witnesses." *Coronet*,
Jan. 1956, pp. 129-133.

Lockwood, Robert. "How Jehovah's Witnesses Attack Catholicism."
Our Sunday Visitor, Vol. 62, Dec. 2, 1973, pp. 1, 2.

————. "Latin Catholics Target for Jehovah's Witnesses."
   Our Sunday Visitor, Vol. 62, Nov. 25, 1973, pp. 1, 6.

Luchterhand, Elmer. "Prisoner Behavior and Social System
   in the Nazi Concentration Camps." *International Journal
   of Social Psychiatry*, Vol. 13, No. 4, 1967, pp. 245-264.

MacGowan, Gault. "Jehovah's Witnesses (They Sell Books)."
   Catholic Digest, Vol. 3, Nov. 1938, pp. 71-76.

McGinnis, H.C. "Russell, Then Rutherford Spawn Jehovah's
   Witnesses." *America*, Vol. 64, Feb. 8, 1941, pp. 481-482.

————. "Rutherford and His Witnesses Find Your Catholics a
   Bad Lot." *America*, Vol. 64, Feb. 15, 1941, pp. 512-513.

————. "Rutherford in a Palace, His Witnesses in the Slums."
   America, Vol. 64, March 1, 1941, pp. 569-570.

————. "Rutherford Warns His Dupes on Religion and Government." *America*, Vol. 64, Feb. 22, 1941, pp. 542-543.

McLoughlin, William G. "Is There a Third Force in Christendom?" *Daedalus*, Vol. 96, No. 1, Winter 1967, pp. 43-68.

"Malawi Expels Witnesses." *Church and State*, Vol. 22, No. 1,
   Jan. 1966, p. 10.

"Marching to Armageddon." *Time*, Aug. 11, 1958, pp. 39, 40.

"Marriages Performed by Jehovah's Witnesses Not Valid."
   Church and State, Vol. 24, No. 2, Feb. 1971, p. 19.

Martin, Walter R. "Herbert W. Armstrong the All-American
   Cultist." *Youth Illustrated*, Oct., Nov., Dec. 1970, pp.
   34-39.

"Massing of the 'Witnesses.'" *Newsweek*, Aug. 4, 1958, p. 49.

Meisler, Stanley. "Jehovah's Witnesses in Africa--Martyrdom
   Safari!" *Nation*, Vol. 217, July 16, 1973, pp. 51, 52.

Melrose, K.M.C. "Reply." *Spectator*, Vol. 195, Aug. 12,
   1955, p. 221.

Mitchell, R.J. "Jehovah's Witnesses in Cuba." *Worldview*,
   Vol. 20, No. 4, 1977, p. 2. Reply to a previous article.

"Modern Crusaders." *Ave Maria*, Vol. 48, Sept. 24, 1938, p. 407.

Moley, Raymond. "The Boot Is on the Other Leg." *Newsweek*, June 29, 1942, p. 68.

Moyle, Peter-Simon Olin. "The Legal Case Against the Watch-tower Exposed by a Former 'Insider.'" *United Israel Bulletin*, Vol. 29, No. 1, Feb. 1972, pp. 1, 2.

————. "More Light on the Watchtower's Deviation." *United Israel Bulletin*, Vol. 29, No. 3, Dec. 1972, p. 1.

Muller, Albert. "These Jehovah's Witnesses." *America*, Vol. 105, June 2, 1961, pp. 464-465.

"Needless New Religions." *Literary Digest*, March 23, 1912, p. 596.

Nelkin, Dorothy. "The Science-Textbook Controversies." *Scientific American*, Vol. 234, No. 4, April 1976, pp. 33-39.

"New York Court Tax-Exempt." *Christianity Today*, Vol. 19, Sept. 13, 1974, p. 88.

"New York Witnesses the Witnesses." *America*, Vol. 99, Sept. 9, 1958, p. 483.

Nichols, Beverly. "Wimbley Assembly." *Sunday Chronicle*, Dec. 16, 1951.

"Nigeria." *Journal of Church and State*, Vol. 15, No. 3, Autumn 1973, p. 491.

"No Fiery Hell." *Newsweek*, Aug. 4, 1958, p. 49.

"Non-Jewish Reader Says the 'Jews Are God's Time-Clock.'" *United Israel Bulletin*, Spring 1975.

O'Brien, John A. "Jehovah's Witnesses—A Visit to Head-quarters." *Catholic Digest*, Vol. 27, Dec. 1962, pp. 61-63.

————. "A Visit to Jehovah's Witnesses." *Pastoral Life*, Vol. 2, Nov. 1963, pp. 20-24.

"On from Yankee Stadium." *Time*, Aug. 2, 1963, p. 40.

Ostling, Richard N. "Witness under Persecution." *Time*, Feb. 22, 1982, p. 66.

"Pastor Charles T. Russell Article Evokes National Interest;
    Noted Bible Scholars React Favorably; Events Vindicate
    Founder." *United Israel Bulletin*, Vol. 28, No. 2, July
    1971, p. 1.

"Pastor Charles T. Russell's Famous Pro-Zionist 1910 Hippo-
    drome Speech Recalled." *United Israel Bulletin*, Vol. 37,
    No. 2, Summer 1980, pp. 1, 4.

"Pastor Charles Taze Russell Evokes National Interest." *United
    Israel Bulletin*, Vol. 28, No. 2, July 1971, p. 4.

"Pastor Russell Cheered by Audience of Hebrews." *United Israel
    Bulletin*, 1971.

"Pastor Russell Cited at UI's Founders' Meeting in 1944."
    United Israel Bulletin, Vol. 29, No. 3, Dec. 1972, pp. 1, 2.

"Pastor Russell, in 1897, Spoke of Herzl's 'Jewish State.'"
    United Israel Bulletin, Vol. 28, No. 3, Nov. 1971, pp. 1, 3.

"Pastor Russell's 'The Restoration of Israel.'" *United Israel
    Bulletin*, Vol. 28, No. 1, March 1971, p. 4.

Paulus, Jean Pierre. "Le Kitawala au Congo Belge." *Revue
    de l'Institut de Sociologie*, Nos. 2-3, 1956, pp. 257-270.
    (The Watchtower in the Belgian Congo.)

Payton, G.H. "Witnesses of the Millennium." *New Statesman
    and Nation*, No. 1074, Oct. 6, 1951, pp. 342-362.

"A Peculiar Investigation of Missions." *The Missionary Review
    of the World*, Vol. 25, July 1912, p. 538.

Pelletier, Pam. "Scaling the Jehovah's Witnesses Watchtower."
    Reprinted from *Moody Monthly*, Aug. 1977. *The Lookout*, Vol.
    40, No. 9, Feb. 26, 1978, pp. 6, 7.

Penton, M. James. *Jehovah's Witnesses in Canada: Champions
    of Freedom of Speech and Worship*. Reviewed by J.L. Granat-
    stein. *Quill and Quire*, Nov. 1976, p. 36.

————. *Jehovah's Witnesses in Canada*. "The Watchtower
    People: Review of *Jehovah's Witnesses in Canada: Champions
    of Freedom of Speech and Worship*" by Bryan Wilson. *Times
    Literary Supplement*, April 1, 1977.

————. *Jehovah's Witnesses in Canada: Champions of Freedom of Speech and Worship*. Reviewed by John W. Netter. *Church History*, Vol. 47, No. 1, March 1978, pp. 98, 99.

————. *Jehovah's Witnesses in Canada: Champions of Freedom of Speech and Worship*. Reviewed by J.K. Zeman. *Journal of Church and State*, Vol. 20, No. 2, Spring 1978, pp. 341-343.

————. "Jehovah's Witnesses and the Secular State: A Historical Analysis of Doctrine." *Journal of Church and State*, Vol. 21, No. 1, Winter 1979, pp. 55-72.

"Persecution in Malawi." *Church and State*, Vol. 21, No. 2, Feb. 1968, p. 10.

Porter, Thomas. "Star of 'Get Christie Love' Now Preaching Door-to-Door." *National Enquirer*, April 27, 1976, p. 8.

Pottersman, Arthur. "The Terrible Mr. Spillane, and the Girl He Married Right off a Book Jacket." *Detroit Free Press--Sunday Magazine*, June 11, 1976, pp. 45, 46. Spillane was a Witness.

Quick, Griffith. "Some Aspects of the African Watchtower Movement in Northern Rhodesia." *International Review of Missions*, Vol. 29, April 1940, pp. 216-226.

Quotation from *Awake! Playboy*, Feb. 1969, p. 22.

"Raymond Jolly, Associate of the Late Pastor Russell, Recalls His Years Working with Noted Bible Scholar." *United Israel Bulletin*, Vol. 34, No. 3, Winter 1977, p. 4.

"Record of Witnesses." *Life*, Vol. 45, Aug. 11, 1958, pp. 117, 118. Rally.

"Record Record." *Newsweek*, Oct. 29, 1951, p. 78.

"Reign of Terror in Malawi." *Church and State*, Vol. 26, No. 2, Feb. 1973, p. 53.

Review of Two Books on Jehovah's Witnesses. *Ms.*, Vol. 29, March 1948, pp. 70-74.

Rogerson, Alan Thomas. "Témoins de Jéhovah et Etudiants de la Bible. Qui Est Schismatique?" (intro. in English and article in French) (English translation mimeographed, 7 pp.). *Social Compass*, Vol. 24, No. 1, 1977, pp. 33-43. (Jehovah's Witnesses and Bible Students--Who Is Schismatic?)

Roll, William G. "Prankish Ghost Puts on Eerie Display for
    Investigators." *National Enquirer*, Feb. 25, 1975, p. 6.
    About a Witness family.

Ross, J.J. "Editorial: Being 'Labelled.'" *The Gospel Witness*,
    July 14, 1927, pp. 8-13.

"Russellism Admitting Its Mistakes." *The Watchman*, Vol. 25,
    Dec. 1916, pp. 11-15.

"Russellism--or the Coming of a False 'Christ.'" *The Watch-
    man*, Vol. 24, April, June, Aug., Sept., Oct. 1915, pp. 162-
    166, 267-272, 363-367, 406-410, 454-458.

Russell, Charles T. *The Plan of the Ages*. Reviewed by J.B.
    Rotherham. *The Rainbow*, Dec. 1886, pp. 507-517.

Rutherford, J.F. "The Late Pastor Russell: Biographical
    Sketch by His Successor." *Overland Monthly*, Vol. 69, April
    1917, pp. 296-302.

"Rutherford's Flock." *Newsweek*, Aug. 5, 1940, p. 42.

"Salvation at the Door Step." *Detroit Free Press--Sunday
    Magazine*, April 18, 1976, pp. 6-10.

"Say Yeah!" *Time*, Jan. 5, 1976, pp. 76, 77. About ex-Witness
    Patti Smith.

Schnell, William J. *Thirty Years a Watchtower Slave*. Reviewed
    by Stanley Rowlean, Jr. *Nation*, Vol. 182, Nov. 24, 1956,
    p. 464.

————. "When They Come to Your Door." *Lutheran Standard*,
    Aug. 18, 1970, pp. 6+.

"School Board Reverses Ban." *Church and State*, Vol. 12, No.
    10, Nov. 1959, p. 8.

Schorr, Jose. "You Be the Judge." *Saturday Evening Post*.

Semprun, Jorge. "A Day in Buchenwald." *Dissent*, Fall 1982,
    pp. 425-430.

"Short History of Jehovah's Witnesses." *Sign*, Vol. 38, Sept.
    1958, p. 50.

"Singapore De-Registered Jehovah's Witnesses." *Church and State*, Vol. 25, No. 3, p. 20.

Smith, Theodore A. "Regarding Founder of Jehovah's Witnesses." *United Israel Bulletin*, Vol. 28, No. 2, Dec. 1972, pp. 1, 2.

"Smoking." *Christianity Today*, Vol. 19, Jan. 18, 1974, p. 52. Discusses the new expulsion rule for Jehovah's Witnesses who smoke.

Southworth, H.R. "Jehovah's 50,000 Witnesses." *Nation*, Vol. 151, Aug. 10, 1940, pp. 110-112.

Standerwick, D. "Report on the Witnesses." *Jubilee*, Vol. 6, Aug. 1958, pp. 2-4.

Sterling, Chandler W. *The Witnesses: One God, One Victory*. Reviewed by D.W. Dayton. *Library Journal*, Vol. 100, May 1, 1975, p. 863.

Stevenson, W.C. *The Inside Story of Jehovah's Witnesses*. Reviewed by Peter Sedgwick. *New Statesman and Nation*, Vol. 75, Jan. 12, 1968, p. 48.

————. *The Inside Story of Jehovah's Witnesses*. Reviewed by Edith French. *Library Journal*, Vol. 93, Oct. 1, 1968, p. 3566.

Stewart, E.C. "Life of Pastor Russell." *Overland Monthly*, Vol. 69, Dec. 1917, pp. 126-132.

Stroup, Herbert. *The Jehovah's Witnesses*. "The Religion of Hate: Review of *The Jehovah's Witnesses*" by S. Pritchett. *New Statesman and Nation*, Vol. 30, Oct. 13, 1945, p. 248.

————. *The Jehovah's Witnesses*. Reviewed by Theodore Tappert. *Lutheran Church Quarterly*, Vol. 19, No. 2, April 1946, pp. 219-220.

Tedo, James. "This We Believe." *Color*, c. 1951, pp. 128, 129.

Tennant, Hal. "Jehovah's Witnesses: The New Look of a Turbulent Sect." *MacLean's (Canada's National Magazine)*, Vol. 75, Aug. 25, 1962, pp. 40, 41.

"A 'Terrible Upheaval.'" *Newsweek*, July 4, 1955, p. 58.

Testa, Bart. "Bearing Witness to a Mass Exodus." *MacLean's (Canada's National Magazine)*, Vol. 94, March 16, 1981, pp. 47-49.

"Testimony by Mr. Overman and Others Relative to the Charges of Sedition Against Rutherford and Others." *Congressional Record of the United States*, May 4, 1918, pp. 6050-6053.

Thurston, H. "Rutherford and the Witnesses of Jehovah: Are They Apostles of Anarchy?" *Catholic Mind*, Vol. 37, Aug. 8, 1939, pp. 769-787.

"Tidings" (Malawi). *Time*, Dec. 18, 1972, p. 98.

"20 Jehovah's Witnesses Sentenced to Long Prison Terms." *Church and State*, Vol. 27, No. 11, Nov. 1974, p. 13.

"Upholds Right to Attack Religions" (in Mineola, N.Y.). *Church Management*, May 1940.

Walker, Charles R. "Fifth Column Jitters." *McCall's Magazine*, Jan. 1940, pp. 9, 10, 116.

Watt, David. "Two Cheers for Theocracy." *Spectator*, Vol. 195, Aug 5, 1955, p. 190.

Whalen, William J. "All About Jehovah's Witnesses." *U.S. Catholic*, Vol. 73, April 1979, pp. 93-99.

———. "Jehovah's Witnesses: Gonna Take a Fundamental Journey." *U.S. Catholic*, Jan. 1979, pp. 29-34.

———. "Jehovah's Witnesses' New Look." *Lamp*, Vol. 59, Oct. 1961, pp. 8, 9, 29, 30.

———. "Jehovah's Witnesses: They Expect the Battle of Armageddon to Start Any Day." *Our Sunday Visitor*, Vol. 65, April 3, 1977.

———. "What I Like About Jehovah's Witnesses." *U.S. Catholic*, Vol. 30, July 1964, pp. 17-19.

———. "When Jehovah's Witnesses Call." *Marriage*, Vol. 45, March 1963, p. 42.

———. "Who Are Jehovah's Witnesses?" *Sign*, Vol. 39, April 1960, pp. 29-31.

"What Happened to Pastor Russell's Original Will?" *United Israel Bulletin*, Vol. 28, No. 3, Nov. 1971, p. 4.

"What Price Syncretism?" *Time*, May 6, 1957, p. 89.

White, Timothy. "Book Notes: *A People for His Name: A History of Jehovah's Witnesses and an Evaluation.*" *Church History*, Vol. 38, No. 1, March 1969, p. 128.

"Whither the Witnesses?" *Newsweek*, July 19, 1950, p. 46.

"Will the Real Teresa Graves Please Stand Up?" *Ebony*, Dec. 1974, pp. 68, 70. Subtitled "Star of 'Get Christie Love' series is devout Bible student."

"Witness Angle." *Newsweek*, Vol. 21, March 22, 1943, pp. 68, 69.

"A Witness Explanation." *Christianity Today*, Vol. 24, Feb. 6, 1981, pp. 8, 9.

"The Witnesses." *Time*, June 30, 1961, p. 47.

"The Witnesses Hear the Word." *Life*, Vol. 29, Aug. 14, 1950, pp. 32, 33.

"Witnesses, Jehovah's." *America*, Vol. 54, Dec. 7, 1935, p. 196.

"Witnesses of Jehovah." *The Sign*, Vol. 25, Dec. 1945, p. 645.

"Witnesses' Spartan Trials." *Time*, Sept. 9, 1966, pp. 84, 86.

"Witnesses Vindicated." *Newsweek*, Oct. 19, 1953, p. 100.

"Witnesses Want Windham to Teach Creationism." *Newsletter on Intellectual Freedom*, Vol. 31, No. 1, p. 5.

"Witnesses Win." *Church and State*, Vol. 27, No. 9, Sept. 1974, p. 22.

"Witnessing for Jehovah." *Newsweek*, Aug. 3, 1953, pp. 44, 45.

"Witnessing the End." *Time*, July 18, 1969, pp. 62, 63.

Woodward, E.P. "Another Gospel: An Exposure of the System
    Known as Russellism." *The Safeguard and Armory*, Vol. 19,
    1914, pp. 1-123.

"The Word and the Way According to Victor Wierville." *Chris-
    tianity Today*, Vol. 20, Sept. 26, 1975, pp. 40, 42.

"The World's Worst Woman." *Saturday Evening Post*, July 2,
    1955, pp. 24, 74-77.

"Wrath." *Newsweek*, Nov. 8, 1943, p. 70.

"Zambia and Malawi: Whose Witnesses?" *The Economist*, Vol.
    245, No. 6747, Dec. 16, 1972, pp. 40-41.

"Zambia Paper Attacks Jehovah's Witnesses." *Church and State*,
    Vol. 22, No. 7, July-Aug. 1969, p. 10.

Zygmunt, Joseph F. "Jehovah's Witnesses in the U.S.A.--
    1942-1976" (intro. in French and article in English).
    Social Compass, Vol. 24, No. 1, 1977, pp. 45-47.

Theology, Doctrine, and General Discussions

"Armageddon--Cancelled until Further Notice?" *Eternity*, Vol.
    26, May 1975, p. 6.

Armstrong, Arthur. "Antichrist Answered." *Logos*, 1978, pp. 240,
    241.

--------. "The Truth vs. Jehovah's Witnesses." *Logos*, Vol. 43,
    No. 9, June 1977, p. 272.

"Attend Bible Classes of The Jehovah's Witnesses?" *Extension*,
    Vol. 53, June 1956, p. 37.

"The Authority of the Scriptures." *The Discerner*, Vol. 2,
    No. 2, Oct.-Dec. 1955, pp. 5-7.

Baldus, S.A. "Witnesses of Jehovah." *Extension*, Vol. 35,
    Nov. 1940, p. 19.

Bales, James D. "The Godhead." *The Spiritual Sword*, Vol. 6,
    No. 1, Oct. 1974, pp. 1-3.

Barclay, William. "An Ancient Heresy in Modern Dress." *The
    Expository Times*, Vol. 65, No. 2, Nov. 1953, pp. 31, 32.

Bechtle, John D. "And the Word Was What?" *The Discerner*, Vol. 8, No. 8, Oct.-Dec. 1975, pp. 7-10.

Beenken, Gilbert. "Misinterpretations of the Biblical Subject of Eternity." *The Discerner*, Vol. 5, No. 4, Oct.-Dec. 1965, pp. 6-11.

Bevins, John. "A Loyal Witness, but a Stranger to Grace ... In the Organization, but Outside the Pale." *Evangelical Times, special issue, Christ and the Watchtower*, Vol. 1, 1974, p. 6.

"Bible (in) Version." *Eternity*, Nov. 1981, p. 14.

Binsse, H.L. "Religion and a Liquor License." *Commonweal*, Vol. 45, Jan. 10, 1947, pp. 317-318.

Blackford, Dick. "Jehovah's Witnesses." *Precepter*, Vol. 23, No. 8, 1974.

"Boom in Doom." *Logos*, Vol. 43, No. 5, Feb. 1977, pp. 158, 159.

Braden, Ruth. "Jehovah 1975." *New Society*, Vol. 14, 1969, pp. 201, 202.

Button, L.C. "No Longer a Mormon." *The Discerner*, Vol. 5, No. 8, Oct.-Dec. 1966, p. 7. Discusses the author's experience with the Witnesses.

Canedy, Herbert V. "The Hazards of Date-Setting." *The Discerner*, Vol. 2, No. 11, July-Sept. 1976, pp. 8, 10-12.

————. "Quintuplet Cults, or Brothers Under the Skin." *The Discerner*, Vol. 1, No. 2, July-Aug. 1947, p. 5.

————. "Satan's Strategy in His War of Worlds." *The Discerner*, Vol. 2, No. 11, July-Sept. 1958, pp. 13, 14.

Carter, Cecil J. "The New American Standard Version and the Deity of Christ." *Plains Baptist Challenger*, Vol. 36, No. 1, Feb. 1977, pp. 1, 3.

Cetnar, William. "Kicked Out of the Watchtower." *Eternity*, Vol. 31, No. 9, Oct. 1980, pp. 40-42.

Clevenger, Eugene W. "Sin and Salvation." *The Spiritual Sword*, Vol. 6, No. 1, Oct. 1974, pp. 18-20.

Cohen, D. "Let's Hear It for Doomsday." *The Humanist*, July-Aug. 1976, pp. 22-26.

Cole, Marley. Review of *Jehovah's Witnesses--The New World Society*. *The Discerner*, Vol. 2, No. 2, Oct.-Dec. 1955, p. 14.

Cotton, Richard E. "In the Watchtower Movement for 18 Years, When God Rode Out to Conquer My Heart." *Evangelical Times, special issue, Christ and the Watchtower*, Vol. 1, 1974, pp. 4, 5.

————. "Will the World End This Year?" *Evangelical Times*, Vol. 9, No. 1, Jan. 1975, pp. 1, 2.

Countess, R.H. "Translation of 'Theos' in the New World Translation." *Journal of the Evangelical Theological Society*, Vol. 10, Summer 1967, pp. 153-160.

Dahlin, John E. "Common Characteristics of Cults." *The Discerner*, Vol. 2, No. 11, July-Sept. 1958, pp. 2-4.

————. "Cultists Are Past Masters in Distorting the Scriptures." *The Discerner*, Vol. 2, No. 2, April-June 1959, pp. 12-14.

————. "The Great Success of Cults in Our Time." *The Discerner*, Vol. 5, No. 10, April-June 1967, pp. 2-5.

————. "I Saw Jehovah's Witnesses at Work in Europe." *The Discerner*, Vol. 2, No. 8, Oct.-Dec. 1955, pp. 12, 13.

————. "The Jehovah's Witnesses." *The Discerner*, Vol. 6, No. 9, Jan.-March 1970, pp. 3, 4.

————. "The Jehovah's Witnesses as Dangerous Innovators." *The Discerner*, Vol. 4, No. 11, July-Sept., 1964, pp. 2-5.

————. "Some Guidelines in Dealing with Cultists." *The Discerner*, Vol. 6, No. 12, Oct.-Dec. 1970, pp. 2-5.

————. "The Tragic Errors of Present-Day Cultists." *The Discerner*, Vol. 4, No. 8, Oct.-Dec. 1963, pp. 2-5.

————. "Unscriptural Cults of Our Time--a Review." *The Discerner*, Vol. 2, No. 8, Oct.-Dec. 1957, pp. 2-6.

Dalyik. "Jehovah's Witnesses." *Information*, Vol. 69, Dec. 1955, pp. 25-30.

d'Anjou, M.J. "Actualité Religieuse." *Relations*, Vol. 20, Nov. 1960, pp. 300, 301. (Religious News.)

Darby, George. "Cultist Activity in the Last Days." *The Discerner*, Vol. 4, No. 6, April-June 1963, pp. 5-8.

"Darkness vs. Light." *Regular Baptist Press*, April 1953, pp. 63-67.

Davies, Horton. "Centrifugal Christian Sects." *Religion in Life*, Vol. 25, Summer 1956, pp. 328, 329.

Deaver, Roy. "Christ--His Person." *The Spiritual Sword*, Vol. 6, No. 1, Oct. 1974, pp. 4-11.

————. "The Witnesses and 1 Peter 3:18." *The Spiritual Sword*, Vol. 6, No. 1, Oct. 1974, pp. 14-16.

"A Defense of the True Bible Chronology." *The Present Truth and Herald of Christ's Epiphany*, March-April 1970, pp. 23-28.

"The Deity of Our Lord." *The Discerner*, Vol. 3, No. 8, Oct.-Dec. 1960, pp. 9-13.

Dencher, Ted. "Do Not Slam Your Door to a Jehovah's Witness." *Herald of His Coming*, Vol. 38, No. 5 (449), May 1979, pp. 7-8.

————. "From Watchtower to Christ." *The Evangelical Christian*, Feb. 1962, pp. 18-20.

————. "How Can We Help Jehovah's Witnesses?" *Church Herald*, July 26, 1974, pp. 14ff.

————. "The Watchtower Heresy Versus the Bible, Reviewed by John Dahlin." *The Discerner*, Vol. 4, No. 7, July-Sept. 1963, pp. 14, 15.

"Devils That Tempt." *Megiddo Messenger*, Vol. 62, No. 2, Feb. 1975, pp. 9-11.

Dixon, A.C. "Russellism under the Searchlight." *The Life of Faith*, May 5, 1915, pp. 519, 520.

Doherty, J.E. "Jehovah's Witnesses." *Liquorian*, Vol. 41, March 1953, pp. 151-157.

Donovan, Oswald M. "The Jehovah's Witnesses." *Ministry*, Vol. 22, June 1949, pp. 17-19.

Dugre, Alexandre. "Sur le Front de l'Heresie." *Ma Paroisse*, Feb. 1954, pp. 8, 9. (At the Front of Heresy.)

————. "Faux témoins d'un Faux Jehovah." *Relations*, Vol. 14, Feb. 1954, pp. 34-37. (False Witnesses of a False Jehovah.)

————. "Sur le Front Jehovah." *Relations*, Vol. 14, March 1954, pp. 80-83. (On the Jehovah's Witness Front.)

Duncan, Homer. "Jesus Christ Is Not God." *The Discerner*, Vol. 9, No. 3, July-Sept. 1977, pp. 11-13.

Eddy, G. Norman. "The Jehovah's Witnesses: An Interpretation." *Journal of Bible and Religion*, Vol. 26, 1958, pp. 115-121.

"80,000,000 Books." *Logos*, Vol. 144, No. 6, March 1978, pp. 176, 177.

Emch, William N. "What Do Jehovah's Witnesses Teach?" *Lutheran Standard*, Vol. 112, No. 38, Sept. 17, 1955, p. 3.

————. "Who Are Jehovah's Witnesses?" *Lutheran Standard*, Vol. 117, May 23, 1959, pp. 13, 14.

Estes, T. "Jehovah's Witnesses Won't Tell Who Translated Their Bible." *Gospel Defender*, Vol. 3, No. 7, 1962, p. 4.

Feyles, G. "Los Testigos de Jehova." *Didascalia*, Vol. 18, July 1964, pp. 297-305. (The Jehovah's Witnesses.)

Fisher, Ronald. "Why and How of Reaching Jehovah's Witnesses." *Evangelical Missions Quarterly*, Vol. 12, No. 4, Oct. 1976, pp. 227-238.

Fisk, Samuel. "Meeting a Jehovah's Witness at the Door." *The Discerner*, Vol. 7, No. 3, July-Sept. 1971, pp. 9-13.

Fletcher, Austen G. "The Only Begotten: How Does This Term Apply to Christ?" *Ministry*, Vol. 50, April 1977, pp. 40-42.

Gager, Leroy. "Who Are Jehovah's Witnesses?" *The Discerner*, Vol. 2, No. 2, Oct.-Dec. 1955, pp. 3, 4.

Garner, Carl B. "What Is Man According to the Witnesses?" *Thrust*, Vol. 1, No. 1, 1980, pp. 23-29.

Gilbert, Richard R. "Waiting for Armageddon: Jehovah's Witnesses." *Presbyterian Life*, Aug. 15, 1962, pp. 5, 6, 31-34.

Goedelman, Kurt. "Jehovah's Witnesses and the Gospel of the Resurrection." *The Journal of Pastoral Practices*, Vol. 3, No. 2, 1979, pp. 128-130.

Gruss, Edmond E. "Is the Watchtower Society God's Channel?" *The Discerner*, Vol. 7, July-Sept. 1973, pp. 11-14.

————. "Jehovah's Witnesses." *Moody Monthly*, 1971.

————. "Now a Witness for Jesus Christ, Not a Jehovah's Witness." *The Discerner*, Vol. 6, No. 9, Jan.-March 1970, pp. 8-11.

————. "Review of *Jehovah's Witnesses: Apostles of Denial*." *Moody Monthly*, Jan. 1971, pp. 40-41. Reprinted in *The Discerner*, Vol. 7, No. 10, Jan.-March 1971, p. 12.

————. "The Watchtower Society and Prophetic Speculation." *The Discerner*, Vol. 7, No. 5, Jan.-March 1972, pp. 13-15.

Haas, Samuel. "Review of New World Translation of Hebrew Scriptures." *Journal of Biblical Literature*, Vol. 74, March 1955, pp. 282, 283.

Hassell, J.W. "The Truth About Jehovah's Witnesses." *Southern Presbyterian Journal*, Vol. 12, May 2, 1951, pp. 6, 7.

Hawk, Ray. "Salvation and the Witnesses." *Thrust*, Vol. 1, No. 2, 1980, pp. 48-51.

Hebert, Gerard. "Les Témoins de Jehovah." *Relations*, Vol. 20, Oct. 1960, pp. 259-262. (The Jehovah's Witnesses.)

————. "Où en sont les Témoins de Jehovah." *Relations*, Vol. 23, Sept. 1963, pp. 263-266. (The Present State of Jehovah's Witnesses.)

Hedegord, David, ed. "Kring Jehovas Vitten." *For Biblical Faith*, No. 3, 1958, pp. 107-116. (About Jehovah's Witnesses.)

Henschel, Milton G. "Who Are Jehovah's Witnesses?" *Look*, Vol. 17, July 28, 1953, pp. 76, 77.

The Herald of the Epiphany, special edition, Feb. 15, 1959, 4 pp.

Herrgott, Jean. "French Evangelist Endures Sanatorium, Millennial Dawnists to Serve His Savior." *Greater Europe Report*, Vol. 4, No. 2, March-April 1974, pp. 3, 6.

Hill, William F. "Are Jehovah's Witnesses Really Witnessing for Jehovah?" *The Discerner*, Vol. 8, No. 6, April-June 1975, pp. 12-14.

Higgins, J. "Jehovah's Witnesses at Your Door." *Liquorian*, Vol. 60, Oct. 1972, pp. 16-19.

Hobbs, A.G. "A General Look at Jehovah's Witnesses." *The Spiritual Sword*, Vol. 6, No. 1, Oct. 1974, pp. 41-46.

Hoekema, Anthony. "Assessing Jehovah's Witnesses." *Christianity Today*, Vol. 11, July 21, 1967, pp. 14-17.

————. *The Four Major Cults.* Reviewed by David Larson. *The Discerner*, Vol. 5, No. 2, April-June 1965, pp. 14, 15.

Hope, S. "Be Prepared for Jehovah's Witnesses." *Presbyterian Journal*, May 7, 1975, p. 13.

"How to Spot a Cult." *Moody Monthly*, Aug. 1977, p. 32.

"Is Armageddon Imminent?" *Insight*, Vol. 6, Oct. 28, 1975, p. 17.

"Is It a Sin to Change Religions?" *Evangelical Times, special issue, Christ and the Watchtower*, Vol. 1, 1974, p. 2.

"Is It Wrong to Refuse to Argue with Jehovah's Witnesses?" *Messenger of the Sacred Heart*, Vol. 91, Feb. 1956, pp. 50, 51.

"Is Something Happening in the Watchtower Movement?" *Evangelical Times, special issue, Christ and the Watchtower*, Vol. 1, 1974, p. 1.

Jackson, Wayne. "The Church (The Kingdom)." *The Spiritual Sword*, Vol. 6, No. 1, Oct. 1974, pp. 22-24.

————. "The Lord's Return." *The Spiritual Sword*, Vol. 6, No. 1, Oct. 1974, pp. 25-27.

"Jehovah's Witnesses." *The Expository Times*, Vol. 55, Feb. 1944.

"Jehovah's Witnesses." *Catholic Mind*, Vol. 43, July 1945, p. 421.

"Jehovah's Witnesses Do Not Believe." *The Discerner*, Vol. 4, No. 11, July-Sept. 1964, pp. 14, 15.

"Jehovah's Witnesses Refuted by the Bible." *Herald of the Coming Age*, Vol. 20, No. 3, Oct. 1969, p. 48.

"Jehovah's Witnesses: The Christian View--Personal Freedom Outreach of St. Louis, Missouri." *The Journal of Pastoral Practice*, Vol. 3, No. 1, 1979, pp. 95-113.

"Jehovah's Witnesses vs. Scripture." *Megiddo Messenger*, Vol. 53, No. 10, Oct. 1966, pp. 14-16.

Johnson, Andrew E. "Laymen's Home Missionary Movement." *The Discerner*, Vol. 6, No. 1, Jan.-March 1968, pp. 6, 7, 15. About an offshoot of the Jehovah's Witnesses.

————. "Witness with False Evidence." *Good News Broadcaster*, Jan. 1973, pp. 10ff.

————. "Witnesses with False Evidence." *The Discerner*, Vol. 7, No. 9, Jan.-March 1973, pp. 9-12.

Jones, Jerry. "Baptism." *The Spiritual Sword*, Vol. 6, No. 1, Oct. 1974, pp. 20-22.

Kelcy, Raymond C. "Punishment of the Wicked." *The Spiritual Sword*, Vol. 6, No. 1, Oct. 1974, pp. 38-40.

Knuteson, Roy E. "The God of the Jehovah's Witnesses." *The Discerner*, Vol. 4, No. 7, July-Sept. 1963, pp. 6-9.

————. "The Kingdom Concept of the Jehovah's Witnesses." *The Discerner*, Vol. 4, No. 11, July-Sept. 1964, pp. 10-14.

"La Cour Suprême et les Témoins de Jehovah." *Relations*, Vol. 13, Nov. 1953, p. 286. (The Supreme Court and Jehovah's Witnesses.)

"La Divinidad de Jesus Frente a los 'Testigos de Jehova.'" *Didascalia*, Vol. 21, No. 2, 1967, pp. 97-102. (The Divinity of Jesus Face to Face with the Jehovah's Witnesses.)

Larsen, David L. "Cultic Distortion of the Holy Scriptures." *The Discerner*, Vol. 6, No. 12, Oct.-Dec. 1970, pp. 5-9.

Larsen, Robert L. "Where Is Elijah?" *Ministry*, Vol. 44, Nov. 1971, pp, 32, 33.

Laursen, Gerald A. "How to Witness to Jehovah's Witnesses." *Evangelical Beacon*, Aug. 10, 1971, pp. 10, 11.

Ledit, J.H. "Les Témoins de Jehovah." *Relations*, Vol. 6, Feb. 1947, pp. 43-46. (The Jehovah's Witnesses.)

————. "Les Témoins se reorganisent." *Relations*, Vol. 3, Aug. 1943, pp. 212-214. (The Witnesses Reorganize.)

Lewis, Jack P. "The New World Translation of the Holy Scriptures." *The Spiritual Sword*, Vol. 6, No. 1, Oct. 1974, pp. 32-36.

Lusk, Maurice, III. "Christ--His Resurrection." *The Spiritual Sword*, Vol. 6, No. 1, Oct. 1974, pp. 14-16.

McCluskey, N.G. "Who Are Jehovah's Witnesses?" *America*, Vol. 94, Nov. 19, 1955, pp. 204-208. Reprinted in *Catholic Digest*, Vol. 20, March 1956, pp. 56-61.

McCord, Hugo. "Man--His Nature and Death." *The Spiritual Sword*, Vol. 6, No. 1, Oct. 1974, pp. 16-18.

McGinnis, H.C. "Who Are the Holy Crusaders Joining Jehovah's Witnesses?" *America*, Vol. 64, March 22, 1941, pp. 651-652. Reprinted as "Witness Jehovah's Witnesses." *Catholic Digest*, Vol. 51, July 1941, pp. 53-59.

McInerney, T.J. "Watchtower Zealots." *Sign*, Vol. 26, Dec. 1946, pp. 39-41. Abridged in *Catholic Digest*, Vol. 11, Feb. 1947, pp. 102-103.

McKinnley, George D. *Theology of Jehovah's Witnesses*. Reviewed by Frank B. Price. *International Review of Missions*, Vol. 52, Oct. 1963, pp. 467-470.

Martin, Walter R. "Jehovah's Witnesses and the Gospel of Confusion." *Eternity*, Vol. 8, Sept. 1957, pp. 22, 23, 36, 37.

Mattingly, J.F. *Jehovah of the Watchtower*. Reviewed by G.D. Young. *Northwestern Pilot*, May 1954.

————. "Jehovah's Witnesses Translate the New Testament." *Catholic Biblical Quarterly*, Vol. 13, Oct. 1951, pp. 438-443.

"The Message of the Revelation in 1942." *Lutheran Church Quarterly*, Vol. 15, 1942, pp. 296-299.

Metzger, Bruce M. "Review of the *New World Translation of the Christian Greek Scriptures*." *Princeton Seminary Bulletin*, Vol. 44, No. 4, Spring 1951.

————. "The Jehovah's Witnesses and Jesus Christ: A Biblical and Theological Appraisal." *Theology Today*, Vol. 10, No. 1, April 1953, pp. 65-85.

Mignard, Robert B. "Fifteen Reasons Why I Cannot Be a Jehovah's Witness" (reprint of tract with same title). *The Discerner*, Vol. 5, No. 6, April-June 1966, pp. 12-15. Reprinted in Vol. 8, No. 12, Oct.-Dec. 1976, pp. 13-16. Also reprinted in *The Voice*, June 1966.

Moffitt, Jerry. "Everlasting Punishment." *Thrust*, Vol. 1, No. 2, 1980, pp. 58-66.

Morey, Robert. "A Jehovah's Witness? Next Time Open the Door." *Christianity Today*, Vol. 26, No. 14, Sept. 1982, pp. 37-39.

Muller, Albert. "Jehovah's Witnesses Call." *Homiletic and Pastoral Review*, Vol. 63, May 1963, pp. 676-683.

"The Name of God." *Herald of Holiness*, June 18, 1969, p. 10. A critical analysis of Witnesses' use of the name Jehovah.

"New Notes." *The Journal of Pastoral Practices*, Vol. 3, No. 2, 1979, pp. 131, 132.

O'Brien, John A. "Challenge of the Witnesses." *American Ecclesiastical Review*, Vol. 117, Oct. 1947, pp. 284-290.

————. "Light on Jehovah's Witnesses." *Our Sunday Visitor*, p. 29.

"Ominous Decision." *Time*, June 22, 1942, p. 55. Jehovah's Witnesses can be forced to pay peddlers' tax.

"Ontario: Jehovah's Witnesses." *Time*, Sept. 25, 1944, p. 17.

"Organizations: Glad Assembly." *Time*, Aug. 19, 1946, p. 24.

Patania, Connie. "From Jehovah's Witnesses to Life in Jesus Christ!" *Deeper Life*, Sept. 1979, p. 5.

Paul, J.M. "Russellism Refuted." *The Christadelphian Advocate*, Nov. 1915, pp. 327-330.

Pelletier, Pam. "Scaling the Jehovah's Witnesses Watchtower." *Moody Monthly*, Vol. 77, Aug. 1977, pp. 33-35.

"People." *Moody Monthly*, Dec. 1977, pp. 20, 22. About Inga Markmiller, a Jehovah's Witness opera singer.

Perry, Victor. "Jehovah's Witnesses and the Deity of Christ." *Evangelical Quarterly*, Vol. 35, Jan.-March 1963, pp. 15-22.

Pickering, Ernest. "Jehovah's Witnesses--The Doctrine of the Church." *The Discerner*, Vol. 3, No. 9, Jan.-March 1961, pp. 11-15.

Plante, A. "L'Incident de Shawinigan." *Relations*, Vol. 10, June 1950, pp. 155-157. (The Incident at Shawinigan [a city in South Quebec].)

Prescott, William W. "Jehovah--Jesus." *Revue de l'Institut de Sociologie*, Vol. 98, April 28, 1921, pp. 3-5.

Price, E.B. "How to Work for Jehovah's Witnesses." *Ministry*, Vol. 35, April 19, 1962, pp. 34-36.

"Pseudo-Science and Pseudo-Theology (A) Cult and Occult." *Journal of the American Scientific Affiliation*, March 1977, pp. 24, 25.

"Quebec: The Witnesses." *Time*, Oct. 1, 1945, p. 42.

"Questions and Answers." *Megiddo Messenger*, Vol. 49, No. 11, May 26, 1962, p. 11.

"Questions and Answers." *Megiddo Messenger*, Vol. 49, No. 14, July 7, 1962, p. 11.

"Questions and Answers." *Megiddo Messenger*, Vol. 54, No. 12, Dec. 1967, p. 23.

"Questions and Answers." *Megiddo Messenger*, Vol. 55, No. 5, May 1968, p. 15.

"Questions and Answers." *Megiddo Messenger*, Vol. 55, No. 7, July 1968, p. 23.

"Questions from Readers." *Epiphany Bible Students Association*, Vol. 251, pp. 6-8.

Read, W.E. "The Name of God (Part I)." *Ministry*, Vol. 42, Feb. 1969.

————. "The Name of God (Part II): Jesus as 'The Lord Thy God.'" *Ministry*, Vol. 42, March 1969.

Rhodes, Oran. "The Holy Spirit and the Witnesses." *Thrust*, Vol. 1, No. 1, 1980, pp. 18-22.

————. "The Kingdom and 1914." *Thrust*, Vol. 1, No. 2, 1980, pp. 70-75.

Rogerson, G. "1914 in Bible Prophecy, Part I." *Signs of the Times* (Australia), Vol. 88, Aug. 1, 1974, pp. 2-4.

————. "1914 in Bible Prophecy, Part II: The Law of Probabilities and 1914." *Signs of the Times*, Vol. 99, Sept. 1, 1974, pp. 10-13.

————. "1914 in Bible Prophecy, Part III: Chronology of the Seventy Years as It Affects 1914." *Signs of the Times*, Vol. 88, Oct. 1, 1974, pp. 10-12.

————. "1914 in Bible Prophecy, Part IV: The Seventy Years in Retrospect." *Signs of the Times*, Vol. 88, Nov. 1, 1974, pp. 10, 11.

————. "1914 in Bible Prophecy, Part V: Do the Signs Indicate 1914?" *Signs of the Times*, Vol. 88, Dec. 1, 1974, pp. 18-20.

Rosen, Moishe. "Titles." *Jews for Jesus Newsletter*, Vol. 10, 1977, p. 1.

Rowley, H.H. "How Not to Translate the Bible." *The Expository Times*, Vol. 65, Nov. 1953, p. 41, 42.

————. "Jehovah Witnesses' Translation of the Bible." *The Expository Times*, Vol. 67, Jan. 1956, pp. 107, 108.

Rumble, L. "Witnesses of Jehovah." *Homiletic and Pastoral Review*, Vol. 54, July 1954, pp. 873-884.

Sage, Wayne. "The War on the Cults." *Human Behavior*, Oct. 1976, pp. 40-49.

Sanders, Evelyn. "When You Meet Jehovah's Witnesses." *Evangelical Beacon*, Vol. 46, No. 3, Oct. 31, 1972, pp. 8, 9.

————. "When You Meet Jehovah's Witnesses." *Presbyterian Journal*, May 15, 1974, pp. 9ff.

————. "When You Meet Jehovah's Witnesses." *Princeton Seminary Bulletin 44*, Vol. 30, No. 3, 1974, pp. 9, 10.

Schmuck, Terry. "Set Free by the Truth." *The Discerner*, Vol. 9, No. 4, Oct.-Dec. 1977, pp. 10-12.

Schnell, William. "Open Letter to Jehovah's Witnesses" (6th letter). *The Discerner*, Vol. 6, No. 3., July-Sept. 1968, pp. 14, 15.

————. "Witnessing for Christ to Jehovah's Witnesses." *United Evangelical Action*, Vol. 19, July 1960, pp. 163+.

"The Second Advent of Christ." *Megiddo Messenger*, Feb. 17, 1962, pp. 13-16.

"The Second Coming--Visible or Invisible." *Megiddo Messenger*, Feb. 17, 1962, pp. 7-9.

Shahan, R. "I Was a Jehovah's Witness." *Lutheran Standard*, Feb. 5, 1977, pp. 8ff.

Simmel, O. "Sind die Ernsten Bibel Forscher Ernst Zu Nehman?" *Stimmen*, Vol. 146, Sept. 1950, pp. 466-469. (Should We Take the Bible Students [J.W.'s] Seriously?)

Smith, Wilbur N. "Jehovah's Witnesses." *Christianity Today*, Vol. 5, Dec. 19, 1960, pp. 16-18.

"Smoking." *Church Management*, Vol. 50, No. 2, April 1974.

So Many Versions? Reviewed in *Eternity*, April 1976, pp. 41, 42.

Spivey, Arnold. "A Look at Jehovah's Witnesses." *Sabbath Recorder*, Vol. 200, No. 3, March 1978, pp. 7, 28.

Sprague, Theodore W. "The 'World' Concept Among Jehovah's Witnesses." *Harvard Theological Review*, Vol. 39, April 1946, pp. 109-140.

Springstead, William A. "Hermeneutics of Jehovah's Witnesses." *The Discerner*, Vol. 3, No. 6, April-June 1960, pp. 8-10.

————. "Jehovah's Witnesses' Amazing Switch in Doctrine." *The Discerner*, Vol. 2, No. 2, April–June 1959, pp. 9–11, 15.

Starkes, M. Thomas. "Armageddon's Army: The Jehovah's Witnesses." *Home Missions*, March 1975.

Starling, Norman W. "The Name 'Jehovah's Witnesses.'" *Thrust*, Vol. 1, No. 2, 1980, pp. 67–69.

Stedman, Ray C. "The New World Translation of the Christian Greek Scriptures." *Our Hope*, Vol. 60, July 1953, pp. 29–39.

Stevens, Josephine. "Witnesses." *New Society*, Aug. 23, 1973, p. 474.

Strelkov, M.S. "Outwitting the Witnesses." *St. Anthony's Messenger*, Vol. 66, Sept. 1958, pp. 37–41.

Stuermann, Walter. "The Bible and Modern Religions III." *Interpretation: A Journal of Bible and Theology*, Vol. 10, No. 3, July 1956, pp. 323–346.

————. "Jehovah's Witnesses and the Bible." *Interpretation: A Journal of Bible and Theology*, Vol. 10, No. 3, July 1956, pp. 323–346.

————. "New World Translation of the Christian Greek Scriptures." *Interpretation: A Journal of Bible and Theology*, Vol. 10, No. 3, July 1956, pp. 323–346.

Swanson, Collene. A Letter which Mentions Jehovah's Witnesses. *Moody Monthly*, Dec. 1977, p. 9.

Swetmon, Bill. "Jehovah's Witnesses Translations of I Peter 3:15." *The Spiritual Sword*, Vol. 6, No. 1, Oct. 1975, pp. 36, 37.

Tarbet, Don. "Jehovah's Witnesses Doctrine About Christ." *Thrust*, Vol. 1, No. 1, 1980, pp. 10–17.

————. "The 'Trinity.'" *Thrust*, Vol. 1, No. 2, 1980, pp. 52–57.

Terry, George. "Jehovah's Witness Presiding Elder Exclaims, 'I've Been Born Again!'" *Evangelical Times, special issue, Christ and the Watchtower*, Vol. 1, 1974, pp. 2, 3.

————. "A Problem Verse for Christians?" *Evangelical Times, special issue, Christ and the Watchtower*, Vol. 1, 1974, p. 3.

Thiele, Edwin R. "Jehovah's Witnesses and the Dates of the Babylonian Captivity." *Ministry*, Vol. 49, No. 2, Feb. 1976, pp. 17-19.

"Thirty Years a Watchtower Slave." *Power*, Vol. 16, No. 1, Jan.-March 1958, 8 pp. Reprinted in *The Discerner*, Vol. 2, No. 11, July-Sept. 1958, pp. 8, 9-12.

Thomas, Stan. *Jehovah's Witnesses and What They Believe*. Reviewed by Gary Wharton. *The Evangelical Christian*, July 1967, p. 22.

Thompson, Robert F. "My Lord and My God. Part 1: Why Jehovah's Witnesses Are Wrong About the Deity of Christ." *Ministry*, Vol. 9, Sept. 1976, pp. 20-23.

————. "My Lord and My God. Part 2." *Ministry*, Vol. 49, No. 11, Nov. 1976, pp. 22-24.

Thomson, Alexander. "An Interesting New Version." *The Differentiator*, Vol. 14, April 1952, pp. 52-57.

————. "An Interesting New Version." *The Differentiator*, Vol. 16, June 1954, pp. 131-136.

————. "An Interesting New Version." *The Differentiator*, Vol. 17, Dec. 1955, pp. 257-262.

————. "Jehovah's Theocratic Organization." *The Differentiator*, Vol. 21, No. 3, June 1959, pp. 98-104.

"To 'Christie Love,' Star Teresa Graves, Religion More Important Than Show Business." *Midnight*, Vol. 22, No. 2, July 14, 1975, p. 4.

Trombley, Charles. "A Wedge in My Foundation." *Voice*, March 1963.

"Twenty Questions on a Witness' Mind." *Evangelical Times, special issue, Christ and the Watchtower*, Vol. 1, 1974, pp. 1-8.

Van der Goes, Catherine. "Why I Quit the Jehovah's Witnesses." *The Discerner*, Vol. 7, No. 9, Jan.-March 1973, pp. 13, 14. Reprinted from *Power for Living*, 1972.

"Victory Without Peace." *Extension*, Aug. 1943, p. 19.

"Waiting for Armageddon." *Time*, Aug. 14, 1950, pp. 68, 69.

Warren, Thomas B. "Editorial: Jehovah's Witnesses: A System of Infidelity." *The Spiritual Sword*, Vol. 6, No. 1, Oct. 1974, inside front cover and pp. 3, 4.

Whalen, William. "What Can the Jehovah's Witnesses Teach Us?" *Ave Maria*, Vol. 95, Feb. 24, 1962, pp. 26-29; also Vol. 94, July 8, 1961, p. 17.

————. "We Can Learn Something from Jehovah's Witnesses." *St. Anthony Messenger*, Vol. 80, May 1973, pp. 18-21.

Wharton, Gary. "I Came Back." *The Evangelical Christian*, July 1967, pp. 19-22. Story of Stan Thomas.

Whittington, John. "History of Jehovah's Witnesses." *Thrust*, Vol. 1, 1980, pp. 10-17.

————. "A Review of the *New World 'Translation'* of the Bible." *Thrust*, Vol. 1, No. 2, 1980, pp. 42-47.

"Who Are God's True Witnesses?" *Herald of the Coming Age*, p. 20.

Wimbish, John S. "What Is a Jehovah's Witness?" *The Sword of the Lord*, Vol. 47, No. 47, Nov. 20, 1981, pp. 1, 8-14.

"Witnesses Deny Christian Tie." *Presbyterian Life*, Sept. 1, 1969.

"Witnesses Examined." *Time*, July 29, 1940, pp. 40, 41.

"Witnesses in Detroit." *Time*, Aug. 5, 1940, p. 39.

"Witnesses in Trouble." *Time*, June 24, 1940, p. 54.

"The Witnesses (Outlawed in Poland)." *Time*, July 17, 1950, p. 71.

Woods, Guy N. "New Heavens—New Earth." *The Spiritual Sword*, Vol. 6, No. 1, Oct. 1974, pp. 27-29.

"Working with Jehovah's Witnesses." *Ministry*, Vol. 42, Aug. 1943, pp. 46, 47.

Workman, Gary. "The Watchtower Doctrine of the Last Things."
    Thrust, Vol. 1, No. 1, 1980, pp. 30-40.

————. "The Watchtower Doctrine of the Last Things (Part 2)."
    Thrust, Vol. 1, No. 2, 1980, pp. 76-88.

"World Scene." *Christianity Today*, Vol. 17, March 3, 1972,
    p. 48.

Young, Douglord. *Jehovah of the Watchtower*. Reviewed in *The
    Discerner*, Vol. 2, No. 2, Oct.-Dec. 1955, p. 15.

Zuck, Ray. "Letter to a Jehovah's Witness." *Moody Monthly*,
    Vol. 73, March 1973, pp. 30-33, 90, 91.

SECTION FOUR

OFFSHOOTS OF THE WATCHTOWER
BIBLE & TRACT SOCIETY

Since its inception the Watchtower Bible & Tract Society
has experienced numerous schisms. The largest and most important of these are discussed in this section.
Some of this literature is difficult to classify in that
some of the dissonants were still technically associated with
the Watchtower Bible & Tract Society when they produced their
literature. Many of these documents relate to internal problems which, in time, resulted in the crystalization of separate
groups. As many of these were papers that circulated internally
and were printed (almost all of them were typeset and commercially printed) for limited circulation, they are grouped here.
As some of the material in this section is of importance to a
study of the Watchtower Bible & Tract Society itself, a few of
the documents in this section are also listed in the previous
section.
It should also be noted that in the case of some early
offshoots such as the Pastoral Bible Institute, even though
the leaders were expelled from Bethel, some were still demo-
cratically elected elders in the local Watchtower ecclesia.
Rutherford could, and often did, forbid dissidents to be
official pilgrims. Thus, in a sense, all the literature produced by the various factions, especially the 1917-1919 splits,
could be considered "official" literature. In time, however,
the divisions became increasingly great until in the United
States four major movements arose at this time--the Watchtower
Bible & Tract Society, the Pastoral Bible Institute, the Layman's Home Missionary Movement, and the Standfast Bible Students. In Britain, a number of other splits occurred at this
time. The Watchtower tried increasingly to differentiate
itself from the offshoots, but it was not until 1931, when
Rutherford introduced the name "Jehovah's Witnesses," that a
clear distinction between the various Bible Student groups
and the Watchtower existed.

Actually, Jehovah's Witnesses is as much an offshoot of the Russell movement as are the Standfasters or Layman's Home Missionary Movement. According to Alan Rogerson, "from 1919 to 1932 [Rutherford] systematically changed all aspects of the sect: [its] norms and values, ideology, patterns of evangelization and worship, internal structure, group commitments and (perhaps inevitably) its membership."

A SHORT HISTORY OF THE BIBLE STUDENT MOVEMENT

After the unexpected death of Pastor Russell on October 31, 1916, multiple divisions rent asunder the International Bible Students Association.

Even before Russell's death several leaders had disagreed with some of Russell's teachings and had led members to separate from the Watchtower. But after Russell's death, this splintering became more and more pervasive. When Russell died, the current directors of the Watch Tower Bible and Tract Society were Vice President A.I. Ritchie; Secretary-Treasurer William E. VanAmburgh, and James D. Wright, Isaac F. Hoskins, Henry Clay Rockwell (replaced on March 29, 1917, by Robert H. Hirsh), and Joseph F. Rutherford. All of these men had been appointed by Russell. Two days after Russell died, Andrew N. Pierson was elected by the committee to fill the vacancy left by Russell. The Executive Board included A.I. Ritchie, William E. VanAmburgh, and Joseph F. Rutherford. The Editorial Committee (which supervised all publications) included William E. VanAmburgh, Joseph F. Rutherford, Fred H. Robison, H.C. Rockwell, and Robert H. Hirsh. The pastoral work (primarily an organized way of following up interest in the IBSA) continued under the direction of Menta Sturgeon. A.H. MacMillan was in charge of the office staff.

The first election of the Society's officers after Russell died took place January 6, 1917, a Saturday, during the two-day Pittsburgh convention. Joseph Franklyn Rutherford was elected President of the Society, A.N. Pierson, Vice President (over A.I. Ritchie), and W.E. VanAmburgh was reelected Secretary-Treasurer. At this time, the Executive Committee was dissolved. This election has been the subject of endless debate.

The First Major Split After Russell Died

A major factor which caused the first division after Russell died was publication of *The Finished Mystery* (the seventh volume of *The Studies of the Scriptures*, thereafter referred to as the Seventh Volume). In November of 1916, at Rutherford's urging, the Executive Committee asked Clayton J. Woodworth and George H. Fisher of Scranton, Pennsylvania, to compile from Russell's notes a volume on Ezekiel and Revelation (and also Canticles), to be published as the "posthumous work of Pastor Russell." Four members of the Watch Tower Board of Directors, R.H. Hirsh, I.F. Hoskins, A.I. Ritchie, and J.D. Wright, objected to the publication of this work and to several other aspects of Rutherford's administration. On July 17, 1917, Rutherford claimed that since the Society charter required the election of directors, only the three officers of the board who had been elected in January were legal board members. He then appointed A.H. MacMillan, G.H. Fisher, J.A. Bohnet, and W.E. Spill to the board positions previously occupied by Ritchie, Hirsh, Wright, and Hoskins. The Seventh Volume was issued the same week.

Hirsh and the other ousted board members published during the summer a protest pamphlet called *Light After Darkness*. In October Rutherford answered this pamphlet with a special *Harvest Siftings No. 2*. Within a month, P.S.L. Johnson published his version (which is probably the most accurate), *Harvest Siftings Reviewed*. A straw poll of IBSA classes in December indicated that 95% backed Rutherford in the dispute (although most Bible Students did not know much about it and few had any first-hand knowledge). The annual election of Society officers and the first election of the Board of Directors since Russell's death was held January 5, 1918, during the January 2-6 Pittsburgh convention. R.H. Barber was nominated for director; other nominees were William E. Van-Amburgh, A.H. MacMillan, J.F. Rutherford, A.N. Pierson, W.E. Spill, J.A. Bohnet, and G.H. Fisher; F.H. McGee of Trenton, New Jersey, nominated the following: Menta Sturgeon, H.C. Rockwell, A.I. Ritchie, R.H. Hirsh, I.F. Hoskins, J.D. Wright, and P.S.L. Johnson (Johnson later withdrew). Rutherford, Mac-Millan, VanAmburgh, Spill, Bohnet, Anderson (not nominated), and Fisher were elected. McGee and W.J. Hollister (who was also not nominated) received about 13% of the total votes. Rutherford was reelected President, Anderson was elected Vice President, and VanAmburgh was reelected Secretary-Treasurer. The convention also voted to request R.H. Hirsh to resign from the Editorial Committee.

Among those who parted with the Society about 1918 were
McGee and his nominees, R.E. Streeter, I.I. Margeson, H.A.
Firese, P.L. Read, and P.E. Thomson. A.E. Burgess wavered
for a year before finally leaving and Raymond G. Jolly sided
with Paul S.L. Johnson.

Those avowing loyalty to the Society at that time (although most later left) include: O.L. Sullivan, F.T. Horth,
M.L. Herr, E.J. Coward, E.H. Thomson, W.E. Page, J.F. Stephenson, E.D. Sexton, H.H. Riemer, W.A. Baker, R.E. Nash, C.P.
Bridges, W.J. Thorn, G.S. Kendall, B.M. Rice, J. Hutchinson,
E.A. McCosh, Jesse Hemery (the British branch manager for half
a century who left in the early 1950s), E.G. Wylam, J.H.
Hoeveler, F.P. Sherman, and J.R. Muzikant. Dr. L.W. Jones
said he was not in opposition, but later left. Also about
this time Edwin Bundy, who had dissented from the Society from
1912 to 1917, returned to its fellowship; he later left again.

Other Endeavors at This Time

There are many viewpoints about Russell's work. Some
groups feel that Pastor Russell's teachings should be strictly
adhered to; others believe they know the date when the Church
will be completed (or feel that a great witness work is now
due the Jews, etc.). Still others believe the Church does
not at this time have any special work or "harvest" message.
Some Bible Students even feel they have received or are re-
ceiving direct revelations from God or Christ. These beliefs
frequently generate publications.

In time most of the well-known Bible Students left the
Watchtower Society. Dr. Leslie W. Jones of Chicago, who from
about 1904 to 1916 published the Souvenir Convention Reports,
and the first Pittsburgh Reunion Convention souvenir reports,
left in the 1920s.

Currently the total number of Bible Students outside the
Society who profess consecration and partake of the Memorial,
the Lord's Supper, the only sacrament the Watchtower and its
offshoots practice, is under 10,000, of whom over half are
overseas. There are perhaps one hundred or more immersions
annually of those who profess the "high calling" (life in
heaven).

These various groups which split from the Watchtower from
1917 to 1931 are very difficult to classify. Some, like the
Dawn Bible Students and the Pastoral Bible Institute, in
contrast to most offshoots, have a general sense of group
cohesiveness. Almost all consider themselves independent
Bible students, and, while they adhere to their doctrinal

particularities, they do not let this adherence interfere with their widespread intermingling and swapping of speakers and each other's literature. The last point is directly related to our bibliographic concerns, as it greatly complicates the task of classifying the literature.

These various movements are usually organized around a periodical, a personality, or both. The periodical serves as a means of communication and group cohesiveness and is often the major polemical organ. Most groups also publish a few books, a voluminous number of booklets and pamphlets, and a veritable flood of ephemera.

Bibliographically, the most frustrating characteristic of this literature is its anonymity. Much of it lists no author and no publisher, place of publication, or date. In many cases this information can be supplied only by chance acquaintance with the author or someone who knows him or her. There are several reasons for this anonymity. First, it was Pastor Russell's practice. His name often did not appear anywhere on his own works. Second, it allows publications to freely move from one group to another without reference to the group or the author.

There are a number of other reasons Bible Students tend to write anonymously. Many of them feel the work should be judged on its own merits and not be rejected solely because the writer may belong to a dissident ecclesia or a group which is not held in favor by mainline Bible Students. Many also wish to encourage the utilization of their work by a variety of Bible Student groups. For this reason they may leave a blank area on the back so that the local ecclesia or group can rubber-stamp its imprint if that ecclesia finds the tract or booklet useful for distribution.

Much of this literature is extremely rare and often only photocopies or references in other bibliographies are available. Thus, many of the listings that follow include no publisher, place of publication, or date. Often publications bear only an insignia, such as "published by Cincinnati Bible Students," or a general title such as "published by Berean Bible Students" (Berean is a popular name for various Bible Student groups). In addition, many non-conforming Bible Students experience difficulty fellowshipping with *any* Bible Student group and thus cannot publish under a group name. The information provided is all that was available even though in the majority of cases this writer has a copy of the original publication.

AMERICAN OFFSHOOTS

A. The Christian Millennial Church

     The New Creation Bible Students (at one time called
Associated Bible Students of L'Aurora Millenniale and later
Millennial Bible Students Church) are related to one of the
earliest offshoots of Russell's movement. They are theo-
logically similar to most other Bible Student groups although
somewhat more liberal. The headquarters is in Hartford,
Connecticut, and the group is associated with the Western
Bible Students. They circulate a national magazine, *The New
Creation*, which was begun in 1940 by its current editor,
Gaetano Boccaccio who left the Society in 1928. A number of
books and booklets are published in several languages. The
branch in Italy is called Mensile della chiesa Cristiana
Millenarista.

A BRIEF HISTORY OF THE WORK IN ITALY

     The work in Italy actually began in Hartford, Connecticut,
in 1939 when the Elders of the Italian Bible Students classes
in Connecticut and Massachusetts voted to expand the work to
Italy through a new magazine published in Italian called
L'Aurora Millenniale (*Millennial Dawn*). Unfortunately,
World War II intervened, and communications to Italy could
not be resumed until after the war ended.
     At that time they contracted with a Baptist publication
in Italy (*Verita Evangelica*) to publish a series of advertise-
ments offering a free copy of their magazine to any one who
requested it. A general description of the subjects dealt
with was also included. Through the magazine and the correspondence that followed, within a short time Mr. and Mrs.
Mario Celenza were converted and, because of their zeal, they
were sent names and addresses of other readers to visit or
contact by mail. Then in 1948, Umberto Spadaccina of Erie,
Pennsylvania, was sent as a pilgrim who, with the Celenzas,
visited readers in various cities and towns in south Italy
and Sicily.
     The fervor of the new converts, especially their denuncia-
tions of immortality of the soul, hellfire, and trinity doctrines, provoked some attacks from the Protestant churches
in Italy. In 1962, it was voted to transfer the publication
of *L'Aurora Millenniale* from Hartford to Pescara, and Gaetano
Boccaccio turned over the editorship of the magazine to Mario
Celenza. A few years later, the name of the magazine was

changed to *La Nuova Creazione* after the American magazine *The New Creation*.

In 1970, Mr. and Mrs. De Palma, after a trip to Italy to visit the brethren, felt a need to establish an Italian head-quarters. An appeal was made for funds, and on July 26, 1971, the brethren bought a five-room condominium in which to hold meetings and other activities.

After their last trip to Italy, De Palma and Celenza started a campaign for the unity of Bible Student groups which resulted in the formation of the "federation of Bible student churches and Bible classes" with a common constitu- tion, interests, and initiatives, having for its goal a true unity of the spirit but letting each group remain fully independent. Gaetano Boccaccio had this goal in mind for years. He also changed the name Associated Bible Students of L'Aurora Millenniale to Millennial Bible Students Church and later to Christian Millennial Church, because of the possibility of the work becoming connected in the minds of the people with the Jehovah's Witnesses (whose governing body, the Watchtower Society, a few years ago started publishing again under their old name, International Bible Students Association).

The New Creation magazine then became the official publication of the Christian Millennial Church. During the past five years, it has expanded and now stresses unity of all Bible Student groups in America.

In Italy today, groups exist from Milan in north Italy to the toe of the peninsula. From time to time, Mario Celenza visits these various groups, leading Bible studies and proselytizing to outsiders. However, since 1939 the Italian-American brethren in America have supplied much of the needed funds since Italy has never been a wealthy nation. However, over the years gradually almost all of the American supporters have died, and of the few still living, most are retired.

LITERATURE OF THE CHRISTIAN MILLENNIAL CHURCH (also called Congregation of Bible Students (Hartford, Conn.). For the first 30 years this group used the name Associated Bible Students. Gaetano Boccaccio has directed this group since the 1930s.)

Magazine

The New Creation. Vol. 1, No. 1, Jan. 1939 to date. The Italian *New Creation* entitled *La Nueva Creazione*, is published in Italy and is similar in content to the English-language edition. Published monthly, the English-language edition is about 30 pp. and the Italian 22 pp. The Italian edition was published in Hartford, Conn., until 1962 and was

named *L'Aurora Millenniale* until about 1965 when the name
was changed to the present title.

Newsletter for Christian Millennial Church Members. Published
semi-monthly (first issue April 1980, Vol. 1), 5 pp.

Booklets

The ABC of Salvation and Eternal Life. Hartford, Conn., n.d.,
24 pp.

Do You Have an Immortal Soul? N.d., 16 pp.

God's Plan for Humanity.

God's Plan of the Ages. Hartford, Conn., n.d., 28 pp.

Has the Church a Share in the Sin Offering? Hartford, Conn.,
n.d., 14 pp.

Justification to Life: When & How?

Knowledge ... Understanding and Wisdom. Hartford, Conn.,
n.d., 16 pp.

The Most Important Three R's.

1000 Years of Peace. Hartford, Conn., n.d., 24 pp.

One World Government. 1981, 8 pp.

The Rich Man and Lazarus. Hartford, Conn., n.d., 20 pp.

"We Believe." Hartford, Conn., 1980, 19 pp.

What Is the Resurrection of the Dead?

When Will Wars, Sickness, Pain and Death Cease?

Boccaccio, Gaetano. *Truth or Tradition?* Hartford, Conn.,
1982, 12 pp.

DiMarco, Sabby. *This One Thing I Do.* Hartford, Conn., n.d.,
12 pp.

Kemp, Roy. *A Treatise on Love.* Hartford, Conn., n.d., 8 pp.

Sadlack, Emil. *Our Lord's Return.* Hartford, Conn., n.d.,
14 pp. (translated from the German).

Tracts

Are You a Real Christian?

Atonement--Ransom--Propitiation--Reconciliation. 4 pp.

"Come Now, and Let Us Reason Together, Saith the Lord." N.d.,
8 pp.

Do You Know? N.d., 1 p.

The Gospel. 2 pp.

Have You Made Your Choice?

The Holy Bible. 2 pp.

Is Hell a Bible Teaching? 4 pp.

A Message of Faith, Hope and Comfort. 1 p.

A Message of Joy. 2 pp.

Overwhelmed? N.d., 1 p.

You Are an Important Person. 1 p.

You Can Have a Happy Home.

Your Dead Shall Rise Again. N.d., 4 pp.

Your Life, Liberty and Happiness. 1 p.

Bishop, Jim. *God: Does He Exist?* 4 pp.

Cyrus, Harry. *The Second Coming or Parousia of Our Lord.*
4 pp.

Bible Correspondence Course (12 parts, as listed)

1. *What Is the Millennium?*

2. *How Well Do You Know God?*

3. *Do You Have an Immortal Soul?*

4. *What Is the End of the World?*

5. *What Is the Resurrection of the Dead?*

6. *Is the Doctrine of the Trinity in the Bible?*

7. *What Is the Truth About Hell & Purgatory?*

8. *How Well Do You Know the Lord Jesus Christ?*

9. *Do You Know What Are the 3 Steps to Your Salvation?*

10. *In the Kingdom of God: Will You Be a Ruler or a Subject?*

11. *Satan and the Origin of Evil Spirits.*

12. *Do You Know God's Wonderful Plan of the Ages?*

B. The Henninges-McPhail Schism

In 1908-09, E.C. Henninges, head of the Australian branch of the Watch Tower Society, and M.L. McPhail, of the Chicago class (a term which means church), united against certain of Russell's ideas concerning the Covenant and Christ's ransom. The resultant schism cost Russell most of his Australian following and much of his U.S. following. The Australian group used the name New Covenant Fellowship (see Australian section), and the U.S. group, Christian Believers Assembly.

1. THE CHRISTIAN BELIEVERS ASSEMBLY

M.L. McPhail led the "New Covenant" people in the United States. His major work was *The Covenants*, published privately in 1909. Out of his leadership grew the New Covenant Believers, now called the Christian Believers Conference. They have relied heavily on Henninges' literature; their own publications are scarce. The Cicero, Illinois, class has been publishing recently under the imprint of the Berean Bible Students Church.

2. BEREAN BIBLE STUDENTS CHURCH (Cicero, Illinois)

Booklets

Berean Bible Study Guide. N.d., 19 pp.

God's Plan for Humanity. 20 pp.

Constas, Constantine J. *Do the Scriptures Teach Universal Salvation?* 1965, 39 pp. A reprint of a work by C.J. Constas of the Free Christian Church in Athens against the *Concordant Version of the Holy Scripture.*

Polychronis, Andrew, and Larry and Wayne Urbaniak. *God and Man*. N.d., 48 pp.

Magazines

The Kingdom Scribe, ed. Charles Loucky. Vol. 1, No. 1, 1908 to Vol. 53, 1975.

Berean News. Vol. 1, No. 1, Feb. 1956 to Vol. 19, No. 11, Dec. 1975, published monthly, each about 9 pp. long.

Tracts

Polychronis, Andrew, and Larry and Wayne Urbaniak. *Briefly, We Believe....* N.d., 6 pp.

Occasional Papers Series

Vol. 1, No. V (1980). Iannaccone, Laurence R. *Women Who Served: Female Deacons in the New Testament*. Xerox, 22 pp.

Vol. 1, No. 2 (1980). Chun, Roland. *Participation of Our Sisters in Christian Service*. 3 pp.

Vol. 1, No. 3 (1975; revised 1980). Iannaccone, Laurence R., and L. Iannaccone. *Shall Women Keep Silent? A Study of 1 Corinthians 14:34-36*. 20 pp.

Vol. 1, No. 4 (March 1981). Frey, Richard. *Paul's View of Women's Function in the Church*. 3 pp; with (Feb. 1981) White, C.A. *Participation of a Sister in Christian Service*. 4 pp.; with *Comments on Women and the Scriptures*. 2 pp.; and letter from Nick and Catherine Nicholson. 2 pp.

Iannaccone, I.A. *I Permit No Women to Teach or Have Authority: A Study of 1 Timothy 2:11-12*. March 1981, 24 pp.

Reply to Occasional Papers, Vol. 1, No. 4, 5 pp. Letter from Sandra Eger, April 1981, 8 pp., and letter from Lee Maria, 1 p.

A *RELATED GROUP*, the Christian Believers Fellowship of Staten Island, N.Y., has published several tracts, which are distributed by the New Creation Bible Students as is all Christian Believers literature.

Booklets

God's Plan for Humanity. N.d., 20 pp.

Tracts

Have You Made Your Choice? N.d., 4 pp.

Hell, a Bible Teaching. N.d., 2 pp.

*Of What Value Is Your Life? Have You Experienced the Abundant
   Life?* N.d., 2 pp.

Series of tracts called The Christian Call, Vol. 1,
No. 1, March 1944 to ?? (published by Nicholas F.
Nicholson)

Are You a Christian? March 1944, 4 pp.

Hear, O Israel! N.d., 4 pp.

Hear, O Israel! The Lord Our God Is One Lord. N.d., 4 pp.

4. OTHER GROUPS RELATED TO THIS OFFSHOOT

   Other groups related to this offshoot include the Milwaukee
Ecclesia of Free Bible Students led by Wesley J. Lodwig. Its
perspective was closest to the Berean Christian Conference but
was independent in outlook.
   Other periodicals by this general group of Bible Students,
but of uncertain date of origin, place of publication, and/or
present status, include:

Berean Forum.

The Candlestick. St. John's, Newfoundland, Canada. 1946-??
   Edited by J.L. Butler.

Stream of Time.

Studies in the New Creature. St. Joseph, Mo. Published by
   M.E. Rumer in the 1930s.

Open Letter: A Word to the Watchers. Irregular; edited by T.
   Contopulos, Bellaire, N.Y., in the 1960s. Some issues are
   72 pp.

                  C. The Pastoral Bible Institute

   The 1917 problems in the WtBTS resulted in an expulsion
of four board members and others, including R.H. Hirsh, I.F.
Hoskins, A.I. Ritchie, and J.D. Wright. Part of this schism

was caused by a power struggle and part by opposition to Volume VII of the *Studies of the Scriptures*, which was supposedly the posthumous work of Charles T. Russell but was actually written by Clayton J. Woodworth and George H. Fisher. The seventh volume expounded a number of new theological ideas which many considered unscriptural; thus, opposition to this work developed. This group opposed Rutherford's attempts to control the Society until the decisive elections at the Convention of 1918.

After Rutherford's conclusive victory, a number of prominent brethren withdrew and, with about fifty colleagues and supporters, began the Pastoral Bible Institute. In 1918 the periodical *The Herald of Christ's Kingdom* was established, edited by R.H. Streeter until his death in December 1924. This periodical is still published today.

The first convention after Russell died that was held independent of the IBSA took place July 26-29, 1918, in Asbury Park, New Jersey. A few months later two to three hundred persons attended the second convention, at Providence, Rhode Island, in November of 1918. At this meeting the Pastoral Bible Institute was formed in order to resume Russell's work independently of the Society.

Ingraham I. Margeson, Harvey A. Friese, Wright, Hoskins, Ritchie, and Hirsh were in the forefront of the PBI work. The PBI later published Streeter's books on Revelation (1925) and (posthumously) Daniel (1928)--see below. The PBI offices were in Brooklyn until the 1960s. The work was then split between St. Louis and Batavia, Illinois, and the 177 Prospect Place, Brooklyn, property was disposed of. An annual convention at Atlantic City, New Jersey, is closely associated with the PBI. The classes at the local churches are largely independent of the "corporation" (or headquarters) although the doctrine is still largely that developed by Russell, and his major works are kept in print. Certain dates and other changes were introduced, but in contrast to some Bible Student groups, such as the Dawn Bible Students, the group is not highly active in proselytizing.

The PBI, since it does not stress proselytizing, has experienced several major setbacks (they had expected the year 1934 to see "the glorification of the saints," for example) and has steadily declined in followers since its founding in 1918. There was not much stress on indoctrinating children because the primary goal was "perfecting the saints" and only adults can be saints. Thus, many young persons lost interest and left the movement.

PBI membership is open to anyone who contributes at least $5. It is managed by a board of seven directors, and has an editorial committee of five. Its annual volume of service work and its net assets since World War II have remained

fairly constant, both over $20,000. Its primary purposes are
the pilgrim work to teach followers and the publication of
The Herald of Christ's Kingdom (10,000 circulation in 30
countries) and related publications. No more than a basic
baptismal confession is enforced either for fellowship or for
the teachers the organization sponsors (called pilgrims).

PBI leaders at various times since World War II include
Percy L. Read, W.J. Siekman, Paul E. Thomson, Horace E. Hollister, James C. Jordan, John T. Read, Benjamin F. Hollister,
Alex L. Muir, Fred A. Essler, James Burpee Webster, Alex
Gonczewski, the Petrans, and others. Leaders before the war
included J.J. Blackburn, Isaac F. and John Hoskins, Dr. S.D.
Bennett, and Dr. John G. Kuehn. Considerable emphasis has
been placed on visiting Bible Students in isolated places and
in the British Isles.

The Pastoral Bible Institute experienced a number of
schisms from its founding to the present. The literature of
the early schisms is extremely rare and there are few, if any,
remaining adherents. Some of the more recent schisms are
still operating, and thus literature can be obtained from the
headquarters or members. Many of the schisms died out as
they often involved only 30, 50, 100 or so members and groups
this small, unless they are aggressive proselytizers, in time
usually disband and their literature is lost or destroyed.
In addition, it is often difficult to recognize the literature
of these schisms and thus much of it was destroyed or will remain unknown and will be lost forever in the history of the
Bible Student movement.

Also used by members and advertised in the *Herald* are
works by non-PBI Russellites and even by non-Russellite
Bible students, such as Werner Keller's *The Bible as History*.
The British-based Bible Fellowship Union works closely with
the PBI and H.O. Hudson's booklets are widely circulated (see
under Bible Fellowship Union).

The PBI is one of the freest of the Bible Student groups
in terms of the latitude of doctrine allowed and its use of
material that is not strictly Russellite in origin. The two
main writers of Institute-sponsored material are R.E. Streeter
and Percy L. Read. The former was the author of several expository books which refigured Russell's chronology (Streeter
based his upon 588 B.C. as the fall of Jerusalem instead of
Russell's date of 606 B.C., giving a different date for the
return of Christ and the end of the world). Read, the single
most influential member of the PBI wrote, until he died in 1983,
a series of pamphlets which are the most advertised works among
the members.

PUBLICATIONS OF THE PASTORAL BIBLE INSTITUTE (St. Louis, Mo.)

<u>Magazine</u>

The Herald of Christ's Kingdom. Vol. 1, No. 1, 1918 to date
(Vol. LXIII, No. 4, July-Aug. 1980).

<u>Convention Reports</u>

*Souvenir Notes from the Reunion Convention of Christian Bible
Students.* Pittsburgh, Pa., Nov. 1, 2, 3, 1929, 135 pp.

Kuehn, Hugo, ed. *Convention Report, Sharon, Pennsylvania,
1937 and Other Helpful Discourses* (Book Six). New York:
Pub. by Ed., 1937, 120 pp.

<u>Booklets Pertaining to the 1918 Split</u>

The Committee Bulletin (Asbury Park Convention Committee).
No. 1, Aug. 1918, 8 pp.; No. 2, Sept. 1918, 7 pp.; No. 3,
Oct. 1918, 7 pp.

*Light after Darkness: A Message to the Watchers, Being a
Refutation of "Harvest Siftings."* Brooklyn, N.Y., Sept. 1,
1917 (reprinted in the late 1970s), 23 pp.

*Facts for Shareholders of the Watch Tower Bible and Tract
Society.* Brooklyn, N.Y., Nov. 15, 1917 (reprinted in the
late 1970s), 16 pp.

A Letter to International Bible Students. Brooklyn, N.Y.,
March 1, 1918, 4 pp. (Written by I.F. Hoskins).

An Open Letter to the People of the Lord Throughout the World.
Nov. 1-15, 1917, 3 pp.; signed by 156 members of the
Brooklyn Ecclesia.

An Open Letter to the Shareholders of the Society. Aug. 15,
1917.

A Brief Review of Brother Johnson's Charges. 1918, 4 pp.

A Timely Letter of Importance to All Brethren. Freehold, N.J.,
Sept. 10, 1918 (printed with response from J.D. Wright,
Sept. 14, 1918), 8 pp.

Letter to Brethren from Brooklyn. July 27, 1917, written by
J.D. Wright, A.I. Ritchie, I.F. Hoskins, and R.H. Hirsh
(also included is a letter to A.I. Ritchie from A.N. Pierson,

July 26, 1917, and a letter from Davies, Auerbach, and Cornell, July 23, 1917), total of 4 pp.

Letter to Brother Charles R. Cox from Brother Frank F. Cook. C. 1917, 2 pp.

Other Booklets

Conversion in the After-life. N.d., 16 pp.

A Message to the Watchers and All That Mourn. N.d., 8 pp.

The Resurrection of the Dead. N.d., 16 pp.

The Second Advent--Its Nature and Purpose. N.d., 16 pp.

That Servant--"Faithful and Wise." Brooklyn, N.Y., n.d., 9 pp.

World Conversion--When? N.d., 16 pp.

Hollister, Horace Edward. *I Will Come Again.* Chicago: Society for Bible Research, 1950, 319 pp.

Jones, L.W. *God's Best Gift.* Chicago: Sacred Lyceum, 1927, 30 pp. A children's book.

Read, P.L. *The ABC of the Bible Prophecy.* N.d., 17 pp.

————. *... After Death the Judgment.* N.d., 16 pp.

————. *Are Wars to Cease?* N.d., 11 pp.

————. *Beliefs That Matter.* N.d., 19 pp.

————. *Do You Know What the Bible Foretells of Today and Tomorrow?*

————. *Elias Shall First Come.* N.d., 20 pp. (condensed from an original by C.T. Russell).

————. *Great World Changes Long Foretold.* N.d., 15 pp.

————. *Has Judgment Day Begun?* N.d., 15 pp.

————. *Heathendom's Hope.*

————. *If a Man Die, Shall He Live Again?* N.d., 16 pp.

————. *Is Israel Emerging from Hell?* N.d., 15 pp.

————. *Israel and the Middle East.* N.d., 25 pp.

————. *Is Israel Emerging from Hell?* N.d., 15 pp.

————. *Our Lord's Return.* N.d., 31 pp.

————. *Parables of the Kingdom.* N.d., 21 pp.

————. *The Place of Israel in the Plan of God.* 1954.

————. *What Is the Soul?* N.d., 15 pp.

————. *What Say the Scriptures about Hell?* N.d., 36 pp. (condensed from an original by C.T. Russell).

————. *Why Does God Permit Evil?* N.d., 15 pp.

————. *The World Tomorrow.*

Siekman, W.J. *The Coming World Potentate.* N.d., 16 pp.

Books

Russell, C.T. *The Divine Plan of the Ages.* Reprinted by the Pastoral Bible Institute in Brooklyn, N.Y., 1922, 354 pp.

Sadlack, Emil, and Otto Sadlack. *The Desolations of the Sanctuary.* Brooklyn, N.Y.: Pastoral Bible Institute, 1930.

Streeter, R.E. *The Revelation of Jesus Christ: Volume I.* Brooklyn, N.Y.: Pastoral Bible Institute, 1923, 571 pp.

————. *The Revelation of Jesus Christ, Volume II.* Brooklyn, N.Y.: Pastoral Bible Institute, 1924, 638 pp.

————. *Daniel the Beloved of Jehovah.* Brooklyn, N.Y.: Pastoral Bible Institute, 1928, 493 pp. (published posthumously).

D. The Stand Fast Bible Students

Most of the adherents of the PBI lived in the New York, New Jersey, and Pennsylvania areas. The Bible Students in the northwestern states who split from the Watchtower Society formed a group called Stand Fasters, Standfasters, or the Stand Fast Bible Student Association.

The Stand Fasters are so called from their determination
to "stand fast on the war principles that our dear Pastor
Russell announced." Charles E. Heard of Vancouver and many
others felt that Rutherford's recommendation in the spring
of 1918 to buy war bonds was "cowardice" and a sacrilegious
perpetuation of the harvest work. They felt that the Society
reneged on its earlier stand on Liberty Bonds (the bonds
which went toward supporting the war) and non-combatant service.
The Stand Fasters felt that a Christian should not support,
in any way, the army, either by buying Liberty Bonds or by
involving himself in non-combatant service (combatant service
was forbidden by both the Stand Fasters and the Watchtower).
In response to this the Stand Fast Bible Students Association
organized on December 1, 1918, at Portland, Oregon. It published *Old Corn Gems* (taken from Josh. 5:11-12) and organized
conventions throughout the United States. Well-known members
included Heard and W.B. Palmer, R.O. Hadley, William H. Wisdom
(the author of the only book-length biography of Russell),
H.A. Livermore, Ian C. Edwards, Allen A. Yeres, and Finley
McNercher. Many, mostly non-doctrinal divisions followed a
Seattle convention held on July 25-27, 1919. Interestingly,
the Stand Fasters accepted the Seventh Volume--one of the main
reasons for the other splits (and in 1919 a split from the
Stand Fasters occurred over the Seventh Volume). At first
they were quite successful, especially attracting adherents
who did not accept what they saw as compromises over the war
issue.

They believe that everything that the Watch Tower Society
taught up to Easter of 1918 was correct, but after that date
the "separation of Elijah and Elisha" had begun and the Stand
Fasters were the Elijah class who "stood fast" on Pastor
Russell's teachings. Of course, all the schismatic groups,
at first at least, claimed to be following Russell's wishes
and, therefore, to be "true followers of Russell," but the
Stand Fasters claimed to follow *only* his teachings, i.e.,
they did not claim that they were legitimate messengers of
his or "God's organization" as did some of the other splits.
The Pastoral Bible Institute, for example, came to believe
that the Watch Tower Society apostatized from the "truth"
and that only they, the Pastoral Bible Institute, taught the
"primitive truth." The Stand Fasters, on the other hand,
felt that leaders and organizations were relatively unimportant.
They were organized simply to help others learn about Russell's
teachings. Their loose organization was probably one of the
main reasons that they were one of the first schismatic groups
to disintegrate.

An interesting aspect of their history was the "westward
movement" when Stand Fasters were encouraged to move to the

west because the rapture (removal of people to heaven much as
Christ ascended to heaven in a "twinkling of an eye") would
take place in 1920, and only in the western states! Thus, if
one did not live in the correct state, he or she would not be
a part of the rapture. In 1923, Heard and Issac Edwards led
a movement which involved about 300 Stand Fasters which,
according to P.S.L. Johnson, "degenerated into communism."

In 1923, Edwards and Heard organized into the Star Con-
struction Company in Victoria, B.C. Fearing the time of
trouble (part of the sign of the end of the world), in 1924
Edwards took over 300 followers to Stookie and the Gordon
River to live a communal existence. When the business failed
in 1927, it was shut down by Alec McCarter and Oscar Kuenzi.
From the original twelve hundred adherents in 1919 in the
Northwest and near Wisconsin, this "Seventh Volume movement"
dwindled to almost no believers and no formal organization
today. Their experiment at communal living, often called
the Stookie Movement because it was located at Stookie Harbor,
British Columbia, ended in failure. The history of its
development and disintegration would make an important sociological study.

PUBLICATIONS OF THE STAND FAST BIBLE STUDENTS ASSOCIATION
  (Portland, Ore.--started Dec. 1, 1918)

Books

Temple Notes: A Helping Hand for the Royal Priesthood. Victoria, B.C., Canada, c. 1922, 142 pp., hb.

Booklets

The Temple of Beauty Foreshadowing Messiah's Kingdom in Earth.
  N.d. (c. 1920), 32 pp.

Heard, C.E. "The Ship's Acts 27th Chapter." Seattle, Wash,,
  1919, 11 pp. Stenographic report of an address at the
  Standfast Bible Students Convention, Jan. 12, 1919.

Tracts

McKercher, F. Letter and Charter of Stand Fast Bible Students
  Association, Dec. 7, 1918.

————. *Circular Letter.* Jan. 6, 1919, 1 p.

Magazine

Old Corn Gems. Ed. F. McKercher. Magazine published from

Jan. 1919, semi-monthly.

        No. 1. 8 pp. mimeo.
        No. 2. 10 pp. mimeo.
        No. 3. Feb. 15, 1919, 16 pp. typeset.
        No. 4. March 1, 1919, 16 pp. typeset.
        No. 5. March 15, 1919, 16 pp. typeset.
        No. 6. April 1, 1919, 16 pp. typeset.
        No. 7. April 15, 1919, 16 pp. typeset.
        No. 8. May 1, 1919, 16 pp. typeset.
        No. 9. May 15, 1919, 16 pp. typeset.
        No. 10. June 1, 1919, 16 pp. typeset.
        No. 11. June 15, 1919, 16 pp. typeset.
        No. 12. July 1, 1919, 16 pp. typeset.
        No. 13. July 15, 1919, 16 pp. typeset.
        No. 14? issued in 1919; no copies known.
        No. 15? issued in 1919; no copies known.

1. ELIJAH VOICE SOCIETY

In 1923, John A. Hardersen, C.D. McCray, and about 300
persons from the Stand Fast Bible Students organized the
Elijah Voice Society to effect an ambitious regathering and
witness work. For several years they published the Elijah
Voice Monthly and many tracts. The E.V.S. became the most
prominent Seventh Volume group; the group is discussed by
Paul Johnson in his Elijah and Elisha.

They felt they were "called to smite Babylon," similar to
the Stand Fasters, only they were more extreme--so extreme
that they refused to contribute to the Red Cross, buy Liberty
Bonds, or salute the flag (many years before the Jehovah's
Witnesses prohibited their members from this act)--all behavior which they felt clearly marked one "of Satan." Their
only publication was the Elijah Voice Monthly. Many tracts
were written, but all are unknown to this researcher.

2. SERVANTS OF YAH

One of the more unusual splinter groups is the Servants
of Yah, led by C.H. Zook and headquartered in Brooklyn, N.Y.,
and later Levittown, N.Y. They also had a branch in Vienna,
Austria. Among other things, they teach that "Jehovah" is
actually the name of Satan and the name of God is "Yah."
From this they conclude that the Jehovah's Witnesses must be
Witnesses of Satan although their doctrine is very similar
to that of the Witnesses. Only the 144,000 are destined to
discover the "hidden meaning of the scriptures" and enter

heaven. The meaning is "hidden" partly because they believe that our Bible texts were altered. The Servants of Yah see the Bible as primarily prophecy, most of which relates to the present century. They deny Bible Student teachings and Witness doctrine about Armageddon, the Genesis Flood, water baptism, the ransom sacrifice, and the existence of Satan. They are Universalists and believe all persons who ever existed (except the 144,000 who will live in heaven) will someday live forever on a perfected earth.

Publications of the Servants of Yah *(Most written by C.H. Zook)*

Armageddon Is As False As Hell. Brooklyn, N.Y., n.d., 2 pp.

The Basis for the Correct Understanding of the Scriptures. N.d., 6 pp.?, hb.

The Glory of God's Character. Levittown, N.Y., n.d., 1 p.

The Kingdom of God Has Begun to Operate in the Earth. Levittown, N.Y., n.d., 2 pp.

The Name of Almighty God. N.d., n.p., 2 pp.

Reincarnation. Levittown, N.Y., n.d., 2 pp.

The Resurrection of the Dead. Brooklyn, N.Y., n.d., 2 pp.

3. WATCHERS OF THE MORNING

In the early 1930s, influenced by the Henninges and McPhail writings, some of the prominent members of the PBI began to feel that the "Church" (the PBI members) was now under the Mediator (Christ) and also under what they call the New Covenant (a new set of relationships between God and man) and that the "Church" had no part in the sin offering of Christ. Some also began to doubt the doctrine that Christ returned in 1914 and that the "sleeping saints" had already been raised from the dead. Others felt that only those fully in harmony with "Present Truth" should engage in the official ministry. Still others, who were in harmony with the PBI in other areas, felt that those who were not could still continue in the work without limitation.

At the PBI annual meeting on June 6, 1936, the "liberal" directors P.L. Read, Dr. S.D. Bennett, J.J. Blackburn, J.C. Jordan, and P.E. Thomson were elected, together with their nominees, Chester A. Stiles of Washington, D.C., and Benjamin Boulter of New Jersey. The "Present Truth" directors, I.F.

Hoskins and B.A. Parkes, were not elected nor were their
nominees, P.A. Gates of Memphis, Tennessee, Dr. Kuehn of
Toledo, Ohio, C.W. McCoy of Spokane, Washington, S.N. McElvany
of Pittsburgh, Pennsylvania, and G.C. Stroke of Buffalo, New
York.

At this time, Isaac F. Hoskins withdrew from the PBI and
in April of 1937 began his own group, publishing *The Watchers
of the Morning*, which emphasized "Present Truth" as opposed
to Russell's truth. Among those cooperating with Hoskins were
H.H. Eddy of Providence, Rhode Island, C.W. McCoy of Spokane,
and Charles F. Moser of Toldeo, Ohio. The journal *Watchers
of the Morning* ceased when Hoskins died in August of 1957
(last issue June 1957).

E. Laymen's Home Missionary Movement

Shortly before Russell died in 1916, he had arranged for
Paul S.L. Johnson to go to England to mediate in some problems
with managers at the Watch Tower Society's British branch.
In the meantime Russell died and Rutherford became President
of the Society. He and the other six Directors of the Society
agreed to Johnson's trip to Britain as Russell planned.

For this assignment, they reportedly gave Johnson the
authority to do what was necessary to solve the problems in
Britain. Among other things, Johnson fired two of the managers
at the London office. Evidently Rutherford was threatened by
Johnson--he was probably one of the most intelligent and
knowledgeable Bible Students. An ordained Lutheran minister
who was born a Jew, Johnson graduated with high honors from
Capital University in Columbus, Ohio, and had a good knowledge
of Hebrew, Greek, and several other languages. In 1917
Rutherford cabled that Johnson was "absolutely without authority" and told him to come home. The majority of the Board
sided with Johnson but Rutherford ousted them on a legal tech-
nicality and then put Johnson out. After the 1918 election
meeting in Pittsburgh, Johnson, Raymond Jolly, and others withdrew from the Watch Tower organization and formed the Pastoral
Bible Institute. This group also had a number of differences,
which resulted in Johnson and Jolly's forming another new
group using a name Russell had once used, the Laymen's Home
Missionary Movement.

Johnson came to believe that Pastor Russell had been a
Parousia messenger but that he himself was a special "Epiphany
messenger" with a commission to announce that the door to the
"high calling" (heaven) was now closed; in later years it was
taught that he was the last member of the Church. After he

organized the Laymen's Home Missionary Movement, in July of
1920 he began publishing *The Bible Standard*. He wrote volu-
minously on the interpretation of types, the multi-meanings
of scriptures and shadows (scriptures which have their major
fulfillment in our day). Adherents feel they constitute a
class of "Youthful Worthies" or an Epiphany Company who will
reign with the Ancient Worthies. Johnson's chief co-worker,
Raymond G. Jolly, was his successor and became the leader of
the movement when Johnson died in October of 1950. Since
Jolly's death in 1979 August Gohlke has headed the movement.

The Laymen's Home Missionary Movement, like most of the
Bible Student movements, still uses almost all of Russell's
writings as its primary study material and is very close to
Russell in theory (probably closer than most Bible Student
groups). The movement has grown, especially in Poland,
where there are probably as many as 5,000 members and many
sympathizers.

Of interest is the fact that Johnson adopted the *Bible
Numerics* of Ivan Panin and bought up the last 300 copies of
his *Numeric Greek New Testament*. Bible numerics is the belief that the Bible can be "proved" to be of divine origin
by adding up the values of various words and sentences,
letters and words (a = 1 pt., b = 2 pts., etc.), etc., to
come up with certain patterns which would be impossible to
occur by chance. This idea has been hotly debated, but is
nonetheless intriguing.

The LHMM movement strongly opposes the Witnesses, especially because they have changed Russell's teachings. The LHMM
also opposed the Witnesses' refusal to salute the flag and receive blood transfusions, and especially the fact that they
have set aside the Biblical scriptures which refer to the
modern nation of Israel (the Witnesses teach that "Israel"
in the New Testament usually refers to symbolic Israel, i.e.,
themselves).

The LHMM has produced a set of sound and color film strips
which are often shown in various churches, bible study classes,
YMCA, YWCA, and similar groups. Members also often comb the
obituaries and send personal letters and LHMM tracts, etc.,
to relatives of the deceased.

In 1951 when Johnson died and his longtime associate
Raymond C. Jolly succeeded to leadership, the bi-monthly
Herald became the monthly *Bible Standard and Herald of Christ's
Kingdom*. A second periodical, primarily circulated among
members, is *The Present Truth and Herald of Christ's Epiphany*,
also monthly and dating from 1920.

PUBLICATIONS BY THE LAYMEN'S HOME MISSIONARY MOVEMENT
(Chester Springs, Pa.)

Books

    Shortly after Johnson set up his organization he began
the publication of a series of books, based upon and supplemental to Russell's *Studies in the Scriptures*. He repudiated
the Seventh Volume as a fraud and began his own completion
of Russell's six volumes called the *Epiphany Studies in Scriptures*. This series ran to some 15 volumes by the time he died.
Jolly also edited some materials of Johnson's after his death,
adding several more volumes to the series.

--1. *Epiphany Studies in the Scriptures* by Paul S. Johnson
    (Vols. 1-15), and Raymond Jolly (vols. 16-17), all
    published in Chester Springs, Pa.

    Vol. 1. *God*. 1938, 547 pp.
    Vol. 2. *Creation*. 1938, 585 pp.
    Vol. 3. *Elijah and Elisha*. 1938, 477 pp.
    Vol. 4. *The Epiphany's Elect*. 1938, 469 pp.
    Vol. 5. *A Miscellany*. 1938, 542 pp.
    Vol. 6. *Merariism*. 1938, 750 pp.
    Vol. 7. *Gershonism*. 1938, 494 pp.
    Vol. 8. *Numbers*. 1938, 494 pp.
    Vol. 9. *The Parousia Messenger*. 1938, 605 pp.
    Vol. 10. *The Epiphany Messenger*. 1941, 829 pp.
    Vol. 11. *Exodus*. 1948, 716 pp.
    Vol. 12. *The Bible*. 1949, 797 pp.
    Vol. 13. *Samuel, Kings, Chronicles*. 1949, 847 pp.
    Vol. 14. *The Parousia Messenger*. Vol. 2 (part 2 of
          Vol. 9), 1949, 573 pp.
    Vol. 15. *Christ--Spirit--Covenants*. 1950, 736 pp.
    Vol. 16. *The Chart of God's Plan*. 1953, 351 pp.
    Vol. 17. *The Millennium*. 1956, 480 pp.

--2. *Other Books (all reprints, some revised)*

    Daily Heavenly Manna and Devotional Service. Revised
       by P.S.L. Johnson, 1937 (original edition WtBTS,
       1907), c. 350 pp. Revised again and enlarged, 1980,
       400 pp.

    Hymns of the Millennial Dawn. Revised by P.S.L. John-
       son, 1937, 346 pp. (republished from WtBTS edition
       of 1905).

    Life-Death-Hereafter. 1st edition, 1920; 4th revised
       and enlarged by Raymond Jolly in 1968, 216 pp.
       Mostly republished C.T. Russell articles.

Poems of Dawn. 1965, 318 pp. Republished from the
WtBTS edition of 1912.

*Tabernacle Shadows of the Better Sacrifices: A Helping
Hand for the Royal Priesthood,* by C.T. Russell, 1936,
168 pp. Republished from the WtBTS edition of 1881.

Studies in the Scriptures by C.T. Russell, 1937, 3,500
pp. Republished with 120 pp. of appendix notes, also
questions. Republished again without appendix and
notes, 1965, 3,380 pp.

--3. *Free Booklet Set* (24 pp. each; contents from *The Bible
Standard,* except as noted. All published at Chester
Springs, Pa.)

Where Are the Dead? (from Pastor Russell).
Life and Immortality. 1954 (from Pastor Russell).
What Is the Soul? (from Pastor Russell).
The Resurrection of the Dead (from Pastor Russell).
Spiritism Is Demonism (from Pastor Russell), from Feb.
1958 *Bible Standard.*
Why Does a Loving God Permit Calamities? (from Pastor
Russell), from July 1956 *Bible Standard.*
The Sabbath Day (from Pastor Russell).
"Faith Healing": Dangers in Hypnotism and Spirit Healing
(partly from Pastor Russell).
"Christian Science Examined." N.d.
Baptism. N.d. (from Pastor Russell).
Present Day "Speaking in Tongues": Is It of God? N.d.
(see May 1954 *Bible Standard*).
The Kingdom of God--Heavenly and Earthly. N.d.
Mormonism--A Modern Delusion. N.d.
The Preservation of Identity in the Resurrection. Re-
printed with slight revisions from the original by
Dr. John Edgar. N.d.
The Evolution Theory Examined. N.d.
Why We Believe in God's Existence.
Time of Jesus' Death and Resurrection.
The Rapture.
Future Life by Resurrection-Not Reincarnation.
Must Christians Pay Tithes?

--4. *Free Leaflets* (tract) Set, listed as published. All
published at Chester Springs, Pa. Most reprinted from
The Bible Standard, date given in parentheses.

What Is Hell? N.d., 6 pp. (Feb. 1958).
What Is the Truth? N.d., 8 pp.
The Great Pyramid. N.d., 8 pp.
Do You Know? N.d., 4 pp. (July 15, 1951).

Israel's Return. N.d., 4 pp. (Nov. 1953).
The New Earth. N.d., 4 pp.
The Bible vs. Evolution. N.d., 4 pp. (Nov. 1958).
Thieves in Paradise. N.d., 4 pp. (Dec. 1958).
"Flying Saucers." N.d., 4 pp. (July 1963).
Jesus' Second Advent. N.d., 4 pp. (April 1961).
The Judgement Day. N.d., 4 pp. (May 1961).
God Loves You! N.d., 4 pp. (May 1961).
Earth's Coming Theocratic Government. N.d., 4 pp. (July 1963).
The War on Poverty. N.d., 4 pp. (April 1965).
The Oath-bound Promise. N.d., 4 pp. (July 1953).
The Pollution Crisis. N.d., 4 pp.
Man's Eternal Destiny. N.d., 4 pp.
Is God or Satan Winning? N.d., 4 pp.
The Laymen's Home Missionary Movement. N.d., 4 pp.
Restitution. N.d., 4 pp.
The Full Gospel. N.d., 4 pp.
Father, Take My Hand. N.d., 2 pp.
Watchman, What of the Night? N.d., 2 pp.
Close Your Eyes. N.d., 2 pp.
Desolation--Restoration. N.d., 2 pp.
Salvation Free to All Mankind. N.d., 2 pp.
Christ's Glorious Reign. N.d., 2 pp.
Studies in the Scriptures. N.d., 2 pp.
Coming By and By. N.d., 2 pp.
How Readest Thou? N.d., 2 pp.
Reputed True Likeness of Jesus. N.d., 2 pp.
A Message for "Jehovah's Witnesses." N.d., 7 pp. (by Raymond Jolly).
A Real Bible Key That Unlocks the Scriptures. N.d., 2 pp.

--5. Magazines

The Present Truth and Herald of Christ's Epiphany. Dec. 1918 to date, 62 years (698 issues), 11,168 pp., published monthly until 1952, then bi-monthly to date, each 16 pp. Bound volumes are as follows: Vol. 1, 1920-1926; Vol. 2, 1927-31; Vol. 3, 1932-35; Vol. 4, 1936-39; Vol. 5, 1940-43; Vol. 6, 1944-47; Vol. 7, 1948-51; Vol. 8, 1952-59; Vol. 9, 1960-67; Vol. 10, 1968-1975.

The Herald of the Epiphany. July 15, 1920 to Dec. 15, 1951, 31 years (312 issues), 588 or 476 issues, total 3,800 pages. Bi-monthly, each 8 pp. Replaced by *The Bible Standard and Herald of Christ's Kingdom.*

The Bible Standard and Herald of Christ's Kingdom.
Jan. 1952 to date, 28 years (336 issues), 2,688 pp.
Published monthly, each 8 pp. For the general
public.

The Herald of the Epiphany and The Bible Standard.
Bound volumes: Vol. 1, 1920-29; Vol. 2, 1930-39;
Vol. 3, 1940-51; Vol. 4, 1952-56; Vol. 5, 1957-61;
Vol. 6, 1962-66; Vol. 7, 1967-71; Vol. 8, 1972-76.
Indexes, 1920-1960; 1961-1970; 1971-1980.

--6. *Priced Booklet* Set (no author given)

Anglo-Israelism--A Strong Delusion. 1975, 80 pp.
The Gift of Tongues. 1975, 80 pp.
Is There Hope for Any of the Unsaved Dead? 1975, 80 pp.
Satan, Satanism, Demonism and Exorcism. 1975, 80 pp.
Born Again. 1975, 48 pp.
The Great Pyramid and the Bible. Reprinted with slight
revisions from the original by Dr. John Edgar, n.d.,
48 pp.
The Restoration of Israel. Reprinted from Vol. 3 of
Studies in the Scriptures, 48 pp.
The Hell of the Bible. 1st ed. c. 1920, latest ed.
1972, 60 pp.
Spiritism, Ancient and Modern. 1st ed. c. 1926, latest
ed. 1972, 67 pp.
Jewish Hopes and Prospects. Israel Commission, 1954,
50 pp.
*The Revised Standard Version of the Bible in the Light
of True Doctrine.* 1952, 32 pp.
*The Teachings of Jehovah's Witnesses Examined in the
Light of the Scriptures.* 1954, 36 pp. From *The
Bible Standard*, March and April 1954.

--7. *Booklets Pertaining to the 1918 Split*

Johnson, Paul S.L. *Harvest Siftings Reviewed.* Brooklyn, N.Y., Nov. 1, 1917, 20 pp.

————. *Another Harvest Siftings Reviewed.* Philadelphia, Pa., Aug. 22, 1918, 12 pp.

F. Offshoots of the Laymen's Home Missionary Movement

1. *EPIPHANY BIBLE STUDENT ASSOCIATION*

After the death of a charismatic leader, a number of schisms
usually occur. This was true of the Laymen's Home Missionary

Movement. When Paul Johnson died in October of 1950 and
Raymond Jolly became the leader of the organization, disagreement occurred between John J. Hoefle and Jolly. Hoefle was a
prominent leader who had spoken at Johnson's funeral and had
also been a pilgrim in Johnson's day. Among other points,
the two men disagreed about the time of Christ's 1,000-year
reign and the nature and validity of John's baptism. There
were personal disagreements, too. Hoefle was formally disfellowshipped on February 8, 1956, from the LHMM after he began
to publish a newsletter called *A Message of Importance to the
Epiphany Elect* which became a regular monthly publication by
the end of 1957. In this newsletter he discussed his position
and tried to defend his doctrine, etc. Actually, Hoefle
agreed with most of the teachings of Russell and Johnson
although much of his newsletter is devoted to discussing the
differences between him and the modern LHMM and other Bible
Student groups including the Watchtower Society. The publications include the following:

Epiphany Bible Students Assn. Journal. Ed. John H. Hoefle.
   June 1955 to date, published monthly, each 8 pp.

Newsletters (specially issued at various times)

The Herald of the Epiphany (10 published)

2. *LAODICEAN HOME MISSIONARY MOVEMENT*

Another offshoot was started by John W. Krewson of Levittown, Pennsylvania, who was disfellowshipped from the LHMM in
1955 after Raymond Jolly took over the LHMM. He then began to
publish his *The Present Truth of Apokalypsis* and several books
and tracts. Sometimes Jolly and Krewson agreed with Hoefle,
and sometimes Hoefle and Jolly united against Krewson. The
arguments concerned what most outsiders feel to be extremely
minor points, and most of the publications are directed
toward those who were affiliated with the LHMM or EBSA movements (Hoefle's group) and not outsiders. They discuss mostly
doctrinal points of concern to the three groups and very few
outsiders.

Magazines

The Present Truth of the Apokalypsis. Vol. 1, No. 1, 1957 to
   date (July-Aug. 1980, No. 153). Issued bi-monthly.

Tracts (all by John W. Krewson and all published in Levittown,
   Pa.)

Are the Dead--Dead? N.d., 8 pp.

Do You Believe in an Earthly Resurrection? N.d., 8 pp.

It Is Later Than You Think! N.d., 10 pp.

On the Stream of Time. N.d., 10 pp.

Books

Krewson, John W. *Apokalypsis Studies in the Scriptures.*
3 vol., hb.

> Vol. I. *Apokalypsis Disclosures.* Levittown, Pa., 1947,
> 480 pp.
> Vol. II. *Laodicean Home Missionary Movement.* Levittown,
> Pa., 1976, 516 pp.
> Vol. III. *Gospel Harvest Testimonies.* Levittown, Pa.,
> 1979, 601 pp.

————. *Harvest Manna for Daily Worship.* Levittown, Pa.,
1972, c. 460 pp.

G. The Dawn Bible Students

In the early 1930s an energetic effort began to regather
the Bible Students outside the Watchtower Society and to again
present to the public Russell's message. This work was spear-
headed by the Brooklyn, N.Y., ecclesia but had support around
the country. William Norman Woodworth and John E. Dawson
left WBBR and the Society in 1929 and later formed the Brooklyn,
New York, Radio Committee which began radio broadcasts in New
York and then Boston on April 12, 1931. The broadcasts were
discontinued after three months due to shortage of funds but
were later reinstated.

Listeners to the Watchtower Society's radio programs
prior to the 1930s no doubt noticed that the message was
often closer to the teachings of Russell than to those of
Rutherford. William Norman Woodworth, who disagreed with
many of Rutherford's "new" ideas, wrote most of the radio
programs. Rutherford unsuccessfully tried to force Woodworth
to conform to his new ideas: Woodworth left and associated
himself with an independent Brooklyn ecclesia, which in 1931
held a convention and elected a central committee that became
the Dawn organization.

Woodworth originally wished to work with the Pastoral
Bible Institute (PBI) but PBI had serious reservations about
a radio ministry. George M. Wilson and William Norman Woodworth in 1931 made an attempt to displace the directors of the

PBI over a disagreement on their passive method of preaching.
The voters, however, reelected the former directors by a
"large majority" and thus in October of 1932 Wilson and Woodworth, with their supporters, founded Dawn Incorporated of
New York and began publishing their own magazine. The Dawn
Bible Students gradually expanded, in time becoming larger
and more important than the Pastoral Bible Institute.

The Dawn Bible Students have always been zealous proselytizers, utilizing both radio and television. Because of this
they are now the second largest movement to owe its origin to
Russell.

The Dawn resumed the "Frank and Ernest" radio broadcasts
in about 1940. The broadcast increased in scope after the
war, and in 1949 the ABC radio network (174 stations) began
broadcasting "Frank and Ernest" throughout the United States
and Canada. The initial rate of mail response was about 5,000
per month. "Frank and Ernest" is currently broadcasting from
approximately 100 stations in America, Europe, Africa, and
Australia.

The low cost and popularity of tape recorders during the
1950s led to the recording and mailing of discourses. Early
in 1953 two brothers in Los Angeles established the Dawn Tape-
Recorded Lecture Service, which prospered. It soon moved
to the Dawn offices in New Jersey, where it has expanded into
an international service. The exchange of tape recordings
between Bible Students is widespread; at times more than 50
recorders are in operation at a single convention.

Over 1,000 *Dawn* subscriptions are supplied without cost
to libraries, schools, hospitals, etc. The *Dawn Magazine* is
an enlarged edition of the four-page weekly tract *The Radio
Echo*, which was published in conjunction with the radio ministry of the Dawn. The *Dawn*, which has a circulation of around
30,000 copies per month, grows at a rate of about 1,000 subscriptions per year. The Dawn advertises in many secular
magazines, as do the Laymen's Home Missionary Movement and
other Watchtower splinter groups. The Dawn representatives
are especially active at local and state fairs and other
places where large numbers of people gather. Members typically
set up a booth, engage in discussion, and hand out literature.
The Dawn also has produced a number of low-budget motion pictures, which have been shown on television hundreds of times.
Their television series "The Bible Answers" is regularly
shown by hundreds of stations. A work entitled *The Unknown
God* has been especially popular in churches, clubs, and
schools. According to some estimates, these films have had
a total attendance of hundreds of thousands. There is also
a recorded lecture service and a pilgrim department which
sends out speakers on request.

The Dawn does not seem to manifest the hatred toward other
religions that some of the offshoots of the Witnesses and the
Witnesses themselves express. Differences of opinion on doctrine are usually tolerated within the organization unless
the ideas are published and begin to create dissension.
Doctrinally, the Dawn is very similar to Pastoral Bible
Institute, but is more conservative, differing primarily in
the matter of adherence to Russell and tolerance to non-
conformity. In recent years, however, the Dawn has introduced
some changes and relaxed its strictness. This has caused a
number of groups to break away, notably the Divine Plan Movement and the other Bible Student movements.
The Dawn offices, originally in Brooklyn (251 Washington
St., then 136 Fulton St.), moved to East Rutherford, New
Jersey, on January 1, 1944. At this time the name Dawn Bible
Student's Association was adopted.
The Dawn corporation is composed of some 72 or so members
managed by a board of 12 trustees to whom the office staff is
responsible. Its annual volume of service work has grown from
a post-war value of $25,000 to over $250,000 today. Its primary purpose has been to regather Bible Students, with increasing emphasis on public witness. A basic baptismal confession is sufficient for fellowship, but the organization
will not sponsor or approve ministers who are not in harmony
with their teachings.
Prime movers of the Dawn at various times since World War
II include William Woodworth, William J. Hollister, and Peter
Kolliman. About one-quarter of the members and one-half of
the trustees of the Dawn live in the New York area; the rest
are spread around the United States, in Canada, and in England.
The individual and collective efforts of the Bible Students were somewhat reduced during the years of wartime economy.
An unsuccessful attempt was made in 1946-47 toward the reunion of the Dawn and the PBI (most of the correspondence
about this is published in the 1947 PBI *Herald*). Shortly
before this, the very important booklet *When Pastor Russell
Died* (1st ed. 1946, 65 pp.; 2nd ed. 1951, 48 pp.) was published. This booklet is the Dawn's statement of their raison
d'être and is essential reading for the researcher. It is
significant that the work contains an attack on the ideas of
R.E. Streeter, one of the PBI founders.
The Dawn's publications have been voluminous but are
frustrating to list due to their lack of dates. Therefore,
an alphabetical arrangement is followed, with dates and editions listed where possible. Prior to 1944, works were published at the Brooklyn headquarters, and later literature was
published at East Rutherford, New Jersey. The pre-1944 publications are listed where known. The Dawn is also an avid

reprinter of Russell's major works and supplies them to many other groups. *Our Most Holy Faith* (1950, 720 pp.) is the Dawn's most challenging publication to date: it is a reprint of many of Russell's most popular articles and sermons.

PUBLICATIONS OF THE DAWN BIBLE STUDENTS

Books

"*Behold Your King,*" *A Herald of Christ's Presence.* East Rutherford, N.J., 1948 (9th ed.), 144 pp., hb.

The Book of Books. East Rutherford, N.J., 1962 (4th ed.), 320 pp.

The Creator's Grand Decision. East Rutherford, N.J., 1969, 240 pp.

God's Promises Come True. East Rutherford, N.J., 1954, 244 pp., hb. A doctrine book for young adolescents.

Our Most Holy Faith. 1948, 719 pp., hb. A collection of Russell's writings.

Songs of the Night. East Rutherford, N.J., c. 1950, 226 pp., hb.

Zionism in Prophecy: The Return of Israel to the Holy Land: A Fulfillment of Biblical Promises. New York: Pro-Palestine Federation of America, 1936, 64 pp., pb.

Hudgings, William. *Evolutionists at the Crossroads.* Brooklyn, N.Y.: Dawn Publishers, Inc., 1935, 128 pp. p. 6.

Russell, C.T. *Tabernacle Shadows of the "Better Sacrifices."* Reprint of the 1881 WtBTS ed., 131 pp., bound with *Berean Questions*, 33 pp.; total 164 pp.

————. Reprints of *Studies in the Scriptures* (originally written by C.T. Russell). All are reset.

Vol. I. *The Divine Plan of the Ages.* Reprinted in 1975, 358 pp., hb., pb.
Vol. II. *The Time Is at Hand.* Reprinted in 1959, 371 pp., hb., pb.
Vol. III. *Thy Kingdom Come.* Reprinted in 1949, 379 pp., hb., pb.
Vol. IV. *The Battle of Armageddon*, n.d., 660 pp., hb., pb.

Vol. V. *At-One-Ment Between God and Man.* N.d., 498 pp., hb., pb.

Vol. VI. *The New Creation.* Reprinted in 1976, 738 pp., hb., pb.

Siebert, Gertrude, and Hattie Woodward. *Daily Heavenly Manna.* Reprinted without birthday section; introduction, scriptural and topic indexes, and several commentary pages added, n.d., c. 200 pp.

——. *Daily Heavenly Manna.* Reprint of the 1907 WtBTS ed., c. 365 pp., hb.

Music Books

Hymns of Dawn. Printed both with and without music, pb., hb.

Booklets (no author listed unless noted)

Archeology Proves the Bible. East Rutherford, N.J., n.d., 60 pp.

Armageddon, Then World Peace (2nd ed., 1952), last ed. 1963, 31 pp. Discusses prophecies of our day.

As Angels of Light. East Rutherford, N.J., n.d. 48 pp.

The Bible and Its Message. East Rutherford, N.J., n.d., 16 pp.

The Bible, the Word of God. East Rutherford, N.J., n.d., 14 pp.

The Birth of a Nation. East Rutherford, N.J., 1951, 62 pp.

The Blood of Atonement. East Rutherford, N.J., 1953.

Born of the Spirit. East Rutherford, N.J., 1959, 32 pp.

Chosen People. 5th ed., 64 pp., 1951.

Christian Hopes and Prospects.

Christ's Thousand-Year Kingdom. East Rutherford, N.J., 1963, 64 pp.; also n.d., 32 pp.

The Church. West Rutherford, N.J., 4th ed. 1959; 5th ed. 1962, 32 pp.

The Church and Its Mission.

Coming Back from Hell Soon.

Convention Report. Hamilton, Ont., Canada, 1936.

"Created He Them." East Rutherford, N.J., 7th ed., 1952,
64 pp.

Creation. East Rutherford, N.J., 1956, 56 pp. Examines the
Genesis Record.

Creation. N.d., 112 pp. Examines the Genesis Record.

The Day of Judgment. East Rutherford, N.J., 1962, 32 pp.

Divine Healing. East Rutherford, N.J., 2nd ed. 1952; also
1957, 32 pp.

Divine Intervention Near. N.d., 30 pp.

Does God Answer Prayer? East Rutherford, N.J., 2nd ed. 1962,
32 pp.

Early Christian View of War and Military Service. East
Rutherford, N.J., 1967, 44 pp.

The Everlasting Gospel. N.d., 64 pp.

Evolution versus the Bible. East Rutherford, N.J., n.d.,
14 pp.

Exceeding Great and Precious Promises. 1954. A selection
reprinted from C.T. Russell's writings.

*Failure to Recognize God's Organization: A Fruitful Cause of
Division Among Christians.* Unpub. Publ. Notes, 1933.

Faith of Our Fathers by Charles Redeker(?) N.d., 104 pp.

Father, Son and Holy Spirit. East Rutherford, N.J., 4th ed.
1950; also 1964, 32 pp.

The Future of Israel and the World. East Rutherford, N.J.,
1961, 32 pp.

God and Reason by Frank Fact Finder (William Norman Woodworth),
Brooklyn, N.Y.: Dawn Publishers, 1st ed., 1934, 124 pp.

God and Reason. 96 pp. Discusses how God will bring peace.

God and Reason. East Rutherford, N.J., n.d., 54 pp.

God Has a Plan. East Rutherford, N.J., n.d., 15 pp.

God's Assurance of Survival. N.d., 16 pp.

God's Hand in the Affairs of Men. N.d., 16 pp.

God's Kingdom Conquers. N.d.

God's Plan. East Rutherford, N.J., 9th ed., 1952, 1963, 48 pp. Illustrated by charts.

God's Plan for Man. East Rutherford, N.J., n.d., 48 pp.

God's Remedy for a World Gone Mad. A Clear and Concise Presentation of the Doctrine of the Kingdom.

The Grace of Jehovah. 1st ed. 1954 (3rd ed. 1961), 64 pp. God's appeal is through love.

Hope. 16 pp.

Hope Beyond the Grave. East Rutherford, N.J., 1963, 94 pp. The Bible's teaching on the soul, spirit, heaven, hell, and paradise.

Hope for a Fear-Filled World. East Rutherford, N.J., n.d., 32 pp.

How God Answers Prayer. East Rutherford, N.J., n.d., 30 pp.

How to Increase Faith. East Rutherford, N.J., n.d., 14 pp.

Israel in History and Prophecy. East Rutherford, N.J., 1961, 64 pp. Significance of the present rebuilding of Palestine.

Jesus--The World's Savior. East Rutherford, N.J., n.d., 32 pp.

Job Sees God. East Rutherford, N.J., n.d., 16 pp.

The Kingdom of God by Charles F. Redeker. N.d., 61 pp. Evidence that it is near.

The Language of the Bible. East Rutherford, N.J., n.d., 14 pp.

Life After Death. East Rutherford, N.J., 1964, 22 pp.

The Light of the World. East Rutherford, N.J., 1957, 32 pp.
Identifies the "true witnesses" of Jehovah and Jesus.

Man's Creation and the Final Destiny. N.d., 16 pp.

A New Manna Book. N.d.

Oh the Blessedness! East Rutherford, N.J., n.d., 26 pp.

Old Time Religion. East Rutherford, N.J., n.d., 15 pp.

Our Day in Prophecy. East Rutherford, N.J., n.d., 14 pp.

Our Lord's Return. East Rutherford, N.J., 1956, 48 pp. Reveals the manner and purpose.

Paradise without Pollution (God's Solution to Man's Problems).

Paul's Letter to the Hebrews. Paul Counsels the Church.

Peace Through Christ's Kingdom. East Rutherford, N.J., 1962, 32 pp.

The People of the Bible. East Rutherford, N.J., n.d., 16 pp.

Reincarnation versus Resurrection. East Rutherford, N.J., 1956, 32 pp.

Revelations of Jesus Christ.

A Royal Nation. East Rutherford, N.J., 1959, 32 pp.

Science and Creation. East Rutherford, N.J., n.d., 32 pp. Harmony of science and the Bible.

Spiritualism. East Rutherford, N.J., n.d., 16 pp.

Three Keys to the Bible. East Rutherford, N.J., n.d., 24 pp.

The Truth About Hell. East Rutherford, N.J., n.d., 24 pp.

The Voice of God. East Rutherford, N.J., n.d., 14 pp.

What Can a Man Believe?

When a Man Dies. East Rutherford, N.J., 1950, 48 pp.

When Pastor Russell Died. East Rutherford, N.J., 1946 (revised ed. n.d., 44 pp.), 63 pp.

Why God Permits Evil. East Rutherford, N.J., n.d., 20 pp.

"Your Adversary the Devil." East Rutherford, N.J., 1964, 32 pp.

Russell, C.T. *The Sin-Offering and the Covenants.* 1954, 32 pp. Reprint of 1907 ed.

Tracts *A Series, listed in order of publication.*

The Scriptures Clearly Teach a Clarification, Question Supplement No. 1.

Are Blood Transfusions Forbidden by God? Question Supplement No. 2. N.d., 4 pp.

Dawn Bible Students Association, Question Supplement No. 3. N.d., 4 pp.

Calamities, Why Permitted; Question Supplement No. 5. N.d., 4 pp.

Has Christianity Failed? New York, n.d., 2 pp.

The World of Tomorrow. New York, n.d., 2 pp.

Hope for a Fear-filled World. New York, n.d., 2 pp.

Hope of Universal Peace. New York, n.d., 2 pp.

Why God Permits Evil. New York, n.d., 4 pp.

God Has a Plan. New York, n.d., 3 pp.

The Homecoming of Our Dead. New York, n.d.

Human Destiny. New York, n.d., 6 pp.

God's World of Tomorrow. New York, n.d.

Do You Know? New York, n.d.

The Truth About Hell. New York, n.d., 6 pp.

Where Are the Dead? New York, n.d.

Prophecies Fulfilled. New York, n.d., 5 pp.

Death Itself Will Die. New York, n.d.

Israel Fulfilling Prophecy. New York, n.d., 4 pp.

Key to the Bible: The Divine Plan of the Ages. East Rutherford, N.J., n.d., 7 pp.

<u>Magazines</u>

Bible Students News. Published from 1935 to 1939, and again
from 1947 to 1950 (semi-yearly), Vol. I, No. 1 to Vol. IV,
No. 2; Vol. III, No. 2 is 40 pp., Vol. IV, No. 2 is 32 pp.

Witness Bulletin. October 1931 to 1934.

Bible Student Radio Echo. Tracts issued from April 29, 1931
to Sept. 1932. Became *The Dawn.*

The Dawn. October 1932–1980. Published monthly, each about
64 pp. Index.

<u>Convention Reports</u> *(Vol. 1, No. 1 to Vol. 4 ?)*

Bible Students News. Vol. 3, No. 2. East Rutherford, N.J.,
1949, 40 pp.

Bible Students News. Vol. 4, No. 2. East Rutherford, N.J.,
1950, 32 pp.

Convention Report. Hamilton, Ont., Canada, 1936.

H. The Bible Student Examiner

Olin R. Moyle, the Society's attorney from about 1930 to
1939 and author of several Watchtower legal publications,
in time became increasingly disenchanted with the moral tone
of Bethel. He was especially discouraged at the harsh and
obscene language Rutherford used (often in print) and what
he considered to be excessive drinking. His personality was
probably the opposite of the bombastic, jovial yet gruff
Rutherford.

When he could tolerate the situation no longer, he wrote
a letter to the President of the Watchtower Society and was
promptly expelled from Bethel. He intended to continue to
associate with the congregation in his hometown of Milwaukee,

Wisconsin, but Rutherford wanted Moyle out of the organization
as well and instructed the local congregation to disfellowship
him, which they did. Moyle later circulated a typeset set of
letters which discussed some of his feelings. He printed his
letter to Rutherford (dated July 21, 1939), his letter to the
Milwaukee, Wisconsin, congregation of Jehovah's Witnesses relative to his excommunication "under orders from the Society's
president" (dated September 25, 1940), and an additional letter
dated May 18, 1940, to Judge Rutherford outlining his objections to life at Bethel. He charged Rutherford with "a glorification of alcohol," "filthy and vulgar language," "ill treatment of the Bethel family," and discrimination as well as unscriptural practices such as "strong criticism of marriage,"
a practice discouraged until Knorr himself married. The
Society's response to this tract was to print in the *Watchtower*
a short announcement condemning Moyle (*Watchtower*, Sept. 1,
1939, p. 258) and a stronger condemnation on October 15, 1939,
pp. 316-317). Moyle, in turn, sued the Watchtower Society
and won (see *The Golden Age*, December 20, 1944, p. 21 and June
23, 1943, pp. 27-28, for the outcome of the trial and appeal
at which damages were reduced from $30,000 to $15,000). It is
interesting to note that, according to a letter by Peter Moyle
published on p. 382 of the 1939 *Watchtower*, he sided with the
Watchtower Society against his father, but he later left the
Society, and still later left his father's group and converted
to Judaism. He is now an agnostic.

Olin Moyle originally associated with the New Covenant
Believers but because they still held to Russell's chronological
system (Christ returned in 1874 and so on), Moyle started his
own group and began publishing his *Bible Student Inquirer*,
which was later called the *Bible Student Examiner*. When Moyle
died in 1959, Henry Wallis took over. The only publication
the group has produced is their magazine. The magazine ceased
publication in 1982 when Wallis died.

Henry Wallis became involved with Russell in 1914 when he
was 22. In response to a circular he found, he attended the
Photodrama and as a result turned from "a skeptic attending a
Presbyterian Church" to a follower of Pastor Russell. He read
the six volumes in two months and began attending the Baltimore
Ecclesia of the ISBA. A year later he was elected an elder
and was viewed by the class as a very capable Bible Student.
When Rutherford became President of the Society, Wallis became
increasingly disenchanted but remained involved until about
1932.

He found Rutherford a "proud, dictatorial autocrat" after
he had worked with Rutherford a number of times. For example,
Rutherford publicly stated that he had never said that the
resurrection would take place in 1925, which he had done in the
"*Millions Book*," among other places.

From 1932 to 1950 Wallis studied the Bible with a small group of friends and in 1950 he was introduced to Moyle's work. He contributed articles for about four years and became an associate editor in 1954 until 1959, when he became the editor, remaining in this position until he died in 1982.

Magazines

The Bible Student Inquirer. Ed. by Olin R. Moyle. Published from about 1940 to 1959 at Baltimore, Md.

The Bible Student Examiner. Ed. Henry Wallis. Vol. 1, No. 1, 1959, to Vol. 22, Nos. 1 & 2, Jan. & Feb. 1982, Baltimore, Md., 16 pp., bi-monthly.

I. Back to the Bible Way

The founder, Roy D. Goodrich, was a pioneer for the Watchtower Society from 1919 (his wife Maud, daughter of Dr. Hodgson, was a pioneer from 1914) until 1945 when both he and his wife were disfellowshipped. Evidently, in 1943 a friend told him that there were certain "demonistic practices" at the Brooklyn headquarters. In an attempt to correct the matter, he sent a letter to the directors of the Society, who did not answer. Further research by Goodrich uncovered many "demonistic practices" that Rutherford and other high-level Watchtower administrators and theorists practiced. The "demonistic practices" were centered around an innovative medical treatment called "radio diagnosis" (a quack method of treating disease by radio waves--see Quacks by Charles Warner). At this time Goodrich was a company servant and as he was quite outspoken about these matters to his congregation, he was disfellowshipped.

After he was disfellowshipped, he involved himself in the various Bible Student groups and in different ways with the Witnesses. Goodrich, his wife, and others were very active passing out tracts at the large assemblies, an action which often resulted in harsh treatment not only from Witnesses but from Bible Students as well. For example, he picketed the 1946 Witness convention in Cleveland and caused such a stir that The Messenger, the official Watchtower assembly report, was forced to discuss the situation.

In 1952 he began the Back to Bible Way magazine, which was published until his death in 1977. Goodrich not only had a falling out with the Witnesses, but later the various Bible Student groups. Evidently he was a difficult person, insistent upon the correctness of his ideas and position and intolerant of others. His literature records the many confrontations he has had with virtually every Bible Student group, most of whom in time tried to ignore him.

Goodrich was a prolific writer, and many of his writings show a great understanding of and insight into religious matters. He was one of few college-educated Witnesses (Goodrich was a high school science teacher for many years). His research eventually caused him to reject a number of Russell's ideas and accept many of George Storr's beliefs, and even some of the teachings of the early Adventists. In contrast to many of the splinter groups' leaders, he was a lively and energetic writer, and his works tend to be informative and useful to the student of Witness history. He has supplied a great deal of new information about the Watchtower Bible & Tract Society. When he and his wife died in 1977 (within months of each other) his movement, always very small, fell apart. Haviland Davis, of Albany, New York, carries some of Goodrich's publications.

Theologically, Goodrich held to the fundamentals advocated by Russell (denial of the trinity, immortality of the soul, hell, the idea that Christendom is apostate, etc.) but he disagreed strongly with the "invisible second presence theory," the belief that Christ's second coming is not visible. He did not view Russell as the faithful and wise servant as do many Bible Student groups nor did he view the ransom as merely a "curse."

Goodrich's involvement in the various Bible Student groups was his main source of converts, although many ex-Witnesses joined him. His mailing list was as large as 3,000. His publications (including his magazine and 440 different brochures) vary from one-page mimeographed items to printed booklets to postcards and form letters used to answer inquiries. Many of these publications deal with the problems of the Witness theology.

PUBLICATIONS OF BACK TO THE BIBLE WAY PUBL. INC. (Roy D. Goodrich. All published by author in Fort Lauderdale, Fla.)

Brochures

A Bible Study Series

1. *The Communion of Saints.* Feb. 1946, 2 pp.

2. *Love's Memorial, A Confession.* April 1946, 8 pp.

3. *"This Do in Remembrance of Me."* April 1946, 13 pp.

4. *Remembrance Versus Denying the Lord.* April 1946, 5 pp.

5. *Private Interpretation.* Sept. 1946, 2 pp.

6. *The True Basis of Christian Fellowship.* Dec. 1946, 15 pp.

7. *The Name "Jehovah's Witnesses"; Its Right and Wrong Use.*
    Dec. 1946, 7 pp.

Back to the Bible Way--Brochures No. 1 to 444.

1. *To N.H. Knorr.* Oct. 1944.

2. *To Fort Lauderdale "Sheep" (if any).* Nov. 1944, 2 pp.

3. *To "Dear Friends."* Nov. 1944, 2 pp.

9. (Nos. 1, 2, 3 revised and mimeographed.)

14. *An Open Letter to N.H. Knorr.* N.d., 2 pp.

15. *Tamp Assembly Highlights.* Feb. 1945.

19. *Something's Hot.* Feb. 1945.

20. *The Spook Cure.* March 1945, 2 pp.

21. *Notes from "The Grape Cure" Book.* March 1945.

22. *Stalks of the Ghost of Wm. Penn to Clayton J. Woodworth.*
    March 1945.

23. *Dare You Face the Facts?* April 1945.

25. *"Radioclast" Reproductions.* April 1945.

27. *Special Meetings.* West Palm Beach, Fla., 1945, 5 pp.

30. *A Letter to a Brother Who Was Grossly Offended and Ex-
    communicated, and with Whom I Disagree.* May 1945,
    22 pp. About Moyle.

31. *"Heavens and Earth--Which Are Now."* Jan. 1946, 3 pp.

32. *Jehovah of Hosts, The God of "Peace."* Sept. 1, 1945,
    15 pp. (same as No. 133).

34. *Response of Hate.* Oct. 1945, 3 pp.

37. *An Open Letter to N.H. Knorr.* N.d., 2 pp. Reprint of
    No. 14.

38. *Bethel Rides the Broom.* Feb. 1946, 18 pp.

39. *An Open Letter to N.H. Knorr--Unanswered Yet.*

40. *To My Anointed Brethren.* Dec. 24, 1944, 4 pp. (same as No. 9).

41. *The "Murder" of a Pioneer.* Dec. 1945, 1 p.

42. *To My Brethren Whom It May Concern.* Jan. 1946, 3 pp.

43. *The Spook Cure as Advocated by Doctor Rollin Jones, Personal Physician to Judge.* N.d., 4 pp.

46a. *An Introduction to, and History of the Manuscript-- "Theocratic Judgment" As Scorned, Unread by N.H. Knorr.* April 1947, 5 pp.

46b. *Dear "Evil Servant" and Brothers and Sisters to Whom This Shall Come.* Sept. 1946, 4 pp.

47a. *Thank God! After 30-odd Years Satan Has Been Compelled to Allow Freedom of Communication among the Enlightened Members of Temple of the God Jehovah!* Revised 1976, 9 pp.

47b. *Shall the Elders of God's Free Church Remain Gagged and Bound by Fear?* June 1946, 12 pp.

48. *Lawrence E. Drew to Directors.* May 1946.

49. *Circular Letter to Miami Friends.* May 1946.

50. *"We Think."* June 1946, 1 p.

56. *Charter of the Watchtower Society of Pennsylvania.* 1945, 8 pp.

57. *Tobacco.* Oct. 1946, 1 p.

59. *Together with God.* Nov. 1946, 7 pp.

60. *Voices, Thunderings, Lightnings, Earthquake.* Dec. 1946, 3 pp.

61. *"Watch and Be Sober."* Dec. 1946, 3 pp.

62. *"Fogh Hysteria": According to C.H. Zook, "The Instrument of Yah."* Dec. 1946, 2 pp.

63. *Reprint of Letter to Mrs. J.H. Donovan.* March 10, 1945, 1 p.

64. *Ouija Boards, Small and Large.* Dec. 1947, 11 pp.

65. *Introduction to KIM.* Jan. 1947, 1 p.

66. *Crawford and Stoneman Letters.* Dec. 1946, 1 p.

67. *Form Letter "A."* N.d., 1 p.

68. *Spoken in Darkness, Heard in Light.* Jan. 1947, 9 pp.

69. *From Letters "B" and "C."* Jan. 1947, 4 pp.

70. *Jehovah's Witnesses.* N.d., 1 p.

71. *Shall We Study the Watchtower?* Jan 1947, 4 pp.

72. *Character Development.* Feb. 1947, 7 pp.

73. *"Great Is Diana of the Ephesians": A Goddess Falls Down from Heaven!* March 1947, 1 p.

74. *Railing, Reviling, Evil Speaking, Scripturally Defined.* Feb. 1947, 2 pp.

75. *Men and Brethren, What Shall We Do When We See the Errors of "Organization."* Feb. 1947, 6 pp.

76. *A Watchtower Study: Remembrance of Jesus vs. "A Memorial of Integrity."* Feb. 15, 1947, 4 pp.

77. *The Memorial of Jesus.* March 1947 (5 pp. revised).

78. *Zion Repents, Do You?* March 1947, 10 pp.

79. *Moyle's Original Letters.* Feb. 1947, 6 pp.

80. *David and His Sin.* March 9, 1946, 5 pp.

81. *Postscript on Bible Chronology.* Nov. 1, 1945, 5 pp.

82. *Copyrights.* May 6, 1946, 3 pp.

83. *"Bethel": The House of God, as Seen from the Inside.* Feb. 1947, 8 pp. By M.P. Fogh.

85. *To the Beloved of God Convention "Meat."* April 1947,
       3 pp.

86. *As Sheep Having no Shepherd.* April 1947, 2 pp.

88. *Ridicule, Sarcasm, Derision and Reproach.* May 1947, 1 p.

89. *Answer to Miller's Tirade.* May 1947, 1 p.

91. *Betrayal.* July 6, 1947, 4 pp.

92. *"What Next?"* Aug. 1947, 2 pp.

94. *For Los Angeles Contacts* (printed post card). Aug.
       1947.

95. (Postcard photo of defaced sandwich sign). Oct. 1946.

96. *The Wabbling "Channel."* Aug. 1947, 1 p.

97. *In the Temple Gate.* Sept. 1947, 11 pp.

98. *Love: What Is It? The Inspired Answer.* Oct. 1947,
       4 pp.

99. *Advice.* Oct. 28, 1947, 1 p.

100. *To Jehovah's Witnesses, Dawn Readers and Others.* Nov.
       5, 1947, 4 pp.

101. *Scripture Please!* Nov. 1947, reprinted 1952, 2 pp.

102. *By What Authority?* Dec. 1947, 1 p.

103. *Parousia vs Presence--Our First Inkling of the Truth on
       This Subject.* Dec. 1947, 10 pp.

104. *Brotherly Love at Philadelphia.* Jan. 1948, 1 p.

105. *"Ye Shall Know Them by Their Fruits."* Jan. 1948, 1 p.

106. *The Christian Controversy.* Jan. 1948, 19 pp.

107. *A Terrible Disturbance.* Feb. 1948, 1 p.

108. *A Flower upon My Mother's Grave.* Feb. 1948, 3 pp.

108a. *To Relatives and Friends of My Mother.* Feb. 1948, 1 p.

109. *Letter.* N.d., 1 p.

111. *Preaching the Word.* Nov. 1948, 1 p.

112. *The Atlanta Assembly of the Watchtower Witnesses of Jehovah.* March 1948, 2 pp.

113. *Preaching the Word, to My Free Brethren.* April 15, 1948, 3 pp.

114. *Contradicting the Almighty--the Watchtower vs. God.* April 1948, 6 pp.

116. *"Freely Ye Have Received, Freely Give" the Gospel--Our Report from 1944 to 1948.* May 1948, 3 pp.

117. *No Going to Heaven, No Baptism, No Lord's Supper.* May 7, 1948, 1 p.

118. *An Answer to "Free" Bible Students.* May 1948, 5 pp.

119. *Contribution Acknowledgement.* N.d., 1 p.

120. *To Those Concerned as to Merwyn Fogh.* N.d., 1 p.

121. *"He Stirreth up the People."* May 21, 1948, 1 p.

122. *Finke Replies.* May 1948, 1 p.

123. *Preaching the Word.* N.d., 1 p.

124. *The Image of Jealousy.* May 1948, 3 pp.

125. *"That Servant--Faithful and Wise."* June 1, 1948 (enlarged in 1957), 8 pp.

126. *Earnestly Contend for the Faith.* June 3, 1948, 3 pp.

127. *Preaching the Word.* July 25, 1948, 1 p.

128. *Established by God's Grace.* N.d., 1 p.

129. *A Witness Among Wolves.* Oct. 1948, 7 pp.

130. *Postscript to Witness Among Wolves.* Oct. 1948, 3 pp.

131. *Judging.* Oct. 1948, 8 pp. (same as No. 130).

133. *Jehovah of Hosts--The God of "Peace."* Oct. 1948, 8 pp.
     (same as No. 32).

134. *N.H. Knorr's Criticism of the Above "Peace" Manuscript.*
     Oct. 1948, 2 pp.

135. *To the P.B.I. Editors and Directors.* Nov. 1948, 1 p.

136. *"Are You Interested?"* (postcard). 1 p.

137. *Established by God's Grace, or Tossed To and Fro?*
     Nov. 1948, 8 pp.

138. *"We Wrestle Not...."* Nov. 1948, 1 p.

139. *In Whose Seat? Christ's or Caesar's?* Dec. 1978, 1 p.

140. *Contribution Acknowledgement.* Dec. 1948, 1 p.

141. *Crucify Him! Crucify Him! An Eye-Witness Account of
     the Scriptural Murder of Olin R. Moyle by 65,000
     J.W.s at St. Louis in 1941.* Dec. 1948, 2 pp.

142. *Financial Report for 1948.* Jan. 1949, 1 p.

143. *Freedom to Do God's Will in 1949.* Jan. 1949, 1 p.

144. *To Russellite and Watchtower Brethren.* Jan. 1949, 1 p.

145. *As to Adam.* Jan. 1949, 2 pp.

146. *"Self-Justification."* Feb. 1949, 2 pp.

147. *"Rather Reprove Them."* Feb. 1949, 1 p.

148. *"The Key to Studying the Bible."* May 1949, 1 p.

149. *God's (Not Man's) Co-Workers.* Feb. 1949, 1 p.

151. *To All Bible Students of the Miami Ecclesia.* April 23,
     1949, 3 pp.

152. *Whom Will You Obey?* May 1949, 1 p.

153. *Proposed Assembly Witness* (letter). May 1949, 2 pp.

154. *Decency Commended.* May 1949, 1 p.

155. *What Would Happen to Jesus Christ If He Attended a "JW" Assembly?* June 11, 1949, 1 p.

156. *To Hayden C. Covington, et al.* May 1949, 1 p.

159. *It Happened in 1949, Visits to JW Assemblies Recounted.* Aug. 1949, 12 pp.

160. *In Welchem Recht?* 2 pp. (No. 102 above, in German.)

161. *The Heavenly Call of Christianity, The "No Heaven" Challenge of Demonism Squarely Met.* Aug. 1949, 4 pp.

162. *Immortality, What Is It?* Aug. 1949, 2 pp.

163. *What Is the Hope of His Calling?* Aug. 1949, 4 pp.

164. *Is Your Heart Right with God?* Aug. 1949, 1 p.

165. *When? How? and Why? Was the Now Infamous "Goodrich" Thrown Out on His Face by Men Less Righteous Than He?* Sept. 1949, 4 pp.

166. *The Zooky Servants of Yah: A "Truth" Cult Denying Everything, Even the Existence of Jesus as a Man.* Sept. 1949, 1 p.

167. *"Berean Study" False and True.* Sept. 1949, 1 p.

168. *Does the Watchtower Answer Goodrich?* Sept. 1949, 1 p.

169. *Have the "Free Brethren" Answered Goodrich?* Sept. 1949, 1 p.

170. *The Kingdom of God Is at Hand.* Oct. 1949, 2 pp.

171. *From the Last Supper to the First Fruits of Them That Slept, in Type and Anti-type.* Oct. 1949, 17 pp.

172. *Present Truth on Parousia.* Nov. 1949, 2 pp.

173. *Chronoligitis, A Dread Disease.* Dec. 1949, 3 pp.

174. *Please.* Dec. 1949, 1 p.

175. *The Day of Atonement.* Dec. 1949, 4 pp.

176. *Christian Science.* Dec. 1949, 1 p.

176a. *Man Dying in Trailer, Unable to Get Word to Officers.* Dec. 1949, 1 p. Merwyn Fogh's death.

177. *Lift up Your Heads! 1950 Is Here!* Jan. 1950, 3 pp.

178a. *Jesus' Soul, the Sin Offering.* Jan. 1950, 2 pp.

179. *Do It Now* (An Interest Form). Jan. 1950, 1 p.

180. *Christian Baptism.* Jan. 1950, 26 pp.

181. *Whence Came Russell's "Secret Presence" Theory?* July 1961, 1 p.

182. *On Seeing Alike.* Jan. 1950, 1 p. On freedom of communication.

183. *Absurdity Masquerading as the "Deep Things of God" Dies Hard.* Feb. 1950, 7 pp.

184. *Questions.* Feb. 15, 1950, 1 p.

185b. (Monthly and yearly summary forms.) March 1950.

186. (Form letter for Britain.) March 1950, 4 pp.

187. *Some Questions* (poem). April 1950, 1 p.

188. *Viceregency: The Great Mistake and Abomination of the Gospel Age.* April 1950, 8 pp.

189. *General Letter of May 1950.* May 1950, 1 p.

190. *Octogenarian Asks Questions.* May 1950, 1 p.

191. *G.R. Pollock Visits Britain.* May 1950, 3 pp.

192. *My Purpose, My Work and Yours.* May 1950 (revised Feb. 1958), 1 p.

193. *Second John Seven--Is Jesus Coming in the Flesh?* June 1950, 1 p.

194. *Comfort All that Mourn in Zion.* June 1950.

195. *The Bible Student Soul-Searcher.* June 1950, 2 pp. Also Aug. 1950, *The Bible Student Soul-Searcher* (no number).

196. *The Bible Student Soul-Searcher.* Supplement No. 1,
     June 1950, 1 p.

197. *The Bible Student Soul-Searcher.* Supplement No. 2,
     June 1950, 1 p.

198. *Dawn General Convention, Bowling Green, Ohio; Watchtower
     International Assembly, Yankee Stadium, New York
     City.* Aug. 16, 1950, 1 p.

199. *Love ... in Work and in Truth.* June 16, 1950, 1 p.

200. *Letter.* July 1950, 1 p.

201. *It Happened at 124 Columbia Heights, Brooklyn, New York.*
     July 24, 1950, 1 p.

202. *It Happened at 177 Prospect Place.* July 25, 1950, 2 pp.

203. *"Dawn" at Bowling Green.* Aug. 26, 1950, 3 pp.

204. *Wresting Universal Salvation unto Destruction.* Sept. 8,
     1950, 10 pp. (revised and enlarged ed., 24 pp.).

205. *A Personal Letter.* Sept. 27, 1950, 1 p.

206. *"Theocracy's Increase" at Yankee Stadium in 1950: Is
     This the Kingdom of God? Or Merely a New and In-
     creasing Religion?* Sept. 27, 1950, 5 pp.

207. *Evil Speaking Defined--Its Creed Examined.* Oct. 1950,
     2 pp.

208. *Patience, Her Work and Her Creed.* Oct. 1950, 3 pp.

209. (Index card checking form). Dec. 1950, 1 p.

210. *JHVH? YHWH? What Is the Creator's Name?* Dec. 1950,
     5 pp.

211. (Advertising slip for No. 204). Dec. 1950, 1 p.

212. *"For the Elect's Sake."* Dec. 21, 1950, 4 pp.

213. *Proclaiming Repentance (1950 report).* Jan. 1951, 2 pp.

214. *The Season's Greetings, 1951.* Jan. 1951, 2 pp.

215. *Jehovah's Memorial Name in the New Testament.* Jan. 21, 1951, 10 pp.

216. *"Let Us Know."* Jan. 1951, 1 p.

217. *The Great Multitude* (by Percy Sidney Pryer). Feb. 1951, 4 pp.

218. *Nekros-Thanatos: An Answer to This Religious Noise.* Feb. 1951, 1 p.

219. *Two Viewpoints* (from England). March 6, 1951, 2 pp.

220. *In Remembrance of Whom?* March 12, 1951, 6 pp.

221. *Contributions Are Now Possible.* March 15, 1951, 1 p.

222. *God's Organization.* March 29, 1951, 6 pp.

223. *To All Who Love His Appearing* (Britain). April 1, 1951, 1 p.

224. *What Shall We Do "Until ..." What.* April 20, 1951, 2 pp.

225. *God's Organization.* April 1951, 4 pp. (Oct. 1957 fourth printing, 8 pp.).

226. (Invitation to circulate No. 225). April 26, 1951, 1 p.

227. *Honest with Yourself and with Your God.* April 29, 1951, 1 p.

228. *"Not Forsaking the Assembling of Ourselves Together."* May 19, 1951, 1 p.

229. *"Destroyed for Lack of Knowledge."* May 20, 1951, 1 p.

230. *"Proclaim Liberty Throughout All the Land."* May 24, 1951, 1 p.

231. (Form letter). June 17, 1951, 1 p.

232. *The New Watchtower Translation of 1950: An Unbiased Evaluation.* June 18, 1951, 4 pp.

233. *The Atlanta District Assembly of Watchtower Witnesses.* June 8-10, 1951, 4 pp.

234. *Atlantic District Assembly of 1951, Addenda.* June 28, 1951, 1 p.

235. *Modern Scribes and Pharisees: Hypocrites!* July 2, 1951, 3 pp.

236. *Opinion--Profanity.* July 1951, 1 p.

237. *Who Is My Brother? The Bible Answer Surprises Many.* 7 pp.

238. *List of Brochures for Bible Students.* July 20, 1951, 1 p.

239. *Complete List of Brochures in Stock.* July 20, 1951, 1 p.

240. *Dear Friends All, from Dan to Beer-Sheba.* Aug. 17, 1951, 1 p.

241. *Reports of Unity Convention.* Sept. 4, 1951, 1 p.

242. (Name and address form). Sept. 4, 1951, 1 p.

243. *The Present Truth on Parousia.* Sept. 10, 1951, 2 pp.

244. *Questionnaire Form with University Convention Report.* Oct. 17, 1951, 1 p.

245. *1951 Unity Convention Report.* Oct. 20, 1951, 8 pp.

246. *Christian Cooperation.* Nov. 2, 1951, 4 pp.

247. *Brother Strongly Advised Against.* Nov. 12, 1951, 1 p.

248. *Fellowship.* Nov. 19, 1951, 3 pp.

249. *New Year's Greetings, 1952.* Jan. 1, 1952, 1 p.

250. *From Australia on the Unity Convention Report and the Sin Offering.* Jan. 1952, 1 p.

251. *Have Fervent Love Among Yourselves: Let's Get Acquainted!* Jan. 1952, 3 pp.

252. *Brethren All, from Dan to Beersheba.* Feb. 7, 1952, 1 p.

253. *Form Inquiring as to Interest.* Feb. 1952, 1 p.

254. *Back to the Bible No. 1.* Feb. 2, 1952.

255. *Back to the Bible, No. 2.* March 12, 1952.

256. *For Polite Discontinue Requesters* (persons who do not want to receive Goodrich's literature). March 20, 1952, 1 p.

256a. (Correspondence-answering form). March 26, 1952, 1 p.

256b. (Correspondence-answering form). May 4, 1952, 1 p.

256c. (Correspondence--convalescence). June 6, 1952, 1 p.

256e. (Letterhead--back to the Bible). June 24, 1952, 1 p.

256f. (Ditto, plus home from hospital letter). July 28, 1952, 1 p.

256g. (Back to Health letter). Oct. 17, 1952, 1 p.

256h. (Back to Health letter). Jan. 12, 1953, 1 p.

257. *"The True Basis of Christian Fellowship."* June 8, 1952, 1 p.

258. *Unity Convention Bible Study on "The True Basis of Christian Fellowship."* June 8, 1952, 4 pp.

258a. *"Petition" to Jehovah's Witness Assembly Here.* April 18, 1952, 1 p.

259. *Jehovah's Witnesses Assemblies--Opportunity of Service.* Aug. 13, 1952, 1 p.

260. *4 Questions to 66 Dawn and PBI Pilgrims.* May 25, 1953.

261. (For distribution at Yankee Stadium). June 1, 1953.

262. *Have Faith in God, Inviting to Help.* June 7, 1953, 1 p.

263. *Letter Reporting Macatawa and Yankee Stadium.* Aug. 10, 1953, 2 pp.

264. *Answering cards, 261 sent in Aug. 1953.*

265. *N.H. Knorr Speaks at Stadium to "Scores of Thousands,"*
      Sept. 5, 1953, 12 pp.

266. *Half-Truth Versus the Whole Truth.* Sept. 20, 1953, 1 p.

267. (Form letter). Oct. 20, 1953, 1 p.

268. *Letter to "Fry List."* Nov. 28, 1953, 1 p.

269. *Love Your Enemies* (Sister Clark's letter). Dec. 4,
      1953, 2 pp.

270. *Seasons Greetings--Back to the Bible.* Dec. 15, 1953,
      2 pp.

270a. *Are You Interested in the Back to the Bible Public?*
      Dec. 18, 1953.

272. *Demonism and the Watchtower* (enlarged ed.). Jan. 1,
      1954, 16 pp. (revised 1969, 36 pp.).

273. *Blood Transfusion--Does It Violate God's Law?* Feb. 12,
      1954, 4 pp.

274. *To Jehovah's Witnesses, Disfellowshipped by Man or Who
      Fear Their Turn Is Next.* Feb. 17, 1954, 4 pp.

276. *"Out of the Mouths of Babes."* March 11, 1954, 2 pp.

277. *Passover Questions--Raised by Our Readers.* May 1, 1954,
      4 pp.

278. *"It's Better Never Late."* May 2, 1954, 1 p.

279. *Problem: To Complete ___ Copies.* May 3, 1954, 1 p.

280. (Form letter). May 6, 1954, 1 p.

281. *Jehovah's Witnesses Assembly* (double postcard). May 6,
      1954, 1 p.

282. *Jehovah's Witnesses* (postcard). May 21, 1954, 1 p.

283. (Form letters, etc.), June 7, 1954.

284. *Mighty as Death Is Love.* Aug. 12, 1954, 2 pp.

285. *To 39 Fellow Elders.* Sept. 12, 1954, 1 p.

286. (Correspondence-Answering form letter). Sept. 12, 1954, 1 p.

287. *"By What Authority" Growled the Elders.* Sept. 12, 1954, 1 p.

288. *Have You Seen the Light? God's Great Covenants in Simple Language.* Oct. 19, 1954, 8 pp.

289. *Circular Letter on Informal Sessions.* Nov. 25, 1954, 1 p.

290. *Open Letter of Psalm 82.* Dec. 18, 1954, 4 pp.

291. *They Shall All Know Me, Jer. 31:31-34.* Dec. 20, 1954, 1 p.

292. *"Salvation" Seasons Greetings.* Dec. 12, 1954, 1 p.

293. *The Holy Spirit of the God Jehovah by Percy Sidney Pryer.* Jan. 20, 1955, 8 pp.

294. (Correspondence "Pre-Script"). Jan. 20, 1955, 1 p.

295. *A Back to the Bible Answer.* Feb. 4, 1955, 1 p.

296. *Twelve Back to the Bible Answers, to an ex-JW.* Feb. 5, 1955, 5 pp.

297. *To Universalists--All Brands.* Feb. 13, 1955, 1 p.

298. *The Whips of Solomon Change to the Scorpions of Rehoboam.* March 6, 1955, 2 pp.

299. (Announcements). March 24, 1955, 1 p.

300. *"Thy Parousia" Honesty vs. Dishonesty.* March 31, 1955, 3 pp.

301. (Form letter). May 15, 1955, 1 p.

302. *Which Son Are You? Harvest Is Great--Laborers Are Few.* June 1955, 1 p.

303. *"Jehovah's Witnesses Win a Right."* June 1955, 4 pp.

304. *"Planned Free Time" Finis.* June 28, 1955, 1 p.

305. *Penetrating the Iron Curtain.* Aug. 4, 1955, 1 p.

306. *Win Recognition in the "World of Satan."* Aug. 10, 1955, 5 pp.

307. (Form to reply to requests for No. 303). Sept. 10, 1955, 1 p.

307b. (Form). Nov. 29, 1955, and Feb. 10, 1956, 1 p.

308. *Funeral Discourse.* Jan. 5, 1956, 6 pp.

309. *Unpardonable Sin.* Feb. 17, 1956, 8 pp.

310. *Myth, Mercy and Martyrdom--or Does Blood Transfusion Break God's Law?* Feb. 1956, 2 pp.

311. (Charles Glass correspondence). March 16, 1956, 5 pp.

312. *The Christian Sabbath.* March 16, 1956, 4 pp.

313. *ABC's of Bible Study.* June 30, 1956, 78 pp.

314. *Cry of the Hungry.* June 4, 1956, 3 pp.

315. *Try the Spirits* (postcard). June 10, 1956, 1 p.

316. *The Ransom of the Bible versus the Ransom of Confusion.* June 12, 1956, 1 p.

317. (Stenofar stencil for big envelopes). June 26, 1956, 1 p.

318. (Slips about advance copies of No. 313). June 30, 1956, 1 p.

319. *The Atonement of Christ versus Spiritual Gangrene.* July 8, 1956, 2 pp.

320. *Behind the Scenes at Green Castle, Indiana in 1956.* Sept. 24, 1956, 12 pp.

321. *The Watchtower Succumbs to Occult Control.* Sept. 24, 1954, 1 p.

322. (Correspondence-answering form). Oct. 19, 1956, 1 p.

323. *What about W.J. Schnell's Book: 30 YEARS A WATCHTOWER SLAVE?* Dec. 7, 1956, 2 pp.

324. (Mailing list double postcard). Dec. 20, 1956, 2 pp.

325. *The Authority of the Watchtower Society Examined.* Jan. 1, 1957, 4 pp.

325a. (Auf Deutsch). Feb. 15, 1958.

326. *A Happy Back to the Bible Greetings New Year to You!* Dec. 27, 1956, 1 p.

327. *The Night Cometh When No Man Can Work.* Jan. 15, 1957, 1 p.

328. *How to Reach Jehovah's Witnesses and Why.* Feb. 18, 1957, 4 pp.

329. *Dear Back to the Bible Reader.* Feb. 20, 1957, 1 p.

329a. (Newsletter). April 6, 1957, 1 p.

330. *The New Covenant in the Book of Hebrews.* May 5, 1957, 16 pp. (later ed. 28 pp.).

331. *Challenge of the Hour, Bible Week.* May 20, 1957, 1 p.

331. (Bible Week forms for Laura Bridge). June 21, 1957, 1 p.

332. *Bible Week Suggestions.* July 1, 1957, 1 p.

334. *Song Book.* July 10, 1957, 19 pp.

335. *"Home Again"--A Brief Outline of Our 1957 Missionary Journey.* Sept. 14, 1957, 1 p.

336. *New York Watchtower Charter.* Oct. 15, 1957, 8 pp.

337. *Parental Discipline.* Nov. 14, 1957, 4 pp.

338. (Correspondence-answering form letter). Dec. 28, 1957, 1 p.

339. *The Rich Man and Lazarus.* Feb. 1958, 8 pp.

341. (Reply form letter). Feb. 13, 1958, 1 p.

341a. (Corporation receipt form). April 10, 1958, 1 p.

342. *"Auf Deutsch"* (form letter). March 10, 1958, 1 p.

343. *Parable of the Unjust Steward.* April 16, 1958, 8 pp.

344. (Bible Week reservation request card). May 10, 1958, 1 p.

345. *Trying to Serve "Other Lords" and Christ.* May 12, 1958, 4 pp.

346. *The "Canon" of Scripture Chopping Down the Ransom. Are Scholars Wrong? John 1:1.* May 28, 1958, 8 pp.

347. *Charter of the Bible Way Publications, Inc.* June 6, 1958, 10 pp.

348. *"Trembling at Men, Is What Lays a Snare."* June 15, 1958, 2 pp.

349. (Form letter on convention trip). Aug. 15, 1958, 2 pp.

350. *"Bird"* (form). *"Are You Alive."* Oct. 15, 1958, 1 p.

351. (Correspondence-answering form). Jan. 27, 1959, 1 p.

352. *Invitation to Fort Lauderdale Memorial Assembly.* June 27, 1959, 1 p.

353. *Dear Modesto California Friends, and Others Everywhere.* Feb. 23, 1959, 1 p.

354. *Remember the Patience of Job.* March 15, 1959, 1 p.

355. *The Symphony of Parousia and Mello.* April 4, 1959, 8 pp.

356. *BTTBW Index 1952-1956.* April 4, 1959, 13 pp.

357. *BTTBW Index 1957, 1958.* April 4, 1959, 5 pp.

358. *"The Tabernacle of David"* (for class study). April 6, 1959, 4 pp.

358a. (Collect rev. chart).

359. *Type and Antitype. The Law and the Faith.* April 6, 1959, 10 pp.

359a. (As above with Scriptures printed in full). July 15, 1961, 12 pp.

360. *Dual Fulfillment.* June 22, 1959, 8 pp.

361. *"The Tabernacle of David."* Sept. 30, 1959, 8 pp.

362. *Our Lord's Last Days Chart Explained.* June 22, 1959, 2 pp.

363. *"Great Signs and Wonders" in the Parousia-Time.* Aug. 24, 1959, 1 p.

364. *"House to House."* Sept. 1, 1959, 2 pp.

365. *As a Snare ... Watch ... Stand ....* March 3, 1960, 8 pp.

366. (Envelope negative). March 5, 1960, 1 p.

367. *Letter.* N.d., 2 pp.

368. *The P.S.L. Johnson Affair of 1917.* June 5, 1960, 5 pp.

369. *"Thou Shalt Love Thy Neighbor as Thyself"* (Archer thrown out of J.W. Assembly). 1960, 8 pp.

370. *"Finding Peace in This Troubled World"* (Charles Archer thrown out of Assembly). 1960, 4 pp.

371. *Auf Deutsch.* Sept. 17, 1960, 12 pp.

372. *Mission Accomplished* (1960 trip). Sept. 7, 1960, 5 pp.

373. *To All the Ministers and Others Who Attended the Recent Minister's Meeting, August 20, and 21, 1960, at Belleville, Illinois.* Sept. 15, 1960, 2 pp.

374. *The Promise of the Father* (German). Oct. 8, 1960.

375. *The Modern Gift of Tongues* (German). Oct. 8, 1960.

376. *To: Dear Theta Chi Alumnus.* March 15, 1961, 1 p.

377. *Bricht Bluttransfusion Gottes Gesetz?* (No. 310 in German). May 6, 1961, 4 pp.

378. *Not Discerning the "Body" and Worshiping Demons.* July 21, 1961, 4 pp.

379. *Divine Providence.* Aug. 24, 1961, 2 pp.

380. *1962 Memorial Assembly Notes.* 1962, 8 pp.

381. *The Inspired Answer.* May 1962, 2 pp.

382. *Index* (page, date and vol. coordinator), June 1962, 1 p.

383. *Pastor Russell and the Ransom.* July 6, 1962, 4 pp.

384. *To Faith's "Endurers."* July 15, 1962, 4 pp.

385. *The Abomination of Desolation.* June 25, 1962, 16 pp.

386. *"I Morti Non Sanno Nulla."* July 1962, 4 pp. (Italian; Dead Know Not Anything).

387. *Spirito, Animo, E. Corpo.* N.d., 4 pp. (Italian; Spirit, Soul and Body).

388. *Retrenchment* (form letter). Sept. 22, 1962, 1 p.

389. (Form letter). Dec. 16, 1962, 1 p.

390. (Postcard for returned journals). Jan. 29, 1963, 1 p.

391. *Backwards, Turn Backward O Time.* Jan. 10, 1963, 1 p.

392. (Form letter for answering correspondence). Feb. 5, 1963, 1 p.

393. (Letter about Memorial Assembly). April 17, 1963, 1 p.

394. (Form letter, work on cottage). May 9, 1963, 1 p.

395. (Form letter, Mrs. Goodrich's driver's license, etc.). July 9, 1963, 1 p.

396. (Mrs. Goodrich's vacation, etc.). Aug. 25, 1963, 1 p.

397. (Program preview). March 1, 1964, 1 p.

398. *Memorial Assembly--Fort Lauderdale, Florida: Sunday April 26, Thru May 2, 1964.* April 1, 1964, 8 pp.

399. *A Bible Study Outline--Three Great Recent Advances in Bible Knowledge.* Feb. 22, 1965, 10 pp.

400. *A Christian's Attitude Toward War.* July 24, 1964, 2 pp.

401. *Hell, A Bible Teaching.* Oct. 1960, 4 pp.

402. *The Resurrection of Jesus Christ, When?* Oct. 1960, 4 pp.

403. *"The Dead Know Not Anything"--But "There Shall Be a Resurrection of the Dead."* Oct. 1960, 4 pp.

404. *"Spirit and Soul and Body."* Oct. 1960, 4 pp.

405. *Modern Gift of Tongues.* March 24, 1961, 4 pp.

406. *'Lord,' 'God,' 'Jesus,' and 'Christ.'* March 24, 1961, 4 pp.

407. *Ten Year Index to Back to the Bible Way.* N.d., 88 pp.

408. *The Oracle Which Habakkuk the Prophet Did See.* July, Aug., 1961, 4 pp.

409. *After 20 Years--Is This the New World?* (reprint of Dec. 1, 1944 issue). 6 pp.

410. *The ABCs of Bible Study: Primary Information--Knowledge the Youngest Need But Few of the Oldest Have* (enlarged and revised). April 8, 1963, 77 pp.

411. *The Symphony of "Parousia" and "Mello"* (typeset reprint of No. 355). Dec. 21, 1960, 5 pp.

412. *The Resurrection Appearances of Jesus Christ.* Dec. 21, 1960, 8 pp.

413. *The Great Counterfeit.* N.d., 34 pp.

414. *Welcome Jehovah's Witnesses by Mrs. Goodwill.* Aug. 5, 1963, 4 pp.

415. *Watchtower Witness Writes to Jehovah's Witnesses.* Sept. 10, 1963, 4 pp.

416. *Excommunication--1944 by the Watchtower; Vindication--1962 by the Watchtower.* Dec. 1964, 12 pp.

417. *In Trouble from Nuisance Witnesses Mary Seeks Help from Pearl.* July 1964, 4 pp.

418. *"Judge Not"* (disfellowshipping letter of Suresh Madoo). Aug. 12, 1964, 4 pp.

419. *The "False Anointed" "Prophets" and "The Harvest."* N.d., 24 pp.

420. *Christ-Mass, Commonly Called Christmas.* Dec. 1964, 24 pp.

421. *The Olivet Prophecy.* Dec. 1964, 40 pp.

422. *A Review of Otto Sadlack's Book.* May 25, 1964, 32 pp.

423. *The Nightmare* (double postcard). Aug. 7, 1965, 4 pp.

424. (Order blank postcard). Aug. 7, 1965, 2 pp.

425. (Exhortation letter). Aug. 7, 1965, 1 p.

426. *'Nightmare' and 'Sole Channel,'* Large. Oct. 2, 1965, 2 pp.

427. *What Has the Watchtower Kingdom Been Doing Since 1914?* Sept. 25, 1966, 8 pp.

428. (Postcard order). Dec. 23, 1966, 1 p.

429. *The Key to Studying the Bible: As Recommended in February 1st 1949 Watchtower.* Feb. 1969, 2 pp.

430. *Letter* (delaying Memorial date). March 17, 1969, 1 p.

431. *Invitation Card.* April 12, 1969, 2 pp.

432. (Correspondence letterhead explanation). July 10, 1969, 1 p.

433. (Form letter to Church of Christ for Jehovah's Witnesses' names). Sept. 5, 1969, 1 p.

434. *Three Historic Documents: Six Sermons: The Doctrine of Election; the "Seventh Sermon"* by George Storrs (reprint of 1847 ed.). Sept. 10, 1969, 100 pp.

435. *Letter to Interested Church of Christ Responders.* Sept. 27, 1969, 1 p.

436. *The Permission of Evil--Why?* June 26, 1972, 87 pp.

437. *Pergamos Means Watchtower.* June 30, 1972, 1 p.

438. *Back to the Bible Way: Seventeen-Year Index 1952 to 1967.* April 1971, 76 pp.

439. *Back to the Bible Way Index, Vol. 16 to Vol. 19.* Oct. 30, 1972, 3 pp.

440. *Who Is the Antichrist?* Aug. 20, 1974, 1 p.

441. *Rejoice!* March 6, 1975, 1 p.

442. *Olivet Prophecy.* March 20, 1975, 40 pp.

443. *"God's Organization"; J.F.R. Speaks Again; the Hierarchies Compared.*

444. *N.H. Knorr Speaks; Analyzing Yankee Stadium Speech on July 30, 1953.*

Tract

Salvation. N.d., 4 pp.

Magazine

Back to the Bible Way: A Journal of Faith, Love, Sincerity, and Present Truth. Vol. 1, No. 1, Jan. 1952 to Vol. 21, No. 23, Dec. 1973, Whole number, 1945.

J. General Bible Student Movement Publications

Most of these are independent groups or persons associated with the groups listed in the previous section. Most follow basic Russell teachings, and many feel they adhere more closely to Russell than do the larger Bible Student groups.

1. Associated Bible Students, Kearney, Neb.

Series of tracts called The Kingdom Herald, *No. 1 to ?*

One Race, One Color, One Language, One Nation, One Religion.

A Thousand Years of Peace! N.d., 4 pp.

Times and Seasons of the Bible.

Will Adam and Eve Be Resurrected? Does God Torture? 1000 Years of Resurrection and Judgment. Jesus Has Lived on Three Planes.

Series of tracts called Everybody's Paper, *No. 1 to ?*
(listed in order of publication)

Thousand-year Days.

World Distress Precedes Armageddon.

Palestine for the Jews.

After the War--What?

Armageddon Soon?

Series of tracts called The Truth Announcer, *No. 1 to ?*
  (listed in order of publication)
Prophetic Pictures of the Worldwide War.

Are Better Times Just Ahead? N.d., 2 pp.

*Good News--Glad Tidings of Great Joy Unto All People! Christ's
Kingdom on Earth Is Very Near!* N.d., 2 pp.

Miscellaneous tracts
"The Days Are at Hand." N.d., 2 pp. (reprinted from *Zion's
Watchtower and Herald of Christ's Presence*).

Israel Is Here to Stay. C. 1939, 6 pp.

"Love Not the World." N.d., 2 pp.

2. Associated Bible Students
(Waterbury, Conn.)

The Ecumenical Movement in God's Plan. N.d., 21 pp.

*A Helping Hand in the Study of "Tabernacle Shadows of Better
Sacrifices."* N.d., 223 pp.

Pastor Russell Not the Founder of "Jehovah's Witnesses."
Tustin, Cal., n.d., 2 pp.

Truth-Light. N.d., 2 pp.

Booklets
After the War--What?

The Bible Made Plain. N.d., 26 pp.

Distress of Nations Precedes Armageddon. N.d., 24 pp.

Do You Know? N.d., 12 pp.

Thousand-Year Days.

True or False?

3. Associated Bible Students
(Wilmington, Del.)

Booklet

The Kingdom of God. Wilmington, Del., n.d., 14 pp.

4. Associated Bible Students
(Paterson, N.J.)

Booklets

"The Divine Plan of the Ages Epitomized." 16 pp.

If You Are Gods. Paterson, N.J., n.d., 8 pp.

The Mystery Hid from the Ages. 4 pp.

Rawson, Kenneth. *The Association of Bible Students, Background, History, Organization, Ministry.* 24 pp.

————. *The Association of Bible Students, Its Historic Position Toward War.* 10 pp.

————. *The Time to Favor Zion Is Come.* 14 pp.

————. *Truth's Challenge.*

5. Berean Bible Students
(Vancouver, Wash.)

Books *(reprints of the Edgars' works)*

Edgar, John, and Morton Edgar. *Great Pyramid Passages* (a photolithographic reprint of the 1923 [Part 1, 409 pp.] and 1924 [Part 2, 1,310 pp.] eds. of *Great Pyramid Passages* and the 1924 ed. of *The Great Pyramid: Its Scientific Features*). 217 pp. Bound with *The Great Pyramid: Why Was It Built and Who Built It?* by Morton Edgar (reset). 38 pp. Republished in 1976 with publisher's foreword, hb.

Edgar, John; Morton Edgar; and Minna Edgar. *Faith's Foundations* (a reprint of John, Morton, and Minna Edgar's small
booklets; see Edgar's works for a complete list). Republished in 1976 with publisher's foreword; 372 pp.

6. Berean Bible Students
(New York)

*Bible Teachers' Manuals by Herbert N. Brissette (all pub-
lished in New York until June 1977 issue, published in Baldwin
Park, Cal.)*

The Kingdom Reign, Is IT "Now" or "Then"? Etc. Jan. 1961.

And They Murmured. Jan. 1963.

Stumbling-blocks as Stepping-stones. Jan. 1965.

Fact and Philosophy of Justification. Oct. 1965.

Volume Seven and That Servant. March 1966.

The Harvest Message in Conflict. Nov. 1966.

Three Typical Signs of His Parousia. Nov. 1967.

Random Key and the Harvest Message. June 1968.

Zion's Glad Morning Versus Her Night of Trial. Jan. 1969,
97 pp.

A Fountain by Drops from Beneath the Cross. June 1969.

The Peter-Class like Peter Sifted as Wheat. Jan. 1970.

The Way, the Truth and the Life. June 1970.

The Race, the Mark and the Prize. Jan. 1971.

Reaping All Day Were the Virgins Fair. June 1971, 81 pp.

Tabernacle Shadows of the Better Sacrifices. Jan. 1972,
87 pp.

The Ox and the Ass and My People Israel. June 1972, 92 pp.

The Faithful Grow from Strength to Strength. Jan. 1973, 95 pp.

Who May Know the Secrets of God. June 1973, 99 pp.

Type and Antitype of the Two Priesthoods. Jan. 1974, 73 pp.

"The Ministers of God in the Last Days." June 1974, 73 pp.

Harvest Work World-Wide International Bible Students Association in Review. Jan. 1976, 46 pp.

The Glorious Messiah and His Kingdom Reign. June 1976, 63 pp.

The Antitypical Vine and His Faithful Branches. June 1977, 42 pp.

The Mountain of God on Top of the Mountains. Jan. 1978, 21 pp.

Come Out of Her, My People Separate--Distinct. June 1978, 22 pp.

The Church of Christ: Her Scriptural Supremacy. Jan. 1979, 28 pp.

Tract

Do You Know? N.d., 4 pp.

7. Bible Students Newsletter
(Columbus, Ohio)

Booklet

Directory [of] Bible Students' Ecclesia Meetings, June 1979. Centerville, Ohio, 1979, 28 pp.

Newsletter

Bible Students Newsletter. Vol. 1, No. 1, 1972 to date, published quarterly in March, June, Sept. and Dec.

8. Bible Students Publications
(Bensenville, Ill.)

Tracts

And the Desert Shall Blossom.

Can We as Saved-Christians Lose Our Salvation?

God Has a Plan and You Are in It.

God's Plan for Man.

The Great Pyramid and the Bible.

The Great Pyramid of Gizeh.

Have You Ever Wondered?

If You Are God's.

Israel: Born to Destiny.

The Lord Is Present Now!

A Man Wonders about Many Things, But Can He Find Answers?

Booklets

... For This Cause. C. 1979, 47 pp.

9. Chicago Bible Students
(Chicago)

The most active publishers are the Chicago Bible Students. They have established a book republishing committee that is actively reprinting all of Russell's works (as noted above).

The Chicago group has been most creative and diverse in its own publications, while still relying heavily on Russell. In addition to a number of attractive tracts, they have published such things as *Time Is at Hand*, a pocket-purse calendar booklet and *Food for Thinking Christians*, not to be confused with Russell's work by the same name.

Magazine

The Harvest Youth (now *Harvest Youth News*). Vol. 1, No. 1,
    1960 to date.

Booklets

Comfort & Consolation. N.d., 28 pp.

"Exceeding Great and Precious Promises." 1954, 96 pp. A collection of writings from the early *Watchtowers*, *Studies in the Scriptures* (Vols. 1, 5, 6), and *Tabernacle Shadows*.

Excerpts from the Divine Plan of the Ages. N.d., 16 pp.

In the Beginning God.... N.d., 8 pp.

Rejoice, O Israel! N.d., 15 pp.

This Land Is Mine! N.d., 16 pp. About Israel, ancient and modern.

Where Are the Dead? (reprint of original written in 1900, with footnotes added). N.d., 108 pp. Reprinted later with different cover and slightly larger.

Tracts

Christianity, Conflict & Crisis. 1967, 7 pp.

The Days of Noah. N.d.

The Divine Plan of the Ages. N.d., 4 pp.

Food for Thinking Christians. N.d., 4 pp.

Food for Thinking Christians. N.d., 8 pp. This tract contains excerpts from the book *The Divine Plan of the Ages.*

God's Plan for Man. N.d.

Scientific, Historic and Prophetic Facts about the Great Pyramid of Gizeh. N.d.

Why Have Jews Been Persecuted? N.d., 3 pp.

Books

Bible Students Manual. Reprinted from original 1909 Edition.

Convention Report Sermons: Pastor Russell's Convention Discourses. C. 1970, 515 pp. A collection of sermons, testimony, meetings, and special services by Pastor Charles T. Russell as found in the "Convention Reports" from 1906 to 1916, plus press coverage of the various conventions, interviews with Pastor Russell, and an exhaustive account of his 1912 world missionary tour.

Daily Heavenly Manna. N.d., c. 208 pp. Contains the text of the original 1905 ed., *Watchtower* comments, but not the birthday record.

Harvest Gleanings. Vol. 1, c. 1979, 780 pp. A collection of Charles T. Russell's writings which have been reset and with a Scripture Index added. The works included in this volume are *The Three Worlds*, *The Russell vs. Eaton Debates*, *The Russell vs. White Debates*, *Old Theology Quarterly Tracts*, and *Bible Students Monthly Tracts*.

Pastor Russell's Sermons (reprint of 100,000 ed. 1917). 803 pp.

Photodrama of Creation. 1976 (reset, minor corrections, and new illustrations; originally published in 1914 by WtBTS), 110 pp., hb., pb.

Reprints of the Original Watchtower and Herald of Christ's Presence. Vol. 1, 1879-1887, pp. 1-996; Vol. 2, 1888-1895; Vol. 3, 1896-1901; Vol. 4, 1902-1906, pp. 2,929-3,912, Vol. 5, 1907-1911, Vol. 6, 1912-1916; Index (also republished loose-leaf, and also bound in a 12-volume ed. These reprints are reprints of the original *Watchtower* reprints.

What Pastor Russell Said (reprint of 1917 ed., edited by L.W. Jones). 894 pp., hb.

What Pastor Russell Taught on the Covenants, Mediator, Ransom, Sin Offering, Atonement (reprint of 1919 ed., edited by Leslie W. Jones). 398 pp., hb.

What Pastor Russell Wrote for the Overland Monthly. 456 pp., hb. Also includes table of contents, scriptural index, and consecutive pagination.

Original Publications (Books)

Book Republishing Committee. *Expanded Biblical Comments 1879-1916 Old Testament*. 1982, 402 pp. An index of all of Russell's commentary listed by Scripture; producing an extensive Bible commentary taken from Russell's published works similar to *The Bible Students Manual*. As Russell was the editor, this index includes all unsigned articles and those by other writers that he used in his publications; the Committee felt that if Russell printed something, he agreed with it.

————. *Expanded Biblical Comments 1879-1916, New Testament*. Same as above, except on the New Testament, which the Committee expects to be complete by 1985.

Poole, Laura K. *The Ten Camels*. 1955, 144 pp. The Divine Plan presented in language for children six to ten years of age.

————. *The Son of the Highest.* C. 1965, 384 pp.

Stracy, Phyllis. *Gems from the Mine.* C. 1979, 698 pp.

————. *Songs of the Night.*

10. Christian Bible Students
(Warren, Mich.). Similar to Dawn.
The group disbanded in 1978.

Magazine

Harvest Message "A Herald of Christ's Presence." Monthly, about 36 pp.

Tracts

The Way, the Truth, and the Life. N.d., 4 pp.

The Late News: Is Jesus Coming Soon? N.d., 4 pp.

11. Detroit Bible Students
(Detroit, Mich.)

Tract

Food for Thinking Jehovah's Witnesses. Detroit, Mich.: Zion's Tower of the Morning Tract Publications, n.d., 4 pp.

Booklets

Satan's Occult Kingdom. N.d., 16 pp.

This Thing Is from Me. Detroit, Mich.: Zion's Tower of the Morning Publications, n.d., 8 pp.

12. Fort Worth Bible Students
(Fort Worth, Texas)
(all by Charles T. Russell [all reprints])

The Bible versus the Evolution Theory. Photolithographic reprint of 1912 ed., reprinted 1973, 47 pp.

The Divine Plan of the Ages. Reprinted, reset, from an early 1900 ed., c. 1973, 88 pp.

A Ray of Hope on a Troubled Sea. N.d., 10 pp. The contents are selected from Pastor Russell's writings as a consolation message.

Our Lord's Return: His Parousia, Apokalupsis and Epiphania. Photolithographic reprint of 1900 ed.; also reprinted with author's foreword from the book *The Time Is at Hand* (1916), reprinted 1972, 73 pp.

Studies in the Scriptures. Photolithographic reprint, 1970, 800 pp. The six volumes and *Tabernacle Shadows* are bound in one volume.

What Say the Scriptures about Spiritism? Photolithographic reprint of 1897 ed., reprinted 1972, 119 pp.

What Say the Scriptures Concerning Hell? Reprinted, reset; from 1900 ed., c. 1973, 23 pp., pb.

Other Tract

The Divine Plan for Human Salvation: Why Evil Was Permitted. N.d., 9 pp.

13. Jewish Bible Students

Since Pastor Russell's positive response to Zionism shortly after the turn of the century, various Bible Students have felt a need for special work with Jews. A few worked toward conversion, but most simply gave their support to Zionism.

Magazines

Jews in the News. Grand Rapids, Mich., Vol. 1, No. 1, 1942. In 1968 moved to Paradise, Cal., and changed its name to *Israel Restoration News.*

Israel Digest. Published in Jerusalem.

Book

Ben-Hanan, Shelam. *This Is the Millennium.* 96 pp.

14. New Albany Bible Students
(New Albany, Ind.)

Booklet

"*What on Earth Is a Kingdom?*" 1982, 24 pp. A well-illustra-
ted, introduction to *The Divine Plan*; mostly pictures.

15. New Brunswick Bible Students
(Edison, N.J.) (also called the
Associated Bible Students)

Booklets

Glossolalia (Tongues-Speaking); What Are Its Implications?
N.d., 39 pp.

What Is This World Coming To? N.d., 39 pp.

Where Are the Dead? N.d., 108 pp.

Rawson, Kenneth. *The Time to Favor Zion Is Come!* 1971,
31 pp.

Tracts

For Me to Live Is Christ.

If You Are God's. Paterson, N.J., n.d., 8 pp.

The Lord Is Present ... Now! N.d., 8 pp.

Books

Reprints of *Studies in the Scriptures* (by C.T. Russell).
All are reset.
  Vol. I. *The Divine Plan of the Ages.* Reprinted in 1975
  with new preface, 356 pp., hb., pb.
  Vol. II. *The Time Is at Hand.* Reprinted in 1977, 371 pp.
  hb.
  Vol. III. *Thy Kingdom Come.* Reprinted in 1977, 380 pp.,
  hb.
  Vol. IV. *The Battle of Armageddon.* Reprinted in 1978,
  661 pp., hb.
  Vol. V. *At-One-Ment Between God and Man.* Reprinted in
  1977, 499 pp., hb.
  Vol. VI. *The New Creation.* Reprinted in 1978, 738 pp.

16. Ohio Bible Students
(Columbus, Ohio)

Tracts

And the Desert Shall Blossom. N.d.

"Israel!--Born to Destiny." N.d.

The Day of Judgment. N.d., 3 pp.

The Great Pyramid and the Bible. N.d.

The Lord Is Present Now! N.d., 8 pp.

A Man Wonders about Many Things, But Can He Find Answers?
N.d.

17. The Pastor Russell Memorial Association

The Pastor Russell Memorial Association of San Francisco
was founded by Guy Bolger, who parted with Rutherford shortly
after Russell's death.

Magazine

Berean Bible Student. Ed. Guy Bolger. 8 pp., monthly (ended
in 1940).

Book

Berean Poems. San Francisco, Cal., 1941, 56 pp.

18. San Diego Bible Students
(San Diego, Cal.)

Tracts (Millennial Morning series, listed in series order)

1. *Israel.* N.d., 4 pp.

2. *Baptism--What's It All About?* N.d., 4 pp.

3. *God's Creative Work-Week.* N.d., 4 pp.

4. *Are You Ready for the Judgement Day?* N.d., 4 pp.

5. *Why Does God Permit Evil?* N.d., 4 pp.

6. *The Living and True God.* N.d., 4 pp.

7. *If This Is Morning, When Will Day Break?* N.d., 4 pp.

8. *Christ Isn't Coming Soon. He's Present.* N.d., 4 pp.

9. *The Return of Elijah.* N.d., 4 pp.

10. *Caution: Glossolalia.* N.d., 4 pp.

11. *The New Day Dawns. Good Morning.* N.d., 4 pp.

12. *"If We Kill Men...."* N.d., 4 pp.

13. *Who Is Millennial Morning?* N.d., 4 pp.

14. *Where Are the Dead?* N.d., 4 pp.

15. *If I Were Elected....* N.d., 4 pp.

16. *Ye Were Bought for a Price.* N.d., 4 pp.

17. *"Is There No End...."* N.d., 4 pp.

18. *If It's Morning, Why Is Everything So Dark? Because It's Morning.* N.d., 4 pp.

19. *A Clamor for Rights--Step 1.* N.d., 4 pp.

20. *If It's Morning, Why Is Everything So Dark? Because It's Morning.* Vol. 3, No. 5, n.d., 4 pp. (same as Tract No. 18 above).

21. *Once Saved, Always Saved?* Vol. 3, No. 6, n.d., 4 pp.

22. *Father = Son = Holy Spirit or Father ≠ Son ≠ Holy Spirit.* Vol. 3, No. 7, n.d., 4 pp.

23. *Everyone's Baby.* Vol. 3, No. 8, n.d., 4 pp.

24. *The Hidden Mystery.* Vol. 3, No. 14, n.d., 4 pp.

25. *Christ Isn't Coming Soon. He's Present.* Vol. 3, No. 15, n.d., 4 pp. (same as Tract No. 8 above).

Other Tracts

The Healing Sun. N.d., 4 pp.

"The Lord Shall Be King Over All the Earth." N.d., 4 pp.

Booklets

The Manner of Christ's Return and Appearing. N.d., 59 pp.

K. Bible Student Literature by Individuals
(both books and booklets)

Charles Taze Russell 1852-1916. N.d., 1916.

The Church of the Living God (by C.T. Russell). 36 pp.

The Divine Plan of the Ages Epitomized. N.d., 16 pp.

The Time to Favor Zion Is Come. N.d., 14 pp.

Berean Questions: The Atonement Between God and Man. N.d.,
70 pp.

God's Best Gift. Chicago: Sacred Lyceum, 1927, 30 pp.

Millions Now Living Will Never Die! Brooklyn: International
Bible Students Association, n.d., 128 pp. Reprinted privately from original.

Berean Bible Student. "That Faithful and Wise Servant." San
Francisco, Cal., 18 pp.

Bible Research Council. The Time of the End. Manitoba, Canada,
84 pp.

Bible Student's Association. If Jesus Had Not Been Born.
Petersham, New South Wales.

Bible Students Council. God's Plan for Human Redemption.
Cheshire, B.S.C.

Black, Margaret Harris. Paradise in Eden--How Lost and How
Redeemed. San Antonio, Texas: Naylor Company, 3rd ed.,
1963, 109 pp.

Bricker, R.H., and Samuel McComb. *Who Is That Wise and Faithful Steward?* Pittsburgh, Pa., n.d., 29 pp.

Bundy, Walter H. *Evil, Its Origin, Purpose and End.* Los Angeles, Cal.: Concordant Pub. Concern.

————. *Paul's Inspired Letter to the Romans.*

————. *The Sacred Scrolls of the Scriptures.*

————. *Studies in the Scriptures, Investigating Bible Statements Analytically.* Los Angeles, Cal.: Concordant Pub. Concern, c. 1928, 160 pp.

Bunker, Laurence H. *The Book and the Chosen People.* London, England: Chosen Books.

Carrington, Arthur. *Bible Versus Bank Rate.* Leeds, England: pub. by author, 1969, 4 pp.

————. *God and the Common Market.* Great Britain: John H. Hirst & Co., n.d., 8 pp.

————. *Is God Helping Israel?* 1967, 4 pp.

————. *Perfecting Holiness in the Fear of God.* Great Britain: Headley Brothers, Ltd., n.d., 8 pp.

Christian Bible Students. *Briefly We Believe.* N.d., 8 pp.

————. *Come Now, and Let Us Reason Together: Saith the Lord.* N.d., 8 pp.

————. *Have You Made Your Choice?* N.d., 4 pp.

————. *Is Hell a Bible Teaching?* 4 pp.

————. *Overwhelmed.* N.d., 1 p.

————. *Souvenir Notes from the Reunion Convention of Christian Bible Students.* 1929, 122 pp.

Christian Fellowship. *Christ's Second Coming "The Hope of the World."* Manchester, England.

Coshocton Ecclesia. *Timely Excerpts from the Harvest Message.* Coshocton, Ohio, n.d., 124 pp., pb.

Cupertino Ecclesia. *Hope of the World*. Cupertino, Cal., n.d.

Eddington, W. Clark. *A Letter to the Watford International Bible Student Association Class*. April 13, 1916.

Falkner, Carl G. *A Review, God's Wisdom versus Man's Wisdom*. Christian Fellowship Associates, Ohio, Jan. 1968.

Flood, Robert L. *Our Lord's Second Coming--Return to Earth Due for Our Time*. Roseville, Mich., 1962.

Frey, Richard. *Tabernacle Notes*.

Gaunt, Bonnie. *Stonehenge ... A Closer Look*. Ann Arbor, Mich.: Braun-Brumfield, 1979, 222 pp. Reprinted with corrections by Bell Publishing Co., New York, 1982.

Gilbert, J.W. *In God's Own Words: A Useful Handbook for a Subject Study of the Bible*. Philadelphia, Pa.: pub. by author, n.d., 36 pp.

Gray, Julian T. *The Authorship and Message of the Great Pyramid*. Cincinnati, Ohio: E. Steinman and Co., 1953, 306 pp.

————. *The Year 1958 A.D. in Prophecy*. Claremont, Cal.: the author, 1969, 8 pp.

————. *The Ark of the Testimony--A Treasure--Love of Truth*. Claremont, Cal.: the author, 1968, 4 pp.

————. *The Creation of the Universe in Six Days*. 1968, 4 pp.

————. *A Great Biblical Prophecy and Its Hidden Message*. 1964, 4 pp.

————. *The Handwriting on the Wall--Its Hidden Meaning*. 1968, 2 pp.

————. *The Harmony of the Ages*. 1968, 4 pp.

————. *The Precious Vessels That Were Brought Back from Babylon; Their Number and Remarkable Significance (Ezra 1:7-11)*. 1964, 4 pp.

————. *The Rites of Atonement Performed by the High Priest of Israel on the Day of Atonement--Type and Antitype*. 1969, 8 pp.

————. *The Universe--A Witness to Jehovah and His Plan (I).* N.d., 4 pp.

————. *The Universe--A Witness to Jehovah and His Plan (II).* 1967, 2 pp.

————. *Which Is the True Chronology?* Cincinnati, Ohio, 1934, 154 pp., hb.

Greaves, Arnold E. *Are Wars to Cease on Earth?* Brooklyn, N.Y., 1965, 14 pp.

————. *"That Servant."* New York, 1932, 22 pp.

Harris, C.J. *When Will Wars, Sickness, Pain and Death Cease?* Vancouver, B.C., Canada: pub. by author, n.d., 28 pp.

Harry, C. *Justification to Life, When? and How?* Brooklyn, N.Y., n.d., 16 pp.

Holliday, J. *Both Sides of the Veil.* Outline of a talk, Oct. 1966.

Hollister, Horace Edward. *After Thirty Years Pastor Russell Answers 20 Up-to-Date Questions on the Chronology.* Chicago: The Society for Bible Research.

————. *"I Will Come Again"--Jesus? The Five Successive Phases of the Advent.* Chicago: The Society for Bible Research, 1950, 95 pp.

————. *The Chronology and Time-Prophecies and the Bible.* 400 pp.

Hollister, R. Robert. *Meet Our British Brethren.*

Hollister, W.J. *Notes on the Book of Revelation.* Unpub. dupl. notes.

Horwood, Andrew. *Alleluia.*

————. *Bridal Anthem.*

————. *How Pastor Russell Viewed Justification.* Unpub. dupl. notes.

————. *The Revelation.* St. John's Newfoundland, Canada: unpub. dupl. notes, 1973, 41 pp.

Hudgings, Franklyn. Zionism in Prophecy. Unpub. dupl. notes.

Jones, Dr. L.W. Souvenir Notes from Reunion Convention of
Christian Bible Students. Pittsburgh, Pa., 1929.

————. Transcontinental Tour of Pastor Russell.

————. The Jubilee System of Volume Two of Studies in the
Scriptures. Unpub. dupl. notes, c. 1953.

Kuehm, J.G. A Voice from Switzerland. 1932, 94 pp. This is
a translation of Das Tier, a book on Revelation 13 and 17
by Werner Hodler, a Swiss Bible Student.

Kuehn, Hugo F. The Coming of the Lord Draweth Near. Pub. by
author, West Virginia booklet, 32 pp.

Lenfest, Edna T. A Helping Hand for Bible Students.

————. Brief General Monograph of the Prophecies. N.d.,
9 pp. (booklet).

————. Charles Taze Russell 1852-1916. N.d., 8 pp. (booklet).

————. Ezekiel. Acton, Maine, 1965, 142 pp.

————. Fellows of the Order of Royal Priesthood. N.d.,
68 pp. (booklet).

————. God Through Isaiah Speaks to Israel. 1976, 329 pp.

————. Hail to the Brightness of Zion's Glad Morning. N.d.,
12 pp. (booklet).

————. Jeremiah. 1967, 278 pp.

————. Outlines of Bible Chronology. 4 pp. (leaflet).

————. Proofs and Evidences of Messiah's Second Presence.
51 pp.

————. Revelation for the End of the Gospel Age. Sanford,
Maine, 132 pp.

————. The Minor Prophets: Hosea to Malachi. 1967, 290 pp.,
pb. (book).

Livermore. Revelation of John (From the Sinaitic M.S.). Unpub.
dupl. notes, n.d., 15 pp.

Loomis. *Revelation Notes.* Unpub. dupl. notes, n.d.

Maranatha. *The Middle East in Bible Prophecy.* London, B.C.M. (unpub. dupl. notes).

Meggison, J.A. *Echoes of Brother Barton's Discourses.*

————. *Meggison Notes: Genesis-Malachi.*

————. *Notes on Ezekiel's Temple.*

————. *A Search for the Role of the Christian in the Day of Wrath.*

————. *The Song of Solomon.*

————. *Studies in the Book of Hebrews.*

Mitchell, Martin C. *Little Foxes Coloring Book.* Rutherford, N.J., 1965, 44 pp.

————. *Poems of the Way.* Rutherford, N.J., c. 1975, 192 pp. A book of poems, many reprinted from early *Watchtower* literature, especially *Poems of Dawn.*

Moore, John H. *The Day of Vengeance.* Vancouver, B.C., Canada, 59 pp.

————. *Elias Shall First Come.* N.d., 32 pp.

————. *Israel, Type and Antitype.* N.d., 32 pp.

————. *Jerusalem of the New Testament.* Vancouver, B.C., Canada, 1967, 30 pp.

————. *The New Covenant--Made with Whom?* Vancouver, B.C., Canada, 1968, 28 pp.

————. *"Some Questions for Bible Students."* 3 pp.

————. *To the Jew First, Will It Always Be So?* 1966, 28 pp.

————. *Which Things Are an Allegory?* 1967, 30 pp.

New York City Ecclesia. *An Open Letter to the People of the Lord Throughout the World.* 1917.

————. *A Petition to Brother Rutherford and the Four Deposed Directors of the Watch Tower Bible and Tract Society.* 1917.

North London Ecclesia. *Elias Shall First Come.* N.d., 24 pp.

————. *Report of the Broadway Hall Convention.* Dec. 26, 1916.

Norwood, H. Dorothy. *The Bible Tells It Like It Is: The Imminent Fifth Universal Empire.* New York: Vantage Press, 1972, 153 pp.

Olson, Carl W. *The World to Come, A Dissertation on the Divine Plan of God as Found in the Bible.* Minneapolis, Minn.

Ott, Leslie A. *Revelation of the Apostle John.*

Panin, Ivan. *Biblical Chronology.* In two volumes. 328 pp., 1920? Panin was not a Bible Student. An often used supplementary text, mentioned by Paul Johnson in *The Present Truth*, Sept. 1, 1924 (p. 140) and recently reprinted by Canadian Bible Students.

————; A.B. King; et al. *Ivan Panin's Scientific Demonstration of the Inspiration of the Scriptures.* Revised ed. Toronto, n.p., 1924.

Parkinson, James B. *Bible Consistent Chronology.* Mimeo by author, n.d., 5 pp. A listing of the chronology of various Biblical events.

————. *Bible Student Fragments.* N.d., 32 pp.

————. *The Bible Student Movement in the Days of C.T. Russell.* Los Angeles, Cal.: the author, 1965, 72 pp.

————. *Chapters of History.* Mimeo by author, n.d., 10 pp. Discusses the last-day prophecies found in Daniel and Revelation.

————. *Christian Memorial Dates.* Ditto, 10 pp.

————. *Chronological Studies.* Ditto, Los Angeles, Cal., 1963, 10 pp.

————. *Excerpts from Nigerian Correspondence.* Mimeo by author, 1976, 3 pp. Excerpts of letters from Nigeria.

————. *New Testament Manuscript and Translation Studies.* Mimeo, Los Angeles, Cal., 1969, 9 pp.

————. *New Testament Manuscript and Translation Studies.*
Los Angeles, Cal., 1970, 31 pp.

————. *On Resolving the Chronological Problem, I Kings 6:
and Acts 13:19-20.* Mimeo by author, n.d., 5 pp. Discusses
various problems in chronology.

Phoenixville Bible Students. *Facts About the Trinity.* N.d.,
5 pp.

————. *The Lord Our God Is One Lord.* Kimberton, Pa., n.d.,
39 pp.

Pollock, Russell G. *The Jubilee Years.* Unpub. dupl. notes
(see also Prosser below).

Poole, Herbert, and Laura Kathleen Poole. *Palestine--Israel's
Inheritance.*

Prosser, C.E. *Interesting Data on Biblical Subjects.* Los
Gatos, Cal.: pub. by author, n.d., 30 pp.

Sadlack, Otto. *End and Transformation of the Present Evil
World.* 1969.

Sargeant, W. *Liberty in Christ.* Reprint of a talk given
Jan. 29, 1939. 15 pp.

Schroeder, Charles, comp. *Harvest Time and Harvest Work.*
Chicago: mimeo, 1920, 10 pp.

Scripture Study Publishing House. *Sunrise: The Scheme Scripture.* Manchester, England, 1918.

Shallieu, Frank. *God, Angels, and Men.* Southfield, Mich.:
C.L. Thornton, n.d., 69 pp.

Shearn, H.J. *A Review of the Doctrines.* Letchworth, Herts.,
England.

Smith, Wilber M. *Egypt in Biblical Prophecies.* Boston, Mass.:
W.A. Wilde Co., 1957.

Sunbom, Chester A. *Trumpets and Seals of Revelation.* Unpub.,
22 pp.

————. *Notes on the Beast and His Image.* 38 pp.

————. *Baptism.* Unpub. dupl. notes.

Towell, Herbert. *The Book of Revelation.* London, England, 1918.

Transcript of Meeting Held in Chicago. Aug. 1966. Unpub. dupl. notes.

T.S. *The Revelation.* Patmos Yeovil, 1942.

Welch, Edgar, and Gladys Welch. *Ending the Confusion.* Vista, Cal.: New View Publishers, 1976, 292 pp.

West, Wickham. *Private Circulation Sheets.* 1958–1965.

Wiley, C.W. *Blessed Is That Servant!* N.d., 6 pp.

Young, J.W. *The Time of the End.* Winnipeg, Manitoba, Canada: Bible Research Council, n.d., 83 pp., pb.

SECTION FIVE

NON-AMERICAN BIBLE STUDENT GROUPS

I. BRITISH GROUPS

A. Bible Fellowship Union

As in America, in Britain a committee was formed after Pastor Russell's death by H.J. Shearn to carry on work outside of the Watchtower Society. A group of seven formed the Bible Students Committee. This group soon developed friendly relations with the Pastoral Bible Institute and they exchanged publications. Later they changed their name to the Bible Fellowship Union.

The Bible Students Committee in Britain produced the following publications:

Book

Barton, B.H. *God's Covenants*. London, England: Bible Students Committee, c. 1912, 48 pp.

Booklets

Beauty of Holiness. 60 pp.

Parables of the Kingdom. 30 pp.

Promise of His Presence.

The modern group was founded in 1945 to propagate Bible study and especially matters connected with the pre-Millennial advent of Christ and the doctrine of future probation relative to the Millennial reign of Christ. Other goals include the upholding of the historical accuracy of the Bible and investigating matters of history, archaeology, prophecy, etc., as related to the Bible teaching.

At the inception of the Bible Fellowship Union, the magazine *Bible Study Monthly*, founded in 1924, which otherwise
would have ceased publication, was made its chief vehicle.

The Bible Fellowship Union is not organically connected
with any other Christian group or denomination. The group
is headed today by A.O. Hudson who was born around 1890 and
is considered by many the best scholar in the Bible Student
movement, along with P.L. Reed. Hudson writes extensively
not only about Biblical doctrine but also about archaeology,
history, Biblical languages, and science and the Bible. The
circulation of *The Bible Student Monthly* is about 500 copies
per issue in Great Britain, and about the same in America.

Booklets (all published in Hounslow, Middlesex, England)

God's Fulfilling Purpose, An Outline of the Divine Plan.
N.d., 20 pp.

In the Land of Beginning Again. N.d., 22 pp. Four stories
of the Resurrection and the Millennial world.

Jacob's Trouble. 1st ed. 1942; 2nd ed., revised in 1968,
32 pp.

Holmes, T. *From a Prison Cell.* 1969, 40 pp. Reflections on
the prison epistles of Paul.

Hudson, Albert O. *Future Probation in Christian Belief.*
1975, 88 pp.

————. *The Christian Doctrine of Baptism.* 1964, 32 pp.

————. *The Coming of the King.* 1968, 64 pp.

————. *The Cup of Our Lord.* 16 pp. About Christ's passion.

————. *God of All Space.* 1971, 48 pp. The impact of space
science on Christian belief.

————. *The Golden Future.* 1st ed. 1939; 4th ed. 1970,
36 pp. Study of the future as discussed in the Bible.

————. *The Millennial Gospel of Jesus.* 1st ed. 1947; 2nd
ed. 1974, 32 pp. A study of the New Testament on the Millennium.

————. *The Mission of Jonah.* 1st ed. 1946, 2nd ed. 1970,
80 pp.

————. *Obadiah, the Messenger of Judgment.* 1965, 52 pp. An exposition of the prophecy of Obadiah.

————. *Samuel--Greatest of the Judges.* 1975, 38 pp.

————. *Sixteen Scriptural Truths.* N.d., 30 pp.

————. *The Spirit of Prophecy.* 1965, 52 pp. The nature of Biblical prophecy and the principles of its interpretation.

————. *The Tower of Babel.* 1962, 52 pp. The history of the tower of Babel.

————. *The Tragedy of Samson.* 1960, 52 pp.

————. *The Virgin Birth of Christ.* 1972, 24 pp.

————. *Watcher in Gethsemane.* 1969, 16 pp. About Christ in Gethsemane.

Nadal, D. *Shepherd of Salvation.* 1967, 24 pp. An exposition of Gog and Magog chapters in Ezek. 38-39.

Booklets, Numbered Set

No. 31. *The Bible--the Book for Today.* N.d., 11 pp.

No. 32. *World Conversion--When?* N.d., 15 pp.

No. 33. *The Divine Permission of Evil.* N.d., 11 pp.

No. 34. *Everlasting Punishment of Evil.* N.d., 11 pp.

No. 35. *Conversion in the After-life.* N.d., 15 pp.

No. 36. *The Resurrection of the Dead.* N.d., 15 pp.

No. 37. *The Second Advent--Its Nature and Purpose.* N.d., 15 pp.

No. 38. *The Call and Destiny of Israel.* N.d., 15 pp.

No. 39. *The Personality of the Devil.* N.d., 11 pp.

No. 40. *The Gifts of the Spirit.* N.d., 12 pp.

No. 41. *Man--The Image of God.* N.d., 12 pp.

No. 153. *The Call and Purpose of the Church.* N.d., 4 pp.

No. 154. *The Antiquity of the Books of Moses.* N.d., 4 pp.

Magazines

Bible Study Monthly. Ed. A.O. Hudson. Vol. 1, No. 1, Jan.
1924 to date (Vol. 58, No. 6, Nov.-Dec. 1981). 24 pp. each
issue. *The Bible Students Committee Monthly* was begun in
1924, changed to *Bible Students Monthly* in 1927 and later to
Bible Study Monthly (a bi-monthly at present).

Bible Students Broadsheet. Nos. 1, 2, 3, 4. March 1965,
1966, 1967, 1968.

B. New Jerusalem Fellowship
(Ormskirk, Lancs., England)

The New Jerusalem Fellowship is the name of a very loose
group of the Bible Students united by the writings of Dr. F.S.
Edgell, one of the members of the original Bible Students Committee. During World War I he began circulating a mimeographed newsletter at irregular intervals. In 1922, this
then-unnamed periodical was given the name *Fellowship*, later
changed to *New Jerusalem Fellowship*. Most of Dr. Edgell's
works appeared in the magazine.

The New Jerusalem Fellowship is now headed by E.T. Springett
Moxham, who was acquainted with the founder, Dr. Edgell, in
the early 1940s. They worked together until Dr. Edgell's
death in the early 1950s. Dr. Edgell was also well acquainted
with Charles Russell and obviously much influenced by him.

The fellowship stresses "freedom from all parties, sects,
and creeds," and "the man Jesus Christ who gave himself a
ransom for all." The book-length works listed below explain
the particular message of the New Jerusalem Fellowship, which
could be labeled a variety of Anglo-Israelism.

Magazine

New Jerusalem Fellowship: The Church Without Walls. Ed. E.T.
Springett Moxham. Vol. 1, No. 1, 1922 to date, published
monthly, each 14 pp. The forerunner of this magazine was
started in 1914 and was mimeographed and stapled.

Booklets, Books

Edgell, F.B. *Correspondence with Charles Taze Russell and
Others, 1902-1937.* 1938.

————. *A Nation's Inheritance.* 1938; 2nd ed. 1960, 48 pp.

————. *Man's Destiny.* 1946, 200 pp.

————. *Tabernacle Types.* 1952, 36 pp.

————. *Man's Dilemma.* 1961, 68 pp.

C. Old Paths Publications
(Ilford, England)

This group is directed by William Crawford, who was strict in regard to doctrine and felt the harvest was essentially over. He created the first split in the Bible Students Committee (he was one of the original seven) in 1925 and began to publish his views in a series of pamphlets. There were two series: (1) an unnumbered and undated series and (2) a numbered series that evolved into a monthly magazine. This second series began in 1932 and continued until 1961. A polemic against Crawford is found in Paul S.L. Johnson's *Gershonism* (published by the Laymen's Home Missionary Movement). Crawford died in 1948.

Magazine

Old Paths. Ed. William Crawford until his death in 1948. Published 1932 to 1961.

Books (probably by Crawford)

Symbols of Revelation: Their Interpretation. 1953, 131 pp.

Old Paths Publications: Part I. N.d., bound copy of "The End of All Things," 48 pp.; "Supplement," 28 pp.; "Sealing the Servants of God," 28 pp.; "War in Heaven," 72 pp.; and "Thy God Reigneth!," 40 pp.; total of 216 pp.

Booklets (mostly by Crawford and listed in publication order)

Thy God Reigneth! N.d., 40 pp.

Justification by Faith. N.d.

The Three Great Covenants. N.d.

The Ransom and Sin-Offering. N.d.

The Midnight Cry. N.d.

Watchman, What of the Night? N.d.

The Unsearchable Riches of Christ. N.d., 48 pp.

The End of All Things. N.d.

The End of All Things. N.d. (supplement).

Sealing the Servants of God. N.d.

The New Covenant in the Book of Hebrews. N.d.

War in Heaven. N.d.

Thy God Reigneth. N.d.

Gleanings in Revelation I. 1944, 94 pp.

Gleanings in Revelation II. 1948, 152 pp.

Israel's Tabernacle: Shadow and Substance. 1951, 52 pp.

Booklets *(undated but numbered; listed in publication order)*
1. *Day of Atonement--Type and Antitype.*

2. *Justification and Consecration--Their Order.*

3. *The Saints in Glory--Who Are They?*

4. *Millions Who Will Never Die. Why?*

5. *The Harvest, When and What For?*

6. *The Kingdom Witness, What and When?*

7. *The "Channel" Doctrine Examined.*

8. *Sound Doctrine.*

9. *This He Did Once--When and How?*

10. *Strong Delusions. Why Permitted?*

11. *The Ransom for All--Scripturally Defined.*

12. *Tabernacle Figures Explained.*

13. *Things You Should Know.*

14. *Lamps That Are Going Out.*

15. *Three Views of Atonement.*

16. *Back to Babylon.*

17. *The Time of Harvest.*

18. *The Work of Harvest.*

19. *The Harvest Home.*

20. *The Winter Time.*

21. *Questions on Justification.*

22. *Questions on the Covenants.*

23. *Questions on the Ransom.*

24. *False Christs and False Prophets.*

25. *Within the Holy Place.*

26. *The Work of God Today.*

27. *Our Gathering Unto Him.*

28. *Ye Must Be Born Again.*

29. *The Witness Work.*

30. *Steadfast in the Faith.*

31. *War in Heaven--A Criticism Examined.*

32. *The Greater and More Perfect Tabernacle.*

33. *Who Is the Man Child?*

After pamphlet number 33, the *Old Paths Publications* series of booklets had evolved into a monthly periodical which continued numbering from the above pamphlets, ultimately producing over 350 issues. Issue 345-347 was a large pamphlet entitled *The Light of Life.* No new material was produced after 1956. Issues after this date were reprints of significant earlier works.

D. Forest Gate Church
(London, England)

At the time of Russell's death, the Forest Gate Church
was the second largest IBSA Class in England. William Crawford's father-in-law, F.G. Guard, Sr., led the class to withdraw its support from Rutherford. But they were unable to
stand the pressure of further divergent views and in 1939
began their own publication, *The Forest Gate Church Bible
Monthly*. It is advertised in the United States by the Pastoral
Bible Institute.

The Forest Gate Church defines itself today as an autonomous group of Christians who meet regularly to worship God and
study the Bible. The results of their deliberations are presented as a help to others through the *Bible Monthly*. They
believe that Christ died as a "ransom for all" and that, at
the appointed time, still in the future, He will return to
collect His Bride--the Church--and to set up a Kingdom here
on earth. Presently associated with the Forest Gate Church
is S.H. French, who is an excellent writer.

Magazine

The Forest Gate Church Bible Monthly. Secretary: D. Sutcliffe.
  Began publishing in 1939; published bi-monthly. Issues
  average 20 pp. Typeset until Jan. 1979.

Booklets

The Election and Destiny of the Hebrew Nation.

God's Plan for Human Redemption. N.d., 8 pp.

Only Christ's Return Will Bring a Just World Peace. C. 1945,
  8 pp.

Our Lord's Return.

French, S.H. *The Middle East in Bible Prophecy*. London,
  England: B.D.M. "Maran-atha," n.d., 22 pp.

──────. *The Unsealed Book: An Exposition of the Book of
  Revelation*. London, England: Prophetic Light Publications,
  1968, 113 pp.

Hart, Alf A. *Pamphlet on Forest Gate Elders Views*. Cardiff,
  England, 1923. Not an official publication.

E. Bible Student Publishing Company
(Edinburgh, Scotland)

The *Bible Student*, edited by William Robertson, was issued quarterly, Vol. 1, No. 1, March 1914 to Vol. 9, No. 1, March 1924 (48 pp. per issue). There were no issues for the years 1919, 1922, and 1924. Many articles are critical of the IBSA and of both C.T. Russell and Rutherford. The periodical also contains letters to and from various Watchtower officials, the Edgar brothers, Crawford, Patan, Hemery, etc. Also, *New Era Enterprise* was published in the 1920s, possibly in Glasgow.

F. Maran-atha Conference
(London, England)

The Maran-atha (Greek for "Our Lord Cometh") Conference corresponds approximately to the Berean (Grove City) Conference in the United States.

Magazine

Maran-atha: The Lord Cometh! Began publishing in 1951, usually published bi-monthly, each issue 12 pp. S.H. French of Forest Gate Church also publishes in this magazine and under their imprint.

"Bible Student" Series

Do You Know? 16 pp.

Why Did God Give Us a Bible So Difficult to Understand? 16 pp. (revised ed., 32 pp.).

The True Trinity.

The Prince of Life.

Does Death End All Probation? Is There a Second Chance? 32 pp.

The Parables of Our Lord.

The I.B.S.A. or Russellites in Prophecy. 129 pp. (revised ed., 192 pp.).

Biblical Figures of Speech.

The Book of Hebrews.

The Telescope of Faith.

Miracles.

The Book of Romans.

G. Goshen Fellowship

Jessie Hemery became a Bible Student in 1888, and in 1901
Russell appointed him London branch manager, a post he held
until 1951. He was also the vice-president of the International
Bible Student Association (a Watchtower corporation) until
1946. Hemery was probably one of the most prominent Bible
Students (see 1938 Watchtower, pp. 272 and 336), and he maintained his association with the Society for many years although
his relations in later years were strained.

Hemery idealized the early Bible Student movement and
agreed with many of Russell's early beliefs. While doing research for a *Watchtower* article he became convinced that the
fulfillment of most of the Bible book of Revelation was still
in the future (a position that is and was totally unacceptable
to the Society) and that the 1914 invisible return of Christ
was without foundation. He published his ideas in *Revelations
Unfolded* (Hilltop Publishing Company, 1951).

Because he was a "Rutherford man" and not a "Knorr Man"
and because he had some disagreements with the Society, he
was disfellowshipped in 1951. Knorr wanted to appoint a man
who was more in harmony with his leadership. Hemery (who died
in 1955) agreed with many of the pre-1909 Watchtower views on
the covenants and other matters. To disseminate his views, he
founded the Goshen Fellowship in 1951. The group is currently
headed by Frank L. Brown.

*PUBLICATIONS OF THE GOSHEN FELLOWSHIP, ENGLAND (all published
    at Bexleyheath, Kent, England)*

<u>By Frank L. Brown</u> *(booklet series called* Zion's Herald*)*

Christ Jesus Warns His Disciples. 1967, 84 pp.

The Scripture of Truth: The Vision: Its Understanding. 1967,
    84 pp.

The Prophecy of the Book of Esther. 1967, 83 pp.

The Double Song, the Spirit and Bride.

God's Plan and Purpose of Things to Come. 1968, 172 pp.

The Rise of Babylon the Great: Its Time Appointed of God. 1968, 107 pp.

The Judgment of Babylon the Great. 1969, 87 pp.

Laodicea: The Angel and the Church. 1969, 100 pp.

Unity of the Faith: Judgment of the House of God. 1969, 96 pp.

The End of Years. 1969, 90 pp.

The Revelation of Jesus Christ. 1970, 52 pp.

The Ordinances of Heaven. 1970, 99 pp.

The Prophecy of Joel. 1970, 86 pp.

Ministry of the Lamb. 1970, 108 pp.

Wisdom: Her Seven Pillars. 1970, 110 pp.

My Servant Job (Part 1). 1971, 216 pp.

My Servant Job (Part 2). 1971, pp. 223-421.

God's Purpose in the Life of Samson. 1971, 84 pp.

Thine the Kingdom O Lord. 1971, 96 pp.

The Preacher and 'I.' 1971, 163 pp.

Jonah: "Read": In the Light of the Unveiling of Jesus Christ. 1973, 72 pp.

The Revealer of Secrets: Joseph: God's Chosen Interpreter. 1973, 102 pp.

Zechariah and the Heavenly Messenger. 1973, 95 pp.

Elisha, A Change of Ministry: The House of Healing. 1973, 95 pp.

The Lord of the Harvest and the Daughter of Zion: A Message for the Jews. 1973, 79 pp.

Paradise: God's Blessing for the Meek. 1973, 84 pp.

The Kingdom Gospel, What Is It? Teaching: Preaching: Publishing: When? How? Why? 1973, 72 pp.

The Resurrection: Its Priorities, How? Where? When? Will the Dead Be Raised? 1974, 86 pp.

Behold, I Make All Things New. The New Creation. New Heavens. New Earth. Joy in Heaven. God's Footstool Made Glorious. 1975, 100 pp.

The Son of Man His Coming. 1975, 97 pp.

By Jesse Hemery *(books)*

Revelations Unfolded. London, England: Hilltop Publishing Co., 1951.

The Book of Daniel Unfolded. London, England: Hilltop Publishing Co., c. 1951.

The Second Coming of Christ, Earth's New Ruler. London, England: Hilltop Publishing Co., c. 1951.

Christ's Great Prophecy of the Coming Events. London, England: Hilltop Publishing Co., 1951.

The Letters to the Seven Churches in Asia. London, England: Hilltop Publishing Co., 1955.

Magazine

Zion's Herald Journal of the Goshen Fellowship. Ed. Frank L. Brown. Vol. 1, No. 1, July 1965 to date.

Other Publications

La Reunion Prochaine de la Chrétienté (Approaching Reunion of Christendom). 30 pp.

Thou Hast Left Thy First Love. N.d., 23 pp.

H. The Institute of Pyramidology
(Harpenden, Hertfordshire, England)
(this group broke off from
The Bible Student Movement)

Pastor Russell in the *Watchtower* and the *Studies in the Scriptures* introduced speculation on the Great Pyramid of

Egypt into his movement. His late contemporary Morton Edgar
(see Section One) did much to advance this speculation.
This enterprise has been picked up most noticeably in recent
years by Adam Rutherford and the Institute of Pyramidology.
The Institute of Pyramidology was founded in London in 1940
by Dr. Adam Rutherford, who retired at that time from his
work as an accountant to devote all his energies to the Institute. Raised in a strong Christian family, Dr. Rutherford
first became interested in the Great Pyramid at the age of
nine in 1903. It was an interest which was to last all his
life, and his contributions to the subject are notable. His
early professional life as a school teacher helped him impart
his knowledge to others in such a way as to make the matter
easily understandable, and this quality is evident in his most
famous work, *Pyramidology*, a study of the subject in five
volumes.

The object of the Institute of Pyramidology is to advance
knowledge and research in Pyramidology in all its branches--
scientific, prophetic, and religious. In essence, the Institute believes that the information contained in the Great
Pyramid of Egypt is so profound and so revealing that no one
apart from Almighty God could have designed the building.
The basic message of the Great Pyramid is the same as the
basic message of the Bible (so much so, in fact, that the
Great Pyramid is termed "The Bible in Stone" as based on evidence in the Bible itself). Thus, Pyramidology, which its
believers find in many ways easier to understand than the
Bible, portrays the Divine Truth in a simple, logical manner,
bringing comfort to those seeking to understand "the great
mysteries of God in this age of confusion."

Books

Rutherford, Adam. *Pyramidology*. In 4 vols. Various eds.
  from 1957 to present. All published Harpenden, Hertfordshire, England: The Institute of Pyramidology.

  Book I. *Elements of Pyramidology. Revealing the Divine
    Plan for Our Planet*. Dunstable, Bedfordshire: Institute
    of Pyramidology, 1957, 219 pp. 2nd ed., Harpenden,
    Hertfordshire, 1962.
  Book II. *The Glory of Christ as Revealed by the Great
    Pyramid*. Dunstable, Bedfordshire: Institute of Pyramid-
    ology, 1962.
  Book III. *Co-ordination of the Great Pyramid's Chronograph
    Bible Chronology and Archaeology*. Harpenden, Hertford-
    shire: Institute of Pyramidology, 1966.
  Book IV. *The History of the Great Pyramid*. Harpenden,
    Hertfordshire: Institute of Pyramidology, 1939, 400 pp.

—————. *Armageddon Due to Begin in the Autumn of 1928.* Glasgow, 1928.

—————. *Bridegroom Has Come; The Saints Now Entering Into Glory.* London, England, 1928.

—————. *The Midnight Cry--Behold the Bridegroom Come Go Ye Out to Meet Him.* Glasgow, 1928.

—————. *The Great Pyramid: A Scientific Revelation.* London, England, 1939.

—————. *The Great Pyramid.*

Book 1. *The Great Pyramid.* London, England, 1952, 154 pp.
Book 2. *A New Revelation in the Great Pyramid.* London, England, 1945.
Book 3. *Armageddon in 1955-6.* London, England, 1950.
Book 4. *The Saviour of the World as Revealed by the Great Pyramid.* London, England, 1953.

—————. *Hebrew Chronology.* London, England, 1939.

—————. *Iceland's Great Inheritance.* London, England, 1939, 48 pp. Published in both English and Icelandic. The third ed. was published only in Icelandic by Top Stone Books in 1979.

—————. *Israel-Britain or Anglo-Saxon Israel.* London, England, 1934; 1939 ed., 828 pp.

—————. *Outline of Pyramidology.* London, England, 1957, 96 pp.

—————. *Treatise on Bible Chronology.* Harpenden, Hertfordshire, 1957, 555 pp.

Chart

Chart of the Great Pyramid. A Color Chart of the Great Pyramid's Interior Passages and Chambers. 1957.

Magazine

Pyramidology Magazine. Published in 1941 as an untitled monthly letter from the president of the Institute. In 1953 it was published quarterly and named *Pyramidology Magazine.* 20 pp. per issue.

Tracts

Rutherford, Adam. *The Institute of Pyramidology.* C. 1974,
    2 pp.

―――. *What Pastor Russell Taught about the Great Pyramid.
His Remarkable Forecast.* N.d., 8 pp.

I. Other British Writings

Books

God Has a Plan for Mankind. 13-page book published by the
    Associated Bible Students of Ilford, Essex.

Patmos, T.S. *The Revelation.* Yeovil, Somerset, England,
    1942, 229 pp. The author of this book is anonymous, as
    "Patmos" is obviously a pseudonym.

―――. *Foregleams of the Golden Age.* 304 pp.

―――. *Divine Plan of the Ages.* 350 pp.

―――. *Plan of God--In Brief.* 46 pp.

―――. *Some of the Parables.* 90 pp.

Booklets

Christ's Return. 35 pp.

Hell, Death, Spiritism. 26 pp.

Where Are the Dead?

Times of Refreshing and Christ's Return.

Poems of Dawn.

II. EUROPEAN GROUPS

A. The Philanthropic Assembly of the Friends of Man

F.L. Alexander Freytag (1870-1947) was an effective or-
ganizer and a prolific writer, and for a number of years was

the manager of the Swiss branch of the International Bible
Students Association (IBSA) which he joined in 1898.
In the early years of the IBSA there was more tolerance
for individual opinions than today. When Rutherford became
the head of the IBSA, many could not accept his rule and
left. Freytag was one of those who left. As early as 1917
Freytag criticized in print Russell's *Studies in the Scriptures*. As a result Freytag was taken to court around 1919 by
Rutherford and the Watchtower Society.

Sometime before 1920 Freytag withdrew from the Watchtower
Society and set up The Church of the Kingdom of God, also
known as the Philanthropic Assembly of the Friends of Man and
the Geneva London Bible and Tract Society.

After 1919, Freytag wrote the pamphlet *A Message of Love
to Laodicea*, addressing it to the Adventists and the International Bible Students Association. Those who agreed with
Freytag rallied around him. In 1919 he wrote the *Divine Revelation* and in 1922, *The Message to Humanity*, and early in
1930 he finished his third book, *Eternal Life*. During the
course of his ministry he also wrote various pamphlets and
composed almost 380 hymns and tunes. From the beginning, he
published a weekly sermon entitled *The Paper for All*. The
intimate members of the family make daily use of his book
The Dew of Heaven, a Bible text for each day of the year with
commentary by Freytag.

The movement is today especially popular in Switzerland,
France, Germany, Austria, Belgium, and Italy. A number of
periodicals are currently published, the most important being
The Monitor of the Reign of Justice (published once a month
in England and Spain, and twice a month in the other above-
mentioned countries). It has a circulation of some 120,000
copies. Freytag believed that eternal happiness is God's goal
for all of mankind. His newspaper, although of a religious
nature, tends to discuss secular topics in considerable detail.
He also reprints a large number of articles from secular
sources. The movement owns a number of "communities" in
different countries of Europe. Although the movement still
accepts much of Russell's theology, this is not readily apparent from their publications.

<u>Books</u>

The Divine Revelation: The Seven Spirits of God. Volume I.
    Geneva, Switzerland: Disciples of Christ, 1922, 271 pp.,
    pb. (French ed., *La Révélation Divine*, 1920).

The New Earth: The Message to Humanity. Volume II. Geneva,
    Switzerland: Bible and Tract Society, 1922 (French ed.,

La Nouvelle Terre. Paris, France, 1922), 2nd ed. 1923, reprinted in New York, 1944, 301 pp., hb., pb.

Eternal Life: The Restoration of All Things. Volume III. Geneva, Switzerland: The Messenger of the Lord, 1933; 2nd ed. 1969), 350 pp., pb. French ed., *L'Ange de l'Eternal.* Paris, France, 1947.

Resurrection: Hope for the Whole Human Race. Volume IV. Geneva, Switzerland, n.d.

The Dew of Heaven: A Daily Devotional Reading, A Biblical Text and Commentary. N.d.

Booklets

The Establishment of the Reign of Justice. West New York, N.J., 1943, 64 pp.

Populaires de l'Eglise du Royaume de Dieu. 1944.

The Light in the Darkness. North Bergen, N.J., c. 1945, 32 pp.

The Lord's Second Coming: What It Really Means. London, England, c. 1946, 31 pp.

The Mystery of Hell Revealed. London, England, 1946, 23 pp. (also in Spanish).

The Triumph of Good over Evil. London, England, 1953. 32 pp.

Hymns of the Messenger. Complete ed. in French, German, Italian, abridged ed. in English, 1967.

The Destiny of Man. C. 1969. Spanish only.

Consolation. 1976. Spanish.

Beautiful Christmas Stories. C. 1978. Also published in French.

The Morning of the Resurrection (Le Matin de la Résurrection).

The Lord's Second Coming (La Séconde Venue du Seigneur).

A Word of Consolation. C. 1978. *(Un Mot de Consolation).*

The Triumph of Good over Evil. C. 1979. *(Le Triomphe du Bien sur le Mal).*

Is There a God? C. 1980. *(Y âtîl du Dieu?)*

Public Salvation. C. 1981. *(Le Salut Publique).*

The Mystery of Hell Revealed. C. 1980. *(Le Mystère de l'Enfer Devoilé).*

Man's Destiny. C. 1981. *(La Destinée de l'Homme).*

Living Experiences of God's Kingdom. C. 1982. *(Histoires Vecues du Royaume de Dieu).*

B. The Association of Free Bible Students of France
(L'Association Française des
Libres Etudiants de la Bible)

The French *Dawn, Aurore,* began publication c. 1951.
Journal de Sion began near Lille, France, in 1956 and republished C.T. Russell's writings and some current articles.
Polish immigrants constitute the largest proportion of Bible Students in France.

Magazine

Le Journal de Sion et Messenger de la Présence de Christ
(Zion's Journal and the Messenger of Christ's Presence).
Vol. 1, No. 1, 1956, published bi-monthly in Wallers,
France.

Books

Volume 1. *Des Etudes des Ecritures.* (Vol. 1. *Studies in the Scriptures).*

Volume 6. *Des Etudes des Ecritures.* (Vol. 6. *Studies in the Scriptures).*

La "Manne Celeste" ou nourriture spirituelle pour chaque jour.
(The Heavenly Manna or Spiritual Food for Each Day).

Special Numbers of Zion's Journal *listed in order of publication*

Quel est donc le serviteur fidèle et prudent? (Who Really
Is the Faithful and Discreet Servant?).

L'Ecumenisme et la Bible. (Ecumenialism and the Bible).

Le rétablissement d'Israel. (The Reestablishment of Israel).

Rapport de Pilate sur Jesus-Christ. (Dialogue of Pilate
    about Jesus Christ).

Signes de la Présence de Christ. (Signs of Christ's Presence).

Apropos de l'infaillibilité des Papes. (The Purpose of Papal
    Infallibility).

Free Tracts

La Verité Concernant les Morts. (The Truth about the Dead).

Monde ou vas-tu? (World, Where Are You Going?).

C. German Bible Students

In Germany Samuel Lauper published Heroldes des Konig-
reiches Christi (Herald of Christ's Kingdom). Lauper also
published a German translation of Streeter's volumes on revelation. Lauper worked in Switzerland also. Conrad C. Binkele began publishing Der Pilgrim in the 1930s. This work
was suspended while the Hitler government was in power. Binkele
and the Boehmer family moved to Los Angeles in 1934. After
the war many Bible Students again received Watchtower literature for the first time in a decade, and some left the Society
because of the many changes that occurred during the war.
Die Brennende Lampe (The Burning Lamp) began publication.
It was similar to the American Herald and Dawn. Another
publication, Christliche Warte (Christian Watchtower), began
in 1949 and stresses a pre-harvest theology. The Tagesan-
bruch began in Berlin around 1950 and later moved to Freiburg,
Germany. The German general convention began in 1955 and
typically is host to 200 visitors. There are also many Bible
Students in East Germany. Some booklets are as follows:

Burmester, Wilhelm. Geheimnisvolle Aussprüche oder Das,
    2. Kommen des Herrn. Lüneburg, Germany, 1967, 32 pp.
    (Mysterious Sayings of the Second Coming of Our Lord).

————. Erhebet ein Panier! N.d. (Lift a Banner).

————. Die Sonnenuhr Ahas. N.d. (The Sundial of Ahas).

————. Der Göttliche Liebensplan in den Sternbildern. N.d.,
    30 pp. (The Divine Plan of Love in the Constellations).

————. *Die Weisse Wolke.* Lüneburg, Germany, 1971. (*The White Cloud*).

————. *Der Göttliche Steinzeuge.* Lüneburg, Germany, 1949, 20 pp. (*God's Witness Stone*).

————. *Bibel in Stein.* Lüneburg, Germany, 1971, 22 pp. (*The Bible in Stone*).

————. *Das Tier.* Lüneburg, Germany, 1975, 16 pp. (*The Animal*).

————. *Wache auf, meine Seele.* Lüneburg, Germany, 1965, 16 pp. (*Awaken My Soul*).

D. Greek Bible Students
(Athens, Greece) (also called the
Free Christian Church of Greece;
started by C.J. Constas)

Tracts

Has the Book of Revelation Any Special Value for the Student of God's Word? N.d., 2 pp.

Mimeo

An Open Letter of General Interest. N.d., 5 pp.

The Kingdom of Heaven Taking Place in Four Stages. N.d., 10 pp.

Constas, Constantine J. *"Heaven and Earth Shall Pass Away" Luke 21:33.* C. 1954, 13 pp.

————. *A New World under New Heavens and on a New Earth.* C. 1960, 27 pp.

————. *The Part of Israel in the Plan of God in Christ.* C. 1964, 25 pp.

————. *Christ's Great Olivet Prophecy.* Athens, 1967.

————. *An Open Letter.* Athens: unpub. dupl. notes, c. 1970.

Book

Constas, Constantine J. *The Revelation of Jesus Christ.* New York: Carlton Press, n.d., 638 pp.

E. South India Bible Students Committee
(Bangalore, South India) (associated with
the Dawn Bible Students, East Rutherford, N.J.)

In India at the time of Russell's death L.S.P Devasahayam (Davey) and his associates all left the Society and formed the India Bible Students Association. They have held conventions annually since 1921. Currently these conventions last about three days, attract about one hundred persons, and rotate from year to year among a few cities in India. The Bible Students Press publishes a monthly magazine in the Tamil language. Literature is also available in Telugu, Kanada, Canarese, and a few other dialects. The few hundred Bible Students in India are scattered throughout the country, but are primarily in South India.

Correspondence between Sundar Raj Gilbert and H.A. Livermore of Portland, Oregon, led to foreign support of the work in India in 1947. The Northwest India Committee, consisting of one member each from the Vancouver, Seattle, Portland, and Salem Classes, receives cooperation from several Classes and individuals in the United States and Canada. Other assistance comes directly from Germany, France, and Australia. The Indian Bible Students Press has a working arrangement with the *Dawn* in America.

Booklets

Is There a Hope for the Fallen Mankind? N.d., 4 pp.

The Bible Answers on Israel and Palestine. N.d., 34 pp.

The Bible Questions and Answers. 1972, 68 pp.

Magazine

The Indian Bible Students' Association Monthly Magazine. 1971 to date (Vol. 2, No. 5, May 1974), published monthly, each 20 pp.

F. Polish Bible Students

The Polish work outside the Society began with the journals *Strasz* (*Watchman*) in 1923 and *Bzask Nowej Ery* (*Dawn of
a New Era*) in 1930. In Poland most non-Watchtower Society
Bible Student classes formed after 1934. The general convention in Poland is held every two years and attracts over
two thousand. Roughly three thousand have registered with
the government as Bible Students. *Na Straszy* (*The Watch*)
began publication in Warsaw in 1948. A group led by a Mr.
Kaspczykowski (who died around 1960) severed ties with the
Laymen's Home Missionary Movement in the United States and
in 1958 began publishing *Swit* (*Daybreak*) in Warsaw. There
are many Polish Classes throughout the United States and
central Canada. The American Polish General Convention alter-
nates between Chicago and Detroit.

III. CANADIAN GROUP

Christian Fellowships International

Christian Fellowships International was founded in 1981
by M. James Penton, Ph.D., and John Poole, Lethbridge,
Alberta, Canada. This is one of the most recent splits from
the Watchtower Society.

Booklets

Bartley, Colom. *Searching for the Deep Things of God*. Leth-
    bridge, Alberta, Canada, 1982, 32 pp.

Burganger, Karl. *The Watchtower Society and Absolute Chrono-
    logy*. Lethbridge, Alberta, Canada, 1981, 28 pp.

Butt, Steve. *A Christian Letter from Steve Butt*. N.d. [1982],
    14 pp.

Magazine

The Bible Examiner. Ed. M. James Penton, Ph.D. Vol. 1, No.
    1, July 1981 to Vol. 1, No. 4, Oct. 1981. Published month-
    ly. About 18 pp. per issue.

IV. *AUSTRALIAN GROUPS*

The Berean Bible Institute was founded in 1918 by R.E.B.
Nickolson, partially as a result of his rejection of the
Seventh Volume. The Institute has published the *People's
Paper* since 1918 and is very close to the doctrines and beliefs of the Dawn Bible Students.
This Institute has published *People's Paper* in Melbourne
since 1918, and it represents both the PBI and the Dawn there.
There are several associated Berean Bible Student classes (including Polish) in Australia and also a few in New Zealand.
The term Berean has about the same connotation in Australia
as it had in America before World War II. At the same time,
a revival group headed by Henninges in Melbourne has continued to publish the *New Covenant Advocate* for several
decades (see next section).

A. Berean Bible Institute
(Melbourne, Australia)

Magazines

The Voice. Melbourne, Australia: Berean Bible Institute,
published irregularly, usually 2-4 pp.

People's Paper and Herald of Christ's Kingdom. Melbourne,
Victoria, Australia: Berean Bible Institute, began pub-
lishing in 1917 to date (Vol. LXIII, No. 6, Dec. 1980-
Jan. 1981), published bi-monthly, each issue 8 pp.

Books

Main, C.F. *Foregleams of the Golden Age*. Melbourne, Australia:
Temple Court, 1919.

————. *Notes on "The Finished Mystery."* Melbourne, Australia:
Bible Students Tract Society, 1919, 43 pp.

Poole, Laura Kathleen. *Palestine, Israel's Inheritance*. Mimeo,
n.p., n.d., 91 pp.

————. *Sons of the Highest*. C. 1942, 205 pp.

————. *The Ten Camels*. Melbourne, Australia, 1940, 137 pp.
(reprint ed. 1955), 144 pp., pb.

Booklets

Watch Israel--God's Time Clock. C. 1978, 28 pp.

Times of Refreshing and Christ's Return. C. 1978, 34 pp.

The Christian's Joy. N.d., c 1978, 28 pp.

Knowing God. C. 1978, 40 pp.

Earth's New Ruler--Humanity's Only Hope! C. 1978, 32 pp.

The Greatest of These Is Love. C. 1978, 32 pp.

Where Are the Dead? Do They Know Anything? C. 1978, 39 pp.
   (earlier ed., 16 pp. mimeo).

The Lord Is My Shepherd. C. 1979, 34 pp.

Some of the Parables. C. 1979, 58 pp.

The Mystery of Christ. C. 1979, 32 pp.

Our Lord's Great Prophecy. C. 1980, 50 pp.

A Peace Desired--War Continues: Can Christianity Save the
   World? C. 1980, 22 pp.

The Manner of Christ's Return and Appearing. C. 1980, 64 pp.

Christ's Return: His Revealing and Manifestation. C. 1980,
   37 pp.

The Abrahamic Seed of Blessing. C. 1981, 30 pp.

God's Rest Is Yet to Come. C. 1981, 33 pp.

Armageddon--Then Peace on Earth. C. 1981, 22 pp.

Smith, W.A. The Search for Truth--A True Life Story. N.d.,
   35 pp.

                     B. New Covenant Fellowship

     In 1909 three prominent pilgrims, H.G. Henninges, M.L.
McPhail, and A.E. Williamson, broke away from Russell's
group partly because they could not accept Russell's new

teaching on Christ's ransom and atonement. They felt it
elevated the church to the place of Christ as the Redeemer
and Mediator for humanity. They also rejected what they
felt was Russell's heavy handedness and the belief among
Bible Students that Russell was "that servant" mentioned in
Matthew 25:45-47. These men were all prominent pilgrims and
influenced a large number of persons both in Australia and
America to leave Russell and join their groups.

A.M. McPhail was one of the most respected and loved
Bible Students, second only to Russell (Rogerson, 1972:147).
McPhail was quite active in the movement, both as a pilgrim
and in taking charge of the music at conventions. He composed hymns and published a hymn book used by the Society,
Zion's Glad Songs, which is the basis of the Society's
later hymn books. Another reason McPhail (as well as James
Hay) and E.C. Henninges left the Society was the debate on
the New Covenant issue. In 1880 Russell formulated an interpretation of the New Covenant which restricted its application to the Millennial Age. Later he changed this interpretation, producing endless discussion in the movement.
Actually, the real issue was probably over the degree of
authority it was proper for Russell to hold in the movement.
Nonetheless, McPhail left and in 1909 published his famous
booklet. Likewise, both Hay and Henninges left, and then published their views. Henninges and his wife, Roseball (the
girl whom Russell had taken into his house who was involved
in a scandal at Russell's divorce trial) published several
books and tracts and later founded a new group named The New
Covenant Fellowship in Australia. In America the group took
the name of Christian Believers Conference. They published
the *Kingdom's Scribe* and the *Berean* and since 1910 an annual
conference has been held, in recent years at Grove City College in Grove City, Pennsylvania.

Most of these publications, even though no author is listed,
are by Henninges and are published under the auspices of the
Covenant Publishing Company in Melbourne. In the 1920s the
imprint became the New Covenant Fellowship. The main periodical is *The New Covenant Advocate and Kingdom Herald*, a monthly.
Many of the following works, especially the shorter ones,
were published as part of the series *The New Covenant Quarterly*, but some of the individual issues do not particularly
name this series, which is possibly a continuation of the *Old
Theology* series of Russell's. Dates are listed where known
and relative order is attempted for others.

Books

Bible Talks for Heart and Mind. 1909, 354 pp., 2nd ed. 1911.

Miracles of the Past and Future. 1911, 32 pp.

The Parables of Our Lord. C. 1912, 400 pp., hb., pb.

Everlasting Punishments. C. 1912, 112 pp.

The Christian's Comforter. 1913, 82 pp., hb., pb.

Armageddon. 1914, 64 pp.

The Church and Its Ceremonies. 1914, 151 pp., hb., pb.

Sabbath Observance: An Answer to Seventh-Day Adventism.
   31 pp.

The Dead, Where Are They? 1917, hb., pb.

The New Era. 1920, 80 pp.

The Spirits in Person: An Expose of Spiritualism. 1920.

The Inspiration of the Bible. 1926, 40 pp.

Daniel the Prophet in the Latter Days. C. 1927.

Christ's Prophecy on Olivet. C. 1927, 127 pp.

The Divine Healer. C. 1927, 80 pp.

Do the Dead Communicate? C. 1928, 48 pp.

Modernism, Fundamentalism and the Bible. C. 1929, 45 pp.,
   hb.

Christ's Promised Return. 1929, 38 pp.

God's Plan for Humanity. C. 1930.

Peace or War: Our Great Day and Its Issues. C. 1932, 96 pp.,
   hb., pb.

*What Say the Scriptures About the Ransom, Sin Offering,
   Covenants, Mediator, Scapegoat?* C. 1932, 80 pp., pb., hb.

Hay, James. *Rays of Light from the Cross.* London: The
   Backroom, 1909.

Henninges, E.C., and R.B. Henninges. *Everlasting Punishment:
   An Appeal Direct to the Word.* Melbourne, Australia, 1911,

hb., pb. (No. 7 of *New Covenant Quarterly*, 15,000 ed.).

————. *Bible Talks for Heart and Mind*. Melbourne, Australia, 1909, 354 pp., hb., pb.

————. *Daniel the Prophet in the Latter Days*. 1920.

————. *Comparisons and Contrasts*. 1930, c. 434 pp.

McPhail, M.L. *The Covenants: Their Mediators and the Sin-Offerings*. Chicago, 1909, 117 pp.

————. *Types and Antitypes Reviewed*. Chicago, 1919.

McPhail, Mrs. *Three Views of the Ransom*.

————. *The Three Sprinklings of the Precious Blood of Christ*.

Tracts

Death Abolished. 16 pp.

The Wideness of God's Mercy. 4 pp.

Making the World Better. 8 pp.

Believe. 4 pp.

Magazines

The New Covenant Advocate and Kingdom Herald. Ed. E.C. Henninges. 8 Fink's Building, Elizabeth Street, Melbourne, Australia, published monthly; published until at least 1924.

New Covenant Messenger. Ed. H.S. Winbush, Melbourne, Australia.

New Covenant Quarterly.

C. The Christian Truth Institute

Frederick Lardent, who founded the Christian Truth Institute of Melbourne, Australia, and London, England, published a number of booklets, pamphlets, and a periodical, *Gleanings for Truth Seekers*. His booklets, listed in order of publi-

Section Five

cation, include:

The Call of the Bride. N.d., 48 pp.

God's Oath-Bound Promise. N.d., 23 pp.

God's Wonderful Time Clock.

Hidden Meaning of Bible Colours.

An Instrument of Ten Strings. N.d., 47 pp.

Life of Abraham.

Pilate's Report. N.d., 32 pp.

The Story of God's Far Reaching Plan.

These Things Shall Be! N.d., 14 pp.

Comforted of God. London, England: Christian Truth.

Covenants of God. London, England.

Out of Egypt. London, England.

Our Anointing. London, England.

Pilate's Report. London, England.

Significant Forty. London, England.

Then I Understand. London, England.

<u>Tracts</u>

A set of tracts was issued under the name *Grace and Truth Series.* Each tract was numbered. The tracts include:

A Little Child Shall Lead Them. 4 pp.

In the United States, the Laymen's Home Missionary Movement distributes Lardent's literature.

Wilson, John, 152
Wilthy, J., 200
Wimbish, John S., 126, 239
Wimbush, H.S., 351
Windle, Charles P., 126
Wingerd, S., 200
Winnipeg Free Press, 126
Winter, R.B., 192
Wisdom, William N., 91
Witmer v. U.S., 171, 172
Witness, Inc., 164
Woefkin, C., 207
Wolff, Richard, 126
Woloski, Rosalie, 192
Wong, K.C., 192
Woods, A., 126
Woods, Guy N., 239
Woodward, E.P., 224
Woodward, Hattie, 273
Woodward, Kenneth L., 207
Woodworth, Clayton J., 5, 6, 13, 65
Woodworth, William Norman, 275
Words and Phrases, 152
Workman, Gary, 240
Wormser, Migot, 152
Wright, Gerald, 91, 126
Wright, H., 195
Wright, J.D., 65, 66, 67, 68, 255
Wright, J. Stafford, 120, 132, 152
Wyrick, Herbert, 152
Wysong, Randy, 71

Yinger, J. Milton, 152
Young, Douglord, 240
Young, J.W., 324
Youngshusband, Peter, 207
Yuille, Glenn, 164

Zahn, Gordon C., 153
Zaorski, J.R., 192
Zaremski, M.J., 192
Zaretsky, Irving I., 153
Zeigler, Harmon, 153
Zellner, Harold T., 126, 164
Zion's Tower, 164
Zook, C.H., 261

Zuck, Roy B., 164, 240
Zurcher, Franz, 92
Zygmunt, Joseph, 92, 96, 224

ADDRESSES FOR JEHOVAH'S WITNESSES AND THEIR OFFSHOOTS

1. Bible Fellowship Union, 11 Lyncroft Gardens, Hounslow, Middlesex, England.

2. Chicago Bible Students, P.O. Box 6016, Chicago, IL 60690.

3. Christian Koinonia International, P.O. Box 81, Lethbridge, Alberta, Canada T1J 3Y3.

4. Christian Millennial Church, 307 White St., Hartford, CN 06106.

5. Dawn Bible Students, East Rutherford, NJ 07073.

6. Epiphany Bible Students Association, P.O. Box 97, Mount Dora, FL 32757.

7. Forest Gate Church, 8 Marlingdene Close, Hampton-on-Thames, Middlesex, TW12 3BJ, England.

8. Laodicean Home Missionary Movement, Rt. 38, 9021 Temple Road West, Ft. Myers, FL 33908.

9. Maran-atha Fellowship, London WC1N 3XX, New Jerusalem Fellowship, 8 Westview, Ormskirk, Lancs England, L39 2 DJ.

10. New Jerusalem Fellowship, 8 West View Ormskirk, Lanes, England, L39 2 DJ.

11. The Philanthropic Assembly (Freytag Movement) American Branch 709-74th Street, North Bergen, NJ 07047.

12. Watchtower Bible and Tract Society, 25 Columbia Heights, Brooklyn, NY 11201.